DEADLINE ARTISTS
SCANDALS, TRAGEDIES, AND TRIUMPHS

DEADLINE ARTISTS
SCANDALS, TRAGEDIES, AND TRIUMPHS

MORE OF AMERICA'S GREATEST NEWSPAPER COLUMNS

EDITED BY JOHN AVLON, JESSE ANGELO & ERROL LOUIS

THE OVERLOOK PRESS
NEW YORK, NY

This edition published in the United States in 2012 by
The Overlook Press, Peter Mayer Publishers, Inc.

141 Wooster Street
New York, NY 10012
www.overlookpress.com

For bulk and special sales, please contact sales@overlookny.com

PHOTOGRAPH PERMISSIONS:
Nellie Bly: Library of Congress Prints and Photographs Division, Washington, DC; H.L. Mencken:
Library of Congress Prints and Photographs Division, Washington, DC; Will Rogers: Courtesy of the
Will Rogers Memorial Museums, Claremore/Oologah, Oklahoma; Maurine Dallas Watkins: The New
York Public Library for the Performing Arts; Grantland Rice: National Photo Company Collection/
Library of Congress; George S. Schuyler: Library of Congress Prints and Photographs Division, Wash-
ington, DC; Dorothy Thompson: Bettmann/CORBIS; Heywood Broun: Bettmann/CORBIS; West-
brook Pegler: Photo by John Phillips/Time Life Pictures/Getty Images; Marguerite Higgins: Photo by
US Navy/Time Life Pictures/Getty Images; Ernie Pyle: Courtesy of the Indiana University School of
Journalism and the Lilly Library of Indiana University Bloomington; Ruben Salazar: Courtesy of the
Los Angeles Times; William F. Buckley, Jr.: Courtesy of the author; Murray Kempton: Photo by Al
Ravenna, New York World-Telegram and Sun, Courtesy of the Library of Congress; Shirley Povich with
Joe Dimaggio and Yogi Berra: Photo by Allan Gould/Time Life Pictures/Getty Images; Eugene Patter-
son with Martin Luther King, Jr.: Courtesy of the Poynter Institute; Jimmy Breslin: Photo by Yvonne
Hemsey/Getty Images; Mike Royko: AP Photo/Charles Knoblock; Dave Barry: Photo by Daniel Port-
noy; John L. Smith: Courtesy of the author; Colbert King: AP Photo/Rick Bowmer

Cataloging-in-Publication Data is available from the Library of Congress

Book design and typeformatting by Bernard Schleifer
Manufactured in the United States of America

FIRST EDITION

10 9 8 7 6 5 4 3 2 1

ISBN 978-1-4683-0120-5

To Margaret, Rebecca & Juanita—
and Fletch

The columnist must have a sense of humor, and be able to express it; he must do some thinking, even if it hurts or requires effort; he must have a desire to assist in making the world fit to live in; he must know where reason ends and prejudice begins; he must be a poet, a wit, a philosopher, a critic; he must be a visionary and practical, and he becomes a bore as soon as he makes the habit of taking himself seriously.

—S. E. KISER quoted in *The Column*, 1926

Writing is easy—all you have to do is open your veins and bleed.

—RED SMITH

Contents

TRAGEDIES

TRIUMPHS

INTRODUCTION

This is a book of short stories that really happened.

It is now possible to see the outlines of what might be called the Newspaper Era, stretching from the late nineteenth century through the early twenty-first. At this moment of transition from newsprint to the digital age, some legendary columnists and characters are in danger of being forgotten. Their talents helped define their times but they worked in what was considered a disposable medium, best suited to wrapping fish when the next day dawned. This American art form deserves to be saved and savored because the craftsmanship of a classic reported column can still inspire a rising generation of journalists while also entertaining readers on the run.

What makes a newspaper column retain its power after the moment has passed? A clear voice and compelling storytelling—vivid descriptive writing delivered with punch and panache, pitting heroes against villains and offering flashes of wit and wisdom in the balance. It entertains as it educates.

Great newspaper writing combines the urgency of news with the precision of poetry and the best of it rises to the level of literature. It is history written in the present tense, reminding us that our problems are not unique—they have precedents that can offer perspective.

In this second volume of *Deadline Artists*, we've continued to focus on the classic American columnists who provided star power to their newspapers, but we expanded our search criteria to include a few iconic first-person features as well. We crowd-sourced the selections, encouraging fellow journalists, professors, and readers to submit their own suggestions.

The result is a chance to walk with Jack London in the aftermath of the 1906 San Francisco earthquake, ruminate on the assassination of President Lincoln while the blood still dries at Ford's Theater, or take in a bullfight with Ernest Hemingway. Watch as Watergate unfolds, sex scandals explode, the Twin Towers implode, and winning home runs capture the thrill of a comeback World Series victory.

In all cases, part of the marvel is the fact that all these stories were composed on tight deadline, reported and written in the span of a few hours. Newspaper writing is an improvisational art form, a tightrope walk between accuracy and urgency, and columnists add their own colorful perspective into the mix.

For this volume, we chose to focus on scandals, tragedies, and triumphs. The reason was simple: these are the subjects that have always sold newspapers. They are the stuff of breaking news and tabloid fascination, best told with humor, insight, and compassion.

Scandals are stories of sex, drugs, and murder, replayed by each generation with their own variations—from the murder of famed architect Stanford White over showgirl Evelyn Nesbit to the Jazz Age killings chronicled by Maurine Dallas Watkins that inspired the play and movie *Chicago* to the White House seduction of Monica Lewinsky. Scandals are those cautionary tales about what happens when lust, greed, and rage meet consequence.

Tragedies and disasters are often the essence of breaking news—tales of unexpected violence and heartbreak that come on a random Tuesday. But there is more than unrelenting gloom and the voyeurism of viewing others' misfortune. Tragedies can be told with dry emotional detachment, poetic flourish, or even a dose of humor. They are also tales of endurance and defiance, as when a reporter for the *Xenia Daily Gazette* in Ohio finds his home destroyed by a tornado but his family alive and swears, "Dig we will. And survive we will, dammit."

Then there is newspaper writing that fills hearts instead of breaking them— moments that offer unexpected joy and a bit of redemption at the end of the day. Stories of triumph are proof that good news can also be news—no matter what the cynics say. It may be the novelist Richard Wright recounting Joe Louis's first heavyweight championship fight from the streets of Chicago's South Side or GI journalist Ernie Pyle chronicling the liberation of Paris, "the City of Light," from the Nazis. But whether in war or peace, it is the spirit captured by Shirley Povich's immortal lede from the fall of 1956: "The million-to-one shot came in. Hell froze over. A month of Sundays hit the calendar. Don Larson today pitched a no-hit, no-run, no-man-reach-first game in a World Series."

Within each section, the stories are organized chronologically, as we did in the first volume of *Deadline Artists*. This offers the reader a chance to survey the sweep of history, if they wish—and occasionally glimpse at the evolution from problem to solution. The shock of Lincoln's assassination still resonates a century later with the murder of the Kennedy brothers. There is the scandal of all-but-state-sanctioned violence during the Jim Crow era, followed by the rise of the civil rights movement and Dr. Martin Luther King's "I Have a Dream" speech. Readers can witness the birth of flight with the Wright Brothers at Kitty Hawk and the frenzy that followed Charles Lindbergh landing in Paris followed by man walking on the moon, all occurring in the span of a single lifetime. There are echoes even in tragedy—stories of police officers shot in 1907 and 1993—in Frank Ward O'Malley's "A Policeman Walks East to Death" and Mike Barnicle's "Echoes of Grief in the Line of Duty." Finally, there are eyewitness accounts of the disasters that briefly destroyed San Francisco and Galveston at the turn of the last century that offer perspective on New Yorkers' determination to rebuild after 9/11.

In Hollywood's romanticized reimagining of American life, newspaper columnists are sometimes portrayed as reluctant crusaders: cynical, quick-witted, and hard-drinking—but with an inner decency that always leads them to do the right thing, eventually. Columnists generally have a more sober assessment of their profession as being populated by flawed people trying to do their best. Westbrook Pegler had one of the best takedowns of the trade, writing on the absurdity of the "deep-thinking, hair-trigger columnist or commentator who knows all the answers just offhand and can settle great affairs with absolute finality three days or even six days a week." Few of the individuals enclosed in this anthology are private paragons of virtue. Some attracted scandals of their own by placing storytelling above journalistic ethics and accuracy; others were consumed by bitter interpersonal rivalries or ultimately poisoned by their own prejudices. But in the end, the quality of the work is what matters.

This book is intended to be a tribute from one generation to another, communicating the passion that columnists like Pete Hamill had for the work of predecessors like Jimmy Cannon, whose column he lovingly remembered as an "undisciplined personal mixture of New York street talk, soaring elegance, Hemingway and Algren, deep Celtic feeling, city loneliness, prohibition violence, and a personal belief in honor."

It is our hope that this anthology will reintroduce legendary newspaper columnists like Jimmy Breslin, Mike Royko, and Murray Kempton to contemporary readers and bring them alive through a selection of their best work. Some of the voices enclosed also became beloved authors after their newspaper days ended, including Ernest Hemingway, John Steinbeck, Pete Dexter, and Richard Ben Cramer. It is a tradition kept alive by contemporary Deadline Artists like Mitch Albom of the *Detroit Free Press*, Carl Hiaasen of the *Miami Herald*, Steve Lopez of the *Los Angeles Times*, Peggy Noonan of the *Wall Street Journal*, and many others. The best columnists are not limited to a specific beat, like politics or crime – they have the talent to paint on a broader canvas.

At a time when it feels like obituaries for newspapers are being written every day, opinion writing is proliferating like never before online. But the once towering power of individual columnists on the editorial page has faded somewhat with the comparative democracy of different voices available on the Internet. Assumptions about the primacy of print journalism are giving way to the digital age, as new technology replaces the old, offering a combination of lower costs, instant access, and rolling deadlines for breaking news without geographic barriers to readership.

Mediums may change, but the need for news, insight, and analysis remains the same. And by honoring the Newspaper Era and rescuing a bit more of its best from gathering dust in libraries or moldering on microfilm, we hope we can help keep appreciation for this tradition alive—strong personalities telling the stories of their time without fear or favor, leavened with a little humor and human kindness.

We hope that you will enjoy this collection of literary journalism as inspiration, education and entertainment—great reading in digestible doses. It is a reminder of the power and possibilities of the reported column to provide perspective on the news of the day, offering a little light along with the heat that always comes with scandals, tragedies, and triumphs.

SCANDALS

Scandal is human frailty writ large. Greed, lust, anger—they are universal and timeless impulses, fundamental to human nature, the basis of religions and legal codes. But an act that might simply cause tut-tutting in the local pews can become quite another matter when amplified by the mass media.

Scandals emerging from one person's actions—a philandering politician or a bent ballplayer—can be amusing, dispiriting, shocking or sad. Sometimes those scandals are just isolated stories that resonate with the public. Sometimes they can become the symbol of an age, or a larger societal problem.

But there are other scandals that are rooted in entire societies, or the actions of nations and armies. Those can become history.

Scandal and newspapers have had a symbiotic relationship from the very beginning. Some of the earliest circulated printed works that can be considered newspapers were lurid accounts of hangings from England in the 1600s. They would often lay out the details of a heinous crime, report on the scaffold speech of the accused, dwell on the gory particulars of the death itself, and finish with a nice moral lesson.

There is a direct line from those pamphlets to the fabulous Maurine Dallas Watkins columns on two murderesses for the *Chicago Tribune* included in this volume. Those columns tell of two promiscuous Jazz Age women, Belva Gaertner and Beulah Annan, who became famous after they killed their lovers amid seedy circumstances and too much gin. Watkins would turn the two unrelated but similar tales into a play that explored the idea of the celebrity criminal, which became a movie and the musical *Chicago*.

The one and only Nellie Bly kicks off this volume with her famous investigation into the Blackwell's Island insane asylum. Her revelations shocked New York and led to immediate reforms—and made her one of the most famous women of her age.

Stanford White is rightfully remembered as one of the premiere beaux arts architects who created some of New York's iconic masterpieces—but in his day, he was much more famous for being shot to death by Harry Kendall Thaw after having an affair with Thaw's wife. It led to the so-called Trial of the Century—and Irvin S. Cobb's *New York World* account from that trial remains a great read that shows why all of New York was obsessed with the case.

Needless to say, this was hardly the last Trial of the Century. The trials and crimes of Al Capone, the Black Sox, the Scopes trial, Watergate, Bernie Goetz, and O. J. Simpson are all here—reported by the likes of Damon Runyon, H. L. Mencken, Mary McGrory, Pete Hamill, and Carl Hiaasen.

John Dillinger, dubbed the "ace bad man of the world," goes down in a hail of bullets, as does Mata Hari, but in very different circumstances.

Michael Kelly sarcastically destroys Bill Clinton's Monica Lewinksy defense—and at the same time delivers a stinging portrait of the man himself. Nora Ephron's self-deprecating account of her time as an intern in the Kennedy White House is hysterical—and a perfect indictment of a bygone era of chauvinism and lechery.

The reason we love to read about scandals is because they ultimately reassure us of our own decency. Most of us work hard, play by the rules, and do our best to get ahead—so we are constantly delighted to learn that our suspicions were right all along about the politician who cheated the system or the televangelist caught with his pants down. Their very public human failings make us more proud of our own private victories.

—JESSE ANGELO

Ten Days in the Mad House
NELLIE BLY—*New York World*—10/9/1887

[Twenty-three year old Nellie Bly, posing as a Cuban immigrant named Nellie Moreno, had herself admitted into the Blackwell's Island insane asylum as a way of exposing its abuses. This is the last of a series subsequently published in the *New York World* that led to landmark public health reforms.]

The day Pauline Moser was brought to the asylum we heard the most horrible screams, and an Irish girl, only partly dressed, came staggering like a drunken person up the hall, yelling, "Hurrah! Three cheers! I have killed the divil! Lucifer, Lucifer, Lucifer," and so on, over and over again. Then she would pull a handful of hair out, while she exultingly cried, "How I deceived the divils. They always said God made hell, but he didn't." Pauline helped the girl to make the place hideous by singing the most horrible songs.

After the Irish girl had been there an hour or so, Dr. Dent came in, and as he walked down the hall, Miss Grupe whispered to the demented girl, "Here is the devil coming, go for him." Surprised that she would give a mad woman such instructions, I fully expected to see the frenzied creature rush at the doctor. Luckily she did not, but commenced to repeat her refrain of "Oh, Lucifer." After the doctor left, Miss Grupe again tried to excite the woman by saying the pictured minstrel on the wall was the devil, and the poor creature began to scream, "You divil, I'll give it to you," so that two nurses had to sit on her to keep her down. The attendants seemed to find amusement and pleasure in exciting the violent patients to do their worst.

I always made a point of telling the doctors I was sane and asking to be released, but the more I endeavored to assure them of my sanity the more they doubted it.

"What are you doctors here for?" I asked one, whose name I cannot recall.

"To take care of the patients and test their sanity," he replied.

"Very well," I said. "There are sixteen doctors on this island, and excepting two, I have never seen them pay any attention to the patients. How can a doctor judge a woman's sanity by merely bidding her good morning and refusing to hear her pleas for release? Even the sick ones know it is useless to say anything, for the answer will be that it is their imagination." "Try every test on me," I have urged others, "and tell me am I sane or insane? Try my pulse, my heart, my eyes; ask me to stretch out my arm, to work my fingers, as Dr. Field did at Bellevue, and then tell me if I am sane." They would not heed me, for they thought I raved.

Again I said to one, "You have no right to keep sane people here. I am sane, have always been so and I must insist on a thorough examination or be released. Several of the women here are also sane. Why can't they be free?"

"They are insane," was the reply, "and suffering from delusions."

After a long talk with Dr. Ingram, he said, "I will transfer you to a quieter ward." An hour later Miss Grady called me into the hall, and, after calling me all the vile and profane names a woman could ever remember, she told me that it was a lucky thing for my "hide" that I was transferred, or else she would pay me for remembering so well to tell Dr. Ingram everything. "You d—n hussy, you forget all about yourself, but you never forget anything to tell the doctor." After calling Miss Neville, whom Dr. Ingram also kindly transferred, Miss Grady took us to the hall above, No. 7.

In hall 7 there are Mrs. Kroener, Miss Fitzpatrick, Miss Finney, and Miss Hart. I did not see as cruel treatment as downstairs, but I heard them make ugly remarks and threats, twist the fingers and slap the faces of the unruly patients. The night nurse, Conway I believe her name is, is very cross. In hall 7, if any of the patients possessed any modesty, they soon lost it. Every one was compelled to undress in the hall before their own door, and to fold their clothes and leave them there until morning. I asked to undress in my room, but Miss Conway told me if she ever caught me at such a trick she would give me cause not to want to repeat it.

The first doctor I saw here—Dr. Caldwell—chucked me under the chin, and as I was tired of refusing to tell where my home was, I would only speak to him in Spanish.

Hall 7 looks rather nice to a casual visitor. It is hung with cheap pictures and has a piano, which is presided over by Miss Mattie Morgan, who formerly was in a music store in this city. She has been training several of the patients to sing, with some show of success. The artiste of the hall is Under, pronounced Wanda, a Polish girl. She is a gifted pianist when she chooses to display her ability. The most difficult music she reads at a glance, and her touch and expression are perfect.

On Sunday the quieter patients, whose names have been handed in by the attendants during the week, are allowed to go to church. A small Catholic chapel is on the island, and other services are also held.

A "commissioner" came one day, and made the rounds with Dr. Dent. In the basement they found half the nurses gone to dinner, leaving the other half in charge of us, as was always done. Immediately orders were given to bring the nurses back to their duties until after the patients had finished eating. Some of the patients wanted to speak about their having no salt, but were prevented.

The insane asylum on Blackwell's Island is a human rat-trap. It is easy to get in, but once there it is impossible to get out. I had intended to have myself committed to the violent wards, the Lodge and Retreat, but when I got the testimony of two sane women and could give it, I decided not to risk my health—and hair—so I did not get violent.

I had, toward the last, been shut off from all visitors, and so when the lawyer, Peter A. Hendricks, came and told me that friends of mine were willing to take charge of me if I would rather be with them than in the asylum, I was only too glad to give my consent. I asked him to send me something to eat immediately on his arrival in the city, and then I waited anxiously for my release.

It came sooner than I had hoped. I was out "in line" taking a walk, and had just gotten interested in a poor woman who had fainted away while the nurses were trying to compel her to walk. "Good-bye; I am going home," I called to Pauline Moser, as she went past with a woman on either side of her. Sadly I said farewell to all I knew as I passed them on my way to freedom and life, while they were left behind to a fate worse than death. "*Adios*," I murmured to the Mexican woman. I kissed my fingers to her, and so I left my companions of Hall 7.

I had looked forward so eagerly to leaving the horrible place, yet when my release came and I knew that God's sunlight was to be free for me again, there was a certain pain in leaving. For ten days I had been one of them. Foolishly enough, it seemed intensely selfish to leave them to their sufferings. I felt a Quixotic desire to help them by sympathy and presence. But only for a moment. The bars were down and freedom was sweeter to me than ever.

Soon I was crossing the river and nearing New York. Once again I was a free girl after ten days in the mad-house on Blackwell's Island.

A Woman Tells: Seduction Led to Murder
IRVIN S. COBB—*New York World*—2/7/1907

[In this courtroom dispatch, Irvin Cobb captured the testimony of onetime showgirl Evelyn Thaw, whose husband, Harry Thaw, shot the celebrated architect Stanford White at a nightclub on the roof of Madison Square Garden in a belated attempt to defend his wife's honor. According to witnesses, Thaw stood over White's body after firing and said: "You deserved this. You have ruined my wife." This excerpt details White's initial drugged seduction of Evelyn when she was sixteen.]

A pale, slim little woman on the witness stand this afternoon laid bare the horrors of a life such as few women have led, in her effort to save Harry Thaw from the electric chair. The woman was his wife. For nearly two hours during the morning session and for an equal length of time in the afternoon she traced her history from childhood.

Men and women wept as this life-story was unfolded, sometimes artlessly, sometimes with thrilling dramatic force and fervor.

Harry Thaw sobbed unrestrainedly as his wife half-whispered the story of her degradation when she was a slip of fifteen. It was a public rending of a woman's soul, but a powerful argument to substantiate the claim of the defense that brooding over the wrongs his girl wife had suffered shifted the mental balance of Harry Thaw.

The news that Evelyn Thaw was on the witness stand spread over the city during the morning session and the fragmentary reports of her testimony aroused intense interest. While the court was resting at noon a crowd of probably 10,000 persons gathered around and inside the Criminal Courts Building.

There were riotous scenes as the tide of humanity beat against the immovable police lines. A few slipped through—a sufficient number to fill the courtroom to the limit of its capacity. Those who gained entrance heard a story confirming all the rumors that have gained currency about Evelyn Nesbit and Stanford White since the night Harry Thaw ended the architect's life on the roof of Madison Square Garden.

Evelyn Thaw held nothing back; she told all. How as a child, hungry for childhood's playthings, she had carried the weight of a whole shiftless household on her shoulders; how, with all the wiles of a serpent, her elderly seducer had brought hideous shame to her; how, when the chance of honorable wedlock came to her, she bared her secrets to the young lover; how the dreadful news had maddened him; how finally she had seen Stanford White, the seducer, slain by Harry Thaw, the husband.

"Call Mrs. Evelyn Thaw," said Mr. Delmas, chief counsel for the defense of Harry Thaw, as soon as the trial was resumed today.

She came, white and cold and outwardly calm, in her little, plain blue frock, her white turn-down collar, her big, school-boy tie and her black velvet hat. A court officer let her in by the side door, and she slipped down the paneled aisle back to the jury-box and halted alongside the witness-chair and put one of her small hands, with a yellow glove, upon the Book that the usher held out to her. She was sworn to tell the truth, the whole truth and nothing but the truth, so help her God.

The biggest scene in New York's biggest murder trial was at hand.

She slipped into the big oaken chair yawning for her and nestled herself there almost like a tired child. Her hands dropped into her lap. There was something pitiably small and paltry and weak about the girl sitting there ready to crucify herself for the sake of her husband. . . .

"It was a girl friend who first introduced me to Stanford White. When she first came and told me Mr. White wanted to meet me I objected at first. I said my mother wouldn't let me. But she came again and again, and told me Mr. White wanted to meet me, and that he belonged to one of the best families in New York.

"It was in 1901 when I was sixteen years and some months old. This girl friend and I got in a cab and drove to the Waldorf, where I had an errand. Then we drove to a dingy doorway in West Twenty-ninth Street, and the girl told the driver to stop at this door. We got out, my girl friend leading the way."

"When was this?"

"In August, 1901."

"You were how old?"

"Sixteen years. My hair was down my back and I had on short dresses."

"You say that your mother dressed you on this occasion?"

"Yes."

Mrs. Thaw described her climb up the steps. She said the wide door slammed behind them as they climbed the stairs. The girl said she halted twice, alarmed, but her friend reassured her. At length they came, she said, to White's studio. White met them on the stairs and took them into a room where a table was set for four people.

"The room was very gorgeous," said Mrs. Thaw. "It was beautifully decorated."

"There was another gentleman there?" asked Delmas.

"Yes."

"You must not tell his name."

"I will not."

"You wore short dresses, did you, and your hair was down your back?"

"Yes, my skirts were down to my shoe-tops."

"You told Mr. Thaw all about this at the time he proposed to you?"

"Yes, I am repeating to you what I told Mr. Thaw at the time he first proposed to me, when he questioned me about Mr. White."

"You all sat down to luncheon in the studio?"

"Yes, and pretty soon the man who was with Mr. White got up and went away. He said he was going away on business."

"Then Mr. White took me and the young lady upstairs to a room in which there was a big velvet swing. We got in the swing and he pushed it so that it flew up in the air. The swing went so high that our feet kicked through a big Japanese umbrella.

"This luncheon and the swinging fun was in the afternoon," went on the girl under Delman's prompting. "After a while Mr. White's gentleman friend came back. It was suggested that we go for a drive in the Park. We told Mr. White good-bye and went downstairs. We drove around the Park together in an electric hansom—just the two of us, myself and the girl friend. Then we went to a dentist, where the girl had her teeth fixed. Then I went home and told my mamma all that happened.

"The next time I saw Mr. White was after he had written a letter to my mother.

"Mr. White wrote my mother that if I had any teeth which needed fixing to send me to the dentist and he would paly the bill. He told my mother he would have her dentist's bill paid also. Stanford White said he had the teeth fixed of nearly all the girls of the 'Floradora' company.

"He said," continued Mrs. Thaw, "in his letter that it was not at all unusual. The next time I saw Mr. White at the same studio where I first met him. Again we had luncheon. This was several weeks after the first luncheon.

"My mother gave me new dress for this luncheon, and a red cape and a red hat. I put on this red cape because she said I was going to a party and must be nicely dressed. She wouldn't tell me where the party was to take place.

"I was put in a cab and started for the studio. As I was crossing Twenty-fourth Street I saw a man coming out of Park & Tilford's. It was Stanford White. He put me in a hansom and drove me to Madison Square Garden. We went up in the tower to Mr. White's apartment.

"There was another young man there. We had a nice little luncheon. All Mr. White would let me have was a chocolate éclair and a glass of champagne. We stayed there having a nice time until about 12 o'clock that night, or maybe it was 1 o'clock.

"I asked Mr. White to take me home to my mother, and he took me home all the way to my door and up to my mother. I told Mr. Thaw all about these parties. There were three parties like this in the tower of the Garden.

"After one of them Mr. White called on my mother and asked her if she did not want to go to Pittsburg and visit her friends. My mother said she couldn't bear to go away and leave me alone in New York. Mr. White told her to go ahead and have a nice time and he would look after me and see that nothing happened to me.

"Then mamma went to Pittsburgh. The day after she left Mr. White sent a carriage for me. He telephoned that I was to come to his studio in East Twenty-second Street and have some photographs taken. I got dressed about 10 o'clock in the morning.

"I went down to the carriage door and drove to the studio. When I got there the door opened by itself. I think this was in September, 1901. I went upstairs to the studio. Mr. White was there. There was another man there I knew on the top landing. In the studio there was another man whom I also knew, one a photographer."

"Did you tell Mr. Thaw what took place in that studio?"

"Yes, I told him all about it. In the studio was a lot of clothing, including a gorgeous kimono. They told me to dress up in the things and they photographed me many times. I posed until I got very tired.

"Then Mr. White told the other man to go out and get something to eat. We had a lunch then, after I had put on my street dress in a private room and Mr. White gave me only one glass of champagne. Then he sent me home. Nothing had happened except that while I was dressing he had called to me to ask if I needed any help in dressing. I said no.

"The next night Mr. White asked me to come to a party in his studio in West Twenty-fourth Street. I went there after the theatre. There was no one there except Mr. White. He said the others had thrown him down. 'That's too bad,' I said, 'for now we cannot have any party.'

"'Oh, yes,' he said, 'you stay. I want you to see the rest of this apartment. These are three very pretty rooms.' We went into one room where there was a piano and played a little. Then he took me into another room—a bedroom. In this room there was a little table on which there was a bottle of champagne. He gave me one glass.

"He showed me all around the room, which was full of curious and strange things. When we got through looking at the thinks he said, 'Why don't you drink the champagne?' I said, 'I don't want it.' He said. "You drink it.' So I drank it. Then there came a crumming in my ears. Everything began to swim around me. After that everythink turned black.

"When I came to again, I was in the bed all undressed. My clothes were all scattered. Mr. White was alongside of me. He was entirely undressed. I began to scream. He jumped up and put on a big kimono. There were mirrors all around the room. I screamed and screamed. He begged me to be quiet.

"As I got out of the bed, I began to scream more than ever. I screamed and screamed."

"Where was Mr. White when you regained consciousness?"

"He was in the bed beside me."

"When you got out of the bed, what did Mr. White do?"

"He got out, got down on the floor and took the hem of my dress and kissed it and told me not to mind. He said he couldn't help it, I was so nice and young and slim. He said that only young and pretty girls were nice. He told me that I must never get fat, as he did not like fat girls. He said they were loathsome. I asked him if everybody did as he had done. He said yes. He told me that was all that made life worth living, but that I must always keep quiet about ourselves. He told me that I was so sweet and pretty that he had been unable to keep away from me and that he loved me.

"He made me swear that I must never tell my mother. He said I must never talk about it. He said some of the girls in the theatre were foolish and talked about it. He said women in society were clever. They knew that the secret of getting along was to never get found out. He said I must be just as clever. He said he would always be good to me. He kept me there all night talking like that. I would keep screaming, but he would quiet me and tell me everything was alright."

By this time dozens in the court-room were sobbing. Harry Thaw, with his face in his handkerchief, was weeping aloud. His shoulders shook and his hands trembled. Agony was written deep in every line of the wife's face, but she broke down only once.

"What was the effect on Mr. Thaw when you told him all of this?" said Mr. Delman.

"He broke down and sobbed and wept," ran on Mrs. Thaw, herself half sobbing. "He clinched his hands before his face and bit his nails, crying, 'The coward, the coward!'"

The Germans Were Like Men After an Orgy
RICHARD HARDING DAVIS—*New York Tribune*—8/31/1914

[The celebrated war correspondent Richard Harding Davis recounts the brutal Belgian offensive of the German army in the opening days of World War I.]

I left Brussels on Thursday afternoon and have just arrived in London. For two hours on Thursday night I was in what for six hundred years has been the city of Louvain. The Germans were burning it, and to hide their work kept us locked in the railway carriages. But the story was written against the sky, was told to us by German soldiers incoherent with excesses; and we could read it in the faces of women and children being led to concentration camps and of citizens on their way to be shot.

The Germans sentenced Louvain on Wednesday to become a wilderness and with the German system and love of thoroughness they left Louvain an empty and blackened shell. The reason for this appeal to the torch and the execution of noncombatants, as given to me on Thursday morning by General von Lutwitz, military governor of Brussels, was this: on Wednesday, while the German military commander of the troops of Louvain was at the Hotel de Ville talking to the Burgomaster, a son of the Burgomaster with an automatic pistol shot the chief of staff and German staff surgeons.

Lutwitz claims this was the signal for the civil guard, in civilian clothes on roofs, to fire upon the German soldiers in the open square below. He said also the Belgians had quick-firing guns, brought from Antwerp. As for a week the Germans had occupied Louvain and closely guarded all approaches, the story that there was any gunrunning is absurd.

Fifty Germans were killed and wounded. For that, said Lutwitz, Louvain must be wiped out. So in pantomime with his fist he swept the papers across his table.

"The Hotel de Ville," he added, "was a beautiful building; it is a pity it must be destroyed."

Ten days ago I was in Louvain when it was occupied by Belgian troops and King Albert and his staff. The city dates from the eleventh century, and the population was 42,000. The citizens were brewers, lacemakers, and manufacturers of ornaments for churches. The university was the most celebrated in European cities, and still is, or was, headquarters of the Jesuits.

In the Louvain college many priests now in America have been educated, and ten days ago over the green walls of the college, I saw hanging two American flags. I found the city clean, sleepy, and pretty, with narrow twisting streets and smart shops and cafes set in flower gardens of the houses, with red roofs, green shutters, and white walls.

Over those that faced south had been trained pear trees; their branches heavy with fruit spread out against the walls like branches of candelabra. The Town Hall was very old and very beautiful, an example of Gothic architecture, in detail and design more celebrated even than the Town Hall of Bruges or Brussels. It was five hundred years old, and lately had been repaired with great taste and at great cost.

Opposite was the Church of St. Pierre, dating from the fifteenth century a very noble building, with many chapels filled with carvings of the time of the Renaissance in wood, stone, and iron. In the university were 150,000 volumes.

Near it was the bronze statue of Father Damien, priest of the leper colony in the South Pacific, of which Robert Louis Stevenson wrote. All these buildings are now empty, exploding cartridges. Statues, pictures, carvings, parchments, archives—all are gone.

No one defends the sniper. But because ignorant Mexicans when their city was invaded fired upon our sailors, we did not destroy Vera Cruz. Even had we bombarded Vera Cruz, money could have restored it. Money can never restore Louvain. Great architects, dead these six hundred years, made it beautiful, and their handiwork belonged to the world. With torch and dynamite the Germans have turned these masterpieces into ashes, and all the Kaiser's horses and all his men cannot bring them back again.

When by troop train we reached Louvain, the entire heart of the city was destroyed and fire had reached the Boulevard Tirlemont, which faces the railroad station. The night was windless, and the sparks rose in steady, leisurely pillars, falling back into the furnace from which they sprang. In their work the soldiers were moving from the heart of the city to the outskirts, street by street, from house to house. . . .

In other wars I have watched men on one hilltop, without haste, without heat, fire at men on another hill, and in consequence on both sides good men were wasted. But in those fights there were no women and children, and the shells struck only vacant stretches of veldt or uninhabited mountainsides.

At Louvain it was war upon the defenseless, war upon churches, colleges, shops of milliners and lacemakers; war brought to the bedside and fireside; against women harvesting in the fields, against children in wooden shoes at play in the streets.

At Louvain that night the Germans were like men after an orgy.

There were fifty English prisoners, erect and soldierly. In the ocean of gray the little patch of khaki looked pitifully lonely, but they regarded the men who had outnumbered, but not defeated, them with calm and uncurious eyes. In one way I was glad to see them there. Later they will bear witness as to how the enemy makes a wilderness and calls it war. It was a most weird picture.

On the high ground rose the broken spires of the Church of St. Pierre and the Hotel de Ville, and descending like steps were row beneath row of houses, those on the Boulevard de Jodigne. Some of these were already cold, but others sent up steady, straight columns of flame. In others at the third and fourth stories the window curtains still hung, flowers still filled the window boxes, while on the first floor the torch had just passed and the flames were leaping. Fire had destroyed the electric plant, but at times the flames made the station so light that you could see the secondhand of your watch, and again all was darkness, lit only by candles.

You could tell when an officer passed by the electric torch he carried strapped to his chest. In the darkness the gray uniforms filled the station with an army of ghosts. You distinguished men only when pipes hanging from their teeth glowed red or their bayonets flashed.

Outside the station in the public square the people of Louvain passed in an unending procession, women bareheaded, weeping, men carrying the children asleep on their shoulders, all hemmed in by the shadowy army of gray wolves. Once they were halted, and among them marched a line of men. They well knew their fellow townsmen. These were on their way to be shot. And better to point the moral an officer halted both processions and, climbing to a cart, explained why the men were going to die. He warned others not to bring down upon themselves a like vengeance.

As those being led to spend the night in the fields looked across to those marked for death they saw old friends, neighbors of long standing, men of their own household. The officer bellowing at them from the cart was illuminated by the headlights of an automobile. He looked like an actor held in a spotlight on a darkened stage. It was all like a scene upon the stage, so unreal, so inhuman, you felt that it could not be true, that the curtain of fire, purring and crackling and sending up hot sparks to meet the kind, calm stars, was only a painted backdrop; that the reports of rifles from the dark rooms came from blank cartridges, and that these trembling shopkeepers and peasants ringed in bayonets would not in a few minutes really die, but that they themselves and their homes would be restored to their wives and children.

You felt it was only a nightmare, cruel and uncivilized. And then you remembered that the German Emperor has told us what it is. It is his Holy War.

Mata Hari Falls Before Firing Squad
HENRY G. WALES—International News Service—10/19/1917

Mata Hari, which is Javanese for Eye-of-the-Morning, is dead. She was shot as a spy by a firing squad of Zouaves at the Vincennes Barracks. She died facing death literally, for she refused to be blindfolded.

Gertrud Margarete Zelle, for that was the real name of the beautiful Dutch-Javanese dancer, did appeal to President Poincaré for a reprieve, but he refused to intervene.

The first intimation she received that her plea had been denied was when she was led at daybreak from her cell in the Saint-Lazare prison to a waiting automobile and then rushed to the barracks where the firing squad awaited her.

Never once had the iron will of the beautiful woman failed her. Father Arbaux, accompanied by two Sisters of Charity, Captain Bouchardon, and Maître

Clunet, her lawyer, entered her cell, where she was still sleeping—a calm, untroubled sleep, it was remarked by the turnkeys and trusties.

The sisters gently shook her. She arose and was told that her hour had come.

"May I write two letters?" was all she asked.

Consent was given immediately by Captain Bouchardon, and pen, ink, paper, and envelopes were given to her.

She seated herself at the edge of the bed and wrote the letters with feverish haste. She handed them over to the custody of her lawyer.

Then she drew on her stockings, black, silken, filmy things, grotesque in the circumstances. She placed her high-heeled slippers on her feet and tied the silken ribbons over her insteps.

She arose and took the long black velvet cloak, edged around the bottom with fur and with a huge square fur collar hanging down the back, from a hook over the head of her bed. She placed this cloak over the heavy silk kimono which she had been wearing over her nightdress.

Her wealth of black hair was still coiled about her head in braids. She put on a large, flapping black felt hat with a black silk ribbon and bow. Slowly and indifferently, it seemed, she pulled on a pair of black kid gloves. Then she said calmly:

"I am ready."

The party slowly filed out of her cell to the waiting automobile.

The car sped through the heart of the sleeping city. It was scarcely half-past five in the morning and the sun was not yet fully up.

Clear across Paris the car whirled to the Caserne de Vincennes, the barracks of the old fort which the Germans stormed in 1870.

The troops were already drawn up for the execution. The twelve Zouaves, forming the firing squad, stood in line, their rifles at ease. A subofficer stood behind them, sword drawn.

The automobile stopped, and the party descended, Mata Hari last. The party walked straight to the spot, where a little hummock of earth reared itself seven or eight feet high and afforded a background for such bullets as might miss the human target.

As Father Arbaux spoke with the condemned woman, a French officer approached, carrying a white cloth.

"The blindfold," he whispered to the nuns who stood there and handed it to them.

"Must I wear that?" asked Mata Hari, turning to her lawyer, as her eyes glimpsed the blindfold.

M. Clunet turned interrogatively to the French officer.

"If Madame prefers not, it makes no difference," replied the officer, hurriedly turning away.

Mata Hari was not bound and she was not blindfolded. She stood gazing steadfastly at her executioners, when the priest, the nuns, and her lawyer stepped away from her.

The officer in command of the firing squad, who had been watching his men like a hawk that none might examine his rifle and try to find out whether he was destined to fire the blank cartridge which was in the breech of one rifle, seemed relieved that the business would soon be over.

A sharp, crackling command, and the file of twelve assumed rigid positions at attention. Another command, and their rifles were at their shoulders; each man gazed down his barrel at the breast of the woman which was the target.

She did not move a muscle.

The underofficer in charge had moved to a position where from the corner of their eyes they could see him. His sword was extended in the air.

It dropped. The sun—by this time up—flashed on the burnished blade as it described an arc in falling. Simultaneously the sound of the volley rang out. Flame and a tiny puff of grayish smoke issued from the muzzle of each rifle. Automatically the men dropped their arms.

At the report Mata Hari fell. She did not die as actors and moving-picture stars would have us believe that people die when they are shot. She did not throw up her hands nor did she plunge straight forward or straight back.

Instead she seemed to collapse. Slowly, inertly, she settled to her knees, her head up always, and without the slightest change of expression on her face. For the fraction of a second it seemed she tottered there, on her knees, gazing directly at those who had taken her life. Then she fell backward, bending at the waist, with her legs doubled up beneath her. She lay prone, motionless, with her face turned towards the sky.

A noncommissioned officer, who accompanied a lieutenant, drew his revolver from the big, black holster strapped about his waist. Bending over, he placed the muzzle of the revolver almost—but not quite—against the left temple of the spy. He pulled the trigger, and the bullet tore into the brain of the woman.

Mata Hari was surely dead.

---

8 Men Out: Black Sox Indicted
HARVEY T. WOODRUFF—*Chicago Tribune*—9/29/1920

Following the indictment of eight White Sox players on a charge of conspiracy to commit an unlawful act in throwing the 1919 World Series games with Cincinnati, and the confessions of two of them, Eddie Cicotte and Joe Jackson, the grand jury got ready last night for more indictments today.

The jurors intend today to find the missing link—the man who was the go-between—the man who gave the gamblers' money to the ball players. This man is said to be Abe Attel, a former prizefighter.

Those indicted men are:

Eddie Cicotte, pitcher, admitted he received $10,000 from the agent of a gambling syndicate.

Joe Jackson, outfielder, confessed $5,000 was paid to him.

Fred McMullin, utility man.

Oscar (Happy) Felsch, center fielder.

Charles (Swede) Risberg, shortstop.

Claude Williams, pitcher.

George (Buck) Weaver, third baseman.

Arnold (Chick) Gandil, former first baseman, who quit major league baseball at the beginning of the present season.

Jackson said he was promised $20,000, the price he asked, and was given only $5,000.

Claude ("Lefty") Williams, the man who handed Jackson the $5,000, will be the central figure in the investigation today.

Cicotte confessed first to Comiskey. He went to the "Old Roman's" office early yesterday morning.

"I don't know what you'll think of me," he said, "but I got to tell you how I double-crossed you. Mr. Comiskey, I did double-cross you. I'm a crook. I got $10,000 for being a crook."

"Don't tell it to me," said Comiskey. "Tell it to the grand jury."

Cicotte told it to the grand jury in tears and in shame, slowly, haltingly, hanging his head, now and then pausing to wipe his streaming eyes.

"Risberg and Gandil and McMullin were at me for a week before the World Series started," he said. "They wanted me to go crooked. I didn't know. I needed the money. I had the wife and the kids. The wife and kids don't know this. I don't know what they'll think.

"I bought a farm. There was a $4,000 mortgage on it. There isn't any mortgage on it now. I paid it off with the crooked money.

"The eight of us—the eight under indictment—got together in my room three or four days before the games started. Gandil was master of ceremonies. We talked about throwing the series—decided we could get away with it. We agreed to do it.

"I was thinking of the wife and kids, and how I needed the money. I told them I had to have the cash in advance. I didn't want any checks. I didn't want any promises. I wanted the money in bills. I wanted it before I pitched a ball.

"We all talked quite a while about it, I and the seven others. Yes, all of us decided to do our best to throw the games to Cincinnati.

"Then Gandil and McMullin took us all, one by one, away from the others and we talked turkey. They asked me my price. I told them $10,000. And I told them that $10,000 was to be paid in advance.

"It was Gandil I was talking to. He wanted to give me some money at the time, the rest after the games were played and lost. But it didn't go with me.

"Well, the arguments went on for days—the arguments for 'some now and some later.' But I stood pat. I wanted that $10,000, and I got it.

"How I wish that I didn't!

"The day before I went to Cincinnati I put it up to them squarely for the last time that there would be nothing doing unless I had the money.

"That night I found the money under my pillow. I don't know who put it there. But it was there. It was my price. I had sold out 'Commy'; I had sold out the other boys. Sold them for $10,000 to pay off a mortgage on a farm, and for the wife and kids.

"Ten thousand dollars. What I had asked—what I had demanded. Ten thousand dollars, cash in advance, there in my fingers. I had been paid, and I went on. I threw the game.

"If I had realized what that meant to me! The taking of that dirty, crooked money—the hours of mental torture, the days and nights of living with an unclean mind; the weeks and months of going along with six of the seven other crooked players, and holding a guilty secret; and of going along with the boys who had stayed straight and clean and honest—boys who had nothing to trouble them—say, it was hell!

"I got the $10,000 cash in advance. That's all."

Joe Jackson last night described his confession to the grand jury as follows:

"I heard I'd been indicted. I decided that those men couldn't put anything over on me. I called up Judge McDonald and told him I was an honest man and that he ought to watch this thing. He said to me, 'I know you are not.' He hung up the receiver on me.

"I thought it was over. I figured somebody had squawked. I got the idea that the place for me was the ground floor. I said, 'I'll tell him what I know.'

"He said, 'Come on over and tell it to me.' I went over.

"I got in there and I said: 'I got $5,000 and they promised me $20,000. All I got was $5,000 that Lefty Williams handed me in a dirty envelope. I never got the other $15,000.' I told that to Judge McDonald.

"He said he didn't care what I got, that if I got what he thought I'd ought to get for crabbing the game of the kids I wouldn't be telling him my story. I don't think the judge likes me. I never got that $15,000 that was coming to me.

"Before we broke up I climbed Gandil, McMullin, and Risberg about it. They said to me, 'You poor simp, go ahead and squawk. Where do you get off if you do? We'll all say you're a liar. And every honest ball player in the world will say you're a liar. You're out of luck. Some of the boys were promised a lot more than you and got a lot less.'

"That's why I went down and told Judge McDonald and told the grand jury what I know about this frameup.

"And I'm giving you a tip. A lot of these sporting writers that have been roasting me have been talking about the third game of the world's series being square. Let me tell you something. The eight of us did our best to kick it and little Dick Kerr won the game by his pitching. Because he won it, these gamblers double-crossed us for double-crossing them.

"They've hung it on me. They ruined me when I went to the shipyards, but I don't care what happens now. I guess I'm through with baseball. I wasn't wise enough like Chick to beat them to it, but some of them will sweat before the show is over.

"Who gave me the money? Lefty Williams slipped it to me the night before I left Cincinnati and told me I'd get the other $15,000 after I delivered the goods. I took Lefty's word for it. Now Risberg threatens to bump me too if I squawk. That's why I had all the bailiffs with me when I left the grand jury room this afternoon."

Woman Plays Jazz as Victim Dies
MAURINE DALLAS WATKINS—*Chicago Tribune*—4/4/1921

For more than two hours yesterday afternoon Mrs. Beulah Annan, a comely young wife, played a foxtrot record named "Hula Lou" in her little apartment at 817 East 46th Street. Then she telephoned her husband and reported that she had killed a man who "tried to make love" to her.

The Hawaiian tune was the death song of Harry Kolstedt, 29 years old, of 808 East 49th Street, whom Mrs. Annan shot because he had terminated their little wine party by announcing that he was through with her. His body lay hunched against the wall in her bedroom as she played the record over and over again.

When taken to the Hyde Park station by the police Mrs. Annan protested tearfully that she had killed Kolstedt to save her honor.

MADE HIMSELF AT HOME
"He came into my apartment this afternoon," she said, "and made himself at

home. Although I scarcely knew him, he tried to make me love him. I told him I would shoot. He kept coming anyway, and I—I did shoot him."

Soon after midnight, however, after the fumes of the liquor had worn away, she told a different story to Assistant State's Attorneys Bert A. Cronson and William F. McLaughlin. For hours they had questioned her without breaking down her story.

Then, with Capt. Edward Murnane of the Hyde Park station, they took the woman back to her apartment. There she was forced to stand in a dim light, facing the scene of the murder, while questions were fired at her in monotonous succession.

BREAKS DOWN UNDER QUIZ

"What about the blood on the phonograph record? What about the wine and gin bottles and empty glasses? How come that Kolstedt was shot through the back?" Mrs. Annan was asked.

Finally she broke down.

"You are right; I haven't been telling the truth," the young woman admitted. "I'd been fooling around with Harry for two months. This morning, as soon as my husband left for work, Harry called me up. I told him I wouldn't be home, but he came over anyway.

"We sat in the flat for quite a time, drinking. Then I said in a joking way that I was going to quit him. He said he was through with me and began to put on his coat. When I saw that he meant what he said, my mind went in a whirl and I shot him. Then I started playing the record. I was nervous, you see."

As she played, Mrs. Annan began to wonder about her husband. What would he say when he came home and found a dead man lying in his bedroom? So at ten minutes before 5 she telephoned him at the garage at 9120 Baltimore Avenue, where he is employed.

"I've shot a man, Albert," she told him. "He tried to make love to me."

HUSBAND HURRIES HOME

Annan hurried home in a taxicab and found his wife in a hysterical condition. Kolstedt, in his shirt sleeves, was hunched against the wall. Near by were his coat, hat, vest, and overcoat. Mrs. Annan's clothing was stained with blood.

Annan picked up the telephone to call the police. His wife threw herself on him, imploring him not to. At that instant the connection was completed, and the voice of Sergt. John O'Grady sounded over the wire from the Wabash Avenue station. Mrs. Annan snatched the receiver.

"I've just killed my husband!" she shrieked. In reply to the sergeant's question she mumbled her address. The receiver clicked.

When detectives reached the apartment they found Mrs. Annan—a beautiful woman of 28, slim and tall, with reddish brown hair bobbed to the mode—waiting with a fanciful story of having fainted after shooting Kolstedt.

The Klan Holds a "Klavern"

LINDSAY DENISON—*New York World*—5/3/1923

The Knights of the Ku Klux Klan, Invisible Empire, held a "klavern" on the farm of John Hobbs, a half-mile east of Middlebush, a hamlet five miles out of New Brunswick, N.J., early this morning. It couldn't have been earlier, for the proceedings which were supposed to be nearly over at midnight did not begin until then. It was not until nearly half past 2 o'clock that the 62-foot cross flared up against the sky and faded out again and a small army of Klansmen from every county in New Jersey started streaming out over the road toward home.

With all the theatric effect of white robes and Alice-in-Wonderland terminology, the deepest impression of last night's ceremonies upon outsiders had to do with the numbers in which they turned out. The Klan estimate of members of the order present was 10,000. Unofficial observers guessed it as from 10,000 to 6,000.

There was not a road in Somerset County that was not at some time after dark traversed by long trails of automobile headlights; sometimes one counted ten or fifteen cars; at other times there were fifty or sixty. There was never a time between 10 o'clock and midnight when the main streets of New Brunswick were not filled with the slow-moving processions. They blinked and glared their way through the lanes and highways, often losing their bearings so that columns passed each other on the same road. They were in fine limousines, in delivery trucks, in speed cars, in milk wagons, in touring cars and in great omnibuses.

Somewhere behind each car, on the end of the mudguard, on the license plate rack or on the spare tire case, hung a white streamer. Sometimes it was a silken knotted ribbon like the decoration of a bridal car; more often it was merely a strip of cheesecloth, and frequently it was a bunch of cotton waste tied with string.

On the brightly lighted business streets of New Brunswick the significance of the white streamer was quickly recognized. It put a stop for an hour or two to ordinary night activities of the town, while whispering groups gathered back from the curb in the comparative shadows of the curb line and store doors. Comment was not always friendly.

The Klansmen had meant to keep their meeting secret. No one except the twelve invited guests "from the alien world," as one *World* writer, who had been invited weeks ago with a pledge to hold their knowledge in confidence, were supposed to know there was to be a "klavern." But, after the attack of anti-Klansmen on a recruiting meeting at Bound Brook, ten miles from New Brunswick, night before last, there was not a taxicab driver, hotel clerk, bootlegger or night policeman in Somerset or Middlesex County who was not eager to be the first to tell strangers about the Middlebush meeting. There are many Negroes in New Brunswick's population. They vanished from the streets soon after 10 o'clock.

The guests of the Publicity Committee were separated in the traffic jam in front of the Pennsylvania Railroad Station in New Brunswick. Two of us, with a committeeman, found ourselves in a motorbus marked Long Branch and Red Bank, filled with men who were obviously fisherfolk, truck growers, garage keepers and workmen, and here and there an austere, thin-lipped person in a high collar who might have been a bank clerk or a rising young lawyer. The lumbering bus got off the road three times and there was plenty of time to get acquainted.

It was a good-natured company. There were just two topics of conversation aside from neighborhood gossip that a stranger could not always get a drift of. One was what each man's wife would say to him when he got home along about daylight—he having promised to be in about midnight. The other was that awe and horror which the gathering of the Klans must be producing at the roadsides upon which the travelers peered through the steam-coated windows.

One thing was clear then and remained clear throughout the night. The members of the Klan take themselves very seriously, even in their friendly chat. It is no frolicsome lark for them. They are quite sure that they "are getting this country on the right road at last." They keep saying it.

"Where's Jim," asked a man in a sheepskin coat; "thought he was coming."

"Why, say, I thought you knew," was the answer. "His wife wouldn't let him."

"Why, what's the matter with her?" asked the inquirer, "always thought she was a kinder sensible woman."

The other man whispered something.

"Is that so? Well, now, do you know I never knew she follered the Pope. What do you know about that!"

They let us out in a field overgrown with low underbrush through which the lights of hundreds of cars could be seen twinkling. The road ahead was jammed with cars. More were piling in behind. It was a little after 11 o'clock.

A man apparently having some authority took the committeeman off into the dark and whispered with him. They brought papers to the headlight of the bus and discussed them. The man of authority said he guessed he'd have to take us in. We set out across the underbrush until we came to a woven wire fence. On the other side of it, out of a stubble field, appeared eight or ten stocky-looking youths. Some of them had handkerchiefs tied across the lower half of the face; others wore no concealment.

Every one of them carried a club, a twisted weapon from three to four feet long, often knotted, twisted and gnarled with the bark on. They shooed us down outside of the fence for half a mile until a gate was reached. . . .

On the other side of the automobile screen was a circle of white-robed figures enclosing a space of perhaps three or four acres. To the east of it rose against the moonlit sky the poles of a cross, the upright apparently sixty feet high. Beneath it was rostrum. On it stood an imposing white-robed figure.

Standing or kneeling on one knee in a row at his feet were twenty closely-guarded, robed men. Many had red-lined caps turned back. The invited visitors were led behind the rostrum and the cross. They could make out, back of the robed men, triple and quadruple lines of men in dark clothes with handkerchief masks. All along the woods at the end of the cornfield stalked clubmen.

We were told the person on the rostrum was the Exalted Cyclops. It was explained that he was the master of ceremonies. He had a tiny electric drop-light over the desk by which he read the ritual. His voice was strong and penetrating.

In the center of the great ring was an altar at which another robed figure stood. The Exalted Cyclops addressed him as "Night-Hawk," if one's ears served right, and told him to look into the matter of the "aliens" who were to be naturalized.

"I have your orders, sir," said Night-Hawk, and with arms folded on his breast he stalked out to the rear.

There followed a sonorous colloquy between the Exalted Cyclops and one he addressed as Kotop, who appeared at the altar. The wording of the mutual expressions of patriotism, devotion to clean living and to mutual adherence sprinkled along the way of this antiphony was remarkable in its musical cadence and the clear simplicity of its diction.

A gasoline-lighted small torch appeared at the altar. The Kotop was instructed to usher in the "aliens awaiting naturalization." The cross-bearer—they spoke of him, I think, as a "Klextor"—with an assistant carrying the tank of illuminating gas, marched over to the edge of the ring.

The unmistakable pipe organ tones of the voice of G-1 was heard reciting the lines of "God give us men," followed by preliminary instructions.

Then a dark column of men poured through a gap in the line. From a distance of 300 feet they looked like a huddled flock of frightened herded prisoners. They were in columns of fours. The committeemen told us there were

2,000 of them. The A.E.F. man said he wouldn't know how to pack many more than 800 men into the "road space" they filled.

They were marched across the rear of the circle, which now became a square, and were lined up like soldiers at inspection, in widely separated ranks. The Exalted Cyclops announced that they would be "subjected to the Eye of Scrutiny."

All the robed members marched in single file in and around them, putting the eyeholes in their hoods close to the faces of the "aliens."

After an hour ten hapless persons whose features or speech or appearance of general intelligence seemed to have indicated that the Eye of Scrutiny did not like them were plucked out and escorted in a hollow square before the rostrum. The Exalted Cyclops informed them that they had been found lacking in the essential qualities of Klansmen; he assured them a mistake might have been made and that they would be received in the order later if they were all right. They were then escorted off the premises by an additional guard of clubmen.

Facing east, north, south and west on the sides of the big square, addresses on the high purposes of the Invisible Empire were made to the "aliens" who marched from place to place stumbling through corn stubble. It was impressed upon them that only men of undoubted loyalty to the Government, to God, to their fellow Klansmen were desired. They were invited, if they felt themselves unfit, to withdraw before it was too late, because of their unfitness later they would, without fear or favor, be ejected from the order.

At the end of the instructions the "aliens" were massed across the altar from the cross and oaths and obligations were read to them to which they swore successively with their right hands on their hearts and their left hands uplifted. Those who followed the reading of the pledges noted that they emphasized especially "white supremacy," adhesion to the law and Government of the community, State and Nation, unswerving and unquestioning, demanded the separation of church and state, free schools and free seats in schools, and that no prejudice of church or fraternal organization should stand between Klansman and his duty to the Government, the Invisible Empire and his fellow Klansmen.

The words "white supremacy" were nearest to a direct reference to the reputed object of the Klan, to combat all things in the Negro, the Catholic, the Jew and the foreign-born generally.

At the end of a prayer the great cross was lighted. A strong breeze was setting in to the south. The upright and the arm of the south blazed up so they were seen, it was learned later, seven miles away. The north arm merely smoldered.

The lighting of the cross was apparently the signal for the last onslaught of those who wanted to get into the meeting without authority. There were successive short whistle signals all along the north edge of the farm. At least a thousand men with and without clubs dashed into the scrub pines. The whistles blew again.

"Klansmen!" cried the Exalted Cyclops sharply. "Klansmen are calling for help. Go in there."

Five hundred more dashed into the brush. Two rather light revolved shots sounded. One of the guests declared he saw a Klansman fire them at the sky. They seemed to come from within the farm.

The voice announced that a few things were to be said to the newly naturalized citizens of the Invisible Empire in private. The visitors were escorted out and back to New Brunswick, arriving there after 3 o'clock. All the Klansmen from Southern, Northern and Western New Jersey were directed to find their way home through Bound Brook, passing through its streets in silent protest against the assault on the Klan meeting there by aggrieved members of the community the night before last. No robes were worn on this parade. It was explained that no Klansman may wear a robe outside of a Klavern unless on a special mission to a funeral or a church or "something like that," and then only on authority from the State or the national organization.

At half past 3 o'clock this morning automobiles were still going through New Brunswick like traffic at 42d Street and Broadway at 3 o'clock in the afternoon.

Wanted: A Wet Nurse for the Oil Industry
WILL ROGERS—*Tulsa Daily World*—2/10/1924

[The Teapot Dome scandal brought disgrace to President Warren G. Harding, as members of his administration were found to have accepted bribes from oil company executives in exchange for no-bid drilling contracts at a remote Wyoming petroleum reserve field known as Teapot Dome. It was regarded as the greatest political scandal up to that time and led to the first imprisonment of a cabinet official, Secretary of the Interior Albert B. Fall. Will Hays, who Will Rogers suggests could be appointed "Wet Nurse for the Oil Industry," had been brought in to clean up the fledgling film industry after a scandal involving silent screen star Fatty Arbuckle and subsequently imposed the first "decency codes" on American movies.]

The Exposure is generally very prompt to detect any shortcomings in our national affairs and to chastise them editorially through the columns of this very valuable and able periodical. But this week we have been saved the trouble of exposing them, as, through the stupidity of their own actions, they have exposed themselves.

I am referring of course to the Coffee Pot or Tea Pot Dome, or some such contrivance of kitchen apparel.

Tea started one war we had, but nobody ever thought that a Tea Pot would boil over enough to scald some of our most honorable financiers. The only lamentable thing about it, as I am writing now, is that the U.S. Senate is investigating it. Statistics have proven that the surest way to get anything out of the public mind and never to hear of it again is to have a Senate Committee appointed to look into it.

You read where they go in session, and then you never hear any more of them unless one of them dies. Then it may come out that he held an appointment on this certain Committee. Now if they had turned this thing over to some Justice of the Peace, and give him power to act, with no appeal, why we would be reading this morning what millionaire so and so had served in his cell from the outside for breakfast.

Now I see only one way out of this lamentable scandal—that is to do as the movies did, appoint a Will Hays to wet nurse the oil industry, and see if he can keep their nose clean.

When you come to think of it there is a great similarity between the two industries. Both of them, with the exception of bootlegging, are the newest industry we have. Neither one is a public necessity. We got along great a few years ago without either. But the minute something shows its head in the movies that smacks of scandal, why a howl goes up like a pet coon.

The great criticism of the movies is that people are suddenly thrown into possessions of money who were never accustomed to handle it before, and that they lose their heads. Did you ever think of oil people? Why they are rich so quick they are millionaires before they have time to get the grease off their hands. They jump from a Ford to a Rolls Royce so fast that they try cranking the Rolls through force of habit. . . .

Our history honors many names whose morals would not stand the acid test, but our history honors no man who betrayed, or attempted to have betrayed a government trust. I don't want the patriotism of my children endangered by driving around in a car that is propelled by gasoline manufactured from profits derived from tampering with the integrity of those noble officials whom we trust with not only our lives, but our oil.

No Sweetheart Worth Killing
MAURINE DALLAS WATKINS—*Chicago Tribune*—3/14/1924

No sweetheart in the world is worth killing—especially when you've had a flock of them—and the world knows it. That is one of the musings of Mrs. Belva Gaertner in her county jail cell and it is why—so she says—a "broad minded" jury is all that is needed to free her of the charge of murdering Walter Law.

The latest alleged lady murderess of Cook County, in whose car young Law was found shot to death as a finale to three months of wild gin parties with Belva while his wife sat at home unsuspecting, isn't a bit worried over the case.

"THERE ARE PLENTY MORE."

"Why, it's silly to say I murdered Walter," she said during a lengthy discourse on love, gin, guns, sweeties, wives, and husbands. "I liked him and he loved me—but no woman can love a man enough to kill him. They aren't worth it, because there are always plenty more. Walter was just a kid—29 and I'm 38. Why should I have worried whether he loved me or whether he left me?"

Then the double divorcee of frequent newspaper notoriety turned to the question of juries.

"Now, that coroner's jury that held me for murder," she said. "That was bum. They were narrow minded old birds—bet they never heard a jazz band in their lives. Now, if I'm tried, I want worldly men, broad minded men, men who know what it is to get out a bit. Why, no one like that would convict me."

THIS WORRIES HER.

A long laugh and then a frown.

"But, I wish I could remember just what happened. We got drunk and he got killed with my gun in my car. But gin and guns—either one is bad enough, but together they get you in a dickens of a mess, don't they. Now, if I hadn't had a gun, or if Walter hadn't had the gin—Of course, it's too bad for Walter's wife, but husbands always cause women trouble."

No attempt yesterday was made to get Mrs. Gaertner out on bail and it is not likely one will be made before the grand jury acts. Prosecutor Stanley Klarkowski hopes to get the case before the jury tomorrow or Monday and is convinced there will be an indictment.

And, while Mrs. Gaertner chortled in jail, plans were completed for young Law's funeral today. It will be held from his home and will be private.

Arguments at the Scopes-Monkey Trial
H. L. MENCKEN—*Baltimore Sun*—7/14/1925

The net effect of Clarence Darrow's great speech yesterday seems to be precisely the same as if he had bawled it up a rainspout in the interior of Afghanistan. That is, locally, upon the process against the infidel Scopes, upon the so-called minds of these fundamentalists of upland Tennessee. You have but a dim notion of it who have only read it. It was not designed for reading, but for hearing. The clanging of it was as important as the logic. It rose like a wind and ended like a flourish of bugles. The very judge on the bench, toward the end of it, began to look uneasy. But the morons in the audience, when it was over, simply hissed at it.

During the whole time of its delivery the old mountebank, Bryan, sat tight-lipped and unmoved. There is, of course, no reason why it should have shaken him. He has those hillbillies locked up in his pen and he knows it. His brand is on them. He is at home among them. Since his earliest days, indeed, his chief strength has been among the folk of remote hills and forlorn and lonely farms. Now with his political aspirations all gone to pot, he turns to them for religious consolations. They understand his peculiar imbecilities. His nonsense is their ideal of sense. When he deluges them with his theological bilge they rejoice like pilgrims disporting in the river Jordan.

The town whisper is that the local attorney-general, Stewart, is not a fundamentalist, and hence has no stomach for his job. It seems not improbable. He is a man of evident education, and his argument yesterday was confined very strictly to the constitutional points—the argument of a competent and conscientious lawyer, and to me, at least very persuasive.

But Stewart, after all, is a foreigner here, almost as much so as Darrow or Hays or Malone. He is doing his job and that is all. The real animus of the prosecution centers in Bryan. He is the plaintiff and prosecutor. The local lawyers are simply bottle-holders for him. He will win the case, not by academic appeals to law and precedent, but by direct and powerful appeals to the immemorial fears and superstitions of man. It is no wonder that he is hot against Scopes. Five years of Scopes and even these mountaineers would begin to laugh at Bryan. Ten years and they would ride him out of town on a rail, with one Baptist parson in front of him and another behind.

But there will be no ten years of Scopes, nor five years, nor even one year.

Such brash young fellows, debauched by the enlightenment, must be disposed of before they become dangerous, and Bryan is here, with his tight lips and hard eyes, to see that this one is disposed of. The talk of the lawyers, even the magnificent talk of Darrow, is so much idle wind music. The case will not be decided by logic, nor even by eloquence. It will be decided by counting noses—and for every nose in these hills that has ever thrust itself into any book save the Bible there are a hundred adorned with the brass ring of Bryan. These are his people. They understand him when he speaks in tongues. The same dark face that is in his own eyes is in theirs, too. They feel with him, and they relish him.

I sincerely hope that the nobility and gentry of the lowlands will not make the colossal mistake of viewing this trial of Scopes as a trivial farce. Full of rustic japes and in bad taste, it is, to be sure, somewhat comic on the surface. One laughs to see lawyers sweat. The jury, marched down Broadway, would set New York by the ears. But all of that is only skin deep.

Deeper down there are the beginnings of a struggle that may go on to melodrama of the first caliber, and when the curtain falls at least all the laughter may be coming from the yokels. You probably laughed at the prohibitionists, say, back in 1914. Well, don't make the same error twice.

As I have said, Bryan understands these peasants, and they understand him. He is a bit mangy and flea-bitten, but no means ready for his harp. He may last five years, ten years or even longer. What he may accomplish in that time, seen here at close range, looms up immensely larger than it appears to a city man five hundred miles away. The fellow is full of such bitter, implacable hatreds that they radiate from him like heat from a stove. He hates the learning that he cannot grasp. He hates those who sneer at him. He hates, in general, all who stand apart from his own pathetic commonness. And the yokels hate with him, some of them almost as bitterly as he does himself. They are willing and eager to follow him—and he has already given them a taste of blood.

Darrow's peroration yesterday was interrupted by Judge Raulston, but the force of it got into the air nevertheless. This year it is a misdemeanor for a country school teacher to flout the archaic nonsense of Genesis. Next year it will be a felony. The year after the net will be spread wider. Pedagogues, after all, are small game; there are larger birds to snare—larger and juicier. Bryan has his fishy eye on them. He will fetch them if his mind lasts, and the lamp holds out to burn. No man with a mouth like that ever lets go. Nor ever lacks followers.

Tennessee is bearing the brunt of the first attack simply because the civilized minority, down here, is extraordinarily pusillanimous.

I have met no educated man who is not ashamed of the ridicule that has fallen upon the State, and I have met none, save only Judge Neal, who had the courage to speak out while it was yet time. No Tennessee counsel of any importance came into the case until yesterday and then they came in stepping very softly as if taking a brief for sense were a dangerous matter. When Bryan did his first rampaging here all these men were silent.

They had known for years what was going on in the hills. They knew what the country preachers were preaching—what degraded nonsense was being rammed and hammered into yokel skulls. But they were afraid to go out against the imposture while it was in the making, and when any outsider denounced it they fell upon him violently as an enemy of Tennessee.

Now Tennessee is paying for that poltroonery. The State is smiling and beautiful, and of late it has begun to be rich. I know of no American city that is set in more lovely scenery than Chattanooga, or that has more charming homes. The civilized minority is as large here, I believe, as anywhere else.

It has made a city of splendid material comforts and kept it in order. But it has neglected in the past the unpleasant business of following what was going on in the cross roads of Little Bethels.

The Baptist preachers ranted unchallenged.

Their buffooneries were mistaken for humor. Now the clowns turn out to be armed, and have begun to shoot.

In his argument yesterday Judge Neal had to admit pathetically that it was hopeless to fight for a repeal of the anti-evolution law. The Legislature of Tennessee, like the Legislature of every other American state, is made up of cheap job-seekers and ignoramuses.

The Governor of the State is a politician ten times cheaper and trashier. It is vain to look for relief from such men. If the State is to be saved at all, it must be saved by the courts. For one, I have little hope of relief in that direction, despite Hays' logic and Darrow's eloquence. Constitutions, in America, no longer mean what they say. To mention the Bill of Rights is to be damned as a Red.

The rabble is in the saddle, and down here it makes its first campaign under a general beside whom Wat Tyler seems like a wart beside the Matterhorn.

A Woman Burns
GENE FOWLER—*New York American*—*1/12/1928*

[The electric chair execution of Ruth Brown Snyder, for the crime of killing her husband with her lover Judd Gray, was captured in a grisly photograph on the front page of the *New York Daily News* and remains reprinted to this day.]

SING SING PRISON—They led Ruth Brown Snyder from her steel cage tonight. Then the powerful guards thrust her irrevocably into the obscene, sprawling oaken arms of the ugly electric chair.

This was about 30 minutes ago. The memory of the crazy woman in her last agony as she struggled against the unholy embrace of the chair is yet too harrowing to permit a calm portrayal of the law's ghastly ritual. Ruth was the first to die.

The formal destruction of the killers of poor, stolid, unemotional Albert Snyder in his rumpled sleep the night of March 20, 1927, was hardly less revolting than the crime itself. Both victims of the chair met their death trembling but bravely.

Each was killed by a sustained, long-drawn current that rose and fell at the discretion of the hawk-eyed State executioner, Robert Elliott. In Ruth's case, he administered three distinct increases of current. For Judd, Elliott had two climactic electric increases.

Ruth entered the death chamber at 11:00 o'clock. She was declared dead at 11:07. Less than three minutes after her limp body was freed from the chair, Gray entered—not wearing his glasses and rolling his unhandsome eyes rapidly from right to left and then upward. The current was applied to Gray at 11:10 o'clock. He was pronounced dead by Dr. C. C. Sweet, chief prison physician, at 11:14.

Brief as the time was for the State to slay Ruth and Judd, it seems in retrospect to have been a long, haunting blur of bulging horror—glazed eyes, saffron faces, fear-blanched, that became twisted masks; purpling underlips and hands as pale as chalk, clenching in the last paroxysms.

And as these woeful wrecks passed from life the shadows of attendants, greatly magnified, seemed to move in frantic array along the walls, the silhouettes nodding and prancing in a sepulchral minuet.

The football helmet, containing the upper electrode, was pressed to the skulls of Ruth and Judd, one after the other, in a manner suggesting a sordid coronation of the King and Queen of Horror. A passing noise emanating from the bodies of the current-paralyzed victims rose like a hideous hymn by a serpent choir. No regal incense for these wretched beings, but from the skull of each in turn there curled upward thin, spiral wisps of pale smoke where their scalps were seared by the killing flame.

As Ruth entered the room she responded to the prayer for the dying given her by Rev. Father John T. McCaffrey.

Ruth's voice, bereft of the maddening, hysterical scream that sometimes had risen from her throat in the condemned cell, now was high pitched, but soft in texture. It sometimes was the voice of a little girl—such a one as might be seen and heard during the Times Square rush hour, lost from her parents and among big, strange men.

In response to the prayer of the priest, who wore his black cassock and stood sadly over her, Ruth muttered parts of the responses, the last one being:

"Father, forgive them, for they know not what they do."

The leather helmet was pressed to her blonde hair, a patch of which had been clipped to make a place for the electrode. Two matrons who had walked, one on either side of the woman, departed from the room before Elliott shot the hot blast into her once white, lovely body.

The matrons and Principal Keeper John J. Sheehy had stood before the pitiful woman to shield as much as possible her helpless form from the gaze of the witnesses. Ruth wore a brown smock of the sort stenographers and women clerks used in their office work. It had white imitation pearl buttons. She had on a short, washable black cotton skirt.

Ruth had black cotton stockings, the right one of which was rolled down to her ankle. On her feet were brown felt slippers. She wore blue bloomers.

"Jesus have mercy!" came the pitiful cry. Ruth's blue eyes were red with much weeping. Her face was strangely old. The blonde bobbed hair, hanging in stringy bunches over her furrowed brow, seemed almost white with years of toil and suffering as the six dazzling, high-powered lights illuminated every bit of her agonized lineaments.

Ruth's form seemed more slender than usual as she dragged her feet and groped with her hands.

"Father, forgive . . ."

The failing voice was interrupted. The holy litany was stopped short. No priestly ministrations could save her body now. Ruth's felt-slippered feet were at the great abyss, her blanched face, only the lower part of which one could see, was chalky.

She who had pleaded earlier in the day for life—just twenty-four hours more of it—seemed to have lived a thousand years and a thousand torments in the hellish prelude. Tightly corseted by the black leather bands, Ruth was flabby and futile as the blast struck her. It swept into her veins with an insidious buzz. Her body went forward as far as the restraining things would permit.

The tired form was taut. The body that once throbbed with the joy of her sordid bacchanals turned brick red as the current struck. Slowly, after half a minute of the death current, the exposed arms, right leg, throat and jaws, bleached out again.

Executioner Elliott, in his alcove, gazed as dourly as a gargoyle at the iron widow, who now had turned to putty. Then he shut off the current. Dr. Sweet stepped forward. He adjusted the stethoscope, exploring for any chance heart beat. Ruth's right hand had been clenched. The back of that hand rested flush against the chair. The forefinger and thumb were placed together, in the position of one who is holding a pinch of snuff. As the current was opened, the hand slowly turned over in the wrist strap; the forefinger and thumb, which had been pointed upward, now were turned down.

All this time there had been a fizzing, whirring monotone. That was the only sound in the white-walled death chamber except the light rattle in the silvered steam pipes.

Two attendants hastily donned white interns' coats. A porcelain topped wheel stretcher, virtually a mobile operating table—which hitherto had been behind the chair, was brought to Ruth's feet. And now the small audience was nauseated by the repellent work the chair had done.

One attendant screened Ruth's legs with a towel. Water from the moist electrode was dripping down her right leg. As a guard removed the electrode it proved to have been a ghastly garter, one that scalded, branded, and bit deeply.

A greenish purple blister the size of an eggplant had been raised on her well-formed calf. No mawkish sentiment should be expended on lady murderers, we are told, but somehow one did not think of what this woman had done, but of what was being done to her. It was a fiendish spectacle as they lifted her to the white-topped table.

Two men hoisted her. Her arms hung limply. Her head had been burned. Her mouth, the purplish lips now as white as limestone, was agape in an idiotic grin. What a sorry gift the State made to eternity.

No longer was Ruth trussed in those oily black straps. One of those binders had seemed to press her ample bosom cruelly where once a baby daughter had nestled and found life. Another belt had imprisoned her waist. The humble folds of her cheap girlish smock had retreated vainly and formed puffy plaits under the rude familiarity of the chair's embrace.

Ruth was a broken butterfly in a spider's web.

In looking back—back to the death of Ruth—the adjusting of the helmet, imagine a football helmet of regulation brand on a woman's head as an instrument of death; I say, the adjustment of that dripping helmet was such a striking symbol of Ruth's futile search for worldly joys through sin.

It spelled all that she had dared, suffered and paid in leaving her doll's house in staid, home-loving Queens Village. That helmet was death's sordid millinery. No fluffy ribbons or bows or gaily-hued feathers so dear to the fun-loving Ruth.

Just a snaky wire at the top of this hateful hat, a wire that coiled beside her and was ready to dart into the brain with searing fangs. They wheeled her out to the autopsy room. There were three minutes of mopping up, retesting the machinery. Warden Lawes stood sadly aside. Father McCaffrey, his head bowed, departed.

The chair *Moloch* of civilization in this year of enlightenment was yawning for another human sacrifice. Principle Keeper Sheehy left the room to summon the little corset salesman to his doom.

Everyone had expected Judd to die first. But at the final hour Warden Lawes moved Ruth to the last-minute cell only 20 paces from the chair chamber. Judd was shunted to the east wing and had to walk 160 feet.

Judd Gray met his death like a man. It is true he seemed horribly shaken. It is a fact that he was so moved by the enormity of the price he must pay that his voice could not be heard above a guttural, jumbled monotone. His lips framed the words, but the words died in his throat. It was the voice of a man being turned into a mummy-like catalepsy.

Judd, his roving eyes apparently seeing naught before him, looked shabby in the full white light against the background of severely tailored medical men and uniformed guards. Yet there was in his bearing a sense of dignity incompatible with criminality and disgraceful death. Judd came of good people and his breeding now told.

Yes, his dignity as he tried to repeat after the Protestant chaplain, Rev. Anthony Peterson, the phrases from the Sermon on the Mount, was impressive. One forgot his cheap, frowsy gray trousers and the grotesque, flapping right pants leg that had been split at the inner leg to receive the electrode.

He had figured woolen socks of a mauve shade. The right one was rolled down over a brown felt slipper. His knitted long underwear of light buff color had the right leg rolled high above the knee. Gray's leg was well-developed and evidenced his athletic days of tennis and quarterback on his school football eleven. Now he too wore a football helmet, just the sort he used to sport when directing the attack of his team.

"Blessed are the pure in heart," intoned the chaplain.

Gray's white lips moved. A deaf person would have understood the words by the lip-reading system. But only a cackling scramble of sound got past Gray's rather boyish mouth. It seemed that Gray came into the death house supported by a religious ecstasy. His chaplain was wearing his gown as a doctor of divinity. He is a large, finely set-up man with gray hair and a large kindly face.

Gray sought the eyes of his spiritual advisor, both when he walked into the chamber and before his eyes were masked. In walking Gray moved with leaden feet. At times he seemed to be treading on thorns and the two lines between his eyes and at the top of his nose were black streaks in his ashen face. The face seemed to be fed by lukewarm water instead of blood.

Brisk and facile fingers of veteran guards, whose powerful hands displayed an astounding cunning, worked at Gray's straps. The big hands manipulated the buckles and the spidery accouterments of death with the ease of a Paderewski ensnaring the notes of a rhapsody.

Gray had entered the death room at 11:08 o'clock. At first he walked stiffly as if his knees were locked together. His steps sometimes were like those of a person trying to climb a steep hill. His chin, which had a deep cleft in it, was thrust forward and his nostrils were slightly distended.

There was evidence of a terrible inner strain, but there was not one whit of cowardice manifest in the march of the little corset salesman. His jaws were as yellowish white as saffron and his lately-shaved beard still showed enough to lend shadows to his sunken jowls. But there was no saffron and no yellow in his backbone, no matter what his crime was or how brutal he may have been when he held a sashweight over stodgy, middle-aged Albert Snyder.

The doctors, Sweet and Kearney, watched in a detached way as the well-trained prison attendants proceeded to kill Judd in the name of the State. Elliott sent the short copper lever home. Judd, who had been sort of crumpled beneath his leather manacles, now shot forward and remained erect.

A blue spark flashed at the leg electrode. Soon his sock, not quite clear from the current as the water from the electrode dripped down his calf, was singed. Smoke came from the leg. Next the powerful pressure of the death stream singed his rather wavy dark brown hair. Smoke rose on either side of his head. For a moment he seemed a grotesque Buddha with votive incense pouring from his ears.

At the first electric torrent, Judd's throat and jaw were swollen. The chords stood out. The skin was gorged with blood and was the color of a turkey gobbler's wattles. Slowly this crimson tide subsided and left his face paler, but still showing splotches of red, which were mosaics of pain. The electricity was put on just as the chaplain got this far with his comforting words:

"For God so loved the world . . ."

Judd was not conscious, presumably, to hear the rest of the minister's "that he gave his only begotten Son . . ."

Gray's white shirt was open. When Elliott withdrew the lever of the switch, Dr. Sweet walked forward to search the chest of the night's second victim for heart action. He found none. He said:

"I pronounce this man dead."

The chair with its now lifeless burden still held the eyes of many a bewildering fascination. There were not a few, however, who covered their eyes. The men in white coats made their second trip with the wheeled stretcher. Judd did not know that he had been preceded in death by Ruth. They had not seen each other or exchanged notes since they first entered the death house eight months ago. Nor did the former lovers meet tonight in life.

Still these victims, who were known as No. 79892 (Ruth Snyder) and No. 79891 (Judd Gray) on the prison rolls, are again together in death. For their bodies, shrouded in white sheets, are in the prison morgue, a small room not fifty feet from the chair. This, then, was the end of the road, the close of their two years of stolen love. Their bodies are cut open as the first hour of the new day comes hazily over town, prison and broad, half frozen river. Their skulls are opened by medical men, as in the stern letter of the law, and their brains are plucked therefrom by rubber gloved hands and are deftly turned this way and that for inspection beneath the bright prison lights.

It was an unhallowed spectacle, this reduction of a full-bodied woman of thirty-three years to a limp and blubbery cadaver. It was fearful to see a man cooked in the chair. The twenty-four invited witnesses file out of the death house. Warden Lawes' secretary, Clement J. Ferly, signs the death certificates.

A last minute move on the part of Ruth's mother, Josephine Brown, and her brother, Andrew, failed to prevent the autopsy that is being performed as this is written. An order was served on Warden Lawes forbidding the prison physician to make a surgical incision in Ruth's body. On advice of Attorney General Ottinger, Warden Lawes did not obey the order.

No opiates and no sedatives were administered to either of the pair tonight, Warden Lawes said. They ate somewhat heartily of a last dinner of roast chicken, soup, coffee, celery and mashed potatoes. Gray, in ordering his meal, had underlined his written request for "good coffee." As he handed it to the guard, Gray said: "And I mean *good* coffee."

No typewriters and no telegraph wires were permitted in the penitentiary. Immediately after the reporters left the now empty, grasping, greedy chair—which seemed to clamor for still other human sacrifice—they dashed to waiting automobiles and through the tall iron gates. About a thousand persons were massed as close to the prison as the guards would permit. Through a long gauntlet of watchers, who stood anxiously to hear if Ruth and Judd had gone, roared the press cars.

The stories are now being finished in a cramped and crowded back room of a soft drink establishment, which has an old-time bar running the length of the front room, and where the air is thick with tobacco. Then, as the morning comes on, leaving the night with thinning shadows like ghosts departing, the fading click of typewriters comes with less rattle and the buzz of telegraph instruments, too, is subsiding.

Then the calm realization that the law had been obeyed and society avenged, and that the chair remains to jerk and rip and tear and burn those who slay. Then to bed for nightmares to distort your scrambled dreams.

The bodies of Gray and Mrs. Snyder will be released to relatives at 9 o'clock in the morning. Ruth's body will be claimed by her mother, Mrs. Josephine Brown. Judd's mother, Mrs. Margaret Gray, will claim his.

The Trial of Al Capone

DAMON RUNYON—*New York American*—10/6-17/1931

A fragrant whiff of green fields and growing rutabagas and parsnips along with echoes of good old Main Street, crept into the grime-stained Federal Building here today as your Uncle Sam took up the case of Al Capone and gathered a jury in what you might call jigtime.

It is a jury made up mainly of small towners and Michael J. Ahern, chief counsel for Al Capone, frankly admitted dissatisfaction to the Court about it.

He wanted all these people dismissed but Judge Wilkerson overruled his motion. The jury was sworn in with nine veterans of court room juries among the twelve good men and true, and tomorrow morning at ten o'clock the Government of these United States starts work on Al Capone.

Your Uncle Sam says Al Capone owes him $215,000 on an income of $1,038,000 in six years.

Your Uncle Sam hints that Al Capone derived this tidy income from such illegal didoes as bootlegging, gambling and the like.

"Do you hope the government proves the defendant guilty?" was one question asked a venireman at the request of counsel for the defense.

Apparently none cherished that hope.

"Have you any desire that the defendant be sent to jail?" was another question requested by the defense.

"Well no," was the general reply.

Al Capone sat up straight in his chair and smoothed his rumpled necktie. He felt better. The G-men—as the boys call 'em—want to put Al Capone in a Federal pokey, or jail, for anywhere from two to thirty-two years, to impress upon him the truth of the adage that honesty is the best policy.

As Al Capone sat there with the scent of the new-mown hay oozing at intervals from the jury box, he was a terrific disappointment to the strictly-seeing Chicago tourist who felt that Al should have been vested at least in some of the panoply of his reputed office as Maharajah of the Hoods. Perhaps a cartridge belt. Some strangers felt this Chicago has been misrepresented to them.

Capone arrived for the opening session fifteen minutes ahead of time, which is said to be a record of punctuality in him.

A big crowd was gathered on the Clark Street side of the dingy old building waiting to see him, but Al popped out of an automobile and into the building like a fox going into a hole. Not many of the curiosity-seekers got a good peek at him.

He entered the court room alone and was quickly surrounded by a crowd of reporters, male and female, who began bouncing questions about his ears. They asked him if he was worried, and he replied, logically enough, "Who wouldn't be worried?"

He was scarcely the sartorial spectacle familiar to the winter inmates of Florida, where Al's sport apparel is one of the scenes of interest. In fact, he was quietly dressed this morning, bar a hat of pearly white, emblematic no doubt, of purity.

* * *

The soft murmur of the blue breakers caressing old Miami shore sort o' sneaked into Judge Wilkerson's courtroom this afternoon between shrill snorts of the Chicago traffic coppers' whistles outside, as witnesses from the sunny Southland connected Al Capone up with $125,500 transmitted from Chicago to Miami by wire.

Much of the money was traced to the purchase and improvement of the celebrated winter seat of the Hidalgo of the Hoods on Palm Island, in Biscayne Bay, between Miami proper and Miami Beach.

Vernon Hawthorn, a Miami attorney, told of a meeting in which Capone and a number of officials of Miami and Dade County, Florida were present. It was in 1928; Capone had just appeared in Florida and the good citizens of Dade wanted to find out what the celebrated visitor intended in their startled midst. Al said he was there to rest.

The witness said Capone told him he was in the cleaning and pressing business in Chicago. Finally the witness said, "I'll admit that his business was gambling and that he was interested in the Cicero Dog Track." Furthermore, that he had bought a home in Miami.

The question was asked then at that meeting, "What do you do?" And according to the transcript read this morning, Capone said, "I'm a gambler. I bet on horses."

"Are you also a bootlegger?"

"No, I was never a bootlegger in my life."

* * *

A gleaming diamond belt buckle, one of a batch of thirty purchased by Al Capone at $277 apiece, or $8,310 for the lot, was flashed before the astonished eyes of the jury today.

Al bought these buckles for his friends. One of the buckles is said to have been worn by Alfred (Jake) Lingle, Chicago underworld reporter, who was assassinated in June of last year, for which crime Leo V. Brothers is now doing a stretch in the penitentiary.

The jurors peered at the buckle with interest. Each buckle is said to have been engraved with the initials of the recipient, but markings on the buckle displayed today were not revealed, a fact that is doubtless causing someone to heave big sighs of relief.

* * *

We had a slight diversion after Judge Wilkerson adjourned the court until Monday. The diversion consisted of the seizing of the mysterious Phillip D'Andrea, Capone's bodyguard who had been sitting behind Al Capone since this trial started, by a United States deputy marshal and the discovery on his person of a .38 caliber John Roscoe, or pistol. D'Andrea was ordered by Judge Wilkerson to stand trial for having a revolver in the courtroom and was taken to jail.

D'Andrea is a short, stout bespectacled individual who dresses well and looks like a prosperous professional man. He has been described as a friend of Capone's and Al seemed much disturbed by his seizure. He waited around while D'Andrea was in the marshal's office with Capone attorneys Ahern and Fink trying to get him out of his trouble. Al said he didn't know D'Andrea carried a gun and didn't believe he did.

* * *

That Al Capone is the victim of a wicked plot, conceived in Washington and partially hatched in Miami, was the substance of an utterance by Michael J. Ahern, as he addressed those 12 tired good men and true in Judge Wilkerson's court this afternoon.

Ahern was making the closing address on behalf of Al, whose trial on a charge of beating your Uncle Sam out of his income tax is nearing a close and ought to be handed over to the jury about noon tomorrow.

Ahern went back to the Punic Wars and the time of Cato, the censor, whose cry was "Carthage must be destroyed" and said there are a lot of Cato's around nowadays especially around Washington whose cry is "Capone must be destroyed."

* * *

"This case will determine whether any man is above the law." So said George E. Q. Johnson, United States Attorney in the final argument on behalf of your Uncle Sam this morning.

"Gentlemen, the United States Government has no more important laws in force than revenue laws. Thousands upon thousands of sources go to work daily and all of them who earn more than $1,500 a year must pay income tax. If the time ever comes when it has to go out before the collection of taxes the Army and Navy will disband. Courts will be swept aside, civilization will revert to the jungle days when every man was for himself."

Johnson warned the jury to remember the men and women who pay a tax on incomes over $1,500.00 a year in contrast to those of Capone who should be splayed for evading taxes during "this time of national deficit."

The Burning of the Books
HEYWOOD BROUN—*New York World-Telegram*—5/12/1933

They burned the books, but there remains a red glow in the sky. The fuel of the foolish was curiously assorted. Upon the Nazi bonfire were piled the works of some who never glowed before. I had not thought to live into a day when sparks would fly from Morris Hillquit.

The names of the great, the near and never great came to the crucible along with the words of the lame, the halt and the blind. Side by side the magnificent and the feeble words of those who merely meant well ascended into heaven.

Unconsciously the Nazis paid a singular tribute of respect to certain authors of small fame and rather meager merit. What wouldn't I give to have some forgotten book of my own suddenly become fortuitously a part of a pillar of fire by night! I really must buckle down to work and write something which Hitler does not like in order to be in on the next illumination. Yes, and I will even consent to call it to his attention.

Remarque, Ludwig, Mann, Karl Marx, Jack London and Ben Lindsey! It sounds almost like what some of the book critics call a "balanced ration." But why Ben Lindsey? He seems to me one of God's noblemen and also among the most fearsomely bad writers who ever set an earnest pen to paper.

They burned the books of Dr. Sigmund Freud. One of the barkers at the bonfire explained that the little man from Vienna had put too much stress upon the "animal qualities of human nature."

I cannot understand at all the philosophy of these nascent Nazis. They seem to be engaged upon a rather pitiful attempt to combine the school of blood and iron with sweet violets. If I can make it out the accepted author must be a combination of Nietzsche and Harold Bell Wright. It's a swell trick if they can do it.

But most of all I was interested in the burning of Dr. Freud. Sigmund Freud, like Karl Marx, is a writer who has been vastly discussed by millions who have never read a line he ever wrote. To paraphrase a familiar spiritual: "Everybody talking about Marx ain't gwine there. Revolution! Revolution! Gwine to walk all over Karl Marx's revolution!"

And in some respects Sigmund Freud is in an even better position than Karl Marx to get a pretty good chuckle for himself out of Nazi goings-on. The little man who led the first expedition into the darkest subconscious can afford to smile at the most amazing demonstration of national neuroticism the world has seen in our time.

An American correspondent who reported the address which Herr Gutjahr made as the books burned writes, "It was a boy's speech, and it was received with boyish enthusiasm."

I think Mr. Birchall might have gone further than that. It was, as a matter of sober fact, a child's set piece, and the whole enterprise represented a retreat from reality into infantilism. The I.Q. of the Hitler movement can hardly rate anything above six years of age. At that stage any one of us would like to dress up in a uniform and play with matches.

But somebody really ought to tell Adolf's adolescents that it isn't funny anymore.

The first time I meet a Nazi fooling around writing things with chalk on nice, clean walls and sticking his penknife into the furniture I propose to fetch him a cuff over the side of the head and exclaim in a firm voice, "Naughty, Naughty."

Dillinger "Gets His"
JACK LAIT—International News Service—7/23/1934

John Dillinger, ace bad man of the world, got his last night—two slugs through his heart and one through his head. He was tough and he was shrewd, but he wasn't as tough and shrewd as the Federals, who never closed a case until the end. It took twenty-seven of them to end Dillinger's career, and their strength came out of his weakness—a woman.

Dillinger was put on the spot by a tip-off to the local bureau of the Department of Justice. It was a feminine voice that Melvin H. Purvis, head of the Chicago office, heard. He had waited long for it.

It was Sunday, but Uncle Sam doesn't observe and the NRA works seven days a week.

The voice told him that Dillinger would be at a little third-run movie house, the Biograph, last night—that he went there every night and usually got there about 7:30. It was almost 7:30 then. Purvis sent out a call for all men within reach and hustled all men on hand with him. They waited more than an hour. They knew from the informer that he must come out, turn left, turn again into a dark alley where he parked his Ford-8 coupe.

Purvis himself stood at the main exit. He had men on foot and in parked inconspicuous cars strung on both sides of the alley. He was to give the signal. He had ascertained about when the feature film, *Manhattan Melodrama*, would end. Tensely eyeing his wristwatch he stood. Then the crowd, that always streams out when the main picture finishes, came. Purvis had seen Dillinger when he was brought through from Arizona to Crown Point, Indiana, and his heart pounded as he saw again the face that had been studied by countless millions on the front pages of the world.

Purvis gave the signal. Dillinger did not see him. Public enemy No. 1 lit a cigarette, strolled a few feet to the alley with the mass of middle-class citizens going in that direction, then wheeled left.

A Federal man, revolver in hand, stepped from behind a telegraph pole at the mouth of the passage. "Hello, John," he said, almost whispered, his voice husky with the intensity of the classic melodrama. Dillinger went with lightning right hand for his gun, a .38 Colt automatic. He drew it from his trousers pocket.

But, from behind, another government agent pressed the muzzle of his service revolver against Dillinger's back and fired twice. Both bullets went through the bandit's heart.

He staggered, his weapon clattered to the asphalt paving, and as he went three more shots flashed. One bullet hit the back of his head, downward, as he was falling, and came out under his eye. Police cleared the way for the police car which was there in a few minutes. The police were there not because they were in on the capture, but because the sight of so many mysterious men around the theater had scared the manager into thinking he was about to be stuck up and he had called the nearest station.

When the detectives came on the run, Purvis intercepted them and told them what was up. They called headquarters and more police came, but with instructions to stand by and take orders from Purvis.

Dillinger's body was rushed to Alexian Brothers' hospital in a patrol wagon. There were no surgeons in it. But the policemen knew he was dead, and at the entrance of the hospital, where a kindly priest in a long cassock had come to the door to see who might be in need of help, the driver was ordered to the morgue.

I was in a taxi that caught up with the police car at the hospital, and we followed across town to the old morgue. No one bothered us, though we went fifty miles an hour.

There was no crowd then. We pulled in. Strong arms carried the limp, light form of the man who had been feared by a great government through that grim door of many minor tragedies. It lay on a rubber stretcher.

In the basement, the receiving ward of the last public hospice of the doomed, they stripped the fearsome remains.

What showed up, nude and pink, still warm, was the body of what seemed a boy, the features as though at rest and only an ugly, bleeding hole under the left eye, such as a boy might have gotten in a street fight. His arms were bruised from the fall and the bumping in the wagon.

But under the heart were two little black, bleeding holes, clean and fresh. These could not have been anything but what they were. That part of John Dillinger did not look as though it was a boy's hurt—it was the fatal finish of a cold-blooded killer and not half of what he had given Officer O'Malley in East Chicago, Indiana, in the bank robbery when he cut the policeman almost in half with a machine gun.

Louisiana's Kingfish Lies in State
JOSEPH COOKMAN—*New York Post*—9/12/1935

[Louisiana's populist governor and senator Huey Long—called by some an American Mussolini and immortalized in Robert Penn Warren's novel *All the King's Men*—was assassinated in the statehouse he commissioned.]

The Louisiana peasant who became Louisiana's king is on view in his Capitol in his coffin today.

The face which in life never held the same expression for more than two seconds is fixed in a studied smirk—an undertaker's idea of how Huey Long should have looked.

Here, set forth in a dinner suit, is the man who sold lard substitute to hookwormed sharecroppers.

The shirt front is as smooth as a planed board, as white as a jailbird's face. The black tie flares with the nonchalant perfection of a drawing in a fashion magazine.

You look down at it for the brief moment that the guards, uniformed and plain clothed, permit. You can't believe that here is anything but a bad wax sculpture of a super-humanly alive man—and painted at that.

It is so much like one of those figures you see in store windows which remind you of somebody, but you can't be quite sure of just whom. Huey wouldn't have liked it, and his words wouldn't have been fit to print.

The setting is superb. When Huey Long decreed the building of a new State Capitol he specified it should have an entrance hall that would impress people, all kinds of people.

It does impress. Brass doors with bas-relief of such historical happenings as the defeat of the British by Andrew Jackson; huge Sevres vases, the gift of

France to its former possession, Louisiana; mural paintings in fine and subdued colors; a high and delicately tinted ceiling—don't let anybody tell you that it isn't an ornate rotunda.

Last night people flocked to see the genius the State has produced.

But it was a surprisingly small crowd. A fraction of the Long office-holders of this capital city would have made a larger one.

About 2,000 waited. True, it was drizzling, the hot, weakening drizzle of the Louisiana swamps, through the afternoon. But when, according to the widespread information, the Kingfish was to be seen lying in state, the crowd was still small.

This reporter became a part of the crowd. He wanted to know what was being said by the man in the street and the man on the dusty rural road.

This is what he heard:

"It sho' is hot heah with all these folks jammin' in thisaway."

"Do you heah about that lil' baby, honey? What kind of a fool would be bringin' a baby to see this?"

"I do declare, we is getting closer all the time. Yoo hoo, Clairmont, how yu doin', chil'?"

In short, this reporter didn't hear a single reference to Huey Long or his policies.

This reporter hazards no guess as to the meaning of last night's lack of enthusiasm.

He merely reports that the crowd was much more interested in the fact that movie men were taking a picture of the scene than in the fact that a great man of their State, the man who would make Louisiana the Empire State, was no more.

Some laughed and waved to friends, others pushed and shoved exactly as they would at a bargain sale.

The mourners' line curled into the front door and past the coffin.

As they departed they had to go past a half dozen carpenters who had opened their kits and spread their tools on the expensive marble floor of the rotunda. They were building two wooden fences to keep in line the crowds moving slowly past the coffin today.

Outside there was a clang of picks and spades. Grave diggers were hacking away at the turf in the sunken garden outside the Capitol.

"It's unlucky to leave a grave open at night," a man in the crowd muttered.

National Guardsmen, unarmed but straight and tall in their brown uniforms, stood guard at the coffin. The wall behind the casket was smothered with flowers, and they, too, were a sort of history of Huey Long's life.

"Eleventh Ward of New Orleans," read a gilt ribbon across a cluster of roses and asters.

"New Orleans Clearing House Association," proclaimed another one.

At dusk the 2,000 persons had drifted past the coffin, taking hurried looks at the body and turning to gape at the carpenters. One of the latter whistled softly as he sawed—a torch song called "When I Grow Too Old to Dream."

Earlier, Mrs. Long, swathed to the chin in dark, melancholy blue, went to the funeral parlor and came out dabbing her eyes. Her daughter, Rose, twenty, and a younger son, Russell, walked by her side. Rose clenched her handkerchief in her right hand.

High officials of the State Government, including Governor O. K. Allen and Speaker Allen Ellender, visited the funeral parlor, too.

But the scene in the rotunda was for the people who did not know Long—people who probably never saw him except in death. Farmers, red-necked from the sun and with the mud of bayous caked on their boots, stood in line in the rain for a two-second glimpse at the coffin.

The high French heels of young girls, going clickey-clack across the marble floor, challenged the din raised by carpenters.

Generally, Long's enemies stayed away. Some of them were in the crowd outside the Capitol when the body was brought from the funeral parlor. They took off their straw hats, limp and drooping from the rain, as the coffin was carried up the sweeping flight of steps.

One of the first persons past the coffin was Mrs. Josephine Fohn of New Orleans, an elderly woman in a shapeless brown dress. At the neck of her dress sparkled a pin—a gilt ornament in the shape of a fish. On the fish's head was a crown.

Rap, rap, rap, went the carpenters' hammers, and still Mrs. Fohn talked.

"See," she said while waiting to pass the coffin, "See, a kingfish."

"I don't know whether he was right all the time," she said, "but I guess he was for poor folks. I'm poor folks. He said 'every man's a king,' and I guess he meant it."

"Maybe he was wrong some time, but when I read where he had died, I said to my two boys, 'You've got to take me up to Baton Rouge in your car so I can go to the funeral.' They couldn't get away. I came on the bus."

Now Mrs. Fohn was abreast of the coffin. There was steam on the lenses of her horn-rimmed glasses, and she brushed at them angrily. Mrs. Fohn took a quick look at the coffin and doddered out into the rain. The crowd swallowed her. Inside a carpenter whistled and pounded a nail.

Mussolini's Tough Guys
WESTBROOK PEGLER—Scripps Howard—12/1/1935

One rainy afternoon in Rome I went out in a taxi to circle the huge park, surrounded by a high wall, where Mussolini's house stands alone amid a grove of trees. The house was hidden from view, and the trip would not have paid out in results except for the presence along the sidewalk beneath the wall of a detail of cutthroats the like of which has not been assembled under one command since the days of His Majesty's British Black and Tans.

Mussolini's household guards were stationed at intervals of about fifty yards all around the park, each under his umbrella in a drizzle, all keeping up a nominal pretense of waiting for a street car, of which there was none in that vicinity, or for a friend, of which there can be none on earth. There were other secret policemen on the far side, one carrying a suitcase which could have contained the conventional Tommy gun. This one was strolling up the block the first time I passed. When I came around again he was strolling the other way with his suitcase.

They were a homey touch, in a way, for they were the first of that type that I had seen in several weeks in Italy, and for a moment I thought I was back in Miami Beach, Fla., in the winter colony of the artichoke and slot-machine aristocracy of our Northern cities.

At a distance, and in print, the castor-oil treatment with which the Black Shirts overcame political doubt seems not very brutal and even slightly humorous. But at close quarters, as the boys peered out from underneath their dripping umbrellas, it was not so easy to see the joke.

The customary procedure of these missionaries is to call at night in a body on the victim of a political error, twist his arms and legs until the bones crack, then pour down his neck a quart of castor oil which may be mixed with kerosene. It is inartistic to use kerosene, however, for enough castor oil taken all at once is almost certain to rupture the human plumbing and to bring about death from natural causes within a few days. There is always plenty of castor oil.

A few days later, on a trip to Pontinia, the tailor-made village which Mussolini built on a reclaimed swamp somewhat resembling the Florida glades, the strong-arm detail was out again, this time in greater numbers, and the scene was pleasantly reminiscent of those Kentucky Derbies at Louisville in the days of prohibition when all the Italian alky cookers and bootleggers east of the Rocky Mountains gathered for their annual convention.

They were everywhere. They mingled with the crowd and climbed the steps to overlook the press of people. They sidled up and looked earnestly into your eyes and gazed at your camera and studied your overcoat for bulges.

I felt nervous, for we had left Rome in the dark at 7 a.m. without breakfast, and I had in my pocket an eating apple whose contour might have suggested the hoodlums' pineapple.

This trip was organized after the fashion created by the late Tex Rickard when he was conducting ballyhoo parties for sports writers to the training camps of his fighters. Mussolini has a special preference for the foreign press on such occasions, for he has the natural desire that his achievements in this great reclamation work shall be known in other lands.

He has salvaged the swamps, built several towns, and lifted whole communities out of their old surroundings, to set them down in a new country where everything is ready for life. It is the kind of work that we in America are always going to do. Consequently, the petty Mussolinis of Mussolini's foreign press bureau, so lazy and stupid most of the time, round up all the foreign representation they can find when the Duce is about to put on one of his shows. If they don't turn up with enough foreign press, Mussolini gets sore and gives them hell.

So there were about fifty of us on this trip, and we all had a long look at the Duce putting on his No. 3 routine. This is the one in which he is a kindly man of the people, and the living spirit of a proud and mighty but friendly race demanding only justice for Italy. It is said to be the best act in his repertoire, and I will say that I have never seen anything of its kind, although Red Mike Hylan, when he was Mayor of New York, resembled Mussolini around the ears.

After the act Mussolini received us in the council room of the new town hall. He is not as tall as I had expected, being about 5 feet 10 and thick in the barrel, but not fat. He moves around with the quick, jerky motions of a major general tearing along a company street on an inspection trip, and his yes men, like the humble shave-tail, are frightened speechless in his presence except to throw back their heads and yell, "Doo-chay, Doo-chay."

His face surprised me, for I had expected a popeyed glare, an undershot jaw and the generally bloodthirsty mien, whereas there was a soft expression in Mussolini's eyes, he spoke in a quiet, civil tone, and his lips parted in a smile three or four times. His eyelids were red, as though he had been working nights. But the Black Shirts told me Mussolini never gets tired. His eyelids are naturally red.

A Frenchwoman journalist stepped out and dropped her wedding ring into his hand for his gold collection. Mussolini said he was touched, and went away in a pleasant mood. It was strange to feel drawn to this man, knowing that a word from him might cause another world war any minute, and that down in the village street and all over the place were those plain-clothes missionaries of his who might rub against that apple any minute and take impulsive steps.

Mr. Welles and Mass Delusion
DOROTHY THOMPSON—*New York Herald Tribune*—11/2/1938

[Orson Welles and the Mercury Theatre On the Air's radio play version of H. G. Wells's *War of the Worlds* created mass panic when listeners believed that America was being invaded by Martians. Columnist Dorothy Thompson turned the incident into a meditation on the dangers of propaganda in an age of mass media.]

All unwittingly Mr. Orson Welles and the *Mercury Theatre On the Air* have made one of the most fascinating and important demonstrations of all time. They have proved that a few effective voices, accompanied by sound effects, can so convince masses of people of a totally unreasonable, completely fantastic proposition as to create nationwide panic.

They have demonstrated more potently than any argument, demonstrated beyond question of a doubt, the appalling dangers and enormous effectiveness of popular and theatrical demagoguery.

They have cast a brilliant and cruel light upon the failure of popular education.

They have shown up the incredible stupidity, lack of nerve and ignorance of thousands.

They have proved how easy it is to start a mass delusion.

They have uncovered the primeval fears lying under the thinnest surface of the so-called civilized man.

They have shown that man, when the victim of his own gullibility, turns to the government to protect him against his own errors of judgment.

The newspapers are correct in playing up this story over every other news event in the world. It is the story of the century.

And far from blaming Mr. Orson Welles, he ought to be given a Congressional medal and a national prize for having made the most amazing and important contribution to the social sciences. For Mr. Orson Welles and his theater have made a greater contribution to an understanding of Hitlerism, Mussolinism, Stalinism, anti-Semitism and all the other terrorisms of our times than all the words about them that have been written about reasonable men. They have made the reductio ad absurdum of mass manias. They have thrown more light on recent events in Europe leading to the Munich Pact than everything that has been said on the subject by all the journalists and commentators. Hitler managed to scare all Europe to its knees a month ago, but he at least had an army and an air force to back up his shrieking words.

But Mr. Welles scared thousands into demoralization with nothing at all.

That historic hour on the air was an act of unconscious genius, performed by the very innocence of intelligence.

Nothing whatever about the dramatization of the *War of the Worlds* was in the least credible, no matter at what point the hearer might have tuned in. The entire verisimilitude was in the names of a few specific places. Monsters were depicted of a type that nobody has ever seen, equipped with "rays" entirely fantastic; they were described as "straddling the Pulaski Skyway" and throughout the broadcast they were referred to as Martians, men from another planet.

A twist of the dial would have established for anybody that the national catastrophe was not being noted on any other station. A second of logic would have dispelled any terror. A notice that the broadcast came from a nonexistent agency would have awakened skepticism.

A reference to the radio program would have established that the "War of the Worlds" was announced in advance.

The time element was obviously lunatic.

Listeners were told that "within two hours three million people have moved out of New York"—an obvious impossibility for the most disciplined army moving exactly as planned, and a double fallacy because only a few minutes before, the news of the arrival of the monster had been announced.

And of course it was not even a planned hoax. Nobody was more surprised at the result than Mr. Welles. The public was told at the beginning, at the end and during the course of the drama that it *was* a drama.

But eyewitnesses presented themselves; the report become second hand, third hand, fourth hand, and became more and more credible, so that nurses and doctors and National Guardsmen rushed to defense.

When the trust became known the reaction was also significant. The deceived were furious and of course demanded that the state protect them, demonstrating that they were incapable of relying on their own judgment.

Again there was a complete failure of logic. For if the deceived had thought about it they would realize that the greatest organizers of mass hysterias and mass delusions today are states using the radio to excite terrors, incite hatreds, inflame masses, win mass support for policies, create idolatries, abolish reason and maintain themselves in power.

The immediate moral is apparent if the whole incident is viewed in reason: no political body must ever, under any circumstances, obtain a monopoly of radio.

The second moral is that our popular and universal education is failing to train reason and logic, even in the educated.

The third is that the popularization of science has led to gullibility and new superstitions, rather than to skepticism and the really scientific attitude of mind.

The fourth is that the power of mass suggestion is the most potent force today and that the political demagogue is more powerful than all the economic forces.

For, mind you, Mr. Welles was managing an obscure program, competing with one of the most popular entertainments on the air!

The conclusion is that the radio must not be used to create mass prejudices and mass divisions and schisms, either by private individuals or by government or its agencies, or its officials, or its opponents.

If people can be frightened out of their wits by mythical men from Mars, they can be frightened into fanaticism by the fear of Reds, or convinced that America is in the hands of sixty families, or aroused to revenge against any minority, or terrorized into subservience to leadership because of any imaginable menace.

The technique of modern mass politics calling itself democracy is to create a fear—a fear of economic royalists, or of Reds, or of Jews, or of starvation, or of any outside enemy—and exploit that fear into obtaining subservience in return for protection.

I wrote in this column a short time ago that the new warfare was waged by propaganda, the outcome depending on which side could first frighten the other to death.

The British people were frightened into obedience to a policy a few weeks ago by a radio speech and by digging a few trenches in Hyde Park, and afterward led to hysterical jubilation over a catastrophic defeat for their democracy.

But Mr. Welles went all the politicians one better. He made the scare to end scares, the menace to end menaces, the unreason to end unreason, the perfect demonstration that the danger is not from Mars but from the theatrical demagogue.

Union Thugs
WESTBROOK PEGLER—Scripps Howard—1/19/1940

Mr. William Green
American Federation of Labor
Washington, D.C.

Dear Mr. Green: A few days ago I wrote that the roster of officials in unions in the American Federation of Labor contained the nucleus for a good, major league rogues' gallery. In case you thought I was mistaken I am going to tell you today that the head of one of your big international unions was sentenced to Atlanta Penitentiary for four years and six months for white slavery. This is not Willie Bloff, the Chicago racketeer and vice monger who was and remains boss of the movie and theatrical crafts. Willie is not the union president but just the personal, appointed representative of George Browne, who is, nominally at least, the president of the union.

The man I mean is George Scalese, a Brooklyn racketeer who has become president of the Building Service Employees International Union. Scalese is a criminal of the vilest type that it is impossible to imagine and a member of an old mob in Brooklyn. He used to be a bodyguard for Frankie Uale, alias Yale, the Capone mobster who was killed, nevertheless, and since the repeal of prohibition he and other hoodlums of the same type in Brooklyn and New York have gone into the labor movement.

**

This Building Service Employees Union is no cheap little local, Mr. Green, but one of your big international unions, and Scalese has been moving out the old officials of little subsidiary unions which have existed for years and moving in himself. He is a big shot in Chicago and San Francisco, but I suppose you don't need to be told how big he is. You know all that, but I can't see how you can fail to know what he is or, if you do know what he is, why you haven't had him thrown out of the American Federation of Labor. Do you think it is doing the American Federation of Labor any good to permit such a man to be president of one of your big international unions or doing the rank and file working stiffs any good to subject them to the rule of a vicious mobster?

Have it your own way, Mr. Green. If you lose your own job for stringing along with such people that is your affair.

This Scalese, Mr. Green, was convicted in the federal court in Brooklyn in September, 1913, on four out of eight counts. He and another hoodlum named Joe Alfano, alias Fox, transported a girl from Brooklyn to Boonton, N.J., to work her as a prostitute for their profit. The reason why they received such heavy sentences—Alfano got four years—was that the crime was unusually vicious. And Judge Veeder, in his charge to the jury, spoke of the details of the case as "nauseating" and told the jurymen that they were to disregard evidence that the girl was beaten, seduced and persuaded to live with your distinguished colleague in the labor movement on false promises of marriage. Scalese wasn't on trial for those amiable little acts of rudeness.

Your Mr. Scalese served about four years and put in for a Presidential pardon in 1923, but was turned down on the recommendation of the acting Attorney General of that time on the ground that the evidence was "of a most revolting character." He has now put in another application for a Presidential pardon, and I have information that some prominent politico-labor leaders think he should be pardoned. You wouldn't happen to know anything about that, would you, Mr. Green? Of course it is ironic that a man who can't hold public office or even vote, who lost his citizenship for a rotten crime, should be eligible to hold the presidency of a big union.

***

Well, there you are, you great, big, gorgeous, pious friend of the workingman. There is your colleague, George Scalese, to keep your noted co-worker, Willie Bloff, company. They would understand each other. They have everything in common.

That makes two I have given you, Mr. Green.

Do you want some more?

Okay, Mr. Green. I will give you background on plenty of your American Federation of Labor colleagues. It must be interesting work—your job as president of the American Federation of Labor. You meet such nice people.

Yours very truly,

WESTBROOK PEGLER.

When American Citizens Murder U.S. Soldiers
GEORGE S. SCHUYLER—*Pittsburgh Courier*—5/8/1943

I wish the United States would wreak vengeance on those people within the confines of this country who have killed American soldiers in uniform and gone unpunished to date.

There is, for example, the case of Pvt. Raymond Carr, a colored citizen of the United States. Private Carr while in the uniform of the U.S.A., and while on duty as directed by his superior officers, was killed in cold blood by an officer of the State Police department of Louisiana in Alexandria, La., because he refused to leave his post of duty. The grand jury in Louisiana refused to act, so Wendell Berge, Assistant Attorney General of the United States, has recommended to the Attorney General that no further action be taken concerning this murder of a uniformed American soldier on duty by a member of the Louisiana armed forced. The killing of Private Carr was contrary to the laws of the United States and Louisiana, and yet the Department of Justice is going to forget the whole matter!

On March 22, 1942, Sgt. Thomas B. Foster of the United States Army was shot to death at the doorstep of the Allison Presbyterian church in Little Rock, Ark., by a member of the armed forces of that city. The U.S. government halted prosecution of this white murderer because he was inducted into the U.S. Army! Would we excuse the murderers of the three Army aviators because the Japanese government transferred them to the ambulance corps!

On July 28, 1942, Pvt. Charles J. Rico of the United States Army was murdered in cold blood by a member of the armed forces of Beaumont, Texas. The local U.S. Attorney announced in January 1943, that the case against the murderer would not be prosecuted because "it is lacking in those elements promising a successful prosecution." When the NAACP legal department protested in February against this attitude, the Attorney General replied that the case "would not be opened or investigated."

Of course there have been countless cases of Negro soldiers in the uniform of the United States being beaten to a pulp by civilian police, sometimes resulting in death or permanent injury. There are few if any instances of the culprit or culprits being punished. Certainly none of the members of the armed forces of Arkansas nor any of the citizens who joined them in assaulting colored soldiers and their white officers have been prosecuted for this outrageous violation of U.S. laws. After elaborate investigation the Department of Justice told the NAACP that "the department's files in this matter have been closed."

In other words, when the Japanese murder captured U.S. soldiers in uniform and performing their duties, the United States seethes with indignation and horror, and the government vows to spare no expense in wreaking vengeance upon the yellow murderers who have flouted international law.

But when American citizens murder U.S. soldiers in uniform and in some instances performing their duties, the crimes get brief and often obscure notice in the daily press, and after a certain legal shadow-boxing, Uncle Sam throws up his hands and says "case closed." Meanwhile the murderers walk the streets and scoff at the law, knowing it will not be enforced when non-whites are involved.

Would you not think that the most powerful government on earth could more easily punish its citizens who murder men wearing its uniform than it could punish the nationals of a great military power 7,000 miles across the Pacific who were guilty of the same crime?

Is the statement of Justice Taney still true, that "a Negro has no rights that a white man is bound to respect"? If so, where is the "progress" in race relations to which orators and editorial writers are always referring?

The Liberation of Dachau
MARGUERITE HIGGINS—*New York Herald Tribune*—5/1/1945

Troops of the United States 7th Army liberated 33,000 prisoners this afternoon at this first and largest of the Nazi concentration camps. Some of the prisoners had endured for eleven years the horrors of notorious Dachau.

The liberation was a frenzied scene: Inmates of the camp hugged and embraced the American troops, kissed the ground before them and carried them shoulder high around the place.

The Dachau camp, in which at least a thousand prisoners were killed last night before the SS (Elite Guard) men in charge fled, is a grimmer and larger edition of the similarly notorious Buchenwald camp near Weimar.

This correspondent and Peter Furst, of the Army newspaper, *Stars and Stripes*, were the first two Americans to enter the enclosure at Dachau, where persons possessing some of the best brains in Europe were held during what might have been the most fruitful years of their lives.

While a United States 45th Infantry Division patrol was still fighting a way down through SS barracks to the north, our jeep and two others from the 42d Infantry drove into the camp enclosure through the southern entrance. As men of the patrol with us busied themselves accepting an SS man's surrender, we impressed a soldier into service and drove with him to the prisoners' barracks. There he opened the gate after pushing aside the body of a prisoner shot last night while attempting to get out to meet the Americans.

There was not a soul in the yard when the gate was opened. As we learned later, the prisoners themselves had taken over control of their enclosure the night before, refusing to obey any further orders from the German guards, who had retreated to the outside. The prisoners maintained strict discipline among themselves, remaining close to their barracks so as not to give the SS men an excuse for mass murder.

But the minute the two of us entered, a jangled barrage of "Are you Americans?" in about 16 languages came from the barracks 200 yards from the gate. An affirmative nod caused pandemonium.

Tattered, emaciated men weeping, yelling and shouting "Long live America!" swept toward the gate in a mob. Those who could not walk limped or crawled. In the confusion, they were so hysterically happy that they took the SS man for an American. During a wild five minutes, he was patted on the back, paraded on shoulders and embraced enthusiastically by the prisoners. The arrival of the American soldier soon straightened out the situation.

I happened to be the first through the gate, and the first person to rush up to me turned out to be a Polish Catholic Hlond, Primate of Poland, who was not a little startled to discover that the helmeted, uniformed, begoggled individual he had so heartily embraced was not a man.

In the excitement, which was not the least dampened by the German artillery and the sounds of battle in the northern part of the camp, some of the prisoners died trying to pass through electrically charged barbed wire. Some who got out after the wires were decharged joined in the battle, when some ill-advised SS men holding out in a tower fired upon them.

The prisoners charged the tower and threw all six SS men out the window.

After an hour and a half of cheering, the crowd, which would virtually mob each soldier that dared to venture into the excited, milling group, was calmed down enough to make possible a tour of the camp. The only American prisoner, a flyer, with the rank of major, took some of the soldiers through.

According to the prisoners, the most famous individuals who had been at the camp had been removed by SS men to Innsbrueck. Among them were Leon Blum, former French Premier, and his wife; the Rev. Martin Niemoeller, German church leader; Kurt Schuschnigg, Chancellor of Austria at the time of the anschluss (he was said to have been alive a few days ago); Gabriel Piquet, Bishop of St. Etienne; Prince Leopold of Russia; Baron Fritz Cirini, aide to Prince Leopold; Richard Schmitz, former Mayor of Vienna; and Marshal Stalin's son, Jacob.

The barracks at Dachau, like those at Buchenwald, had the stench of death and sickness. But at Dachau there were six barracks like the infamous No. 61 at Buchenwald, where the starving and dying lay virtually on top of each other in quarters where 1,200 men occupied a space intended for 200. The dead—300 died of sickness yesterday—lay on concrete walks outside the quarters and others were carried out as the reporters went through.

The mark of starvation was on all the emaciated corpses. Many of the living were so frail it seemed impossible they could still be holding on to life.

The crematorium and torture chambers lay outside the prisoner enclosures. Situated in a wood close by, a new building had been built by prisoners under Nazi guards. Inside, in the two rooms used as torture chambers, an estimated 1,200 bodies were piled.

In the crematorium itself were hooks on which the SS men hung their victims when they wished to flog them or to use any of the other torture instruments. Symbolic of the SS was a mural the SS men themselves had painted on the wall. It showed a headless man in uniform with the SS insigne on the collar. The man was astride a huge inflated pig, into which he was digging his spurs.

The prisoners also showed reporters the grounds where men knelt and were shot in the back of the neck. On this very spot a week ago a French general, a resistance leader under General Charles de Gaulle, had been killed.

Just beyond the crematorium was a ditch containing some 2,000 bodies, which had been hastily tossed there in the last few days by the SS men, who were so busy preparing their escape they did not have time to burn the bodies.

Below the camp were cattle cars in which prisoners from Buchenwald had been transported to Dachau. Hundreds of dead were still in the cars due to the fact that prisoners in the camp had rejected SS orders to remove them. It was mainly the men from these cattle cars that the SS leaders had shot before making their escape. Among those who had been left for dead in the cattle cars was one man still alive who managed to lift himself from the heap of corpses on which he lay.

Veteran Kills 12 in Camden
MEYER BERGER—*The New York Times*—9/6/1949

CAMDEN, N.J.—Howard B. Unruh, 28 years old, a mild, soft-spoken veteran of many armored artillery battles in Italy, France, Austria, Belgium and Germany, killed twelve persons with a war souvenir Luger pistol in his home block in East Camden this morning. He wounded four others.

Unruh, a slender, hollow-cheeked six-footer paradoxically devoted to scripture reading and to constant practice with firearms, had no previous history of mental illness, but specialists indicated tonight that there was no doubt that he was a psychiatric case, and that he had secretly nursed a persecution complex for two years or more.

The veteran was shot in the left thigh by a local tavern keeper, but he kept that fact secret, too, while policemen and Mitchell Cohen, Camden County prosecutor, questioned him at police headquarters for more than two hours immediately after tear gas bombs had forced him out of his bedroom to surrender.

BLOOD BETRAYS HIS WOUND
The blood stain he left on the seat he occupied during the questioning betrayed his wound. When it was discovered he was taken to Cooper Hospital in Camden, a prisoner charged with murder.

He was as calm under questioning as he was during the twenty minutes that he was shooting men, women and children. Only occasionally excessive brightness of his dark eyes indicated that he was anything other than normal.

He told the prosecutor that he had been building up resentment against neighbors and neighborhood shopkeepers for a long time. "They have been making derogatory remarks about my character," he said. His resentment seemed most strongly concentrated against Mr. and Mrs. Maurice Cohen, who lived next door to him. They are among the dead.

Mr. Cohen was a druggist with a shop at 3202 River Road in East Camden. He and his wife had had frequent sharp exchanges over the Unruhs' use of a gate that separates their back yard from the Cohens'. Mrs. Cohen had also complained of young Unruh's keeping his bedroom radio tuned high into the late night hours. None of the other victims had ever had trouble with him.

Unruh, a graduate of Woodrow Wilson High School here, had started a GI course in pharmacy at Temple University in Philadelphia some time after he was honorably discharged from the service in 1945, but had stayed with it only three months. In recent months he had been unemployed, and apparently was not even looking for work.

MOTHER SEPARATED FROM HUSBAND

His mother, Mrs. Rita Unruh, 50, is separated from her husband. She works as a packer in the Evanson Soap Company in Camden and hers was virtually the only family income. James Unruh, 25 years old, her younger son, is married and lives in Haddon Heights, N.J. He works for the Curtin Publishing Company.

On Monday night, Howard Unruh left the house alone. He spent the night at the Family Theatre on Market Street in Philadelphia to sit through several showings of the double feature motion picture there—*I Cheated the Law* and *The Lady Gambles*. It was past 3 o'clock this morning when he got home.

Prosecutor Cohen said that Unruh told him later that before he fell asleep this morning he had made up his mind to shoot the persons who had "talked about me," that he had even figured out that 9:30 a.m. would be the time to begin because most of the stores in his block would be open at that hour.

His mother, leaving her ironing when he got up, prepared his breakfast in their drab little three room apartment in the shabby gray two-story stucco house at the corner of River Road and Thirty-Second Street. After breakfast he loaded one clip of bullets into his Luger, slipped another clip into his pocket, and carried sixteen loose cartridges in addition. He also carried a tear-gas pen with six shells and a sharp six-inch knife.

He took one last look around his bedroom before he left the house. On the peeling walls he had crossed pistols, crossed German bayonets, pictures of armored artillery in action. Scattered about the chamber were machetes, a Roy Rogers pistol, ash trays made of German shells, clips of 30-30 cartridges for rifle use and a host of varied war souvenirs.

Mrs. Unruh had left the house some minutes before, to call on Mrs. Caroline Pinner, a friend in the next block. Mrs. Unruh had sensed, apparently, that her son's smoldering resentments were coming to a head. She had pleaded with Elias Pinner, her friend's husband, to cut a little gate again. Mr. Pinner finished the gate early Monday evening after Howard had gone to Philadelphia.

At the Pinners' house at 9 o'clock this morning, Mrs. Unruh had murmured something about Howard's eyes; how strange they looked and how worried she was about him.

A few minutes later River Road echoed and re-echoed to pistol fire. Howard Unruh was on the rampage. His mother, who had left the Pinners' little white house only a few seconds before, turned back. She hurried through the door.

She cried, "Oh, Howard, oh, Howard, they're to blame for this." She rushed past Mrs. Pinner, a kindly gray-haired woman of 70. She said, "I've got to use the phone; may I use the phone?"

But before she had crossed the living room to reach for it she fell on the faded carpet in a dead faint. The Pinners lifted her onto a couch in the next room. Mrs. Pinner applied aromatic spirits to revive her.

Panic Grips Entire Block

While his mother writhed on the sofa in her house dress and worn old sweater, coming back to consciousness, Howard Unruh was walking from shop to shop in the "3200 block" with deadly calm, spurting Luger in hand. Children screamed as they tumbled over one another to get out of his way. Men and women dodged into open shops, the women shrill with panic, men hoarse with fear. No one could quite understand for a time what had been loosed in the block.

Unruh first walked into John Pilarchik's shoe repair shop near the north end of his own side of the street. The cobbler, a 27-year-old man who lives in Pennsauken Township, looked up open-mouthed as Unruh came to within a yard of him. The cobbler started up from his bench but went down with a bullet in his stomach. A little boy who was in the shop ran behind the counter and crouched there in terror. Unruh walked out into the sunlit street.

"I shot them in the chest first," he told the prosecutor later, in meticulous detail, "and then I aimed for the head." His aim was devastating—and with reason. He had won marksmanship and sharp-shooters' ratings in the service, and he practiced with his Luger all the time on a target set up in the cellar of his home. Unruh told the prosecutor afterward that he had Cohen the druggist, the neighborhood barber, the neighborhood cobbler and the neighborhood tailor on his mental list of persons who had "talked about him." He went methodically about wiping them out. Oddly enough, he did not start with the druggist, against whom he seemed to have the sharpest feelings, but left him almost for the last.

NEWLYWED WIFE SHOT DEAD

From the cobbler's he went into the little tailor shop at 3214 River Road. The tailor was out. Helga Zegrino, 28 years old, the tailor's wife, was there alone. The couple, incidentally, had been married only one month. She screamed when Unruh walked in with his Luger in hand. Some people across the street heard her. Then the gun blasted again and Mrs. Zegrino pitched over, dead. Unruh walked into the sunlight again.

All this was only a matter of seconds and still only a few persons had begun to understand what was afoot. Down the street at 3210 River Road is Clark Hoover's little country barber shop. In the center was a white-painted carousel-type horse for children customers. Orris Smith, a blond boy only 6 years old, was in it, with a bib around his neck, submitting to a shearing. His mother, Mrs. Catherine Smith, 42, sat on a chair against the wall and watched.

She looked up. Clark Hoover turned from his work, to see the six-footer, gaunt and tense, but silent, standing in the doorway with the Luger. Unruh's brown tropical worsted suit was barred with morning shadow. The sun lay bright in his crew-cut brown hair. He wore no hat. Mrs. Smith could not understand what was about to happen.

Unruh walked to "Brux"—that is Mrs. Smith's nickname for her little boy— and put the Luger to the child's chest. The shot echoed and reverberated in the little 12 by 12 shop. The little boy's head pitched toward the wound, his hair, half-cut, stained with red. Unruh said never a word. He put the Luger close to the shaking barber's hand. Before the horrified mother, Unruh leaned over and fired another shot into Hoover.

The veteran made no attempt to kill Mrs. Smith. He did not seem to hear her screams. He turned his back and stalked out, unhurried. A few doors north, Dominick Latela, who runs a little restaurant, had come to his shop window to learn what the shooting was about. He saw Unruh cross the street toward Frank Engel's tavern. Then he saw Mrs. Smith stagger out with her pitiful burden. Her son's head lolled over the crook of her right arm.

Mrs. Smith screamed, "My boy is dead. I know he's dead." She stared about her, looking in vain for aid. No one but Howard Unruh was in sight, and he was concentrating on the tavern. Latela dashed out, but first he shouted to his wife, Dora, who was in the restaurant with their daughter Eleanor, 6 years old. He hollered "I'm going out. Lock the door behind me." He ran for his car, and drove it down toward Mrs. Smith as she stood on the pavement with her son.

Latela took the child from her arms and placed him on the car's front seat.

He pushed the mother into the rear seat, slammed the doors and headed for Cooper Hospital. Howard Unruh had not turned. Engel, the tavern keeper, had locked his own door. His customers, the bartender, and a porter made a concerted rush for the rear of the saloon. The bullets tore through the tavern door paneling. Engel rushed upstairs and got out his .38 caliber pistol, then rushed to the street window of his apartment.

Unruh was back in the center of the street. He fired a shot at an apartment window at 3208 River Road. Tommy Hamilton, 2 years old, fell back with a bullet in his head. Unruh went north again to Latela's place. He fired a shot at the door, and kicked in the lower glass panel. Mrs. Latela crouched behind the counter with her daughter. She heard the bullets, but neither she nor her child was touched. Unruh walked back toward Thirty-second Street, reloading the Luger.

Now the little street—a small block with only five buildings on one side, three one-story stores on the other—was shrill with women's and children's panicky outcries. A group of six or seven little boys or girls fled past Unruh. They screamed, "Crazy man!" and unintelligible sentences. Unruh did not seem to hear, or see, them.

AUTOIST GOES TO HIS DEATH

Alvin Day, a television repair man who lives in near-by Mantua, had heard the shooting, but driving into the street he was not aware of what had happened. Unruh walked up to the car window as Day rolled by, and fired once through the window, with deadly aim. The repair man fell against the steering wheel. The car seemed to wobble. The front wheels hit the opposite curb and stalled. Day was dead.

Frank Engel had thrown open his second-floor apartment window. He saw Unruh pause for a moment in a narrow alley between the cobbler's shop and a little two-story house. He aimed and fired. Unruh stopped for just a second. The bullet had hit, but he did not seem to mind, after the initial brief shock. He headed toward the corner drug store, and Engel did not fire again.

"I wish I had," he said, later. "I could have killed him then. I could have put a half-dozen shots into him. I don't know why I didn't do it."

Cohen, the druggist, a heavy man of 40, had run into the street shouting "What's going on here? What's going on here?" but at sight of Unruh hurried back into his shop. James J. Hutton, 45, an insurance agent from Westmont, N.J., started out of the drug shop to see what the shooting was about. Like so many others he had figured at first that it was some car backfiring. He came face to face with Unruh.

Unruh said quietly, "Excuse me, sir," and started to push past him. Later Unruh told the police: "That man didn't act fast enough. He didn't get out of my way." He fired into Hutton's head and body. The insurance man pitched onto the sidewalk and lay still.

Cohen had run to his upstairs apartment and had tried to warn Minnie Cohen, 63, his mother, and Rose, his wife, 38, to hide. His son Charles, 14, was in the apartment, too. Mrs. Cohen shoved the boy into a clothes closet, and leaped into another closet herself. She pulled the door to. The druggist, meanwhile had leaped from the window onto a porch roof. Unruh, a gaunt figure at the window behind him, fired into the druggist's back. The druggist, still running, bounded off the roof and lay dead in Thirty-second Street.

Unruh fired into the closet where Mrs. Cohen was hidden. She fell dead behind the closed door, and he did not bother to open it. Mrs. Minnie Cohen tried to get to the telephone in an adjoining bedroom to call the police. Unruh fired shots into her head and body and she sprawled dead on the bed. Unruh walked down the stairs with his Luger reloaded and came out into the street again.

A coupe had stopped at River Road, obeying a red light. The passengers obviously had no idea of what was loose in East Camden and no one had a chance to tell them. Unruh walked up to the car, and though it was filled with total strangers, fired deliberately at them, one by one, through the windshield. He killed the two women passengers, Mrs. Helen Matlack Wilson, 43, of Pennsauken, who was driving, and her mother, Mrs. Emma Matlack, 66. Mrs. Wilson's son John, 12, was badly wounded. A bullet pierced his neck, just below the jawbone.

Earl Horner, clerk in the American Stores Company, a grocery opposite the drug store, had locked his front door after several passing men, women and children had tumbled breathlessly into the shop panting "crazy man***killing people.***" Unruh came up to the door and fired two shots through the wood paneling. Horner, his customers, the refugees from the veteran's merciless gunfire, crouched, trembling, behind the counter. None there was hurt.

"He tried the door before he shot in here," Horner related afterward. "He just stood there, stony-faced and grim, and rattled the knob, before he started to fire. Then he turned away."

Charlie Petersen, 18, son of a Camden fireman, came driving down the street with two friends when Unruh turned from the grocery. The three boys got out to stare at Hutton's body lying unattended on the sidewalk. They did not know who had shot the insurance man, or why and, like the women in the car, had no warning that Howard Unruh was on the loose. The veteran brought his Luger to sight and fired several times. Young Petersen fell with bullets in his legs. His friends tore pell-mell down the street to safety.

Mrs. Helen Harris of 1250 North Twenty-eight Street with her daughter, Helen, a 6-year-old blonde child, and a Mrs. Horowitz with her daughter, Linda, 5, turned into Thirty-second Street. They had heard the shooting from a distance but thought it was auto backfire.

Unruh passed them in Thirty-second Street and walked up the sagging four steps of a little yellow dwelling back of his own house. Mrs. Madeline Harrie, a woman in her late thirties, and two sons, Armand, 16, and Leroy, 15, were in the house. A third son, Wilson, 14, was barricaded in the grocery with other customers.

Unruh threw open the front door and, gun in hand, walked into the dark little parlor. He fired two shots at Mrs. Harrie. They went wild and entered the wall. A third shot caught her in the left arm. She screamed. Armand leaped at Unruh, to tackle him. The veteran used the Luger butt to drop the boy, then fired two shots into his arms. Upstairs Leroy heard the shooting and the screams. He hid under a bed.

By this time, answering a flood of hysterical telephone calls from various parts of East Camden, police radio cars swarmed into River Road with sirens wide open. Emergency crews brought machine guns, shotguns and tear gas bombs.

Sergeant Earl Wright, one of the first to leap to the sidewalk, saw Charles Cohen, the druggist's son. The boy was half out the second floor apartment window, just above where his father lay dead. He was screaming, "He's going to kill me. He's killing everybody." The boy was hysterical.

Wright bounded up the stairs to the druggist's apartment. He saw the dead woman on the bed, and tried to soothe the druggist's son. He brought him downstairs and turned him over to other policemen, then joined the men who had surrounded the two-story stucco house where Unruh lived. Unruh, meanwhile, had fired about thirty shots. He was out of ammunition. Leaving the Harrie house, he had also heard the police sirens. He had run through the back gate to his own rear bedroom.

GUNS TRAINED ON WINDOW

Edward Joslin, a motorcycle policeman, scrambled to the porch roof under Unruh's window. He tossed a tear gas grenade through a pane of glass. Other policemen, hoarsely calling on Unruh to surrender, took positions with their machine guns and shotguns. They trained them on Unruh's window.

Meanwhile, a curious interlude had taken place. Philip W. Buxton, an assistant city editor on *The Camden Evening Courier* had looked Unruh's name up in the telephone book. He called the number, Camden 4-2490W. It was just after 10 a.m. and Unruh had just returned to his room. To Mr. Buxton's astonishment Unruh answered. He said hello in a calm, clear voice.

"This Howard?" Mr. Buxton asked.

"Yes, this is Howard. What is the last name of the party you want?"

"Unruh."

The veteran asked what Mr. Buxton wanted.

"I'm a friend," the newspaper man said. "I want to know what they're doing to you down there."

Unruh thought a moment. He said, "They haven't done anything to me—yet. I'm doing plenty to them." His voice was still steady without a trace of hysteria.

Mr. Buxton asked how many persons Unruh had killed.

The veteran answered: "I don't know. I haven't counted. Looks like a pretty good score."

"Why are you killing people?"

"I don't know," came the frank answer. "I can't answer that yet. I'll have to talk to you later. I'm too busy now."

The telephone banged down.

Unruh was busy. The tear gas was taking effect and police bullets were thudding at the walls around him. During a lull in the firing the police saw the white curtains move and the gaunt killer came into plain view.

"Okay," he shouted. "I give up. I'm coming down."

"Where's that gun?" a sergeant yelled.

"It's on my desk, up here in the room," Unruh called down quietly.

"I'm coming down."

Thirty guns were trained on the shabby little back door. A few seconds later the door opened and Unruh stepped into the light, his hands up. Sergeant Wright came across the morning-glory and aster beds in the yard and snapped handcuffs on Unruh's wrists.

"What's the matter with you," a policeman demanded hotly. "You a psycho?"

Unruh stared into the policeman's eyes—a level, steady stare. He said, "I'm no psycho. I have a good mind."

Word of the capture brought the whole East Camden populace pouring into the streets. Men and women screamed at Unruh, and cursed him in shrill accents and in hoarse anger. Someone cried "lynch him" but there was no movement. Sergeant Wright's men walked Unruh to a police car and started for headquarters.

Shouting and pushing men and women started after the car, but dropped back after a few paces. They stood in excited little groups discussing the shootings, and the character of Howard Unruh. Little by little the original anger, born of fear, that had moved the crowd, began to die.

Men conceded that he probably was not in his right mind. Those who knew Unruh kept repeating how close-mouthed he was, and how soft spoken. How he took his mother to church, and how he marked scripture passages, especially in prophecies.

"He was a quiet one, that guy," a man told a crowd in front of the tavern. "He was all the time figuring to do this thing. You gotta watch them quiet ones."

But all day River Road and the side streets talked of nothing else. The shock was great. Men and women kept saying: "We can't understand it. Just don't get it."

The Southern Gentlemen
MURRAY KEMPTON—*New York Post*—11/14/1955

The come-on flyers for the Southern Gentlemen's organization of Louisiana are tricked out rather drearily with a stock drawing of an antebellum colonel, goateed and string-tied. Their living expression, as in most of the South, is thicker of blood and closer to the earth.

J. B. Easterly, Southern Gentleman No. 1, is a spike-haired, square-bifocalled, heavy-necked man of sixty-one, alternating explosions of laughter and indignation. His grandchildren call him "Pop-Pop" and he's totally impossible to dislike.

The Southern Gentlemen are Louisiana's militant symbol of the counter-attack against racial integration. As such, they maintain warm fraternal relations with a brotherhood of resistance ranging from the Citizens Councils of Mississippi to the Apartheid Bund of South Africa.

Its Mississippi and Capetown brothers are, of course, the government; in Baton Rouge at least, J. B. Easterly commands a ragged outpost in the shed next to his bungalow which serves both as home office of the Southern Gentlemen and his own modest, prefabricated concrete step business.

As tycoon and opinion-maker, J. B. Easterly is his own secretary, turning from time to time to assault the typewriter with his thick fingers and render his accounts. As opinion-maker, J. B. Easterly's expression is somewhat inhibited by his two youngest grandchildren who toddle around the office step and have to be shooed out of hearing whenever he wants to advert to the prime subject of miscegenation.

"I'm a very illiterate man," says J. B. Easterly. "My daddy went broke when I was in college. I was raised on a cotton and cane plantation; when I was a boy, I hardly knew what a white child was.

"We have no secrets here; all we want to do is maintain segregation by legal means. We're definitely opposed to rough stuff. We believe the Negro race should advance. Look, boy, it's an accident you're a white man. We think the Negro should be proud to be a Negro and be just as good as God gave him the brainpower to be. If we got rough on them, we feel we'd be doing an injustice to 95 per cent of the race.

"But we're definitely goin' to apply economic pressure to white people who contribute to the white Communist NAACP. There's a lot of 'em. They don't come out openly—these rotten politicians slip 'em cash, no checks. We got them people down here. Look at this."

He fished among his papers and came up with a leaflet headed "The White Sentinel—official organ of the National Citizens Protective Association" and pointed to a picture of shadows purporting to be the vice president of the Falstaff Brewing Co. presenting a $500 check to the NAACP.

"See that. We're putting that all over East Baton Rouge. We're not gonna buy their beer. Let the niggers buy it."

The finger poked around and found another paper. It was the *South African Observer*, a magazine for realists, featuring the news that the message had reached the States and, for spiritual comfort on the lonely veldt, an article called "A Christian View of Segregation" by a Mississippi college president emeritus.

It costs 10 shillings a year. Realist Easterly asked his visitor how much that was in dollars so he could subscribe, and the visitor thought it might be $1.60.

"You know there's a lot of science in this. They've found out that there's a difference in the blood. There's no one smarter than a little nigger kid. But, when they get to be sixteen, they just stop. You don't see the AP, the UP and the NAACP printing that.

"That northern press is still fighting the Civil War. We forgot it down here. But our sentiment is gonna be all over the United States. There's Citizens Councils in twenty-three states. I get letters from up there saying that, if we lose, the North is lost. A woman from Illinois told me"—he looked to see if his grandchildren were out of hearing—"that in her child's school, the little nigger boys were always pulling up the little white girls' dresses."

W. L. Lawrence, secretary of the Southern Gentlemen, came into the office carrying membership applications decorated with the stars and bars. (This, like the Southern colonel, is stock for mimeograph stencils and turned out in some commercial art salt mine on our own West Side.) This was fortunate, because just after Lawrence, there came a recruit.

He was R. B. Davidson who said he had reached the shotgun stage. "We don't want none of that," said J. B. Easterly. R. B. Davidson wanted to know what we were gonna do about our parks and playgrounds now that the niggers were coming in. "Turn 'em over to the weeds and dogs," said J. B. Easterly.

R. B. Davidson said he liked a nigger if he stayed a nigger.

"It's all in the Bible. The Lord said of the children of Cain that he'd put a mark on 'em and all their children would be the servants of servants. We're God's servants and they're our servants."

"Sign this," said J. B. Easterly. "It says you never were a Communist. You couldn't be a Communist; you talk too much.

"And don't forget our big parade. We're going to drive up to L.S.U. and let 'em see how we feel about those nigger graduate students they have. We gonna roll this thing back. Put any sign you want on your car, so long as it's not obscene or anything."

The militant Mr. Davidson said that he didn't know about no parades; he had to worry about civil service. "But, civil service or no civil service, I'm with you in the showdown."

Secretary Lawrence said, no, he couldn't say how many members he had. "That's one of the strengths of our organization," said J. B. Easterly, "we have ministers; we have school superintendents."

There would be dangers in making membership public, Lawrence pointed out. "If a member was known, these agitating Negroes might do something to him.

"They do put economic pressure on our boys." But the Southern Gentlemen exact no reprisals. "When a Negro signs a school petition, we just try to persuade him he's wrong. Sometimes, we get his employer to talk to him just to encourage him to take his name off."

Lawrence handed over a mimeographed letter. "I just got this up; do you think it will work?" It was a protest to Philco against a recent television play about a Negro married to a white woman. "I have a number of appliances in my home manufactured by your company." The visitor said it had worked in Queens.

"The worst thing was," said J. B. Easterly, "the girl was from New Orleans." He was looking through the yellow pages for a cab. "I got a lot of right talking about niggers," he said, "I can't even read." He found a number and called a cab, and struck his huge hand out to the invader. "I'm glad you came; this sort of thing is real educational."

The Death of Senator McCarthy

HARRY GOLDEN—*Carolina Israelite*—5/5/1957

The conservatives nearly always tolerate the demagogue while he is destroying liberals. The conservatives may even know that their turn will come next, but they usually take this calculated risk. "Let him knock their heads together," they say, "we'll take care of him in good time." ("Let him keep going," said Senator Taft. "He's hurting the Democrats.")

But it never works out the way the conservatives would like to have it; especially if the demagogue knows how to consolidate his position before he finally goes after his early "allies." Hitler understood the mechanisms of perfect timing. The Thyssens and the Krupps loved him because he was destroying the Weimar Constitution, the liberals, the trade unions, the political heretics—all in one shot. But the conservatives made their move too late. They fell before him like ripe apples off a tree.

But how did McCarthy know to use this oldest, most heinous, and most effective weapon of the demagogue? "I hold a piece of paper in my hands with some names on it . . ." and here his voice trails off to another subject with perfect timing; and suddenly this blank piece of paper becomes a living document, a terrifying document. It becomes a document of potential destruction because *my* name is on it; and so is *yours*; and so are the names of Senator Taft, and Dwight D. Eisenhower. We are all on it, because none of us is on it.

Do you remember that slightly ajar briefcase always resting on its haunches in front of his right foot as he stood on the platform? "I have in my briefcase a list . . ." and again the voice trails off to something else, but every eye rests on that briefcase which may now hold our political destiny and our human dignity. Soon, soon, it will become the symbol of the New Order; instead of a swastika, this time it will be a briefcase.

"Let me see that list," asked one or two of the more courageous reporters of those days.

"What do you take me for?" replied McCarthy. "Do you expect me to betray America to these razor-at-the-throat Reds?" And indeed how can you induce a man to betray America?

But how did McCarthy know to use this oldest gimmick of the demagogue? Had he also read the history of the world? Or do these fellows come by all this stuff by instinct?

"The High Sheriff will come next week with his list of the traitors (Puritans)," said the notice on the bulletin boards of England after the Restoration. There was no list, of course; but when the Sheriff came he knew exactly whom to pick up. He picked up the wives of the men who weren't home. The men who had run away included "real" Puritans, fellows who had an enemy in town, and men who get scared when the Bill of Particulars is a blank piece of paper on which the sheriff may impose as he goes along.

What makes a McCarthy tick? It is one of the oldest stories of mankind. When you have succeeded in creating a devil, the people begin to lose faith in themselves. They even begin to despise their intellectual selves in dealing with the devil who is closing in on them from all sides; and now they are literally pleading for help—anything and anybody, even a young squirt of a lawyer, and his side-kick, a young assistant hotel clerk; these will now lead America by the nose, the America of Franklin, Adams, Jefferson, Pinckney, and Robert E. Lee.

And so the liberals of America hoped for a miracle. They hoped that the conservatives would come to their rescue before it was too late. And this time they prayed for a miracle, and they got the miracle. Senator McCarthy overplayed his hand. At that single moment when he said that General Zwicker was not fit to wear the uniform of the United States Army, that was the precise moment of McCarthy's destruction. He had made a move against the "nobility" a year, maybe even two years, too soon; and they knew they had to finish him right then and there. A few necessary formalities were all that remained.

The Harlem Riot
JIMMY BRESLIN—*New York Herald Tribune*—7/20/1964

The shirtless children ran through the gutters and played with the broken glass and the dull brass cartridge shells from the riot of the night before. The flat sky was an open oven door and its heat made people spill out of the tenements and onto the stoops, or onto milk boxes set up on the sidewalk, and they sat and watched the children pick up the brass shells and pocket them as if they were prizes.

They watched the cops too. The cops were everywhere, four and five of them on a street corner, wearing white steel helmets, and the people of Harlem watched them and hated them yesterday afternoon.

"When I see a white cop, I can't help myself, I just can't stand looking at one of them," Livingston Wingate was saying. "I'm supposed to be a responsible person and I try to rub it from my mind. But right now, when I look across the street here and see those white cops, I get disturbed. I just can't stand looking at them."

Wingate is an official. He is a lawyer who has worked for the government in Washington. He now is one of the major figures in running HARYOU-ACT, which has been formed to help young people in Harlem. When people of position talk the way he did, the trouble is bad. And yesterday afternoon, while everybody in Harlem waited for the sun to go down and night to cloak the streets and make moving around easier, you wondered just how bad it would become.

Some of them wanted to get at it in the daylight. The fire trucks had 129th Street, between Madison and Fifth, tied up during an alarm at 2:15 in the afternoon, and to make room for a hook and ladder coming through, the guy driving us pulled in to the curb in the middle of the block.

Right away, somebody moved off the stoop: a kid with a shaved head and a gold polo shirt. He was about nineteen and he went to another stoop, where three other kids were sitting. He said something to them and they looked at the car. Then they got up and came onto the sidewalk and the one with the shaved head walked across the street and spoke to a crowd on another stoop.

Then he came walking back, looking at the car; and when you stared back at him, his eyelids came down and made his eyes narrow.

"What are you lookin' at, you big fat white bastard?" he said.

"Oh, come on, it's too hot for this nonsense," we told him.

"We're goin' to show you what's nonsense," he said. "We're goin' to stick some nonsense right into your fat white belly."

A fireman, rubber boots flopping on the melting tar street, walked over from an engine. He had an ax in his hand. A new ax. Big, with a light yellow wooden handle. The kid with the shaved head didn't even notice him. He just kept walking past the car and went back to the stoop where three waited for him.

"What the hell are you doing here?" the fireman said. "Don't you listen to the newspapers?"

"We're trying to get through."

"They were stoning us last night," the fireman said. "You don't know what it was like here. They were trying to kill us. Get out of here if you got any brains."

Then he went back to the truck. The other firemen came out of the tenement and climbed onto the trucks. There had been no fire and now the three trucks were starting to pull away.

"Hey, fat white bastard," the shaved head called out. "Why don't you stay around here till these trucks leave?"

"Oh, come on," he was told.

Two trucks left, and then the hook and ladder moved by, and the minute it did, the guy driving us in the car pulled away from the curb and started up the block. The kids came out from both sides. They were walking at first, but then one of them ran and tried to get in the back door on the right-hand side, but now the car was moving too fast and he couldn't make it and then, with the car heading up the block, you saw his bare black arm pull back and then come up and something came through the air at the car.

Whatever it was, it exploded when it hit the street behind the car. Who knows what it was? Molotov cocktails were all over the place Saturday night. Maybe it was nothing more than a firecracker. You couldn't tell. If somebody snapped his fingers on 129th Street in Harlem yesterday afternoon, the noise made you jump.

It all came down to this in Harlem. All the talk and all the speeches and all the ignorance and all the history of this deep vicious thing of black against white which they classify under the nice name of civil rights came crashing down from the rooftops inside garbage cans. The symbol of a couple of hundred years of sinful history became a black arm pulling back and then coming around to throw something at a white cop.

And there seemed to be no way to talk to anybody. For a while the big main avenues of Harlem seemed quiet and police-state orderly yesterday afternoon, the people sitting on the side streets with a bitterness which went right through you when you saw it in their faces.

There seemed to be nobody who could stop what everybody thought the night would bring.

At 4:15 p.m. we drove to the Mount Morris Presbyterian Church with Judge James Watson to hear Jesse Gray address a rally. Gray is an irrational man who is a force in Harlem only because of the white press, which failed in its obligation to check out people it writes of. Publicity made Jesse Gray, and yesterday afternoon was to be his great chance for rabble-rousing.

Then Jesse Gray got up and this church turned into something you've never seen before.

"Before today is over, we'll be able to separate the men from the boys," Gray said when he got up.

"Only one thing can solve the problem in Mississippi, and that's guerrilla warfare," Gray said. "I'm beginning to wonder what's going to solve the problem here in New York."

He threw the line out into the hot airless church and he waited for the answer he knew would come. He got it.

"Guerrilla warfare," they shouted.

"Oh, my God," Judge Watson said in the back of the church.

"Oh, my God."

Alabama Literacy Test
ART BUCHWALD—*Washington Post*—3/18/1965

Getting to vote in Bull Whip, Ala., isn't as easy as one would think. First, you have to sneak around a mounted sheriff's posse, then fight your way through a cloud of state tear gas, and then you have to leap over a hundred cattle prods. And finally, if you still want to vote in Bull Whip, you have to register, and the registration office in the courthouse is open only from 11:55 p.m. to midnight on every sixth Saturday of the month.

The problem is that, although the registration office is open, the courthouse is closed, and it's kind of hard to get into the building.

Even so, Mr. George Abernathy, a Negro, manages, much to the surprise of the registrar, to get in and asks to register to vote.

"Fine, George, fine. Ah'd be glad to register you as soon as you answer a few of these here questions," the registrar says. "Now, first off, what is your educational background?"

"I was a Rhodes scholar, I received a B.A. from Columbia, a master's from Harvard, and a Ph.D. from MIT."

"That's just fine, George. Now let me ask you this. Can you read an' write?"

"I've written three books on cybernetics, Christian philosophy, and advanced political theory."

"Ah'd appreciate it if you didn't use such big words, George. If there's anything Ah hate it's an uppity voter."

Abernathy says, "I believe I have a right to register."

"Yes, you do, George, but I have to give you this here from our great Governor, George Wallace, if you know what Ah mean. Now, first off, would you please read somethin' from this here newspaper?"

"It's in Chinese."

"That's right."

Abernathy reads three stories from the Chinese paper. The registrar is thrown, but he doesn't want to show it.

"All right, now will you read the hieroglyphics off this here Rosetta Stone?" he says.

Mr. Abernathy reads the hieroglyphics and the registrar begins to get nervous.

"George, here is the constitution of Finland, in Finnish. Would you please interpret the first 14 articles for me?"

"What has that got to do with voting in Alabama?"

"We got to keep out agitators and the like. Now, you going to take the test or not?"

Mr. Abernathy interprets the 14 articles and the registrar becomes truly frightened. He telephones the Governor's office and reports what is happening. An aide comes back in a few minutes and says, "The Governor says to give him Part 4 of the test."

The registrar goes to his safe and takes out a clay jar. "George, there's only one more thing you're obligated to do for this here literacy test. Would you be so kind to read for me any two of these Dead Sea Scrolls?"

Mr. Abernathy reads the first one but stumbles on a word in the second one.

"Ah'm sorry, George. You've failed the literacy test, but you can come back next year and try again."

As Abernathy leaves the office, a white Alabaman comes in to register to vote. The registrar says to him, "Would you please spell cat for me?"

The white voter says, "K-A-T."

"Try it again. You're getting warm."

Zodiac Killer Gives Gilbert & Sullivan Clue

PAUL AVERY—*San Francisco Chronicle*—10/21/1970

[The Zodiac serial killer terrorized the Bay Area in the late 1960s and early 1970s and corresponded with the columnist Paul Avery. He was never captured.]

One year and one day ago, the killer who calls himself Zodiac put a 9-mm. bullet through the brain of San Francisco cab driver Paul Stine and then posted a letter to *The Chronicle* boasting of the slaying.

Stine, he wrote, was victim number five. He bragged he would continue his killing spree—choosing victims at random—and that he wouldn't get caught.

Zodiac is still at large today.

And he is now claiming he has murdered 13 persons.

Homicide detectives who've been hunting Zodiac for nearly two years frankly admit he is as much an enigma now as he was on Dec. 20, 1968, when he chalked up his first two victims.

ARIA

In fact, just about the only thing they feel they know for certain is that Zodiac is a Gilbert and Sullivan buff.

That bizarre conclusion came as a result of two letters Zodiac sent to *The Chronicle* last July 27. At the request of investigators, the contents have been kept a secret until now.

In the longer of the two letters, Zodiac penned in poetic style a list of types of people he would like to put "underground."

It was immediately apparent that Zodiac had plagiarized several stanzas from an aria in the Gilbert and Sullivan operetta *The Mikado*.

It is the entrance aria of Ko-Ko, the Lord High Executioner.

* * *

Because of numerous misspellings and occasional variations from the original lyrics of W. S. Gilbert, police are positive Zodiac put the words on paper from memory rather than copying them from the libretto.

This has prompted serious speculation that Zodiac—perhaps in the days when he was a student—once performed the role of Ko-Ko.

Here is part of the executioner's aria as remembered with errors, by Zodiac.

"I've got a little list. I've got a little list.

"Of society offenders who might well be underground.

"Who would never be missed, who would never be missed.

"There is the pestulentual nucences who whrite for autographs.

"All people who have flabby hands and irritating laughs. . . .

"There's the banjo seranader and the others of his race.

"All people who eat pepermint and phomphit (blow it) in your face.

"And the Idiout who praises with inthusastic tone.

"Of centuries but this and every country but his own."

* * *

A quiet search for onetime Ko-Kos has turned up none that could be Zodiac. Obvious differences in physical description and handwriting comparisons have cleared all Ko-Kos tracked down since the arrival of the July 27 letters.

There has never been any shortage of Zodiac suspects.

San Francisco homicide inspectors William Armstrong and David Toschi have, they say, checked out, and cleared, "literally thousands of suspected Zodiacs" named by "wives, mothers, acquaintances, friends, fellow workers, delivery men . . . not to mention police agencies throughout the world."

Sheriff's detective sergeant Kenneth Narlow of Napa County has fruitlessly followed up another 900 tips as to Zodiac's identity since the Sept. 27, 1969, knife slaying of coed Cecilia Ann Shepard at Lake Berryessa.

Hundreds of other leads have been checked out by Solano County authorities because of the murders Zodiac committed near Vallejo. On Dec. 20, 1968, he gunned down teen-agers David Faraday and Betty Lou Jensen and on July 5, 1969, he fatally shot waitress Darleen Ferrin, in each instance at local lovers' lanes.

With Stine, these are the five known victims of Zodiac.

Detectives doubt Zodiac's claim he has murdered eight other persons, mostly because he has never identified any victims but the first five.

* * *

They believe he came so close to getting caught while carrying out the slaying of Stine that he is wary of actually killing again and is content to deluge *The Chronicle* with correspondence in which he keeps upping his score—on paper only.

The Zodiac investigators concede, however, that there are far more than eight unsolved murders in Northern California and that some of these might indeed be the work of the boastful killer.

They also recall that last November Zodiac said he was going to "change the way" of committing murders he'd followed until then.

"I shall no longer announce to any when I commit my murders, they shall look like routine robberies, killings of anger, & a few fake accidents, etc." Zodiac wrote on dime-store stationary.

* * *

In his letters of last July, Zodiac warned that future victims will be tortured before being killed.

Some victims, he said, will be tied over anthills so he can "watch them scream and twitch and squirm."

"Others," he continued, "shall have pine splinters driven under their nails and then burned. Others shall be placed in caves and fed salt beef until they are gorged.

"Then I shall listen to their pleas for water and I shall laugh at them."

There is no doubt the July Zodiac letters are authentic. Crime Lab hand-writing experts have made comparisons with other known messages from the killer and say the hurried printing and crossed-circle signature are identical.

* * *

For this reason inspectors Armstrong and Toschi are puzzled by what they believe to be still another piece of correspondence from Zodiac.

Last Wednesday, *The Chronicle* received a postcard-like note signed "Zodiac." It actually was a plain white, 3-inch by 5-inch file card onto which the author has pasted words cut from an edition of *The Chronicle* itself. Dated "Mon., Oct. 5, 1970," it read:

"Dear Editor:

"You'll hate me, but I've got to tell you.

"The pace isn't any slower! In fact it's just one big thirteenth.

"Some of Them Fought It Was Horrible."

It ended with a P.S., pasted onto the card upside down.

"P.S. There are reports city police pig cops are closeing in on me. Fk. I'm crackproof. What is the price tag now."

Thirteen holes were punched in the card and a small cross, in which blood was used as ink, was pasted on next to the signature.

The detectives studied the card for two days and for reasons they decline to make public say they feel it "highly probable" it came from Zodiac.

The post card is now locked in a fireproof steel filing cabinet, four-drawers high, which is jammed full of reports, suspect investigations, and evidence relating to the Zodiac case, unsolved after almost two years.

The Pentagon Papers: Freedom versus Security
JAMES RESTON—*New York Times*—6/19/1971

> *"Here various news we tell, of love and strife,*
> *Of peace and war, health, sickness, death and life . . .*
> *Of turns of fortune, changes in the State,*
> *The falls of favorites, projects of the great,*
> *Of old mismanagements, taxations news,*
> *All neither wholly false, nor wholly true."*
> New London (Conn.) *Bee*, March 26, 1800

Great court cases are made by the clash of great principles, each formidable standing alone, but in conflict limited, "all neither wholly false nor wholly true."

The latest legal battle, *The United States v. The New York Times*, is such a case: The Government's principle of privacy, and the newspaper's principle of publishing without Government approval.

This is not essentially a fight between Attorney General Mitchell and Arthur Ochs Sulzberger, publisher of the *New York Times*. They are merely incidental figures in an ancient drama. This is the old cat-and-dog conflict between security and freedom.

It goes back to John Milton's pamphlet, *Areopagitica*, in the seventeenth century against Government censorship or, as he called it: "for the liberty of unlicenc'd printing." That is still the heart of it: the Government claim to prevent, in effect to license, what is published ahead of publication, rather than merely to exercise its right to prosecute after publication.

Put another way, even the title of this case in the U.S. District Court is misleading, for the real issue is not the *New York Times* versus the United States, but whether publishing the Government's own analysis of the Vietnam tragedy or suppressing that story is a service to the Republic.

It is an awkward thing for a reporter to comment on the battles of his own newspaper, and the reader will make his own allowances for the reporter's bias, but after all allowances are made, it is hard to believe that publishing these historical documents is a greater threat to the security of the United States than suppressing them or, on the record, as the Government implies, that the *Times* is a frivolous or reckless paper.

The usual charge against the *New York Times*, not without some validity, is that it is a tedious bore, always saying on the one hand and the other and defending, like *The Times* of London in the thirties, "the Government and commercial establishment."

During the last decade, it has been attacked vigorously for "playing the Government game." It refused to print a story that the Cuban freedom fighters were going to land at the Bay of Pigs "tomorrow morning." It agreed with President Kennedy during the Cuban missile crisis that reporting the Soviet missiles on that island while Kennedy was deploying the fleet to blockade the Russians was not in the national interest.

Beyond that, it was condemned for not printing what it knew about the U.S. U-2 flights over the Soviet Union and, paradoxically, for printing the Yalta Papers and the Dumbarton Oaks Papers on the organization of the United Nations.

All of which suggests that there is no general principle which governs all specific cases and that, in the world of newspapering, where men have to read almost two million words a day and select a hundred thousand to print, it comes down to human judgments where "all [is] neither wholly false nor wholly true."

So a judgment has to be made when the Government argues for security, even over historical documents, and the *Times* argues for freedom to publish. That is what is before the court today. It is not a black-and-white case—as it was in the Cuban missile crisis when the Soviet ships were approaching President Kennedy's blockade in the Caribbean.

It is a conflict between printing or suppressing, not military information affecting the lives of men on the battlefield, but historical documents about a tragic and controversial war; not between what is right and what is wrong, but between two honest but violently conflicting views about what best serves the national interest and the enduring principles of the First Amendment.

Attica Prison Riot: Night in the Yard
Том WICKER—*The New York Times*—9/14/1971

ATTICA, N.Y.—Broken glass underfoot, piled barricaded tables, a faint lingering whiff of tear gas; and in the echoing darkness the still figures of men with heads swathed in towels to resemble Arab headdress: "Right on, brother!" someone mutters.

We pass through a door and stumble two-by-two down concrete steps past a burnt-out guard post to a shadowy exercise yard. This is No Man's Land, "controlled" by convicts in revolt but too exposed to guards' rifles and binoculars and too far from the prisoners' hostages to be safe territory.

Fires flicker from oil drums atop low, flat rooftops surrounding the exercise yard, and here and there flashlight beams pick out alert faces, many of them framed in football helmets painted white or orange.

Rapidly, convict "security" takes over and with much counting of heads and almost exaggerated courtesy hurries the long line of invited "visitors"—more than twenty of them—past two steel doors and into the midst of the prison rebellion at Attica Correctional Facility, one of the biggest such uprisings on record.

Curving in a long line from the entrance toward the dark rise of D-Block are the inmates—arms locked, shoulder to shoulder, each man facing in the opposite direction from the two to which he is linked. Beyond this solid human barrier are the faceless hundreds of others—and somewhere in the darkness, huddled on mattresses within a tight ring of wooden benches, the thirty-odd corrections officers being held hostage.

This is another world—terrifying to the outsider, yet imposing in the strangeness—behind those massive walls, in this murmurous darkness, within the temporary but real power of desperate men. "Nobody gonna be hurt," the helmeted security men are saying soothingly, but it is not reassuring; it only reminds that in this dark world, the powerless have taken power.

A few feet from the D-Block building, a long line of tables has been set up. On the wall side, in the light from reading lamps taped to the wall, and that from a few regular outdoor lamps higher up, what appears to be a leadership committee is waiting. Its members are warily cordial, shaking hands firmly, welcoming the visitors as "brothers," but watching them with hard, suspicious eyes.

Brother Herb, a veteran of revolt in the infamous Tombs, is holding the single small microphone in the glare of a floodlamp; like most of the inmates, he is wearing a prison blanket cut like a poncho. Bull-shouldered and hoarse, with the remarkable eloquence that characterizes most of the inmate speakers, Herb has told the visitors in an earlier, daylight visit: "I am Attica."

Now, laying down the prisoners' demands to loud cheering and shouts of "Right on!" Herb is skillfully heightening his brothers' morale; what the visitors are hearing, he says, is "but the sound before the fury of those who are oppressed; when you are the anvil you bend but when you are the hammer you strike."

And Brother Richard, his brown impassive face glistening in the strange light, tells his listeners that it is the guards and the troopers outside who have the bullets and the machine guns, and it is the inmates who are safeguarding the lives of the hostages—"We are the only civilized men here."

But Brother Flip—in fact, he confides to a visitor, his name is Charles Horatio Crowley—is the most eloquent, and the most realistic. "We no longer wish to be treated as statistics, as numbers. We want to be treated as human beings, we *will* be treated as human beings!"

But Flip knows better, in his prison-wise heart. "If we cannot live as people," he concludes, in a silence so deep his voice rings back from the walls, "we will at least try to die like men."

Suddenly, from the lighted windows of C-Block in the distance, shouts, screams, a strange banging and clashing of metal against metal.

"Our brothers!" someone shouts. "They beatin' up our brothers!"

Voices take up the cry, running feet pound along the top of the low surrounding corridor buildings. The lights go out. On top of the table between the committee and the visitors, men appear as swiftly and silently as cats, and stand with feet braced apart, tense, staring beyond the human chain of "security." One man on the table is holding a teargas launcher, with a canister in place.

"Just step around the table, brother," a voice murmurs. "Just step around there now. Nobody gonna get hurt."

With the table, too, between the visitors and the unseen yelling masses of men in the yard, long tense minutes pass. Gradually the din from C-Block fades, and beyond the table and the security chain, an eerie quiet returns to the yard. The lights come on, and the visitors scramble back to their side of the table.

"They not coming in," says Brother Flip. "Not yet awhile."

Murder in Munich
RED SMITH—*The New York Times*—9/6/1972

Olympic Village was under siege. Two men lay murdered and eight others were held at gunpoint in imminent peril of their lives. Still the games went on. Canoeists paddled through their races. Fencers thrust and parried in make-believe duels. Boxers scuffled. Basketball players scampered across the floor like happy children. Walled off in their dream world, appallingly unaware of the realities of life and death, the aging playground directors who conducted this quadrennial muscle dance ruled that a little bloodshed must not be permitted to interrupt play.

It was 4:30 a.m. when Palestinian terrorists invaded the housing complex where athletes from twelve nations live, and shot their way through into the Israeli quarters.

More than five hours later, word came from Avery Brundage, retiring president of the International Olympic Committee, that sport would proceed as scheduled. Canoe racing had already begun. Wrestling started an hour later. Before long, competition was being held in eleven of the twenty-two sports on the Olympic calendar.

Not until 4:00 p.m. did some belated sense of decency dictate suspension of the obscene activity, and even then exception was made for games already in progress. They went on and on while hasty plans were made for a memorial service.

The men who run the Olympics are not evil men. Their shocking lack of awareness cannot be due to callousness. It has to be stupidity.

Four years ago in Mexico City when American sprinters stood on the victory stand with fists uplifted in symbolic protest against injustice to blacks, the brass of the United States Olympic Committee couldn't distinguish between politics and human rights. Declaring that the athletes had violated the Olympic spirit by injecting "partisan politics" into the festival, the waxworks lifted the young men's credentials and ordered them out of Mexico, blowing up a simple, silent gesture into an international incident.

When African nations and other blacks threatened to boycott the current games if the white supremacist government of Rhodesia were represented here, Brundage thundered that the action was politically motivated, although it was only through a transparent political expedient that Rhodesia had been invited in the first place. Rhodesia and Brundage were voted down not on moral grounds but to avoid having an all-white carnival.

On past performances, it must be assumed that in Avery's view Arab-Israeli warfare, hijacking, kidnapping, and killing all constitute partisan politics not to be tolerated in the Olympics.

"And anyway," went the bitter joke today, "these are professional killers; Avery doesn't recognize them."

The fact is, these global clambakes have come to have an irresistible attraction as forums for ideological, social, or racial expression. For this reason, they may have outgrown their britches. Perhaps in the future it will be advisable to substitute separate world championships in swimming, track and field, and so on, which could be concluded in a less hysterical climate.

In the past, athletes from totalitarian countries have seized upon the Olympics as an opportunity to defect. During the Pan-American Games last summer in Cali, Colombia, a number of Cubans defected and a trainer jumped, fell, or was pushed to his death from the roof of the Cuban team's dormitory.

Never, of course, has there been anything like today's terror. Once those gunmen climbed the wire fence around the Olympic Village and shot Moshe Weinberg, the Israeli wrestling coach, all the fun and games lost meaning. Mark Spitz and his seven gold medals seemed curiously unimportant.

A Faceless Man's Plea
Mike Royko—*Chicago Sun-Times*—12/10/1972

Leroy Bailey had just turned twenty-one. He was one of seven kids from a broken family in Connecticut. He had been in the infantry in Vietnam for only one month.

Then the rocket tore through the roof of his tent while he was sleeping and exploded in his face.

He was alive when the medics pulled him out. But he was blind. And his face was gone. It's the simplest way to describe it: He no longer had a face.

That was in the spring of 1968. He went to an Army hospital, was discharged and shipped to Hines Veterans Administration Hospital, west of Chicago.

After three years and much surgery, they told him there was little more they could do for him. He still had no face.

Now Bailey spends most of his life in the basement of his brother's home in suburban La Grange. The brother moved here from the East to be near him while he was hospitalized.

He knits wool hats, which a friend sells for him. He listens to the radio or to a tape player.

Because of his terrible wound, most of the goals and pleasures of men his age will always be denied him.

But there is one thing he would like to be able to do someday. It isn't much, because most of us take it for granted.

He would like to eat solid foods.

Since 1968, he has eaten nothing but liquids. He uses a large syringe to squirt liquid foods down his throat.

Last year, through some friends of his brother, Bailey met a doctor who specializes in facial surgery.

The doctor, Charles Janda, of Oak Brook, said he believed he could reconstruct Bailey's face so that he could eat solid foods.

But it would require a series of at least six separate operations, possibly more.

Bailey eagerly agreed, and the first operation was performed at Chicago's Mercy Hospital.

Then Dr. Janda and the hospital sent their bills to the Veterans Administration.

They did this because Bailey and his brother were under the impression that the VA would pay for any treatment he needed that wasn't available in the VA.

The VA refuses to pay the bills. The reason was explained in a remarkable letter sent to Bailey by a VA official:

Dear Mr. Bailey:

Reference is made to the enclosed invoice for services given to you for selective plastic surgery done on Sept. 22, 1972.

It is regretted that payment on the above cannot be approved since the treatment was for a condition other than that of your service-connected disability.

Outpatient treatment and/or medication may only be authorized for the treatment of a disability which has been adjudicated by the Veterans Administration as incurred in or aggravated by military service.

Any expense involved for this condition must be a personal transaction between you and the doctor.

It is astonishing, I know, but the VA actually told him that he was being treated for something "other than that of your service-connected disability."

Until he was hit by a rocket, Bailey had teeth. Now he has none. He had eyes. Now he has none. He had a nose. Now he has none. People could look at him. Now most of them turn away.

Bailey believes that the VA thinks he wants the surgery just to look better, that it is "cosmetic" surgery.

Even if that were so, then why the hell not? If we can afford $5,000,000 to make Richard Nixon's San Clemente property prettier, we can do whatever is humanly possible for this man's face.

But Bailey insists it isn't his appearance that concerns him. He knows it will never be normal.

He explains his feelings in an appeal he filed months ago with the VA:

The only thing I am asking for is the ability to chew and swallow my food.

This was the purpose for the whole series of painful and unsuccessful operations I underwent in Hines Hospital between the day of my injury in May, 1968, and my eventual discharge from the hospital in 1971.

At the time, I was told the very depressing news that nothing further could be done.

I will never be able to accept this decision. . . .

In some bureaucrat's file cabinet is Bailey's appeal. It has been there for many months.

Every day that it sits there, Bailey takes his syringe and squirts liquid nour-ishment down his throat.

If his appeal is turned down, he will spend the rest of his life doing that. Not even once will he be able to sit down and eat at the dinner table with his brother's family, before going back down to the basement to knit hats.

The Phony-Tough Meet the Crazy-Brave
STEWART ALSOP—*Washington Post*—9/7/1973

The second round of the Watergate hearings will begin in a few days. Per-haps this time the senators will find the answer to the great unanswered question of the whole sordid business: How could people have been such goddam fools?

The Nixon men who testified in the first round said a good many inherently unbelievable things, and often they seemed to have respectable intelligence quotients. Yet these people risked the ruin of the Nixon presidency, which has now occurred, in order to bug Larry O'Brien's office, from which absolutely nothing was to be gained. Why?

I have come up with a theory to answer that question, which I herewith offer with due modesty. My theory derives from the peculiar relationship between two minority categories of the human race—the crazy-brave and the phony-tough. Most people who have been in a war, and a lot of people who haven't, have come across specimens of both breeds.

The crazy-brave, who are a lot rarer than the phony-tough, are always doing crazy things that ought to get them killed, or at least maimed, but nothing ever seems to happen to them. They also exercise a kind of hex or double whammy on the phony-tough, and they keep getting the phony-tough into terrible trouble.

What came out with awful clarity in the first round of Watergate hearings was that almost all the Nixon men were classical phony-toughs. The phony-toughs are easily identifiable by their manner of speech.

The Watergate testimony abounds with examples of phony-tough talk. John Dean's memorandum on how to "screw our enemies"; Chuck Colson's memo-randum on how he would "walk over my grandmother" to re-elect Nixon and his suggestion that someone (not Colson) blow up the Brookings Institution; John Mitchell's various vulgarisms, and his "when the going gets tough, the tough get going"; John Ehrlichman's proposal for poor Pat Gray, to "let him hang there, let him twist slowly, slowly in the wind"; and many more.

Phony-tough talk always shares the same basic characteristic—it is talk designed to show the toughness of the talker, but requiring no painful or dangerous action on his part. This is why the crazy-brave have a hex on the phony-tough—the crazy-brave challenge the phony-tough to translate tough talk into dangerous action.

Enter G. Gordon Liddy. Liddy is the archetype of the crazy-brave. In the testimony of Jeb Stuart Magruder, there is a nice example of the relationship between the crazy-brave and the phony-tough. Magruder, who has been trying to work up the courage to fire Liddy, meets him in a hallway:

"Magruder: . . . I simply put my hand on Mr. Liddy's shoulder and he asked me to remove it and indicated that if I did not serious consequences would occur.

"Dash: Was he more specific than serious consequences?

"Magruder: Well, he indicated he would kill me. . . ."

The phony-toughs in the Nixon entourage were uneasily aware that Liddy often carried a gun and was quite capable of using it. Magruder told how Liddy, spying out McGovern's headquarters in the dead of night, pulled a pistol and shot out a light. When they heard about this, Magruder says, "Both Mr. Strachan and I became very concerned." Spying is fine. But no loud bangs, please.

On another occasion, Magruder was complaining in Liddy's presence about some "enemy" and muttered something about "getting rid" of him. A few minutes later, a Magruder subordinate met a grim-faced Liddy, who mentioned the well-known name of the "enemy" and remarked that "I have been ordered to kill him." A horrified Magruder finally persuaded Liddy that murder was not quite what he had in mind.

John Dean testified about a chance chat with Liddy after the break-in had been discovered. "Liddy was very apologetic for the fact that they had been caught. . . . He also told me that he was a soldier and would never talk. He said that if anyone wished to shoot him on the street he was ready." One can imagine how this notion must have astonished a phony-tough like John Dean who, far from being ready to be shot, was ready instead to squeal on all his former friends and colleagues in the hope of escaping jail.

It is clear from the testimony and other evidence that the Nixonian phony-toughs were scared sick of the crazy-brave Liddy, and kept trying to get rid of him. He kept getting tossed around like a hot potato from the Treasury Department to the White House to the Committee for the Re-Election of the President to the Finance Committee, but no one had quite the guts to fire him.

No one—according to my theory—had quite the guts, either, to tell him to his face to forget his wild schemes for doing in the Democrats. His first and most memorable scheme, to cost a mere million dollars, involved such modest proposals as mass kidnappings and launching a floating whorehouse at Miami Beach to entice the Democrats into whispered indiscretions.

This scheme, it appears, was fairly firmly squelched by John Mitchell. So a frustrated Liddy had to cut back his dream schemes, first to a half-million-dollar operation, finally to a mere quarter million. This third, chicken-feed scheme would allow only for bugging the Democratic National Committee and the headquarters of the chief presidential contenders at Miami Beach.

This is the scheme that ruined the Nixon presidency, and there is a lot of conflicting testimony about whether Mitchell or anyone else approved or disapproved it. My theory is that nobody did either—that, not being morons, none of the phony-toughs in the Nixon high command gave Liddy an unequivocal green light, but that none of them had the guts to tell Liddy to can it, or to deny him the money for the operation when he asked for it.

If this theory is correct, the President was the victim of the hex the crazy-brave exercise on the phony-tough. This is not reassuring. Phony-toughs are dangerous people to have around, above all in or near the White House—for one example, President Kennedy approved the Bay of Pigs fiasco because none of his chief advisers had the courage to seem timid. Most dismaying of all, it seems reasonable to assume that a man who, like Nixon in his first term, surrounds himself with phony-toughs may be a phony-tough himself.

Watergate: For a Lot of People, It Has Changed Everything
MARY MCGRORY—*Washington Star*—1/2/1975

Guilty, guilty, guilty, guilty.

The word stabbed the still, close air of the courtroom fifteen times, spoken mildly, noncommittally by the gray-haired clerk, James Capitanio, no one's first choice for the voice of doom.

John Mitchell, guilty; H. R. Haldeman, guilty; John Ehrlichman, guilty; Robert Mardian, guilty. Was it the only word in the English language? Finally, another was heard. "Not guilty," twice for Kenneth Parkinson, whom the jury believed when he said he had fallen among evil companions.

Parkinson's right hand, which had been twitching uncontrollably, went quiet. His lawyer, Jacob Stein, reached up to clap him on the back. Mitchell, his face still flushed from the jolt he had taken, looked over and mouthed the words "good boy" at the lucky man.

Only Mardian seemed surprised. When "guilty" hit him, he flung his head to one side like an angry horse about to bolt.

Mardian's cover-up career had been the briefest of the five. But he had been surly and contemptuous on the stand, and he may have been judged as much for that as for participation in the panic that followed June 17, 1972.

The verdict in the second Watergate trial, the real one, came unexpectedly on a quiet, sunny New Year's Day afternoon at 4:25. The judge, who had, to the open mouthed amazement of a British correspondent, gone downstairs an hour earlier to pose with the whole cast, minus the defendants, for what was billed on the pressroom blackboard as a "class foto," was sitting in his chambers with seven reporters he had invited in for a chat and reminiscence. He was midway in a recital of a forty-year-old arson case when the marshal appeared at the door.

He broke off, apologized and said casually, "There's another note from the jury."

It was indeed a note, the long-awaited, long-deferred judgment of Watergate. The jury, which had not been in any hurry for sixty-four days, had abruptly packed it up.

The defendants, their defenders, a handful of holiday spectators, and the reporters trooped into the large blank room where since October 1 they have sat together and listened to the history of the Nixon administration and its efforts to "keep the lid on" the greatest political scandal in the country's history.

Haldeman knew what was coming. His oblong face was set. He folded his arms on the table, braced himself for it. Mitchell's dread took the form of an unprecedented animation. He chatted with his second lawyer, Plato Cacheris. The usually pleasant face of his chief attorney, William G. Hundley, was stiff with melancholy. Ehrlichman's back, which was to the room, seemed relaxed. Only Mardian looked genuinely expectant.

The room was so quiet the only sound was the whirring of the air-conditioning. The judge who presided at both trials took his place. The jury, led by its foreman, John Hoffar, came in, appearing serene and relieved. Hoffar's election had sent the last days' one quiver of hope through the demoralized ranks of the defense. A former park policeman, the only white male and the only registered Republican of the twelve, he was figured for an Archie Bunker.

His pale face never registered the slightest interest, his pale blue eyes had played coldly on the witnesses. The dramatic, sometimes hilarious summing-up of Chief Prosecutor James F. Neal had roused him from torpor, but his general demeanor had cried for the caption, "Everybody does it."

But Hoffar, the foreman, was changed. His eyes glinted, he smiled a bit. He had become purposeful. He was carrying judgment under his arm in a large manila envelope.

He stood up. Yes, he was the foreman. Yes, the jury had reached a verdict. The envelope, followed by a hundred eyes, was handed over. In his diffident tones, Capitanio instructed the best and the brightest of the Nixon administration to rise. Then he tonelessly began his reading. The "guilties" and the gasping began.

Andrew Hall, Ehrlichman's second lawyer—his chief advocate, William Frates, had flown back to Florida—asked for a poll of the jury. Some of the yeses were barely audible, others in voices that suggested they should be asked again.

David Bress, Mardian's ailing counsel, who had been absent for most of the trial, noted the stricken conditions of his client—who was indeed slumped down as if he had been shot in the stomach—and asked for another poll. The judge brusquely denied it.

The judge thanked the jury and Mrs. Mardian formed a Bronx cheer. Mrs. Ehrlichman, sitting beside her, was composed.

The heavy scene dissolved. A little congratulatory group formed around Parkinson. John Mitchell reached for his pipe. On his way out, he collided with a junior attorney. Mitchell apologized profusely and put a solicitous hand on the youth's shoulder. Mrs. Ehrlichman made her way to her husband. They stood with an arm around each other, their backs to the room.

But Mardian would not leave the seat which he had taken as a free man. He held his bald head in his hands, he bent it almost to the level of the table. Bress leaned over and tried to console him. Mrs. Mardian, fresh from an encounter with Neal and Assistant Prosecutor Richard Ben-Veniste—she is said to have told them both she would "get" them—was summoned. She put a supporting hand under her husband's elbow. With some of the gentility he had displayed on the stand, he flung it off. She tried again and got him to his feet. He seemed barely able to walk to the door.

Outside the court, a storm of Shakespearean fury had suddenly blown up. Haldeman went out in the rain to say he was the only man who could judge his innocence. Ehrlichman sent word he would talk to the reporters. He came into the littered pressroom—the poker chips and the cards for the long waiting game were whisked out of sight against his arrival—and while the rain lashed the windows and the wind howled, he waxed philosophical, judicious, dispassionate, and compassionate. A friend to all men, including Richard Nixon, he declared himself innocent.

"As far as the verdict is concerned," he said, "it changes nothing."

For a lot of people, though, it has changed everything. A judgment that seemed inevitable had finally been rendered.

You Can Bet on Sinatra
MIKE ROYKO—*Chicago Daily News*—5/5/1976

A short man with a thick neck just walked in and handed me an envelope and said: "Dis is fum Mr. Sinatra."

Sure enough, it was—a letter from Ol' Blue Eyes himself, telling me off good for my column about how he has a 24-hour police guard outside his hotel suite while he's in Chicago.

Here's what he says:

Let me start this note by saying, I don't know you and you don't know me. I believe if you knew me:

First, you would find immediately that I do not have an army of flunkies.

Secondly, neither myself, nor my secretary, nor my security man put in the request for police protection. It is something that's far from necessary.

It's quite obvious that your source of information stinks, but that never surprises me about people who write in newspapers for a living. They rarely get their facts straight. If the police decided that they wanted to be generous with me, I appreciate it. If you have any beefs with the Chicago Police Force, why not take it out on them instead of me, or is that too big a job for you?

And thirdly, who in the hell gives you the right to decide how disliked I am if you know nothing about me?

The only honest thing I read in your piece is the fact that you admitted you are disliked, and by the way you write I can understand it. Quite frankly, I don't understand why people don't spit in your eye three or four times a day.

Regarding my "tough reputation," you and no one else can prove that allegation. You and millions of other gullible Americans read that kind of crap written by the same female gossip columnists that you are so gallantly trying to protect: the garbage dealers I call hookers, and there's no doubt that is exactly what they are, which makes you a pimp, because you are using people to make money, just as they are.

Lastly, certainly not the least, if you are a gambling man:

(a) You prove, without a doubt, that I have ever punched an elderly drunk or elderly anybody, you can pick up $100,000.

(b) I will allow you to pull my "hairpiece." If it moves, I will give you another $100,000; if it does not, I punch you in the mouth.

How about it?

(signed) Sinatra.

cc: The Honorable Richard J. Daley
Police Supt. James Rochford

Mr. Marshall Field, Publisher

Mr. Charles Fegert, Vice President

This material has been copyrighted and may not be reproduced unless used in its entirety and sets forth the following copyright notice: (copyright) Frank Sinatra, 1976.

Before I respond, I have to admit that receiving a signed, hand-delivered, copyrighted letter from Frank Sinatra was a thrill. Even if he did call me a pimp.

Way back, when we were both young, Sinatra was one of my heroes because (a) he was real skinny (b) he had a big Adam's apple (c) he had greasy hair, and (d) all the girls loved him. Me too, except for (d).

For thirty years I considered him the master of pop singers. Why, in 1953, I played his great record of "Birth of the Blues" so often that a Korean houseboy learned every word. And he probably taught that song to his children. So if Sinatra has a fan club in the Korean village of Yong Dong Po, it's because of me.

I mention this only to show how deeply it pained me to be critical of him. The pain may have been brought on by the french fries at lunch, but I prefer to think it was sentiment.

Anyway, here is my point-by-point response to his point-by-point response to my column:

If you say you have no flunkies, I take your word and apologize. I even apologize to the flunky who delivered the letter.

You say you didn't ask for the police guard. I'll buy that. But I didn't say you asked. I quoted the police public relations man who said you did. I now suspect that what actually happened is that some politician sent the cop over to impress you. This point could have been easily cleared up before I wrote the column, but every time we called your suite, your secretary got snippy and hung up. I thought you didn't like smart-aleck broads.

I didn't say you were disliked; the police PR man said it to justify the guard. I like you, Frank, honest. When you wore big bow ties, I wore big bow ties. When you wore big lapels and baggy pants, I wore big lapels and baggy pants. When you dated Ava Gardner, I dated Agnes Grobnik. We're a lot alike.

The reason people don't spit in my eye three or four times a day is that I duck fast.

After rereading your massive file of news clippings, I agree that you never punched any "elderly drunks." Most of the drunks you punched were younger.

If you can prove, without a doubt, that I have ever been a pimp, I will give you $11.69. In cash. You're not the only high roller in town.

I don't want to pull your hair. People would think we're a couple of weirdos.

However, for the sake of a sporting proposition, I'll do it. But only if I can make new terms for the bet.

If your hair doesn't move, you can give me a punch in the mouth. (I figure that fans who can't get tickets for your show will pay 50 cents to touch my swollen lip.)

But if it does move, never mind the 100 G's—you give me one of your old bow ties and an original recording of "Birth of the Blues." I still say it was your best song.

Son of Sam: Fear in Queens
JIMMY BRESLIN—*New York Daily News*—5/15/1977

[In the summer of 1977, a serial killer terrorized New York City. Initially known as the .44 Killer and then as the Son of Sam, the murderer communicated with *Daily News* columnist Jimmy Breslin through a series of letters. In the end, David Berkowitz was caught and sentenced to six consecutive life terms in prison.]

At night, on the way home, there was a stop at the 109th Precinct, which is housed in an antiseptic brick building that removes a part of the terror and all of the glamour of being in a police station.

On the wall of an upstairs office was a color photo of a gun, a black gun with a brown handle, and some brass cartridges placed against a sky-blue background. The printing on the picture said this was New York crime lab Case No. 771663. The gun is a .44-caliber Bulldog. Somewhere on the other side of the closed metal Venetian blinds, out in the night-empty neighborhoods of the city, was a guy with frenzy in his eyes and a .44-Bulldog in his pocket. He shoots at young girls with brown hair. In doing so, he has killed five people and wounded four others in the last nine months.

He shot two of the girls within six blocks of my house and the streets where I live are totally deserted at dusk. I know one girl, Mary Benot, secretary, who now wears a blond wig over her brown hair. She says a lot of girls she knows are doing the same thing. Nobody would be cheered by the chart which was on the wall alongside the picture of the gun. The chart said: "Weapons stolen, 667. Stolen weapons checked, 4."

The man in charge of the investigation, Timothy Dowd, an inspector, sat at his desk and answered telephones. Dowd looks much younger than his 61 years. His blue eyes stared at the door as he listened to the phone, said it wasn't enough. On a windowsill, 17 hand radios sat in slots in a recharging machine. This probably is as big an investigation as the New York police have ever run. And Dowd, after hanging up the phone, said it still wasn't enough.

"We need a phone call," he said. "We're doing everything we can. We've got the best homicide men from all over the city working here. But it surprises us we don't hear from the family or from relatives of the killer. Somebody must live with the guy and suspect something." In leaving the room, the eye was attracted by a large stenciled sign above the light switch. In that great police subtleness, the sign above the light switch said: "Turn Off Lights."

We took a cab home. As we passed the place where the killer shot one of the girls, I saw a big guy in a zippered jacket standing with his hands in his pockets. He is a detective I've known for years and I had the cab stop and I got out.

"Getting the feel of the thing?" I said to him.

"That's television s—" he said.

"Well, what do you come out for?"

"Because I'm just starting on the case. I always start at the start. Go to the scene and start walkin' from there. I don't even know the names of the people who got killed. Only name I'm interested in is the name of the man done the killin'. I'd give up a month's drinking if you could arrange the meetin'."

He has spent his life in the slum precincts and his speech patterns come from those streets. "Come on," he said. "We walkin'." And he started down the street, a gun and a radio in his pocket, a man who has spent his life hunting on cement. His target this time is not the ordinary homicidal person we grow so quickly in the slums. The .44 killer is one of those special, twisted people who have been with us through the ages.

He began walking down a street which goes along railroad tracks. There was not a person in sight.

"Look at these lights they got on the houses," he said. "Little carriage lights. That's about as much illumination as you get from my lighter. I could hide nothin'. These murders never could happen in a black neighborhood. Too many people out on the streets. Everybody would see who did it. Man we after is only workin' white neighborhoods. Nobody comes out at night and he can prowl around and catch him a stray girl and do what he has to do.

"Look at these people around here," he said. He waved a hand at a row of attached houses running into an apartment house. It was 11 p.m. and the only sign that there were people inside were windows filled with the pale blue light of television.

"These same people here, you put a lot of kids on the streets here makin' some noise, and these here people call up and complain. If they got any sense, they pay kids to hang out on the sidewalks all night. Hang out and bang garbage cans around. No killer goin' walk around, if you got people out on the streets."

Up at the corner, a man appeared. He was holding a German shepherd on a leash. He stopped as he saw us walking toward him.

"Look at this," the detective said.

The man with the dog bent down and unleashed the dog. He stood there with a hand on the dog.

"I'm continuing to walk by and the dog's goin' to continue to sniff," the detective said. "If the dog don't continue to sniff, he goin' be a dead dog."

The man put the leash back on the dog and stepped out of the way and we went past him.

When we got down to the boulevard, there were some people at the coffee shop and a few coming out of the subway. But much less than normal.

"We got a Jack-the-Ripper case and everybody thinks they're better off hidin' inside the house," the detective said. "All they do is make it easier for this guy to go around killin' people. Black people are the only ones who know what to do about crime. The more people outside the house, the less can happen to you."

He turned around and walked away from the boulevard and back into the dark vacant streets where a killer has hit twice and where people are afraid he will soon hit again. This time, as the detective walked, there wasn't even a man out with a dog.

Endless Talk About Cambodia

WILLIAM F. BUCKLEY JR.—Universal Press Syndicate—9/10/1977

[In the mid-1970s, the Marxist army known as the Khmer Rouge, led by Pol Pot, overran Cambodia and murdered an estimated 2 million people. America, exhausted by the war in Vietnam, did nothing to stop the slaughter.]

I am quite serious: Why doesn't Congress authorize the money to finance an international military force to overrun Cambodia?

That force should be made up primarily of Asians—Thais, notably, but also Malaysians, Filipinos, Taiwanese, Japanese. Detachments from North Vietnam and China should be permitted, and token representatives from voluntary units of other countries that are signatories to the Genocide Convention and to the various protocols on human rights. Our inactivity in respect of Cambodia is a sin as heinous as our inactivity to save the Jews from the holocaust. Worse, actually; because we did mobilize eventually to destroy Hitler. We are doing nothing to save the Cambodians. What is happening in Cambodia mocks every speech made by every politician in the United Nations and elsewhere about our common devotion to human rights.

The idea, in Cambodia, isn't to go there and set up a democratic state. It is to go there and take power away from one, two, three, perhaps as many as a half-dozen sadistic madmen who have brought on their country the worst suffering brought on any country in this bloody century.

Father François Ponchaud, who lived in Cambodia from 1965 to 1975, estimates that 800,000 Cambodians have died since the Khmer Rouge took over two years ago. And he is thought to be inaccurate on the low side. Richard Holbrooke, our assistant secretary of state for East Asian affairs, puts the figure as high as 1.2 million.

Hundreds of thousands of these deaths were by execution. The balance was worse: death mostly by starvation. We finally mustered the judicial energy to execute Gary Gilmore last January. We could not have found one American, short possibly of Son of Sam, who would have voted to starve him to death. Others die of malaria and other diseases. The Khmer Rouge disdains to accept medical aid from the West, or food.

As for the death figures, what do they mean to those for whom human life means nothing? Mr. Stéphane Groueff, of *France Soir*, went to within a dozen kilometers of Cambodia recently and talked with hundreds of refugees. It is the deepest mystery what actually is the composition of Cambodia's evil leadership, as no correspondent has been there in two years, and the eight diplomatic legations (seven Communist, plus Egypt), are house-bound, and denied permission to speak to any Cambodians. There is speculation that the strongman running the show is the forty-six-year-old French-educated Khieu Samphan, the head of the Presidium.

When you ask the refugees who is the authority behind the Khmer Rouge, they will tell you, presumably in whispers, "Angkar." What is Khieu Samphan to Angkar? What is the role of the prime minister, Pol Pot? Or of Ieng Sari, the Hanoi intellectual whose real name is Nguyen Sao Levy? Or the Communist Party secretary general, Soloth Sar? Mr. Groueff reports that there is only one known interview with Samphan. It was given to an Italian journalist at last summer's Colombo conference.

"What happened to the other million?" the journalist asked. Samphan was annoyed. "It's incredible," he said, "the way you Westerners worry about war criminals."

Two out of seven Cambodians are already dead. That is the equivalent of 57 million Americans killed. Even Stalin might have shrunk from genocide on such a scale. And what are we doing about it? Waiting for Rolf Hochhuth to write a play? Is there no *practical* idealism left in this world? Only that endless talk, which desecrates the language, and atrophies the soul?

Bernhard Goetz: Notes from the Underground
Pete Hamill—*Village Voice*—5/12/1987

[The trial of "subway vigilante" Bernhard Goetz transfixed New York's tabloids at a time of rising crime and civic decay.]

The slow and tedious processes of justice brought Bernhard Hugo Goetz last week to a fifth-floor courtroom at 111 Centre Street and there, at least, the poor man was safe. Out in the great scary city, the demons of his imagination roamed freely; across the street, many of them were locked away in the cages of The Tombs. But here at the defense table, flanked by his lawyers, protected by a half-dozen armed court officers, the room itself separated by metal detectors from the anarchy of the city, Goetz looked almost serene.

By design or habit, he was dressed as an ordinary citizen: pink cotton shirt and jeans over the frail body, steel-rimmed glasses sliding down the long sharp nose. His hair looked freshly trimmed. You see people like him every day, passing you on the street, riding the subways, neither monstrous nor heroic. From time to time, he whispered to the lawyers. He made a few notes on a yellow pad. His eyes wandered around the courtroom, with its civil service design and the words *In God We Trust* nailed in sans-serif letters above the bench of Judge Stephen G. Crane. Goetz never looked at the spectators or the six rows of reporters. In some curious way, he was himself a kind of spectator.

So when it was time to play the tape-recorded confession that Goetz made to the police in Concord, New Hampshire, on New Year's Eve, 1984, he, too, examined the transcript like a man hoping for revelation. The text itself was extraordinary. Combined with the sound of Goetz's voice—stammering, hyperventilating, querulous, defensive, cold, blurry, calculating—it seemed some terrible invasion of privacy. We have heard this voice before; it belongs to the anonymous narrator of *Notes from the Underground*, that enraged brief for the defense.

Goetz furrowed his brow as he listened to this much younger, oddly more innocent version of himself that had ended the long panicky flight out of the IRT in the second floor interview room of police headquarters in Concord. He started by telling his inquisitor, a young detective named Chris Domian, the sort of facts demanded by personnel directors: name, birth date, social security number, address (55 West 14th Street, "in New York City, and that's, uh, that's zip code 10011"). But it's clear from the very beginning that he realized these would be his last anonymous hours.

GOETZ: You see, I'll tell you the truth, and they can do anything they want with me, but I just don't want to, I just don't want to be *paraded* around, I don't want a circus. . . . I wish it were a dream. But it's not. But, you know, it's nothing to be proud of. It's just, just you know, it just *is*.

Exactly. It wasn't a dream, certainly not a movie; it just was. On December 22, 1984, at about 1:30 in the afternoon, Bernie Goetz boarded a southbound number 2 Seventh Avenue IRT train at 14th Street and his life changed forever. So did the lives of Darrell Cabey, Troy Canty, James Ramseur, and Barry Allen. Within seconds after he boarded the train, they were joined together in a few violent minutes that changed this city. And when you listen to Goetz making his jangled confession, you understand that on that terrible afternoon, there were really five victims.

DOMIAN: Okay, let's start with the person that was, uh, on the right, so to speak, laying down.

GOETZ: Yeah, I think he was the one who talked to me; he was the one who did the talking.

That was Canty. He is now 20, finishing an 18-month drug rehab treatment at Phoenix House. Before he ran into Goetz, he had pleaded guilty to taking $14 from video games in a bar. In his confession, Goetz is trying hard to explain to Domian (and to officer Warren Foote, who joined Domian) not simply what he did, but in context. The resulting transcript reads like a small, eerie play: the man from the big city explaining a dark world of menacing signs and nuances to the baffled outlanders.

GOETZ: I sat, I sat down and just, he was lying on the side, kind of. He, he just turned his face to me and he said, "How are you?" You know, what do you do? 'Cause people joke around in New York a lot, and this and that, and in certain circumstances that can be, that can be a real threat. You see, there's an implication there . . . I looked up and you're not supposed to look at people a lot because it can be interpreted as being impolite—so I just looked at him and I said "Fine." And I, I looked down. But you kind of keep them in the corner of your eye . . .

DOMIAN: Did he say anything else to you?

GOETZ: Yeah, yeah . . . the train was out of the station for a while and it reached full speed. . . . And he and one of the other fellows got up and they, uh—You see, they were all originally on my right hand side. But, uh, you know, two stayed on my right-hand side, and he got up and the other guy got up and they came to my left-hand side and . . . You see, what they said wasn't even so much as important as the look, the *look*. You see the body language. . . . You have to, you know, it's, uh, you know, that's what I call it, *body language*.

That's what started it off: "How are you?" and body language. It just went from there. Goetz remembered: "He [Canty] stood up and the other fellow stood up. And they very casually walked, or sauntered—whatever you want to call it—over to my left side. And the fellow . . . uh, he said, 'Give me five dollars.'"

This is the moment that helps explain the intensity of the public response to the Goetz story. It is one thing to read with detached amusement about Jean Harris or Claus von Bulow; such tabloid soap operas have little to do with our lives. But for millions of New Yorkers, what happened to Goetz is a very real possibility. Being trapped on the subway by four bad guys demanding not a dime or a quarter but *five dollars* is similar to the nocturne about the burglar beside the bed in the dark. A quarter is panhandling; five dollars is robbery. Such scenarios don't often happen, but you wonder what you would do if they did. For Goetz, it happened.

GOETZ: One of the other fellows, he had in his fur coat, he had his hand or something like this and he put a bulge. . . . And even that isn't a threat. Because the people, you see, they, they know the rules of the game, the rules of the game in New York. And you know, they're very serious about the rules. . . . You see you don't know what it's like to be on the other side of violence. It's, it's like a picture. When it happens to you, you see, you *see* it. . . . People have the craziest images; they see, like Captain Kirk or someone like that, getting attacked by several guys and boom, boom, boom, he beats 'em up and—and two minutes later, he's walking arm and arm in, with a beautiful woman or something like that. And that's not what it is. . . .

Goetz was not Captain Kirk. He was a frail bespectacled young man living in New York and he had learned the rules of the game. He knew what was meant when one of four young black men told him he wanted five dollars.

GOETZ: I looked at his face, and, you know, his eyes were *shiny*, you know. He, he, he was, if you can believe that, his eyes were shiny, he was *enjoying* himself. . . . I know in my mind what they wanted to do was *play* with me. . . . You know, it's kind of like a cat plays with a mouse before, you know. . . .

DOMIAN: After you got that impression, what did you wind up doing?

GOETZ: That's not an impression, that's not an impression. . . .

Throughout the confession, Goetz struggles with what he clearly believes is an impossible task: to explain to his rural auditors the terrors of New York.

GOETZ: . . . You have to think in a cold-blooded way in New York. . . . If you don't . . . think in what society's going to brand it, as being you know, *cold-blooded* and murderous and savage and monstrous . . . I feel it's *irresponsible*. . . . How can you understand that here in New Hampshire? How, how, how can you?

He explains to the two New Hampshire cops that he began, in his mind, to lay down "my pattern of fire." He would shoot from left to right. That was the only thing he could do, he insists, because this act wasn't premeditated:

"I never knew those guys were on the train, you know, and like I said, I'm, I'm no good guy or anything like that. But if they had acted a little differently, if they hadn't *cornered* me . . ." Clearly what he feared most from them was humiliation. And so he decided to shoot them with the unregistered nickel-plated featherweight .38 caliber Smith & Wesson Special that he had shoved inside his pants.

DOMIAN: Your, your intention was to shoot these people?

GOETZ: My intention, at the moment, let me explain: when I saw what they intended for me, my intention was, was worse than shooting.

DOMIAN: Okay. Was it your intention to kill these people?

GOETZ: My intention was to do anything I could do to hurt them. My intention —you know, I know this sounds horrible—but my intention was to murder them, to *hurt* them, to make them suffer as much as possible.

No, he explained, he didn't have a pistol permit, because the New York police department had turned him down. And then, recalling all this to the cops in New Hampshire, the core of his rage began to burn. The reason he wanted a pistol permit was because he had been attacked three years before and was left with permanent damage to his knee. The cops caught the man who did it, Goetz said, and two hours and 35 minutes after his arrest, he was back on the street without bail, charged with malicious mischief; Goetz himself claimed he spent six hours and five minutes filing the charges and talking to the bureaucrats in the victim aid program.

"That incident was an education," he said, his voice beginning to tremble. "It taught me that, that the city doesn't care what happens to you. You see, *you* don't know what it's like to be a victim inside."

And he began to explain what it's like to live in an almost permanent state of fear. This can't be sneered away; thousands, perhaps millions of New Yorkers live with this most corrosive emotion. Most of us have adjusted to the state of siege. We are tense, wary, guarded; but most of us function and do not explode. Goetz was different.

GOETZ: . . . I kind of accept my life, as I know it, is finished. But, but, boy, it would be just—to lead a normal life. If, if you can't, I mean, is it too much to ask? . . . To live being afraid is unbearable, you know? It's too much to ask, god-damn it . . ."

All over the tape, Goetz talks about fear and its denial. "I'm not afraid of dying instantly," he says at one point. "I don't have a family or anything like that. What I'm afraid of is being maimed and of, of these things happening slowly and not knowing what's going to happen from moment to moment. The fear, in this case, the fear is a funny thing. You see, this is really *combat*." He then becomes even more analytical, sounding like a man who had mastered the theory before engaging in practice. "The upper level of your mind, you just turn off. That's, that's the important thing. And you, you *react* . . . your sense of perception changes, your abilities change. Speed is everything, speed is everything."

And so, with speed, he shot Canty, Allen, Cabey, and Manseur. "They had set a trap for me," he tells the cops, "and only they were trapped. It was just so bizarre. It was—I know this is disgusting to say—but it was, it was so easy. I can't believe it. God." He insists that he knew exactly what he was doing when he was doing it. "I don't believe in this insanity stuff. Because you know what you're doing. You cannot do something and not know it. I mean how could I do it and not know it? This is, this is all bullshit. . . . But if you can accept this: I was out of control. . . . Maybe you should always be in control. But if you put people in a situation where they're threatened with mayhem, *several times*, and then if, then if something happens, and if a person acts, turns into a vicious animal—I mean, I mean, you know, how are you supposed, you know, it's it's, it's, it's, what, *what do you expect*, you know?"

After firing the first shots, dropping Canty, Ramseur, and Allen, he saw Cabey sitting down.

GOETZ: I wasn't sure if I had shot him before, because he just seemed okay. Now, I said I know this sounds, this is gonna sound vicious, and it is. I mean, how else can you describe it? I said, "You seem to be all right. Here's another." Now, you see, what happens is, I was gonna shoot him anyway, I'm sure. I had made up, I mean, in my mind, that I was gonna pull the trigger anyway. But he jerked his right arm. And on reflex, he was shot instantly. You see, that's the whole thing. You're working on reflex. You don't think. . . .

Scattered through the confession there are many other examples of Goetz's fury and rage, which sound as if they too had become reflexes. "If I had more [ammunition] I would have shot them again and again and again." He says that "I wanted to hurt them as much as I possibly could." But even in his rage, he could recognize the fallen men as humans: "I wanted to look at his eyes, I don't even want to say what may have been in my mind. And I looked at his eyes . . . there was such *fear*." It was as if Cabey's fear was the only sign to Goetz of their common humanity. "You know, the, the, the look had changed. And I started—it was kinda like slowing down. All of a sudden it's like putting on the, screeching of the brakes, and you just start slowing down. . . ."

He talked about the reactions of other passengers, the train slowing down, a conductor coming in and asking what was going on. He talked about jumping out into the tracks after the train stopped in the tunnel, and coming up at Chambers Street and taking a cab home, and then a long drive that night in a rented car to Vermont because "instinctively, somehow I kinda feel like heading north is the way to go if there is a problem."

Goetz stayed in Vermont for a week. And if you can believe the confession, he seems actually to have been happy. What he did in the subway, he thought, would be considered just another New York crime. ". . . When I got back to New York, the stuff was still on the news and people were talking about it. You see, up here people have just forgotten about it. It was one more piece of, excuse me for using the word—one more piece of shit that happened in New York."

Hearing himself say those words, Goetz massaged his temple, and then lifted his glasses and rubbed his eyes. In the end, the eruption that Saturday afternoon on the IRT wasn't just another piece of shit that happened in New York. It was a lot more than that.

A Boldfaced Lie
DAVE BARRY—*Miami Herald*—7/12/1987

Unless you are unemployed, sick, or a journalist, you probably have not had time to keep up with the hearings that have been held, over the course of the past year or two, by the Congressional Committee To Drone On About The Iran-Contra Scandal Until Everybody Involved Is Dead. So today, as a public service, we're going to provide the following convenient summary of the entire affair, putting the names of **Key Elements** in easy-to-read **boldface**. There will be a quiz.

It all started when some **Extremist Maniac Lunatics** took some **American Hostages**, which upset **Ronald Reagan**, who to the best of his recollection **was President Of The United States** at the time, so he naturally sold **Weapons** to the **Extremist Maniac Lunatics** in exchange for **Money**, which was funneled, with the help of various **Courageous Patriots** who received nothing for their efforts except a **Sense Of Satisfaction and Eight Million Dollars**, to the crack **Foreign-Policy Adventure Squad** headed by **Lt. Col. Oliver North** (Secret Code Name "**Manhood Testicle**"), who, with his loyal staff, **Fawn Hall**, who has been offered $500,000 by **Penthouse Magazine** to pose **Naked**, occupied an office in the **White House**, but was in no way whatsoever connected with **Anybody Higher Up**, because of course it is a **Common Practice for Totally Random Unofficial People** such as **Insurance Agents** and **Accordion Teachers** to have **White House Offices**, and thus it was that **Col. North**, acting completely on his **Own**, decided to divert the **Money** to the **Contras**, who are at war with **Iraq**, no wait, sorry, it is **Iran** that is at war with **Iraq**, which is the country that shot one of our ships, which naturally caused **President Reagan** (Code Name "**Grinning Vegetable**"), to speak out angrily against—this is the truth—**Iran**, which as some of you may recall is the very same country he sold the **Weapons** to, but we are drifting away from our **Central Point**, which is that **Col. North** was merely trying to insure that the **Contras** received an adequate supply of **Money** in order to carry out the **Reagan Administration's Secret Plan** (Don't tell **Anybody**!) to overthrow the government of **Nicaragua**, a role in which the **Contras** have proved to be as effective, militarily, as a **Bucket Of Dead Shrimp**.

Now that you're up to date on this important scandal, you might want to take some time off from work and watch a few episodes of The Iran-Contra Hearings TV Show. The best time to tune in is when a Reagan administration official is testifying, and the committee tries to trick him into making a coherent statement:

> CONGRESSPERSON: Please state your name and title, and reveal what the U.S. foreign policy is.
>
> WITNESS: My name is Elliott Abrams; my title is Assistant Administrative Associate Sub-secretary of State for Reminding Everybody of a Small Hairless Nocturnal Rodent; and the U.S. foreign policy is . . .
>
> (The entire committee leans forward in breathless anticipation . . .)
>
> WITNESS: . . . a SECRET!
>
> AUDIENCE: (Loud applause)
>
> CONGRESSPERSON: Ha ha! You really had us going there! Don Pardo, tell our witness what exciting gifts he'll receive for testifying here today!
>
> DON PARDO: Bob, he'll receive . . .

The danger, of course, is that one day a witness will slip up and reveal the foreign policy, which is why the Reagan administration, as a Security Measure, is now changing it on a daily basis. It is also kept in a locked box, for which there is only one key. Which the president, as an added precaution, has misplaced.

QUIZ: TEST YOUR SCANDAL KNOWLEDGE
1. Would you pose naked for $500,000? Me too.

Ignorance Epidemic During AIDS Crisis
MOLLY IVINS—*Fort Worth Star-Telegram*—8/13/1992

What is this? Dog days of August? Full moon? Stars in strange alignment?

There is this outbreak of nuttiness all over the state about AIDS. We are in the tenth year of the AIDS epidemic.

We all know there are still slope-browed, egg-sucking ridge-runners out in the hills who believe that only homosexuals get AIDS and that it serves them right.

But most of us long ago accepted the fact that this virus doesn't give a damn what your sexual preference is.

AIDS started in Africa as a disease sexually transmitted by heterosexuals, and its fastest growth rate in this country is now among teenagers and women. So far, the only groups spared by sexual preference is lesbians, a fact that must give some pause to those who believe that it is all God's plan. Ignorance and fear are still the most important factors in the spread of AIDS, but we have long since come to expect our public officials to be responsible about the epidemic. But nooooo, not in Texas.

Leaping like the virus itself from San Antonio to Houston to Corpus Christi, we are having a merry little round of gay-bashing spread by the resident buffoons on the city councils of those fair towns. It started in San Antone, the town that gave us Benny Eureste and Henry Van Archer as standards of civic intelligence.

Dr. Fernando Guerra, director of the city's Metropolitan Health District, was understandably upset when the Bexar County AIDS Consortium, the umbrella funding group for the area, decided to cut $93,000 from a $119,000 grant to the health district for AIDS management services. The consortium wanted to put money into other organizations doing front-line work with AIDS patients. Dr. Guerra told the *San Antonio Express-News* he thought the decision was affected by the fact that members of the consortium who have the AIDS virus might be suffering from impaired judgment caused by AIDS-related conditions, possibly even dementia.

Dr. Guerra, who knows better, promptly apologized for the remarks. The funding cut may or may not have been bad judgment, but as the citizens of Texas know, bad judgment on the part of our leaders is not limited to those with the human immunodeficiency virus.

But then Councilman Weir Labatt decided to jump in by attacking those with AIDS. "I'm real tired of the AIDS community thinking there's something special about them," he said.

Labatt went on to say: "The reason they have AIDS is their lifestyle—the majority of them being drug IV users or having engaged in male-to-male inter-course. The only people they should be upset at are themselves. I suggest they retract their anger. If the local AIDS community is always making noise, I'd rather see the money used in some other area and not go to AIDS patients."

Die quietly, that's his motto; no raging against the dying of the light for Councilman Labatt.

Now in Houston, Councilman John Goodner, a blustery fellow, up and opined that money being spent on AIDS was going down a one-way tube and that if we'd quarantined these people to begin with, we wouldn't have a problem.

I don't know what it is about people dying of AIDS, but they seem to think they have a serious problem. As Labatt noted, they do make noise. One

Houston AIDS activist was arrested on a charge of aggravated assault for demonstrating against Goodner, which just goes to show how much Houston has to learn from Dallas.

At Dallas City Council meetings, what Houston considers aggravated assault is considered normal citizen input and happens every week. And people think Dallas is an uptight town.

Meanwhile, down in Corpus, Councilman Leo Guerrero got into a fight about whether to charge a buck a head to let folks into Bayfest, the annual civic fandangle. He said on a radio show that it would help keep out undesirables like drunks and homosexuals.

You will not be amazed to learn that Corpus gays made noise. So then Guerrero, who is pretty noisy himself, launched into a soliloquy about gays picking up kids on the Seawall and the police were called in to confirm that such things have been known to happen somewhere in the Shining City by the Sea, and with that everyone got mad just in time for Bayfest, which upset the Junior League.

So next there was a huge demonstration at the City Council meeting with local activists raising hell and a counterdemonstration by kids from what used to be the late Brother Lester Roloff's home, he who added such je ne sais quoi to life in Corpus. The kids, who wore Guerrero T-shirts, kept raising their Bibles in unison, and all in all it was much more entertaining than the average City Council meeting.

Far be it from me to discourage the excellent Texas tradition of lunacy in local government. Long may it continue to add color and entertainment to our civic life. And of course I wish the gay militant groups like ACT-UP and Queer Nation still had the astonishing dignity and theatrical impact of their early demonstrations. But then, it's hard to maintain continuity in an organization when the leadership keeps dying.

I'm afraid we are all going to have to recognize and deal with the quality that distinguishes those with AIDS—desperation. Many of these dying people have been spat on all their lives, called "queer" from the time they were ten, been beaten up with some frequency, and now they're dying before they're thirty from a disease their government keeps trying to ignore.

For some reason, they don't think they have a lot left to lose.

Real-Life Rodmans Have to Work It Out
MITCH ALBOM—*Detroit Free Press*—11/11/1992

[In the fall of 1992, the Detroit Pistons' rebounding champ Dennis Rodman refused to show up for preseason camp, citing a recent divorce and saying the game wasn't fun anymore. He was fined $68,000—a small portion of his superstar salary. In this classic column, Mitch Albom contrasts Dennis Rodman's complaints with the life of real-life rod-men working at a local Ford assembly plant.]

There are no basketballs here, no cheering fans, only the hard, cold smell of factory life. Instead of applause we have the whirring of air tools. Instead of mink coats we have drab cotton overalls. The light is by fluorescent bulb, the color is concrete gray. Wherever you walk, you hear the chug and clang of the assembly line.

They are making trucks here. This is a local Ford assembly plant. Dennis Rodman always calls himself "a regular guy, like everyone else," so I figured I'd go to where regular guys work for a living and see how they felt about Dennis' behavior lately.

Meet Louis. He is a spray painter. Like Rodman, he went through a divorce a little while ago. One night, he learned his ex-wife had taken off with some guy for a quick fling in New Orleans—and left his kids with a friend.

The kids phoned Louis. "We want you, daddy!" They were crying. Louis was distraught. Under the court ruling, he couldn't get them, even though they were staying with a woman he didn't know.

He took their tears to bed that night.

And at 4 a.m., he got up and went to work.

"You think I felt like working that day?" Louis says. "Hell, no. It was damn hard to concentrate, but I had to. If I didn't, I couldn't pay their child support."

Wouldn't your employer let you take a few days or weeks off, like Rodman's did?

"Are you kidding?"

Hmm.

Too little money, too little time

Meet Brian. He's a UAW comitteeman. Been with Ford more than 20 years. Like Rodman, he suffered through a divorce. Like Rodman, he was unable to see his young daughter. Unlike Rodman, Brian didn't make $2.35 million a year.

Instead, he would come home some weeks with a paycheck of less than $20, after child support and bills. Never mind that his ex-wife was living in his old house with a new man. Never mind that she slammed the door on Brian when he went to visit the kids, and that he suffered a year and a half without seeing his daughter before a court intervened.

Never mind that Brian had to fix cars at night, just to make enough money to eat. Using his far-too-extended credit cards, he bought Christmas presents for his little girl one year, but her mother made her call and say she didn't want them.

"That was the lowest moment," Brian says.

But next day, 6 a.m., he went to work.

"I had no choice. Hey, I love basketball, but Dennis Rodman doesn't know what problems are until he comes home with a $20 paycheck."

Wouldn't your company understand if you put out half an effort, or walked out after a few minutes, as Rodman has done with the Pistons?

"Yeah, right."

Hmm.

Meet another Louis, 46. He's in the sealer deck. As we speak, he is applying sealant with a gun, running it along the interior of a truck frame. He can't stop to talk, so he speaks while he works.

"Not too long ago, I lost my brother. He died of cancer. They only gave me two days off. Two days. I thought I had at least three coming to me. I had to fly to California to get my mother, bring her in. I wound up taking extra days off with no pay because it wasn't enough time, you know? Two days, man."

Like Rodman—who misses coach Chuck Daly—Louis misses his brother. He misses the trips they would take, the talks they would have.

For nearly 10 months, Louis would finish his shift at the Ford plant and go directly to a hospital. One day, Louis watched in horror as they hooked his brother to a machine to help him breathe. He knew it was the end. He felt helpless. He felt terrible.

Next day, 4 a.m., he went to work.

"By the way," Louis adds, "I'm divorced, too. Never missed a day for it. But I'll tell you what: Every day I had to go to court, they didn't pay me a dime. I lost all my wages."

RODMAN'S WORK "ISN'T FUN ANYMORE'"

Rodman spent most of the summer thinking about his life. Most of the fall now, too. He missed nearly all of Pistons training camp, without as much as a phone call to explain, yet he was only lightly fined and welcomed back when he returned.

In the two games he has played, he seems to drift in and out of concentration. On Monday, he showed up late for practice, stretched, put some ice on his knees, then abruptly walked out. He says basketball "isn't fun anymore" and that his mind is on his daughter and ex-wife. Some reports say he is only acting this way to get himself traded.

He still has his job today.

Dave would not be so lucky. He is an inspector at the plant. One day he came home to find his entire home emptied out, his kids gone, his clothes thrown in the middle of the floor. Where was his wife? Where were the kids? His world was upside down.

Next day, 6 a.m. . . .

You get the picture. Everyone has problems. Everyone has distractions. But there's an expression here on the assembly line: "If you can't hack it, grab your jacket." It is harsh. It is cold. And for 99 percent of the world, it is very, very real.

Dennis Rodman—the regular guy—might keep it in mind.

The O.J. Effect
CARL HIAASEN—*Miami Herald*—6/19/1994

Say you're Rodney King, watching O. J. Simpson lead Los Angeles police on a 50-mile chase. You've got to be wondering: Why weren't the cops that polite with me?

Because, Rodney, you aren't a football star. Maybe you didn't murder anybody, but you didn't have a Heisman Trophy on the mantle, either.

Fans will be fans. It's hard to say who's more disturbed, O.J. or the yahoos who lined up along the freeway to cheer the accused slasher's flight.

Good luck teaching that American culture is superior to all others. This sorry freak show couldn't have happened in any other country.

It's a fascinating news story with absolutely no cosmic significance. The morgues are loaded with innocents killed by people who loved them. We don't care much about accused murderers who sell widgets or bag groceries, but we're positively obsessed if they're movie stars or sports idols.

Beyond the fact that kids look up to him, O.J. is not a particularly important person. He doesn't hold political office, hasn't discovered a cure for any diseases, doesn't write symphonies or paint masterpieces.

Basically, he's just a good-looking jock with a sportscasting gig. His notable talents are running a football and shilling for a rental-car company. But he's sufficiently rich and famous that he's assumed to be immune to the brute passions and jealousies that can torment ordinary men.

The truth is, famous people go bonkers just like regular folks. Last Friday's ludicrous low-speed chase set a new standard for bizarre theatrics. Certainly one couldn't have laid a stronger foundation for an insanity defense.

Announcers repeatedly reminded us how depressed O.J. has been. A pending murder indictment can have that effect. Rarely have you heard such sympathy for a person accused of such vicious crimes.

Before fleeing, Simpson wrote a letter declaring his innocence and complaining about the media.

Show-biz murders do bring out the beast in us. But don't forget that the media made O.J. a national figure and kept him one long after his football days were over. He makes tons of money because he's recognizable. If he wanted a private life, he shouldn't have signed up to do commercials.

Nobody "convicted" poor O.J. before trial. Journalists reported what the police found—information that's always made public, and for which the public rabidly hungers.

How many of you rushed to switch off your televisions, so (out of fairness to O.J.) you wouldn't hear about the evidence? Nobody. You ate it up, every unofficial leak and rumor.

We're all in the frenzy together. We do the feeding, you get the bloody morsels.

More reporters were camped outside O.J.'s home than accompanied Jimmy Carter to Pyongyang. If that's disgraceful, so is the fact that our audience is infinitely more interested in celebrity homicides than nuclear site inspections.

I shudder to think of the fortune being spent covering the Simpson spectacle, money that could generate other stories more vital to the average reader's health and well-being. Problem is, the average reader wants to know about O.J.

In some sick way, we need celebrities to divert us from our own mundane problems. Fascination with fame is as old as humanity. If Christ were being crucified tomorrow, there'd be satellite dishes bristling from Golgotha, and Pontius Pilate would be on the next cover of *People*.

The media's mob behavior on the streets of Brentwood was fairly appalling, but so is the public's appetite for tragedy. We all deserve each other.

Accused Officer's Girlfriend Stands By Her Man
MIKE MCALARY—*New York Daily News*—8/18/1997

[The assault on Haitian immigrant Abner Louima with a plunger in a New York City police precinct polarized the city during the 1997 mayoral election between Rudy Giuliani and Ruth Messinger. *Daily News* columnist Mike McAlary won a Pulitzer Prize for his coverage of the scandal. The widely reported line "It's Giuliani Time" allegedly said by his assailant, Officer Justin Volpe, was found to have been falsified as a way of gaining attention for the case. Volpe was convicted and sentenced to thirty years in prison.]

A week ago, she walked into the 70th Precinct, past the front desk to the stairs. As she climbed the steps to her office, she felt the eyes of the entire stationhouse on her again. She thought she was past all that.

Susan, a 26-year-old civilian employee, is a black woman in love with a white cop.

She and Justin Volpe are the Seven-O love story and have been so for some time.

Then one of her friends—a cop; it's one big family here—told her why people were staring. Her boyfriend was one of the cops involved in a wild racist fracas over the weekend. One cop had beaten and shoved a bathroom plunger up a suspect's rectum. "They say Justin did it," the cop said.

She hopes it is a lie. Because if the terrible tale of torture that has people referring to the 70th, where she's worked for four years, as The Plunger Precinct is true, Susan has been planning to marry a lie.

"Justin wouldn't do this to our life," Susan said yesterday as we talked over coffee. "If it happened, he didn't do it."

Justin Volpe's hair is longer in Susan's picture than in the NYPD's official photograph. But he looks exactly as Abner Louima, a 30-year-old Haitian immigrant, described Volpe to me from a hospital bed last week—maybe a little hipper, a little better looking.

"We want to be married, still," she said. They have been living together for most of the last two years, and were planning a big wedding.

Susan lives in Brooklyn. She wanted to meet and talk. She doesn't want her last name printed. She is concerned about her family. Many of them live in Brooklyn.

Her lover is a suspect in the most atrocious police torture case in 20 years, and his relationship with an intelligent black woman is confusing.

"Justin a racist? Impossible," she said, answering her own question.

"What color were our children going to be? It's like Justin tells the guys in the station, 'Susan isn't my black girlfriend. She is my girlfriend, period.'"

"I know. I know," she said, shaking her head. "On one hand, in the Seven-O, we are fighting racists who don't want to see a white man and a black woman together. But in the same precinct, he is accused of this.

"I see the looks the cops give me in the precinct. The black guys say to me, 'Has he brought you home to meet his parents? It's just sex, nothing will come of it.'"

She folded her hands and looked into space. Her courage in defending a lover accused of such an atrocity is humbling. From what I've learned, her family and his family cherish each other which makes all this, especially if Volpe is guilty, even sadder.

"Justin has been reluctant for me to come forward," she continued.

"I can't imagine being married to . . .

"It's hard to digest or even understand. Black people will say, 'How can you stand by him and believe he is innocent.' But my family said, 'We are with you. Stand by him.'"

I had to say it: "This is like the cliche, 'I can't be a racist. Some of my best friends are black.'"

"I know," she said, biting her lip. "But I know he is not an evil person. His life with me would have to be a lie. We are planning on getting married and having children. If Justin Volpe did this, he did it to me and his children."

Maybe he snapped.

"I have been to his house many times," she said. "His father, Robert, and Justin's mother treat me like their daughter. His father has come to Brooklyn. We traveled to see my family in Virginia. We stayed with my sister and her kids for a week.

"I work days; Justin works nights. Our worlds revolve. Justin I liked because he is different. He makes me laugh. We are together always. Vacations in the Bahamas and the West Indies. You can't lead one life and then do that, in the precinct bathroom. Racism isn't some switch you can turn on and off."

Maybe Justin Volpe can.

"I am an educated woman," she said. "In the police world at that precinct you have to be aware of racism. There was nothing from Justin. But the others, yes. That's why we were reluctant to make our relationship public. Then one year turned to two and we decided to get married. We had to be bigger than the precinct gossip."

If everyone in the precinct knew them, has the Internal Affairs Bureau contacted her?

"They haven't called me. Perhaps because I don't fit with the version of the monster they are building."

She would marry into a Staten Island cop family. Justin's father, Robert, is a world-class detective. Justin's brother is a cop, too.

"Justin's father was saying this morning, 'You spend your whole life on one side. And then one day you wake up and your son is Public Enemy No. 1.' We are both crushed."

Because the man you love could be the most despised cop in the modern history of the NYPD?

"I asked him, and he says it didn't happen the way they're saying. He is not an evil man."

Susan is attractive and delicate with short hair. She is smaller and has a lighter complexion than Abner Louima does. On Sunday, after church, she wore a short black skirt and a white silk blouse. She had a diamond stud in each ear, a silver thumb ring on her right hand, a silver bracelet on her left wrist and an ankle bracelet under her stockings.

Do you know the cops named so far?

"Justin wasn't working with his regular partner that night," she said. "I know Charles Schwarz a little bit. I know Eric Turetzky. He is a new guy. I know them all, locked away in my room on the second floor. And the monster in the papers is not the man I want to marry."

This whole episode is confusing, especially emotionally. Abner Louima is compelling and didn't hesitate when he said he was violated and called "n———r" by a man who hoped to make a black woman his wife.

"We talked about racism many times. Cried about it at night. Where would we live? We talked about moving to Park Slope. I am from Coney Island. I went to Lafayette High School. We both know what the score is.

"I have seen him come home in the morning and struggle with the weight of being a police officer. Justin is depressed a lot. The sadness of the streets takes its toll."

But it is very possible that this man she loves so much stuck a toilet plunger up the rectum of a human being, nearly ruining the man.

If Justin Volpe is convicted, he will have violated Susan, too.

"Our first date? We went to Caliente Cab [Co.] in Greenwich Village," she said, suddenly warm with the memory. "We went to a place called the Shark Bar on Amsterdam Ave. later. He isn't much of a drinker. We're not club people, really. We were headed for a nice life. And then, this."

You think of Volpe, and Abner Louima lying in bed in Coney Island Hospital keeps popping into your head.

He said a cop, who was calling him a n———r, told him that the blacks in the precinct wouldn't help him, that "all they do is make photocopies."

One of Susan's responsibilities is to make photocopies.

Did you ever hear Volpe say anything about David Dinkins or Rudy Giuliani?

"Never. He is not a political person. The thing about it being Giuliani's time is silly." And then she brought a hand to her tear-streaked face.

"We thought it was our time," she said.

I Still Believe
Michael Kelly—*Washington Post*—3/18/1998

I've just finished reading the 600 pages of material released last Friday by Paula Jones's lawyers, and I've just finished watching Kathleen Willey on *60 Minutes*, and I've just finished reading Bill Clinton's statement that he didn't bother to watch Ms. Willey on TV but that he knows what she says isn't true anyway. And I still believe the president. Truly, madly, deeply, I believe. Also verily.

I believe that the president is "mystified" by Ms. Willey's claim that he sexually assaulted her when she visited him in the Oval Office on Nov. 29, 1993, to ask him for a desperately needed job. I believe the president did not grab Ms. Willey, kiss her, touch her breasts and place her hand on his genitals, against her will. I believe that Ms. Willey is perjuring herself to hurt the president, even though the record shows that she supported and liked Clinton very much, and continued to support and like him even after the alleged assault, and that she only talked in the end because she was compelled to by Jones's lawyers.

I believe Ms. Willey is, like Paula Jones and Gennifer Flowers and Dolly Kyle Browning and Sally Purdue before her, and like the women who will come after her, a baldfaced liar. If Monica Lewinsky sticks to her affidavit that she never had sex with the president, I believe her. If she instead confirms the long hours of recorded conversation in which she detailed a sexual affair with the president and affirmed her intention to lie in the affidavit— well, then, I don't believe.

I believe all this because I am assured of it by Robert Bennett, the president's sexual misconduct mouthpiece, which is a distinguished position. It is distinguished from David Kendall, his personal-finance corruption mouthpiece; from Lanny Davis, his campaign-finance corruption mouthpiece; from James Kennedy, his White House general scandal mouthpiece; from James Carville, his "independent" general scandal mouthpiece; and from Michael McCurry, his don't ask, don't tell mouthpiece. I believe that all presidents require, for the handling of daily press inquiries, enough mouthpieces to outfit the wind section of the National Symphony Orchestra.

I believe, as the White House whispering campaign already has it, that Ms. Willey is a bit nutty, and a bit slutty. I believe that, the way things are going, David Brock will write an article to this effect for *Esquire*.

I believe White House communications director Ann Lewis is right to suggest that Ms. Willey's desire to work in Clinton's 1996 campaign casts doubt on her claim that Clinton abused her in 1993. I also believed Ann Lewis in 1991, when she explained why Anita Hill continued to work for Clarence Thomas after he allegedly harassed her: "You don't know what it's like to be a young working woman, to have this really prestigious and powerful boss and think you have to stay on the right side of him, or for the rest of your working life he could nix another job." I believe Ann Lewis is not a rank hypocrite. I believe that it is not despicable for the president's henchmen and henchwomen to smear the reputations of others in order to protect their boss from allegations of misconduct.

I believe that Clinton-Gore fund-raiser Nathan Landow did not try to pressure Ms. Willey to lie in her deposition in the Jones case, and that there must be some perfectly innocent reason why, after Ms. Willey was subpoenaed in the Jones case, Landow's real estate company chartered a plane to fly Ms. Willey to Landow's Eastern Shore estate.

I believe Ms. Willey is lying even though her account of Clinton's amatory approach is remarkably similar to the account Ms. Jones offers of the Clinton modus operandi on May 8, 1991, in a room in the Excelsior Hotel in Little Rock, Ark. I believe Ms. Jones is lying even though her sworn account of what happened to her that day is supported, in graphic, pathetic detail, by sworn contemporaneous accounts from her sister, Lydia Cathey, and by her friends Pamela Blackard and Debra Lynn Ballentine. I believe Ms. Willey and Ms. Jones are lying even though their stories are buttressed by the sworn deposition of Judy Stokes, alleging a similarly sudden and unwanted sexual approach by Clinton against a former Miss Arkansas, Elizabeth Ward.

I believe that L. D. Brown, Larry Patterson and Roger Perry, three former Clinton bodyguards, were all lying in their sworn depositions in which they described, to varying but conforming degrees, Clinton as a sexual adventurer of great recklessness and a man who used the resources and perks of office to further his sexual pursuits.

I believe everybody is lying except my Bill.

In the Land of Oz with Bad Guys
KATHLEEN PARKER—*USA Today*—9/14/1998

Never has misanthropy held such allure. From Paula and the Supremes to Bill, Monica and Ken, I can't find anyone to like.

As we ponder the concept of sex in the Oval Office, the unrealized pleasures of a cigar, and the true meaning of sex, one flounders for meaning in the universe. How, as Dorothy might have said to Toto, the *heck* did we get here?

Oz, come to think of it, isn't a bad place to start as we try to untangle this icky web. Nothing is as it seems. Poppies turn to poison as sincerest utterances turn to lies. "I did not have sexual relations with that woman, Ms. Lewinsky." Well, except for those 10 times . . . did I mention that I'm sorry? Oh, yeah, and the phone stuff.

The road that brought us to this sordid place is long and pocked with lowlifes, upstarts and, scariest of all, do-gooders. Nearly everyone gets a share of blame for this day when young children ask, "What's oral sex?" and "What's the thing about the cigar, mommy?"

Start with Paula Jones, who, you have to admit, pre-surgery, bore a striking resemblance to a certain Oz character. Hint: *"I'll get you, my little pretty."* Were Jones's claim true—that the then-Arkansas governor invited her to perform a Lewinsky— she should have smirked, thrown back her head and laughed shrilly. Instead, she filed a sexual harassment lawsuit, which might have been ignored, but wasn't.

Back in Munchkin Land, the Supreme Court—apparently having trudged through a poppy field or two—ruled that Jones could pursue her civil case, thus setting a precedent for anyone to attack a sitting president on the basis of little more than a bad mood. The justices also set the stage, inevitably, for a level of prurience that has left almost no one unembarrassed.

Enter the Tin Man, Ken Starr. All brains but no heart. Starr was supposed to investigate Whitewater and wound up instead listening to lurid tape recordings of some raven-haired hussy and her fiendish friend, Linda Tripp, chief of the wicked witch's flying monkeys.

Starr would get to the bottom of the Wizard's tricks no matter what it took. All he needed to make his case was a little DNA, graciously provided by Monica Lewinsky, the only woman in America who saves her stains. But that wasn't enough. Thanks to Starr, we're now privy not only to the president's sexual preferences, perversions and peccadilloes and, not least, his angle of repose.

Did we have to go there?

Absolutely not.

Then there's dear, sweet Dorothy, who at any other time in history would have been properly labeled not the lovelorn lass but just-a-tramp, son. *Stay stay away from girls like that.* Who, pray tell, shows her underwear to the president of the United States at the earliest hint of a flirtation?

"Hi, I'm Monica. Wanna see my thong?"

"No, Monica, we want you to go home and wash out your mouth with Lysol."

That, or something similar, is what the president might have said. How about this from any decent man: "Monica, you're adorable; I'm flattered. I'm also old enough to be your father, now git!"—as they say back home.

Instead, Mr. Wizard pulls back the curtain himself and plays kiddy courtship games in the corridors and cubbyholes of the White House. They, like, "accidentally" bump into each other in the hallways. She, like, brings him pizza and stuff. They like make out and, you know, fool around, only he won't go all the way cuz he doesn't trust me and everything.

Whom to blame? How about everybody. If there's a conspiracy out there, it's a conspiracy to make America stupider—and dirtier—than dirt.

Victory noted.

We've traveled so far from the reality of what America once was, where values were understood and agreed upon, that we hardly notice when someone does wrong.

Clinton says he sinned. What Clinton did wrong was to be himself. From the beginning, he has been a wham-bam-thank-you-ma'am, weather-watching, wind-checking, poll-marking, please-yourself kind of man. All he ever had to do was keep his pants zipped and, failing that, tell the truth and say,

I'm sorry—the first time, not after the polls said he wasn't contrite enough.

Had Clinton owned up to his actions in January when Lewinsky's name first surfaced, our nation wouldn't have suffered through eight months of humiliation. We wouldn't look like fools to the rest of the world. Our children wouldn't be discussing oral sex in fourth-grade civics; and most important, they wouldn't be learning that adultery and lying are OK, as long as you shed a timely tear and hang your head for the camera.

Everybody in this lousy movie has been wrong, and no one, not once, put the welfare of our country first. The key players may deserve each other, but America deserves better.

No Party for Essie Mae
COLBERT KING—*Washington Post*—12/21/2002

Sen. Strom Thurmond's 100th birthday party will go down in the annals of Washington soirees as an event most noted for who was there and, above all, what was said and by whom. But the celebration was also remarkable because of a person not in attendance.

The audience was full of luminaries, including current and former members of Congress, Supreme Court justices and friends and family of the retiring South Carolina senator. But the party failed to include a retired schoolteacher in her late seventies now living in Los Angeles. A widow since 1964, the former teacher, Essie Mae Williams, was born Essie Mae Washington in 1925 in Edgefield, S.C. Washington reportedly is the fruit of a relationship between a white Edgefield school superintendent and a black teenager, Essie Butler, nicknamed "Tunch," who worked as a maid in the superintendent's stately house.

Now, it could have been an oversight, a deliberate snub or maybe Essie Mae Washington was invited but chose not to come. But this much is true: The fair-skinned woman, a member of Delta Sigma Theta sorority and a 1950 graduate of traditionally black South Carolina State College, was not on hand to help honor the man believed by many to be her father, the former Edgefield school superintendent and the oldest and longest-serving senator in U.S. history, Strom Thurmond.

This is not a groundbreaking column on the story of Thurmond's alleged black daughter. Marilyn Thompson, *The Post*'s assistant managing editor for investigations, included a chapter about then-Gov. Thurmond's alleged support for an alleged black daughter named Essie Mae in *Ol' Strom*, an unauthorized biography of Thurmond that she wrote with Jack Bass in 1998. Thompson, a veteran South Carolina reporter who had spent the better part of 10 years tracking the story, also wrote a lengthy article about the senator and his longtime ties with an African-American woman for *The Post*'s Style section in 1992. Both Thurmond and Washington have acknowledged a relationship, but she denies he is her father, though the senator has never issued a categorical denial.

The purpose of today's column is not to rehash the strong circumstantial evidence or to repeat interviews with knowledgeable sources about the long-standing and secret relationship between Thurmond and Washington. Thompson unearthed all that. But this annotation to Thurmond's life is worth highlighting, given that his fiery advocacy of segregation did more to stifle racial progress in America than the actions of any single human being in the postwar era until Alabama Gov. George Wallace came along.

Strom Thurmond was among the vanguard of southerners who passed and enforced laws legalizing segregation and discrimination in virtually every aspect of daily life. And leading the list of noxious Jim Crow laws were statutes specifically put on the books outlawing and punishing interracial cohabitation and marriage.

Thurmond was chief among those who believed and argued that drawing a tight color line and strictly segregating the races was the only way to prevent what Theodore Bilbo of Mississippi called "the mongrelization of the Nation." Thurmond was so motivated that he captured the Senate floor in 1957 and filibustered for 24 straight hours against a civil rights bill and "race-mixing." It was Thurmond who vowed to preserve the integrity of the white race and to keep the races distinct.

And it was Strom Thurmond who, according to published reports, did not practice what he so fervently preached.

The very thing Thurmond condemned, he did. Learn the story of Thurmond, Essie Mae and her mom, and come to understand the true meaning of deception, arrogance and what it means to be unprincipled. But this is not the time to wage war against Strom Thurmond. His day has come and gone. Rather we must address the damage that he did and his legacy of racial ill will that live on.

Thurmond helped create a world with walls separating people from people, the vestiges of which still exist. He was among those who vowed to protect the virtue of the white women of the South even as he allegedly used the back stairs to have his way with a woman of the darker race, surreptitiously exercising a prerogative preserved for Southern white men.

While doing that, he and they preserved an evil social system that used the gun and the noose to say that the gift of love cannot come to people of different races. Segregation, to be sure, left generations of African-Americans with broken dreams and unrealized ambitions, even as others enriched themselves with better schools, jobs, housing, health care and the like. But the official rules and racial customs of Thurmond's Jim Crow era also made it possible for untold numbers of people to miss out on the mystery of love, to never know the pleasure of sharing, if even for a moment. Thurmond stood between the natural coming together of men and women, even as men like him gave themselves a pass.

And now he goes out glorified. Because in Washington, that's the way it is. But the birthday party is not the last word or act. For some of us, this is the season to put aside our agendas and turn to quiet reflection, repentance and recommitment.

This is also a time of giving. So reach out with a thought to the one untouched by the joy of Ol' Strom's birthday party: the woman who wasn't there.

Open Casket Opened Eyes
LEONARD PITTS, JR.—*Miami Herald*—1/10/2003

If you ever saw that picture of Emmett Till, you never forgot it.

Not the one that shows a handsome brown teenager, hat tipped up slightly off his forehead. Not, in other words, the "before" picture. No, I'm talking about the picture that was taken after. After he went from Chicago to visit family in Mississippi in the late summer of 1955. After he accepted a schoolboy dare to flirt with a white woman working behind the counter of the general store. After he called her "baby" and allegedly gave a wolf whistle. After her husband and his half-brother came for him in the dead of night. After his body was fished from the Tallahatchie River.

The picture of him that was taken then, published in Jet magazine and flashed around the world, was stomach-turning. A lively and prankish boy had become a bloated grotesquerie—an ear missing, an eye gouged out, a bullet hole in his head. You looked at that picture and you felt that here was the reason coffins have lids.

But his mother refused onlookers that mercy, refused to give him a closed-casket funeral. She delayed the burial for four days, keeping her son's mutilated body on display as thousands came to pay their respects. "I wanted the world to see what I had seen," she later explained. "I wanted the world to see what had happened in Mississippi. I wanted the world to see what had happened in America."

The world saw and was electrified.

Mamie Till Mobley died in Chicago on Monday of an apparent heart attack. And if one were seeking to sum up her life, it might be enough to say that she spent 47 years keeping the casket open, speaking, writing and agitating in the name of her murdered son. Indeed, her book, *The Death of Innocence*, is due for release this year.

I met her once, maybe 30 years after her son's death, by which point she must have told his story a million times. And she still welled up as she spoke, her voice stammering and turning gray.

At the time, I was writing and producing a radio documentary tracing over 500 years of African and African-American history. I'll never forget my narrator's response when he reviewed a script that recounted Emmett's ordeal and the ordeals of other black men and women who were hanged, burned or hacked to pieces for the crime of being. He jokingly dubbed me "the Stephen King of black history" for my insistence on including the grisly details.

But I happen to believe Mamie Till Mobley was right to keep the casket open.

We're always so eager to hide the horror. Close the casket, turn your eyes, use euphemism to obscure truths too obscene.

Consider Trent Lott's first attempt at apology, when he blithely described segregation as "the discarded policies of the past." If you didn't know any better, you might have thought he was talking about farm subsidies or tax codes, so bloodless and opaque was the language.

But segregation wasn't opaque and it surely wasn't bloodless. It was a Mississippi courtroom where the sheriff sauntered in every day and greeted spectators in the colored section with a cheery, "Hello, niggers." It was two white men freely admitting that they had kidnapped a black Chicago boy. It was witnesses who placed the men at a barn inside which they heard a child being tortured.

And it was a jury of white men who heard this evidence, then deliberated for less than an hour before returning an acquittal. As one of them told a reporter, "If we hadn't stopped to drink pop, it wouldn't have took that long."

This is the fetid truth behind the flowery words, the stinking fact much of the nation would prefer not to know.

But by her very presence, a murdered boy's mother demanded that we be better than that, demanded that we be, at least and at last, brave enough to face the horrors we have made and that have, in turn, made us.

Mamie Till Mobley was 81 years old at the time of her death. Her only child was 14 at the time of his.

Why Truth Matters

NICHOLAS KRISTOF—*The New York Times*—5/6/2003

When I raised the Mystery of the Missing W.M.D. recently, hawks fired barrages of reproachful e-mail at me. The gist was: "You *&#*! Who cares if we never find weapons of mass destruction, because we've liberated the Iraqi people from a murderous tyrant."

But it does matter, enormously, for American credibility. After all, as Ari Fleischer said on April 10 about W.M.D.: "That is what this war was about."

I rejoice in the newfound freedoms in Iraq. But there are indications that the U.S. government souped up intelligence, leaned on spooks to change their conclusions and concealed contrary information to deceive people at home and around the world.

Let's fervently hope that tomorrow we find an Iraqi superdome filled with 500 tons of mustard gas and nerve gas, 25,000 liters of anthrax, 38,000 liters of botulinum toxin, 29,984 prohibited munitions capable of delivering chemical agents, several dozen Scud missiles, gas centrifuges to enrich uranium, 18 mobile biological warfare factories, long-range unmanned aerial vehicles to dispense anthrax, and proof of close ties with Al Qaeda. Those are the things that President Bush or his aides suggested Iraq might have, and I don't want to believe that top administration officials tried to win support for the war with a campaign of wholesale deceit.

Consider the now-disproved claims by President Bush and Colin Powell that Iraq tried to buy uranium from Niger so it could build nuclear weapons. As Seymour Hersh noted in *The New Yorker*, the claims were based on documents that had been forged so amateurishly that they should never have been taken seriously.

I'm told by a person involved in the Niger caper that more than a year ago the vice president's office asked for an investigation of the uranium deal, so a former U.S. ambassador to Africa was dispatched to Niger. In February 2002, according to someone present at the meetings, that envoy reported to the C.I.A. and State Department that the information was unequivocally wrong and that the documents had been forged.

The envoy reported, for example, that a Niger minister whose signature was on one of the documents had in fact been out of office for more than a decade. In addition, the Niger mining program was structured so that the uranium diversion had been impossible. The envoy's debunking of the forgery was passed around the administration and seemed to be accepted—except that President Bush and the State Department kept citing it anyway.

"It's disingenuous for the State Department people to say they were bamboozled because they knew about this for a year," one insider said.

Another example is the abuse of intelligence from Hussein Kamel, a son-in-law of Saddam Hussein and head of Iraq's biological weapons program until his defection in 1995. Top British and American officials kept citing information from Mr. Kamel as evidence of a huge secret Iraqi program, even though Mr. Kamel had actually emphasized that Iraq had mostly given up its W.M.D. program in the early 1990's. Glen Rangwala, a British Iraq expert, says the transcript of Mr. Kamel's debriefing was leaked because insiders resented the way politicians were misleading the public.

Patrick Lang, a former head of Middle Eastern affairs in the Defense Intelligence Agency, says that he hears from those still in the intelligence world that when experts wrote reports that were skeptical about Iraq's W.M.D., "they were encouraged to think it over again."

"In this administration, the pressure to get product 'right' is coming out of O.S.D. [the Office of the Secretary of Defense]," Mr. Lang said. He added that intelligence experts had cautioned that Iraqis would not necessarily line up to cheer U.S. troops and that the Shiite clergy could be a problem. "The guys who tried to tell them that came to understand that this advice was not welcome," he said.

"The intelligence that our officials was given regarding W.M.D. was either defective or manipulated," Senator Jeff Bingaman of New Mexico noted. Another senator is even more blunt and, sadly, exactly right: "Intelligence was manipulated."

The C.I.A. was terribly damaged when William Casey, its director in the Reagan era, manipulated intelligence to exaggerate the Soviet threat in Central America to whip up support for Ronald Reagan's policies. Now something is again rotten in the state of Spookdom.

All the President's Girls
NORA EPHRON—*The New York Times*—5/18/2003

I too was an intern in the J.F.K. White House. I was. This is not one of those humor pieces where the writer pretends to some experience related to the news in order to make an "amusing" point. It was 1961, and I was hired by Pierre Salinger to work in the White House press office, the very same place where Mimi Beardsley, later Fahnestock, was to work the next year. And now that Mimi Fahnestock has been forced to come forward to admit that she had an affair with Kennedy, I might as well tell my story.

I notice that all the articles about poor Mimi (whom I never met) quote another woman in the press office, Barbara Gamarekian, who fingered Ms. Fahnestock in the oral history archives at the Kennedy Library. Ms. Gamarekian cattily pointed out, according to the newspapers, that Mimi "couldn't type." Well, all I can say to that is: Ha. In fact, Double Ha. There were, when I worked there, six women in Pierre Salinger's office. One of them was called Faddle (her best friend, Fiddle, worked for Kennedy) and her entire job, as far as I could tell, was autographing Pierre Salinger's photographs. Fiddle's job was autographing Kennedy's. Typing was not a skill that anyone seemed to need, and it certainly wasn't necessary for interns like me (and Mimi, dare I say), because THERE WAS NO DESK FOR AN INTERN TO SIT AT AND THEREFORE NO TYPEWRITER TO TYPE ON.

Yes, I am still bitter about it! Because there I was, not just the only young woman in the White House who was unable to afford an endless series of A-line sleeveless linen dresses just like Jackie's, but also the only person in the press office with nowhere to sit. And then, as now, I could type 100 words a minute. Every eight-hour day there were theoretically 48,000 words that weren't being typed because I didn't have a desk.

Also, I had a really bad permanent wave. This is an important fact for later in the story, when things heat up.

I met the president within minutes of going to "work" in the White House. My first morning there, he flew to Annapolis to give the commencement address at the Naval Academy, and Pierre invited me to come along with the press pool in the press helicopter. When I got back to the White House, Pierre took me in to meet the president. He was the handsomest man I had ever seen. I don't remember the details of our conversation, but perhaps they are included in Pierre's reminiscences in the Kennedy Library. Some day I will look them up. What I do remember is that the meeting was short, perhaps 10 or 15 seconds. After it, I went back to the press office and discovered what you, reader, already know: there was no place for me to sit.

So I spent my summer internship lurking in the hall near the file cabinet. I read most of the things that were in the file cabinet, including some interesting memos that were marked "'top secret" and "eyes only." The file cabinet was right next to the men's room, where one day the speaker of the House, Sam Rayburn, got locked in. Had I not been nearby, he might be there still.

From time to time I went into the Oval Office and watched the president be photographed with foreign leaders. Sometimes, I am pretty sure, he noticed me watching him.

Which brings me to my crucial encounter with J.F.K., the one that no one at the Kennedy Library has come to ask me about. It was a Friday afternoon, and because I had nowhere to sit (see above) and nothing to do (ditto) I decided to go out and watch the president leave by helicopter for a weekend in Hyannis-port. It was a beautiful day, and I stood out under the portico overlooking the Rose Garden, just outside the Oval Office. The helicopter landed. The noise was deafening. The wind from the chopper blades was blowing hard (although my permanent wave kept my hair stuck tight to my head). And then suddenly, instead of coming out of the living quarters, the president emerged from his office and walked right past me to get to the helicopter. He turned. He saw me. He recognized me. The noise was deafening but he spoke to me. I couldn't hear a thing, but I read his lips, and I'm pretty sure what he said was, "How are you coming along?" But I wasn't positive. So I replied as best I could. "What?" I said.

And that was it. He turned and went off to the helicopter and I went back to standing around the White House until the summer was over.

Now that I have read the articles about Mimi Fahnestock, it has become horribly clear to me that I am probably the only young woman who ever worked in the Kennedy White House whom the president did not make a pass at. Perhaps it was my permanent wave, which was a truly unfortunate mistake. Perhaps it was my wardrobe, which mostly consisted of multicolored dynel dresses that looked like distilled Velveeta cheese. Perhaps it's because I'm Jewish—don't laugh, think about it, think about that long, long list of women J.F.K. slept with. Were any Jewish? I don't think so.

On the other hand, perhaps it's simply because J.F.K. somehow sensed that discretion was not my middle name. I mean, I assure you if anything had gone on between the two of us, you would not have had to wait this long to find it out.

Anyway, that's my story. I might as well go public with it, although I have told it to pretty much everyone I have ever met in the last 42 years. And now, like Mimi Fahnestock, I will have no further comment on this subject. I would request that the news media respect my family's privacy.

Torture, American Style
ANDY ROONEY—Tribune Media—6/3/2004

If you were going to make a list of the great times in American history, you'd start with the day in 1492 when Columbus got here.

The Revolution when we won our independence would be on the list.

Beating Hitler. The unconditional German surrender at Reims on May 8, 1945 was a great day.

The day we put Americans on the moon was a special occasion.

We've had a lot of great days.

Our darkest days up until now have been things like presidential assassinations . . . four of them. The stock market crash in 1929, Pearl Harbor and 9/11, of course.

The day the world learned that American soldiers had tortured Iraqi prisoners should be put high on the list of our country's worst. It's a black mark on our record that will be in the history books in a hundred languages for as long as there are history books. It changed the world's perception of us.

The image printed in every newspaper in the world of one bad young woman with a naked man on a leash did more to damage America's reputation than all the good things we've done ever helped our reputation. Other guards put hoods over the heads of prisoners, stripped them naked, beat them and left them hanging from the bars of their prison cells by their wrists. The hoods made it difficult for them to breathe. Impossible sometimes, and some died of slow asphyxiation.

What were the secrets they were trying to get from captured Iraqis? What important information did that poor devil on the leash have that he wouldn't have given to anyone in exchange for a crust of bread or a sip of water?

One prisoner reported that a guard told him, "I'm going to make you wish you'd die and you're not going to."

Our general in charge said our guards were "untrained." Untrained at what? Being human beings? Should we excuse the Iraqi who chopped off Nicholas Berg's head because he was untrained?

The guards who tortured prisoners are faced with a year in prison. Great. A year for destroying America's reputation as a nation of decent people.

I don't want them in prison anyway. We shouldn't have to feed them. Take away their right to call themselves American, that's what I'd do. You aren't one of us. Get out. We don't want you. Find yourself another country or a desert island. If the order came from someone higher up, take him with you.

In the history of the world, several great civilizations that seemed immortal have deteriorated and died. I don't want to be dramatic, but I've lived a long while and, for the first time in my life, I have this faint, far-away fear that it could happen to us in America as it happened to the Greek and Roman civilizations. Too many Americans don't understand what we have here and how to keep it. I worry for my grandchildren and great-grandchildren. I want them to have what I've had . . . and I sense it could be slipping away from them.

Have a nice day.

Long a Public Scold, Now Facing Life as a Punch Line
CLYDE HABERMAN—*The New York Times*—3/11/2008

He didn't say much, not publicly anyway. But Gov. Eliot Spitzer said just enough on Monday to make shiningly clear that he doesn't get it and perhaps never will.

"I do not believe that politics in the long run is about individuals," he said as he apologized to his family and other New Yorkers after law enforcement officials identified him as a prostitution ring patron. "It is about ideas, the public good and doing what is best for the state of New York."

That is a noble sentiment. It doesn't happen to be rooted in reality.

Long run or short run, politics is always about individuals—their strengths, their weaknesses, their boldness, their anger, their modesty, their vanity. Politicians deal with one another as individuals, not just as members of a particular party or as bearers of a particular ideology. Thus it ever was. Thus it ever will be.

Eliot Spitzer himself has reinforced that verity at almost every turn in his 14 months and 10 days and counting as governor.

Is he smart? Sure. "The world's smartest man," Representative Charles B. Rangel once said of him with a healthy dash of derision. Is he ambitious? No question. Has he shown that he is prepared to knock down walls to get his way, even if it means knocking down people as well? Absolutely.

But character is destiny, as the saying goes, and Mr. Spitzer's flaws as an individual keep getting in his way, particularly his broad moralizing streak.

He was headed for trouble right from his vaunted Day 1 in office, when everything, he promised, would change. His inaugural address, delivered in his usual from-the-mount cadences, stood out for a singular lapse into gracelessness.

With his predecessor of the previous 12 years, George E. Pataki, sitting in front of him, the new governor likened New York to Rip Van Winkle, a state that "has slept through much of the past decade while the rest of the world has passed us by." Even if one accepted that assessment, having it delivered with Mr. Pataki sitting right there reflected both self-righteousness and exceptionally poor manners.

Nor did the questions about Mr. Spitzer's character end on Day 1. They have continuously been obstacles to implementing the ideas and the public good that he holds forth as paramount.

Right off the bat, he treated lawmakers as unworthy hacks, especially after they installed one of their own as state comptroller to replace Alan G. Hevesi, who had been driven from office by scandal.

Mr. Hevesi's sin, it might be noted, was using state money to have his ailing wife driven around. That qualifies as gallantry compared with what Mr. Spitzer's sin seems to be. As his wife, Silda, stood by his side on Monday, New Yorkers got a fresh taste of the public torment that men in high office put their women through, time and again.

Over the months, the tales of Mr. Spitzer's epic temper kept dribbling out.

With a swagger, he warned one assemblyman that he was a "steamroller," modifying that word with a street profanity to show that he was not some effete product of the Upper East Side who could be trifled with. One state senator said the governor threatened during an argument to cut the senator's head off.

For a time, Mr. Spitzer even managed to make a sympathetic figure of a charter member of Albany's Old Guard: the State Senate majority leader, Joseph L. Bruno. It takes a certain genius to manage that. But the governor did it, according to news accounts last year, by referring to Mr. Bruno, 30 years his senior, as "old" and "senile" in startlingly vulgar language.

So Mr. Spitzer's observation on Monday notwithstanding, politics in the long run is very much about individuals and how they behave.

Sanctimony is not listed among the seven deadly sins, but maybe it should be, right next to pride. It, along with his apparent recklessness, may be what does Mr. Spitzer in—not his budget or his health care plan or his proposal to issue driver's licenses to illegal immigrants.

And if he is ultimately forced from office, he may find that his ordeal does not end there. He is doomed to serve as a Leno or Letterman gag. You want to talk about the long run? Being cast eternally as a punch line could be a fate worse than resignation. Mr. Spitzer might want to start asking Monica Lewinsky or Senator Larry Craig what it's like.

Who We (Still) Are
Peggy Noonan—*Wall Street Journal*—12/18/2008

It's become a status symbol in New York to know someone who lost everything, as we now say, with Bernard Madoff, and to provide the details with a tone of wonder that subtly signals, "I of course was too smart for that, but I do feel compassion." It reminds me of the study I was told of years ago of soldiers who had seen a nearby comrade killed in battle. Their first thought tended to be not "Oh no!" or "Poor Joe," but "I'm not shot."

There has been criticism of Mr. Madoff's investors: How could they not have diversified? But people who were receiving quarterly reports on supposedly broad portfolios run by Mr. Madoff thought they were diversified. They didn't know he was the original toxic asset.

The most memorable line came from a Palm Beach, Fla., doyenne who reportedly said of his name last week, "I know it's pronounced 'Made-off,' because he made off with the money." A more sober observation came from a Manhattan woman who spoke, on the night Mr. Madoff was arrested, and as word spread through a Christmas party, of the general air of collapse in America right now, of the sense that our institutions are not and no longer can be trusted. She said, softly, "It's the age of the empty suit." Those who were supposed to be watching things, making the whole edifice run, keeping it up and operating, just somehow weren't there.

That's the big thing at the heart of the great collapse, a strong sense of absence. Who was in charge? Who was in authority? The biggest swindle in all financial history if the figure of $50 billion is to be believed, and nobody knew about it, supposedly, but the swindler himself. The government didn't notice, just as it didn't notice the prevalence of bad debts that would bring down America's great investment banks.

All this has hastened and added to the real decline in faith—the collapse in faith—the past few years in our institutions. Not only in Wall Street but in our entire economy, and in government. And of course there's Blago. But the disturbing thing there is that it seems to have inspired more mirth than anger. Did any of your friends say they were truly shocked? Mine either.

The reigning ethos seems to be every man for himself.

An old friend in a position of some authority in Washington told me the other day, from out of nowhere, that a hard part of his job is that there's no one to talk to. I didn't understand at first. He's surrounded by people, his whole life is one long interaction. He explained that he doesn't have really thoughtful people to talk to in government, wise men, people taking the long view and going forth each day with a sense of deep time, and a sense of responsibility for the future. There's no one to go to for advice.

He senses the absence too. It's a void that's governing us.

And this as much as anything has contributed to the sense you pick up that people feel all trends lead downward from here, that the great days of America Rising are over, that the best is not yet to come but has already been. It is so non-American, so unlike us, to think this, and yet one picks it up everywhere, between the lines and in asides. The other night a man told me of his four children, and I congratulated him on bringing up so many. From nowhere he said, "I worry about their future." At another time he would have said, "Billy wants to be a doctor."

People are angry but don't have a plan, and they'll give the incoming president unprecedented latitude and sympathy, cheering him on. I told a friend it feels like a necessary patriotic act to be supportive of him, and she said, "Oh hell, it's a necessary selfish act—I want him to do well so I survive. We all do!"

This is a good time to remember who we are, or rather just a few small facts of who we are. We are the largest and most technologically powerful economy in the world, the leading industrial power of the world, and the wealthiest nation in the world. "There's a lot of ruin in a nation," said Adam Smith. There's a lot of ruin in a great economy, too. We are the oldest continuing democracy in the world, operating, since March 4, 1789, under a vibrant and enduring constitution that was formed by geniuses and is revered, still, coast to coast. We don't make refugees, we admit them. When the rich of the world get sick, they come here to be treated, and when their children come of age, they send them here to our universities. We have a supple political system open to reform, and a wildly diverse culture that has moments of stress but plenty of give.

The point is not to say rah-rah, paint our faces blue and bray "We're No. 1." The point is that while terrible challenges face us—improving a sick public education system, ending the easy-money culture, rebuilding the economy—we are building from an extraordinary, brilliant and enduring base.

The other day I called former Secretary of State George Shultz, because he is wise and experienced and takes the long view. I asked if he thought we should be optimistic about our country's fortunes and future. "Absolutely," he said, there is "every reason to have confidence." He told me the story of Sumner Schlicter, an economics professor at Harvard 50 years ago. "He was not the most admired man in his department, but he'd make pronouncements about the economy that turned out to be right more often than his colleagues'." After Schlicter died, a friend was asked to clean out his desk, and found the start of an autobiography. "It said, I'm paraphrasing, 'I have had a good record in my comments on and expectations of the American economy, and the reason is I've always been an optimist. How did I get that way? I was brought up in the West, where the future is more important than the past, in a family of scientists and engineers forever developing new things. I could never buy into the idea that we had crossed our last frontier, because I was brought up with people crossing new frontiers.'"

Mr. Shultz laid out some particulars of his own optimism. There is "the ingenuity, the flexibility, the strengths of the national economy." The labor force: "We are so blessed with human talent and resources." And the American people themselves. "They have intelligence, integrity and honor."

We should experience "the current crisis" as "a gigantic wake-up call." We've been living beyond our means, both governmentally and personally. "We have to be willing to face up to our problems. But we have a capacity to roll up our sleeves and get down to work together."

What a task President-elect Obama has ahead. He ran on a theme of change we can believe in, but already that seems old. Only six weeks after his election he faces a need more consequential and immediate. In January, in his inaugural, he may find himself addressing something bigger, and that is: Belief we can believe in. The return of confidence. The end of absence. The return of the suit inhabited by a person. The return of the person who will take responsibility, and lead.

Polanski Backers Lose Sight of Real Victim
STEVE LOPEZ—*Los Angeles Times*—9/30/2009

Q: Did you resist at that time?
A: A little bit, but not really because . . .
Q: Because what?
A: Because I was afraid of him.

That's Roman Polanski's 13-year-old victim testifying before a grand jury about how the famous director forced himself on her at Jack Nicholson's Mulholland Drive home in March of 1977.

I'm reading this in the district attorney's office at the Los Angeles County Criminal Courts Building, digging through the Polanski file to refresh my memory of the infamous case, and my blood pressure is rising.

Is it because I'm the parent of a girl?

Maybe that's part of it.

But I wish the renowned legal scholars Harvey Weinstein and Debra Winger, to name just two of Polanski's defenders, were here with me now. I'd like to invite Martin Scorsese, as well, along with David Lynch, who have put their names on a petition calling for Polanski to be freed immediately.

What, because he won an Oscar? Would they speak up for a sex offender who hadn't?

To hear these people tell it, you'd think Polanski was the victim rather than the teenager.

And then there's Woody Allen, who has signed the petition too.

Woody Allen?

You'd think that after marrying his longtime girlfriend's adopted daughter, he'd have the good sense to remain silent. But at least Soon-Yi Previn was a consenting adult.

I'd like to show all these great luminaries the testimony from Polanski's underage victim, as well as Polanski's admission of guilt. Then I'd like to ask whether, if the victim were their daughter, they'd be so cavalier about a crime that was originally charged as sodomy and rape before Polanski agreed to a plea bargain. Would they still support Polanski's wish to remain on the lam living the life of a king, despite the fact that he skipped the U.S. in 1977 before he was sentenced?

The Zurich Film Festival has been "unfairly exploited" by Polanski's arrest, Winger said. Thanks, Deb. And so sorry the film festival was inconvenienced by the arrest of a man who left the United States to avoid sentencing for forcing himself on a child.

Weinstein, meanwhile, issued an open letter urging "every U.S. filmmaker to lobby against any move to bring Polanski back to the U.S.," arguing that "whatever you think of the so-called crime, Polanski has served his time."

So-called crime?

Let's get back to the grand jury testimony.

Polanski has taken the girl to Nicholson's house to photograph her, ostensibly for a French magazine. The girl's mother, it's clear to me, should have had her head examined for allowing this to happen, but that's another matter.

The girl says Polanski, who was in his 40s at the time, opened a bottle of champagne and shared it with her and with an adult woman who later left for work. That's when Polanski allegedly began taking pictures of the 13-year-old and suggested that she remove her blouse.

Quoting again from the grand jury transcript, with the girl being questioned by a prosecutor:

Q: Did you take your shirt off or did Mr. Polanski?
A: No, I did.
Q: Was that at his request or did you volunteer to do that?
A: That was at his request.

She said Polanski later went into the bathroom and took part of a Quaalude pill and offered her some, as well, and she accepted.

Q: Why did you take it?
A: I don't know. I think I must have been pretty drunk or else I wouldn't have.

So here she is, at 13, washing down a Quaalude with champagne, and then Polanski suggested they move out to the Jacuzzi.

Q: When you got in the Jacuzzi, what were you wearing?

A: I was going to wear my underwear, but he said for me to take them off.

She says Polanski went back in the house and returned in the nude and got into the Jacuzzi with her. When he told her to move closer to him, she resisted, saying, "No. No, I got to get out."

He insisted, she testified, and so she moved closer and he put his hands around her waist. She told him she had asthma and wanted to get out, and she did. She said he followed her into the bathroom, where she told him, "I have to go home now."

Q: What did Mr. Polanski say?
A: He told me to go in the other room and lie down.
She testified that she was afraid and sat on the couch in the bedroom.
Q: What were you afraid of?
A: Him.

She testified that Polanski sat down next to her and said she'd feel better. She repeated that she had to go home.

Q: What happened then?
A: He reached over and he kissed me. And I was telling him, "No," you know, "Keep away." But I was kind of afraid of him because there was no one else there.

She testified that he put his mouth on her vagina.
"I was ready to cry," she said. "I was kind of—I was going, 'No. Come on. Stop it.' But I was afraid."

She said he then pulled off her panties.

Q: What happened after that?
A: He started to have intercourse with me.

At this point, she testified, Polanski became concerned about the consequences and asked if she was on the pill.
No, she told him.
Polanski had a solution, according to her.
"He goes, 'Would you want me to go in through your back?' And I went, 'No.'"
According to her, that didn't stop Polanski, who began having anal sex with her.
This was when the victim was asked by the prosecutor if she resisted and she said, "Not really," because "I was afraid of him." She testified that when the ordeal had ended, Polanski told her, "Oh, don't tell your mother about this."
He added: "This is our secret."

But it wasn't a secret for long. When the victim got home and told her story, her mother called the police.

Now granted, we only have the girl's side of things. But an LAPD criminalist testified before the grand jury that tests of the girl's panties "strongly indicate semen." And a police officer who searched Polanski's hotel room found a Quaalude and photos of the girl.

Two weeks after the encounter on Mulholland Drive, Polanski was indicted for furnishing a controlled substance to a minor, committing a lewd or lascivious act upon a child under 14, unlawful sexual intercourse, rape by use of drugs, perversion (oral copulation) and sodomy.

Three months later, a plea bargain was worked out. Court records indicate that the victim and her family had asked the district attorney's office to spare the victim the trauma of testifying at a criminal trial.

"A stigma would attach to her for a lifetime," the family's attorney argued.

So Polanski pleaded guilty to just one count—unlawful sexual intercourse. The other charges were dropped.

Polanski spent 42 days in prison for pre-sentencing diagnostic tests. After his release, but before his sentencing in 1978, he skipped, boarding a plane for Europe because he feared he would be ordered to serve more time in prison. A warrant for his arrest has been in effect ever since, and Polanski was arrested this week in Switzerland.

He is fighting extradition, but I hope he loses that fight, gets hustled back to California and finally gets a sentence that fits his crime.

There's little question that this case was mishandled in many ways. According to a recent documentary, the now-deceased judge inappropriately discussed sentencing with a prosecutor who wasn't working the case. And Polanski's lawyers allege that the director fled only because he believed the judge would cave under public pressure and renege on a promise that he would serve no more time.

Regardless of whether there was such a deal, Polanski had not yet been sentenced, and under state law at the time, he could have been sent away for many years. Does anyone really believe 42 days was an appropriate penalty given the nature of the case?

Yes, Polanski has known great tragedy, having survived the Holocaust and having lost his wife, Sharon Tate and their unborn son, to the insanity of the Charles Manson cult.

But that has no bearing on the crime in question.

His victim, who settled a civil case against Polanski for an unspecified amount, said she does not want the man who forced himself on her to serve additional time.

That's big-hearted of her but also irrelevant, and so is the fact that the victim had admitted to having sex with a boyfriend before meeting Polanski.

Polanski stood in a Santa Monica courtroom on Aug. 8, 1977, admitted to having his way with a girl three decades his junior and told a judge that indeed, he knew she was only 13.

There may well have been judicial misconduct.

But no misconduct was greater than allowing Polanski to cop a plea to the least of his charges. His crime was graphic, manipulative and heinous, and he got a pass. It's unbelievable, really, that his soft-headed apologists are rooting for him to get another one.

Devil of a Scandal
MAUREEN DOWD—*TheNew York Times*—4/3/2010

The Devil didn't make me do it.

The facts did.

Father Gabriele Amorth, the chief exorcist for the Holy See, said in Rome that the *Times*'s coverage of Pope Benedict, which cast doubt on his rigor in dealing with pedophile priests, was "prompted by the Devil."

"There is no doubt about it," the 85-year-old priest said, according to the Catholic News Agency. "Because he is a marvelous pope and worthy successor to John Paul II, it is clear that the Devil wants to grab hold of him."

The exorcist also said that the abuse scandal showed that Satan uses priests to try to destroy the church, "and so we should not be surprised if priests too . . . fall into temptation. They also live in the world and can fall like men of the world."

Actually, falling into temptation is eating cupcakes after you've given them up for Lent. Rape and molestation of children is far beyond what most of us think of as succumbing to worldly temptation.

This church needs a sexorcist more than an exorcist.

As this unholy week of shameful revelations unfurls, the Vatican is rather overplaying its hand. At the moment, the only thing between Catholics and God is a defensive church hierarchy that cannot fully acknowledge and heal the damage it has done around the globe.

How can the faithful enjoy Easter redemption when a Good Friday service at the Vatican was more concerned with shielding the pope than repenting the church's misdeeds? The Rev. Raniero Cantalamessa, preacher of the papal household, told those at St. Peter's Basilica, including the pope, that he was thinking about the Jews in this season of Passover and Easter because "they know from experience what it means to be victims of collective violence and also because of this they are quick to recognize the recurring symptoms."

Amazingly enough, it turns out that the Franciscan priest was not referring to the collective violence and recurring symptoms of the global plague of Catholic priests who harmed children, enabled by the malignant neglect of the Vatican.

He was talking about the collective violence and recurring symptoms of those critics—including victims, Catholics worldwide and commentators—who want the church to face up to its sins.

Father Cantalamessa went on to quote from the letter of an unnamed Jewish friend: "I am following with indignation the violent and concentric attacks against the church, the pope and all the faithful by the whole world. The use of stereotypes, the passing from personal responsibility and guilt to a collective guilt, remind me of the more shameful aspects of anti-Semitism."

As they say in Latin, "Ne eas ibi." Don't go there.

Mindful of the church's long history of anti-Semitism, Leon Wieseltier, the New Republic literary editor and Jewish scholar, noted: "Why would the Catholic Church wish to defend itself by referring to other enormities in which it was also implicated? Anyway, the Jews endured more than a bad press." This solidarity with Jews is also notable given that Italy's La Repubblica reported that "certain Catholic circles" suspected that "a New York Jewish lobby" was responsible for the outcry against the pope.

It's insulting to liken the tragic death of six million Jews with the appropriate outrage of Catholics at the decades-long cover-up of crimes against children by the very men who were supposed to be their moral guides. Even the Vatican spokesman, the Rev. Federico Lombardi, tried to walk the cat back: "I don't think it's an appropriate comparison."

Father Cantalamessa was expressing the sense of self-victimization permeating the Vatican at a time when more real victims are pouring forth. News reports said that the abuse hot line set up by the Catholic Church in Germany imploded the first day out when more than 4,000 callers charging abuse flooded the lines.

There is the pope's inability to say anything long, adequate and sincere about the scandal and what role he has played, including acceding to the petition of the Wisconsin priest who abused 200 deaf kids that he should not be defrocked in his infirmity, to spare his priestly "dignity." And there is his veiled dismissal of criticism as "petty gossip." All this keeps him the subject of the conversation.

It is in crises that leaders are tested, that we get to see if they succumb to their worst instincts or summon their better angels. All Benedict has to do is the right thing.

The hero of the week, for simply telling the truth, is Ireland's Archbishop Diarmuid Martin. His diocese is Dublin, where four archbishops spent three decades shrugging off abuse cases.

"There is no shortcut to addressing the past," he said during a Holy Week Mass. "This has been a difficult year. We see how damaging failure of integrity and authenticity are to the body of Christ. Shameful abuse took place within the church of Christ. The response was hopelessly inadequate."

Amen.

The Age of Indiscretion
DAN HENNINGER—*Wall Street Journal*—4/25/2012

Past some point, it becomes pointless to ask, What were they thinking? That people exist who still ask this question suggests there's hope. Maybe.

Carousing Secret Service agents, thought to be an oxymoron in a slovenly time, was one we didn't see coming. Former Congressman Anthony Weiner, from a class of humanity that fell long ago, nonetheless broke new ground by frolicking in ghastly color online with unmet women thousands of miles away. The General Services Administration "on retreat" in Vegas was a bottomless joke until you saw five senior GSA officials (not all of them partygoers) standing in front of a congressional committee, their hands raised like characters in *The Godfather*. That would be hitting bottom for most people.

Wondering what were they thinking is a statement, not a question. The better question is: Does *anyone* think anymore that what they are about to do is, at the least, a mistake? Yes, but those who do look before they leap are a dwindling tribe.

Let us stipulate that the GSA and Secret Service scandals involve serious issues of mismanagement and possibly malfeasance. The big bust can't happen, though, until that voice in the individual brain says: Go ahead; do it.

Welcome to the Age of Indiscretion.

Athletes, celebrities, politicians, bureaucrats, reality TV, YouTubers, no doubt co-workers and now even Secret Service agents. We're all in.

Discretion, before its recent death, had many allies—judgment, common sense, prudence, reticence and the two better selfs, self-control and self-discipline.

Indiscretion, of its nature weak, dropped discipline and control to let the self run free. Has it ever. The age of indiscretion even has its own motto, on display at the Resort M in Vegas and the Hotel Caribe in Cartagena: Living large.

Earlier mottos have been discarded as too corny, such as, A word to the wise is sufficient, or, Forewarned is forearmed. Worth noting, though, is how often now one hears cries for "adult supervision."

The reign of indiscretion has been a long time coming. Some say it arrived in the late 1960s or early '70s, when constraints on behavior eased. But the new age's booster rocket, the thing that finally killed discretion, was social media.

Social media is about compulsion and revelation. It empowered the already indiscreet. Some of social media's indiscretions are microscopic ("She tweeted that?"), but holding nothing back has become reflexive, and so the norm.

One big paradox at the center of this great untethering is that digitized photos, audio and video are always along for the ride. I'm looking at snapshots, uploaded by someone to the Web, of disgraced GSA Pacific Rim administrator Jeff Neely and his wife on their "scouting trips" to a Vegas hotel. Of Mr. Neely combing his hair in the hotel-room mirror or soaking in the tub with a glass of what looks like Cabernet.

Going further than one should is one thing, but why the compulsion always to record it in a media format that can be distributed to the whole world? Such is the allure and power of indiscretion. Which group of people more than any other would be aware that any hotel, such as the Hotel Caribe, has 24/7 security cameras recording everyone's movements onto a hard disk?

A big part of the Greatest Generation's mystique was its instinct to self-protect. On balance, they were discreet. Countless intelligence veterans of World War II and the Cold War, for example, have gone to their graves without a public peep about their successes. But when the current generation takes down Osama bin Laden, it releases a photograph of itself in the Situation Room and provides operational details of the Navy Seals' attack plan to the media the next day. That was indiscreet.

The mortgage-securities bubble was fraught with systemic misfeasance. At its core, though, a liar loan was an act of indiscretion, on both sides of the deal. "Honey, do you really think we should be taking out a loan this big?" "Why not?!?!" Yeah, said lenders from Countrywide and mortgage packagers from Citibank, why not?

Or as Rep. Barney Frank said in the spirit of the age, let's "roll the dice a little bit more" on subsidized housing. That is a government living large, and in time the boys and girls at the Government Services Administration and agencies everywhere saw that "roll the dice a little bit more" was the new normal.

An architect of simplicity in design once said, less is more. An irony of the age of indiscretion is that more is less, especially if you get caught. The straightforward truth is that much unusual behavior can be tolerated and absorbed by a free society if discretion is putting speed bumps in the path of excess. It beats hitting the wall.

TRAGEDIES

Newspapers, daily bearers of some bad tidings, occasionally must bring word of horror that crosses into a special category—tales so grim that paper and ink can barely contain the shock. That is where the newsman's duty to tell even the most terrible truths gives rise to some of the most searing works of deadline art: columns about disasters—some natural, others man-made—all sad and gripping, occasionally beautiful, but unmistakably tragic.

In many cases, the historic nature of the event is obvious. Walter Lippmann's 1948 analysis of the assassination of Mahatma Gandhi has a poetic ring to it, as he contemplates the way Gandhi "died by violence as he was staking his life in order to set the example of non-violence." But after watching from yards away as John F. Kennedy was shot to death in Dallas, Merriman Smith of UPI skips the poetry. "I could not see the President's wound," he writes. "But I could see blood spattered around the interior of the rear seat and a dark stain spreading down the right side of the President's dark gray suit." Less than five years later, Jack Newfield ends up at the Los Angeles hotel where Kennedy's brother, seeking the presidency, is cut down and sadly concludes "the stone is once again at the bottom of the hill."

More than a century after the fact, the best columns can make forgotten natural disasters once again come alive in the mind. Winifred Black's description of the hurricane that destroyed Galveston, Texas, in 1900 is a reminder that 2005's Hurricane Katrina, which drowned New Orleans, was not the deadliest in American history (that terrible prize still goes to Galveston, where as many as twelve thousand perished). Jack London's account of the 1906 San Francisco Earthquake is a tribute to local citizens and firefighters hopelessly overwhelmed by an inferno of unthinkable dimensions. In 1974, after a twister destroys the lovely town of Xenia, Ohio, Rich Heiland offers a prayer that echoes through the ages: "I will cry a hundred years from now, no matter how many memories come and go, when I think of what this wind did to my city and its people."

Those tales of men battling nature become all the more poignant when considered alongside the similar heroism following the anything-but-natural terrorist attack of September 11, 2001, which columnists Mike Daly and Steve Lopez skillfully etch into the history books. One hears an echo of the monstrosity of that day in A. M. Rosenthal's 1958 visit to Auschwitz—where, more than a decade after the Nazis' mass murder was ended, the silence on the killing field seems indecent.

Another category of tragedy regularly makes the papers: the loss of a loved one to crime. Vermont Royster's farewell to an accomplished friend who died in an aimless suburban killing spree has an uncanny resemblance to stories by Frank del Olmo and Jimmy Breslin about life senselessly snuffed out in the inner city. Ellen Goodman's classic remembrance of John Lennon's life remains an oft-reprinted tribute to a great artist cut down by a crazed gunman.

Tales of heroes who lose their lives while doing their duty are a sad but inspiring staple of the newspaper columns. In "The Death of Rodriguez," Richard Harding Davis describes a Cuban independence fighter who faces the firing squad "with the nonchalance of a man who meets his punishment fearlessly, and who will let his enemies see that they can kill but cannot frighten him."

Many years later and a world away, John Fetterman won a Pulitzer Prize for the *Louisville Times* describing the homecoming and funeral of a young soldier killed in Vietnam. The death of Bobby Sands, the Irish independence fighter, has an ominous tone; Richard Ben Cramer writes from Belfast of "a grim, lingering rage, a quiet, determined, smouldering smile; these mourners will not be pacified."

Unmistakable echoes of tragedy can be heard in stories of people denied respect and recognition, who never quite get their place in the sun. Murray Kempton's tale of the political tumble taken by Tammany hall political boss Carmine DeSapio is a reminder that even so-called bad guys have their friends and family, and even do some good in the world. Jimmy Cannon's paean to the boxer Archie Moore is a tribute to every fighter who put their hearts and bodies on the line for the briefest flicker of fame—only to be denied even that small measure of tribute.

Even the seemingly ordinary tales of loss are food for thought. Hemingway's description of a bullfight as a tragedy in 1923 remains an eye-opener for those accustomed to thinking of animals as soulless beasts. Sixty years later, Pete Dexter's poignant remembrance of losing his dog as a five-year-old is no less evocative. Even Dick Young's mock-obituary of the Brooklyn Dodgers following the team's sale ("Preliminary diagnosis indicates that the cause of death was an acute case of greed") registers a familiar note: the reality that life is often cruelly unfair, and we must make sense of it in order to continue.

—ERROL LOUIS

The Murder of President Lincoln
NOAH BROOKS—*Sacramento Daily Union*—4/16/1865

No living man ever dreamed that it was possible that the intense joy of the nation over the recent happy deliverance from war could be or would be so soon turned to grief more intense and bitter than ever before the nation had known.

Just while the national Capital was in its brightest garb of joy, and while the nation was all pervaded with a generous exaltation, a heavy woe filling every heart with horror and stiffening once more the relaxing grasps of justice, swept over the land, and all the people stood aghast at the damnable deed which, in our hour of triumph, took away the beloved and revered chief magistrate, Abraham Lincoln.

. . . The performance had begun when the President and the party entered and the reception caused a suspension of the play, the enthusiasm being unusually great. They took seats in a double box on the right of the stage as you face the performers and the door was closed.

Two women only were on the stage and the second scene of the third act was just begun, when the theater, so often the scene of a mock tragedy, was made the scene of the real one of which the world has never seen parallel since Caesar was murdered in the Roman senate.

Ms. Harris looked up and saw Booth enter deliberately but rapidly, walk up behind the president whose face was turned toward the audience and apply a little pistol exactly under the left ear, fire. Oh God! Where was thy providence at that dreadful instant of time? It was but an instant, and dropping his pistol, the murderer flashed out a knife and sprung over the edge of the box and jumped.

The audience had heard the report of the pistol, but did not notice it, as it was very likely supposed to be a part of the stage business; but a sudden movement caused them to look up and there was a marble face, a pair of glittering black eyes and a flashing knife as Booth paused on the gilded cornice of the proscenium long enough to shout "Sic Semper Tyrannis!"

Then he dropped on the stage falling upon his knees but quickly recovering himself he marched across the stage to the left with that stagy, stilted stride peculiar to his class of actors, shouting "Revenge for the South!" as he went. Gaining the first stage entrance left side he pushed aside Ms. Keene who was about to enter, met an attaché of the theater whose coat he slashed open with his knife, dashed out of the door which he had left open, mounted his horse which a boy had been holding for him, and clattered out into the night bearing with him the mark of Cain, which will brand him to the day of his death. All this happened in a moment of time, and so completely paralyzed was every person that it was an easy thing for the wretch to flee almost unpursued; one man only, a lawyer in this city, had a dim idea of what had happened and leaping on the stage he pursued Booth into the alley, saw him knock down the boy who held the horse, mount and ride away into the darkness of the streets.

When the audience were roused by the piercing shrieks of Mrs. Lincoln they rushed upon the stage with shouts of "hang him! hang him!" and for a space all was confusion. . . . Surgeons were on the spot and everything was done that could be done to recall the bleeding, dying President to life. Mrs. Lincoln on hearing the report had turned, when, to her horror, she saw the head of her husband fall forward on his breast; he was laid on the sofa at once, but breathed only with difficulty, rattling in his throat. He never spoke or gave any sign of consciousness. The bullet had gone through the skull, glancing obliquely across the brain and lodging under the right eye, where a great discoloration settled. He was moved to a private house opposite, and instantly mounted couriers were scouring the city; horsemen galloped to and fro; the patrol encircled the city, which was in a state of terror and alarm. Guards kept the people out of the street where the president lay dying, but crowds anxious, tearful and enraged besieged the place all through the night. . . .

The Death of Rodriguez
RICHARD HARDING DAVIS—*New York Journal*—5/5/1897

. . . There had been a full moon the night preceding the execution, and when the squad of soldiers marched from town it was still shining brightly through the mists. It lighted a plain two miles in extent, broken by ridges and gullies and covered with thick, high grass, and with bunches of cactus and palmetto. In the hollow of the ridges the mist lay like broad lakes of water, and on one side of the plain stood the walls of the old town. On the other rose hills covered with royal palms that showed white in the moonlight, like hundreds of marble columns. A line of tiny campfires that the sentries had built during the night stretched between the forts at regular intervals and burned clearly.

But as the light grew stronger and the moonlight faded these were stamped out, and when theirs came in force the moon was a white ball in the sky, without radiance, the fires had sunk to ashes, and the sun had not yet risen.

So even when the men were formed into three sides of a hollow square, they were scarcely able to distinguish one another in the uncertain light of the morning.

There were about three hundred soldiers in the formation. They belonged to the volunteers, and they deployed upon the plain with their band in front playing a jaunty quickstep, while their officers galloped from one side to the other through the grass, seeking a suitable place for the execution. Outside the line the band still played merrily.

A few men and boys, who had been dragged out of their beds by the music, moved about the ridges behind the soldiers, half-clothed, unshaven, sleepy-eyed, yawning, stretching themselves nervously and shivering in the cool, damp air of the morning.

Either owing to discipline or on account of the nature of their errand, or because the men were still but half awake, there was no talking in the ranks, and the soldiers stood motionless, leaning on their rifles, with their backs turned to the town, looking out across the plain to the hills.

The men in the crowd behind them were also grimly silent. They knew that whatever they might say would be twisted into a word of sympathy for the condemned man or a protest against the government. So no one spoke; even the officers gave their orders in gruff whispers, and the men in the crowd did not mix together, but looked suspiciously at one another and kept apart.

As the light increased a mass of people came hurrying from the town with two black figures leading them, and the soldiers drew up attention, a part of the double line fell back and left an opening in the square.

With us a condemned man walks only the short distance from his cell to the scaffold or the electric chair, shielded from sight by the prison walls, and it often occurs even then that the short journey is too much for his strength and courage.

But the Spaniards on this morning made the prisoner walk for over a half-mile across the broken surface of the fields. I expected to find the man, no matter what his strength at other times might be, stumbling and faltering on this cruel journey; but as he came nearer I saw that he led all the others, that the priests on either side of him were taking two steps to his one, and that they were tripping on their gowns and stumbling over the hollows in their efforts to keep pace with him as he walked, erect and soldierly, at a quick step in advance of them.

He had a handsome, gentle face of the peasant type, a light, pointed beard, great wistful eyes, and a mass of curly black hair. He was shockingly young for such a sacrifice, and looked more like a Neapolitan than a Cuban. You could imagine him sitting on the quay at Naples or Genoa lolling in the sun and showing his white teeth when he laughed. Around his neck, hanging outside his linen blouse, he wore a new scapular.

It seems a petty thing to have been pleased with at such a time, but I confess to have felt a thrill of satisfaction when I saw, as the Cuban passed me, that he held a cigarette between his lips, not arrogantly nor with bravado, but with the nonchalance of a man who meets his punishment fearlessly, and who will let his enemies see that they can kill but cannot frighten him.

It was very quickly finished, with rough and, but for one frightful blunder, with merciful swiftness. The crowd fell back when it came to the square, and the condemned man, the priests, and the firing squad of six young volunteers passed in and the line closed behind them.

The officer who had held the cord that bound the Cuban's arms behind him and passed across his breast, let it fall on the grass and drew his sword, and Rodriguez dropped his cigarette from his lips and bent and kissed the cross which the priest held up before him.

The elder of the priests moved to one side and prayed rapidly in a loud whisper, while the other, a younger man, walked behind the firing squad and covered his face with his hands. They had both spent the last twelve hours with Rodriguez in the chapel of the prison.

The Cuban walked to where the officer directed him to stand, and turning his back on the square, faced the hills and the road across them, which led to his father's farm.

As the officer gave the first command he straightened himself as far as the cords would allow, and held up his head and fixed his eyes immovably on the morning light, which had just begun to show above the hills.

He made a picture of such pathetic helplessness, but of such courage and dignity, that he reminded me on the instant of that statue of Nathan Hale which stands in the City Hall Park, above the roar of Broadway. The Cuban's arms were bound, as are those of the statue, and he stood firmly, with his weight resting on his heels like a soldier on parade, and with his face held up fearlessly, as is that of the statue. But there was this difference, that Rodriguez, while probably as willing to give six lives for his country as was the American rebel, being only a peasant, did not think to say so, and he will not, in consequence, live in bronze during the lives of many men, but will be remembered only as one of thirty Cubans, one of whom was shot at Santa Clara on each succeeding day at sunrise.

The officer had given the order, the men had raised their pieces, and the condemned man had heard the clicks of the triggers as they were pulled back, and he had not moved. And then happened one of the most cruelly refined, though unintentional, acts of torture that one can very well imagine. As the officer slowly raised his sword, preparatory to giving the signal, one of the mounted officers rode up to him and pointed out silently that, as I had already observed with some satisfaction, the firing squad were so placed that when they fired they would shoot several of the soldiers stationed on the extreme end of the square.

Their captain motioned his men to lower their pieces, and then walked across the grass and laid his hand on the shoulder of the waiting prisoner.

It is not pleasant to think what that shock must have been. The man had steeled himself to receive a volley of bullets. He believed that in the next instant he would be in another world; he had heard the command given, had heard the click of the Mausers as the locks caught—and then, at that supreme moment, a human hand had been laid upon his shoulder and a voice spoke in his ear.

You would expect that any man, snatched back to life in such a fashion, would start and tremble at the reprieve, or would break down altogether, but this boy turned his head steadily, and followed with his eyes the direction of the officer's sword, then nodded gravely, and, with his shoulders squared, took up the new position, straightened his back, and once more held himself erect.

As an exhibition of self-control this should surely rank above feats of heroism performed in battle, where there are thousands of comrades to give inspiration. This man was alone, in sight of the hills he knew, with only enemies about him, with no source to draw on for strength but that which lay within himself.

The officer of the firing squad, mortified by his blunder, hastily whipped up his sword, the men once more leveled their rifles, the sword rose, dropped, and the men fired. At the report the Cuban's head snapped back almost between his shoulders, but his body fell slowly, as though some one had pushed him gently forward from behind and he had stumbled.

He sank on his side in the wet grass without a struggle or sound, and did not move again.

It was difficult to believe that he meant to lie there, that it could be ended so without a word, that the man in the linen suit would not rise to his feet and continue to walk on over the hills, as he apparently had started to do, to his home; that there was not a mistake somewhere, or that at least some one would be sorry or say something or run to pick him up.

But, fortunately, he did not need help, and the priests returned—the younger one with the tears running down his face—and donned their vestments and read a brief requiem for his soul, while the squad stood uncovered, and the men in the hollow square shook their accouterments into place, and shifted their pieces and got ready for the order to march, and the band began again with the same quickstep which the fusillade had interrupted.

The figure still lay on the grass untouched, and no one seemed to remember that it had walked there of itself, or noticed that the cigarette still burned, a tiny ring of living fire, at the place where the figure had first stood.

The figure was a thing of the past, and the squad shook itself like a great snake, and then broke into little pieces and started off jauntily, stumbling in the high grass and striving to keep step to the music.

The officers led it past the figure in the linen suit, and so close to it that the file closers had to part with the column to avoid treading on it. Each soldier as he passed turned and looked down on it, some craning their necks curiously, others giving a careless glance, and some without any interest at all, as they would have looked at a house by the roadside, or a hole in the road.

One young soldier caught his foot in a trailing vine, just opposite to it, and fell. He grew very red when his comrades giggled at him for his awkwardness. The crowd of sleepy spectators fell in on either side of the band. They, too, had forgotten it, and the priests put their vestments back in the bag and wrapped their heavy cloaks about them, and hurried off after the others.

Everyone seemed to have forgotten it except two men, who came slowly towards it from the town, driving a bullock-cart that bore an unplaned coffin, each with a cigarette between his lips, and with his throat wrapped in a shawl to keep out the morning mists.

At that moment the sun, which had shown some promise of its coming in the glow above the hills, shot up suddenly from behind them in all the splendor of the tropics, a fierce, red disk of heat, and filled the air with warmth and light.

The bayonets of the retreating column flashed in it, and at the sight a rooster in a farmyard nearby crowed vigorously, and a dozen bugles answered the challenge with the brisk, cheery notes of the reveille, and from all parts of the city the church bells jangled out the call for early mass, and the little world of Santa Clara seemed to stretch itself and to wake to welcome the day just begun.

But as I fell in at the rear of the procession and looked back, the figure of the young Cuban, who was no longer a part of the world of Santa Clara, was asleep in the wet grass, with his motionless arms still tightly bound behind him, with the scapular twisted awry across his face, and the blood from his breast sinking into the soil he had tried to free.

Galveston Is Gone

WINIFRED BLACK—*San Francisco Examiner*—*9/14/1900*

I begged, cajoled and cried my way through the line of soldiers with drawn swords who guard the wharf at Texas City and sailed across the bay on a little boat which is making irregular trips to meet the relief trains from Houston.

The engineer who brought our train down from Houston spent the night before groping around in the wrecks on the beach looking for his wife and three children. He found them, dug a rude grave in the sand and set up a little board marked with his name. Then he went to the railroad company and begged them to let him go to work.

The man in front of me on the car had floated all Monday night with his wife and mother on a part of the roof of his little home. He told me that he kissed his wife good-bye at midnight and told her he could not hold on any longer; but he did hold on, dazed and half conscious, until the day broke and showed him that he was alone on his piece of dried wood. He did not even know when the women that he loved had died.

Every man on the train—there were no women there—had lost someone that he loved in the terrible disaster, and was going across the bay to try and find some trace of his family—all except the four men in my party. They were from outside cities—St. Louis, New Orleans and Kansas City. They had lost a large amount of property and were coming down to see if anything could be saved from the wreck.

They had been sworn in as deputy sheriffs in order to get into Galveston. The city is under martial law, and no human being who cannot account for himself to the complete satisfaction of the officers in charge can hope to get through.

We sat on the deck of the little steamer. The four men from out-of-town cities and I listened to the little boat's wheel plowing its way through the calm waters of the bay. The stars shone down like a benediction, but along the line of the shore there rose a great leaping column of blood-red flame.

"What a terrible fire!" I said. "Some of the large buildings must be burning." A man who was passing the deck behind my chair heard me. He stopped, put his hand on the bulwark and turned down and looked into my face, his face like the face of a dead man, but he laughed.

"Buildings?" he said. "Don't you know what is burning over there? It is my wife and children, such little children; why, the tallest is not as high as this"— he laid his hand on the bulwark—"and the little one was just learning to talk.

"She called my name the other day, and now they are burning over there, they and the mother who bore them. She was such a little, tender, delicate thing, always so easily frightened, and now she's out there all alone with the two babies, and they're burning them. If you're looking for sensations there's plenty of them to be found over there where that smoke is drifting."

The man laughed again and began again to walk up and down the deck.

"That's right," said the United States marshal of Southern Texas, taking off his broad hat and letting the starlight shine on his strong face. "That's right. We had to do it. We've burned over 1,000 people today, and tomorrow we shall burn as many more.

"Yesterday we stopped burying the bodies at sea; we had to give the men on the barges whiskey to give them courage to do their work. They carried out hundreds of the dead at one time, men and women, negroes and white people, all piled up high as the barge could stand it, and the men did not go far enough out to sea, and the bodies have been drifting back again."

"Look!" said the man who was walking the deck, touching my shoulder with his shaking hand. "Look there!"

Before I had time to think I did look, and I saw floating in the water the body of an old, old woman, whose hair was shining in the starlight. A little further on we saw a group of strange driftwood. We looked closer and found it to be a mass of wooden slabs with names and dates cut upon them, and floating on top of them were marble stones, two of them.

The graveyard, which has held the sleeping citizens of Galveston for many, many years, was giving up its dead. We pulled up at a little wharf in the hush of the starlight. There were no lights anywhere in the city, except a few scattered lamps shining from a few desolate, half-destroyed houses. We picked our way up the street. The ground was slimy with the debris of the sea. Great pools of water stood in the middle of the street.

We climbed over wreckage and picked our way through heaps of rubbish. The terrible, sickening odor almost overcame us, and it was all that I could do to shut my teeth and get through the streets somehow.

The soldiers were camping on the wharf front, lying stretched out on the wet sand, the hideous, hideous sand, stained and streaked in the starlight with dark and cruel blotches. They challenged us, but the marshal took us through under his protection. At every street corner there was a guard, and every guard wore a six-shooter strapped around his waist.

. . . The abomination of desolation reigns on every side. The big houses are dismantled, their roofs gone, windows broken, and the high-water mark showing inconceivably high on the paint. The little houses are gone—either completely gone as if they had been made of cards and a giant hand which was tired of playing with them had swept them all off the board and put them away, or they are lying in heaps of kindling wood, covering no one knows what horrors beneath.

The main streets of the city are pitiful. Here and there a shop of some sort is left standing. South Fifth Street looks like an old man's jaw, with one or two straggling teeth protruding. The merchants are taking their little stores of goods that have been left them and are spreading them out in the bright sunshine, trying to make some little husbanding of their small capital. The water rushed through the stores, as it did through the houses, in an irresistible avalanche that carried all before it. The wonder is not that so little of Galveston is left standing, but that there is any of it at all.

Every street corner has its story, its story of misery and human agony bravely endured. The eye-witnesses of a hundred deaths have talked to me and told me their heartrending stories, and not one of them has told of a cowardly death. The women met their fate as did the men, bravely and for the most part with astonishing calmness. A woman told me that she and her husband went into the kitchen and climbed upon the kitchen table to get away from the waves, and that she knelt there and prayed. As she prayed, the storm came in and carried the whole house away, and her husband with it, and yesterday she went out to the place where her house had been, and there was nothing there but a little hole in the ground.

Her husband's body was found twisted in the branches of a tree half a mile from the place where she last saw him. She recognized him by a locket he had around his neck—the locket she gave him before they were married. It had her picture and a lock of the baby's hair in it. The woman told me all this without a tear or a trace of emotion. No one cries here.

They will stand and tell the most hideous stories, stories that would turn the blood in the veins of a human machine cold with horror, without the quiver of an eyelid. A man sat in the telegraph office and told me how he had lost two Jersey cows and some chickens. He went into minute particulars, told how his house was built and what it cost and how it was strengthened and made firm against the weather. He told me how the storm had come and swept it all away and how he had climbed over a mass of wobbling roofs and found a friend lying in the curve of a big roof, in the stoutest part of the tide, and how they two had grasped each other and what they said.

He told me just how much his cows cost and why he was so fond of them, and how hard he had tried to save them, but I said: "You have saved yourself and your family; you ought not to complain." The man stared at me with blank, unseeing eyes. "Why, I did not save my family," he said. "They were all drowned. I thought you knew that. I don't talk very much about it."

San Francisco Earthquake: The Story of an Eyewitness
JACK LONDON—*Collier's*—5/5/1906

The earthquake shook down in San Francisco hundreds of thousands of dollars' worth of walls and chimneys. But the conflagration that followed burned up hundreds of millions of dollars' worth of property. There is no estimating within hundreds of millions the actual damage wrought. Not in history has a modern imperial city been so completely destroyed. San Francisco is gone. Nothing remains of it but memories and a fringe of dwelling-houses on its outskirts. Its industrial section is wiped out. Its business section is wiped out. Its social and residential section is wiped out. The factories and warehouses, the great stores and newspaper buildings, the hotels and the palaces of the nabobs, are all gone. There remains only the fringe of dwelling houses on the outskirts of what was once San Francisco.

Within an hour after the earthquake shock the smoke of San Francisco's burning was a lurid tower visible a hundred miles away. And for three days and nights this lurid tower swayed in the sky, reddening the sun, darkening the day, and filling the land with smoke.

On Wednesday morning at a quarter past five came the earthquake. A minute later the flames were leaping upward. In a dozen different quarters south of Market Street, in the working-class ghetto, and in the factories, fires started. There was no opposing the flames. There was no organization, no communication. All the cunning adjustments of a twentieth century city had been smashed by the earthquake. The streets were humped into ridges and depressions, and piled with the debris of fallen walls. The steel rails were twisted into perpendicular and horizontal angles. The telephone and telegraph systems were disrupted. And the great water mains had burst. All the shrewd contrivances and safeguards of man had been thrown out of gear by thirty seconds' twitching of the earth's crust.

By Wednesday afternoon, inside of twelve hours, half the heart of the city was gone. At that time I watched the vast conflagration from out on the bay. It was dead calm. Not a flicker of wind stirred. Yet from every side wind was pouring in upon the city. East, west, north, and south, strong winds were blowing upon the doomed city. The heated air rising made an enormous suck. Thus did the fire of itself build its own colossal chimney through the atmosphere. Day and night this dead calm continued, and yet, near to the flames, the wind was often half a gale, so mighty was the suck.

Wednesday night saw the destruction of the very heart of the city. Dynamite was lavishly used, and many of San Francisco's proudest structures were crumbled by man himself into ruins, but there was no withstanding the onrush of the flames. Time and again successful stands were made by the firefighters, and every time the flames flanked around on either side or came up from the rear, and turned to defeat the hard-won victory.

An enumeration of the buildings destroyed would be a directory of San Francisco. An enumeration of the buildings undestroyed would be a line and several addresses. An enumeration of the deeds of heroism would stock a library and bankrupt the Carnegie medal fund. An enumeration of the dead will never be made. All vestiges of them were destroyed by the flames. The number of the victims of the earthquake will never be known. South of

Market Street, where the loss of life was particularly heavy, was the first to catch fire.

Remarkable as it may seem, Wednesday night while the whole city crashed and roared into ruin, was a quiet night. There were no crowds. There was no shouting and yelling. There was no hysteria, no disorder. I passed Wednesday night in the path of the advancing flames, and in all those terrible hours I saw not one woman who wept, not one man who was excited, not one person who was in the slightest degree panic-stricken.

Before the flames, throughout the night, fled tens of thousands of homeless ones. Some were wrapped in blankets. Others carried bundles of bedding and dear household treasures. Sometimes a whole family was harnessed to a carriage or delivery wagon that was weighted down with their possessions. Baby buggies, toy wagons, and go-carts were used as trucks, while every other person was dragging a trunk. Yet everybody was gracious. The most perfect courtesy obtained. Never in all San Francisco's history, were her people so kind and courteous as on this night of terror. . . .

It was at Union Square that I saw a man offering a thousand dollars for a team of horses. He was in charge of a truck piled high with trunks from some hotel. It had been hauled here into what was considered safety, and the horses had been taken out. The flames were on three sides of the Square and there were no horses.

Also, at this time, standing beside the truck, I urged a man to seek safety in flight. He was all but hemmed in by several conflagrations. He was an old man and he was on crutches. Said he: "Today is my birthday. Last night I was worth thirty thousand dollars. I bought five bottles of wine, some delicate fish and other things for my birthday dinner. I have had no dinner, and all I own are these crutches."

I convinced him of his danger and started him limping on his way. An hour later, from a distance, I saw the truckload of trunks burning merrily in the middle of the street. . . .

THE DAWN OF THE SECOND DAY

I passed out of the house. Day was trying to dawn through the smoke-pall. A sickly light was creeping over the face of things. Once only the sun broke through the smoke-pall, blood-red, and showing quarter its usual size. The smoke-pall itself, viewed from beneath, was a rose color that pulsed and fluttered with lavender shades then it turned to mauve and yellow and dun. There was no sun. And so dawned the second day on stricken San Francisco.

An hour later I was creeping past the shattered dome of the City Hall. Than it there was no better exhibit of the destructive force of the earthquake. Most of the stone had been shaken from the great dome, leaving standing the naked framework of steel. Market Street was piled high with the wreckage, and across the wreckage lay the overthrown pillars of the City Hall shattered into short crosswise sections.

This section of the city with the exception of the Mint and the Post-Office, was already a waste of smoking ruins. Here and there through the smoke, creeping warily under the shadows of tottering walls, emerged occasional men and women. It was like the meeting of the handful of survivors after the day of the end of the world. . . .

San Francisco, at the present time, is like the crater of a volcano, around which are camped tens of thousands of refugees. At the Presidio alone are at least twenty thousand. All the surrounding cities and towns are jammed with the homeless ones, where they are being cared for by the relief committees. The refugees were carried free by the railroads to any point they wished to go, and it is estimated that over one hundred thousand people have left the peninsula on which San Francisco stood. The Government has the situation in hand, and, thanks to the immediate relief given by the whole United States, there is not the slightest possibility of a famine. The bankers and business men have already set about making preparations to rebuild San Francisco.

A Policeman Walks East to Death
FRANK WARD O'MALLEY—*New York Sun*—10/23/1907

Mrs. Catherine Sheehan stood in the darkened parlor of her home at 361 West Fifteenth Street late yesterday afternoon, and told her version of the murder of her son Gene, the youthful policeman whom a thug named Billy Morley shot in the forehead down under the Chatham Square elevated station early yesterday morning. Gene's mother was thankful that her boy hadn't killed Billy Morley before he died, "because," she said, "I can say honestly even now that I'd rather have Gene's dead body brought home to me, as it will be tonight, than to have him come to me and say, 'Mother, I had to kill a man this morning.'

"God comfort the poor wretch that killed the boy," the mother went on, "because he is more unhappy to-night than we are here. Maybe he was weak-minded through drink. He couldn't have known Gene or he wouldn't have killed him. Did they tell you at the Oak Street Station that the other policemen called Gene Happy Sheehan? Anything they told you about him is true, because no one would lie about him. He was always happy, and he was a fine-looking young man and he always had to duck his helmet when he walked under the gas fixture in the hall as he went out the door.

"He was doing dance steps on the floor of the basement after his dinner yesterday noon for the girls—his sisters, I mean—and he stopped of a sudden when he saw the clock and picked up his helmet. Out on the street he made pretend to arrest a little boy he knows who was standing there—to see Gene come out, I suppose—and when the little lad ran away laughing, I called out, 'You couldn't catch Willie, Gene; you're getting fat.'

" 'Yes, and old, Mammy,' he said, him who is—who was only twenty-six—'so fat,' he said, 'that I'm getting a new dress coat that'll make you proud when you see me in it, Mammy.' And he went over Fifteenth Street, whistling a tune and slapping his leg with a folded newspaper. And he hasn't come back again.

"But I saw him once after that, thank God, before he was shot. It's strange, isn't it, that I hunted him up on his beat late yesterday afternoon for the first time in my life. I never go around where my children are working or studying— one I sent through college with what I earned at dressmaking and some other little money I had, and he's now a teacher; and the youngest I have at college now. I don't mean that their father wouldn't send them if he could, but he's an invalid, although he's got a position lately that isn't too hard for him. I got Gene prepared for college, too, but he wanted to go right into an office in Wall Street. I got him in there, but it was too quiet and tame for him, Lord have mercy on his soul; and then, two years ago, he wanted to go on the police force, and he went.

"After he went down the street yesterday I found a little book on a chair, a little list of the streets or something that Gene had forgot. I knew how particular they are about such things, and I didn't want the boy to get in trouble, and so I threw on a shawl and walked over through Chambers Street toward the river to find him. He was standing on a corner someplace down there near the bridge, clapping time with his hands for a little newsy that was dancing; but he stopped clapping, struck, Gene did, when he saw me. He laughed when I handed him the little book and told that was why I'd searched for him, patting me on the shoulder when he laughed—patting me on the shoulder.

" 'It's a bad place for you here, Gene,' I said. 'Then it must be bad for you, too, Mammy,' said he; and as he walked to the end of his beat with me—it was dark then—he said, 'They're lots of crooks here, Mother, and they know and hate me and they're afraid of me'—proud, he said it—'but maybe they'll get me some night.' He patted me on the back and turned and walked east toward his death. Wasn't it strange that Gene said that?

"You know how he was killed, of course, and how—now let me talk about it, children, if I want to. I promised you, didn't I, that I wouldn't cry any more, or carry on? Well, it was five o'clock this morning when a boy rang the bell here at the house and I looked out the window and said, 'Is Gene dead?' 'No, ma'am,' answered the lad, 'but they told me to tell you he was hurt in a fire and is in the hospital.' Jerry, my other boy, had opened the door for the lad and was talking to him while I dressed a bit. And then I walked down stairs and saw Jerry standing silent under the gaslight, and I said again, 'Jerry, is Gene dead?' And he said, 'Yes,' and he went out.

"After a while I went down to the Oak Street station myself, because I couldn't wait for Jerry to come back. The policemen all stopped talking when I came in, and then one of them told me it was against the rules to show me Gene at that time. But I knew the policeman only thought I'd break down, but I promised him I wouldn't carry on, and he took me into a room to let me see Gene. It was Gene.

"I know today how they killed him. The poor boy that shot him was standing in Chatham Square, arguing with another man, when Gene told him to move on. When the young man wouldn't but only answered back, Gene shoved him, and the young man pulled a revolver and shot Gene in the face, and he died before Father Rafferty of St. James got to him. God rest his soul. A lot of policemen heard the shots, and they all came running with their pistols and clubs in their hands. Policeman Laux—I'll never forget his name or any of the others that ran to help Gene—came down the Bowery and ran out into the middle of the Square where Gene lay.

"When the man that shot Gene saw the policemen coming, he crouched down and shot at Policeman Laux, but thank God he missed him. Then policemen named Harrington and Rourke and Moran and Kehoe chased the man all around the streets there, some heading him off when he tried to run into that street that goes off at an angle—East Broadway, is it?—a big crowd had come out of Chinatown now and was chasing the man, too, until Policemen Rourke and Kehoe got him backed up against a wall. When Policeman Kehoe came up close the man shot his pistol right at Kehoe, and the bullet grazed Kehoe's helmet.

"All the policemen jumped at the man then, and one of them knocked the pistol out of his hand with a blow of a club. They beat him, this Billy Morley, so Jerry says his name is, but they had to because he fought so hard. They told me this evening that it will go hard with the unfortunate murderer, because Jerry says that when a man named Frank O'Hare, who was arrested this evening charged with stealing cloth or something, was being taken into headquarters, he told Detective Gegan that he and a one-armed man who answered to the description of Morley, the young man who killed Gene, had a drink in a saloon at Twenty-second Street and Avenue A and that when the one-armed man was leaving the saloon he turned and said, 'Boys, I'm going out now to bang a guy with buttons.'

"They haven't brought me Gene's body yet. Coroner Shrady, so my Jerry says, held Billy Morley, the murderer, without letting him get out on bail, and I suppose that in a case like this they have to do a lot of things before they can let me have the body here. If Gene only hadn't died before Father Rafferty got to him I'd be happier. He didn't need to make his confession, you know, but it would have been better, wouldn't it? He wasn't bad, and he went to Mass on Sunday without being told; and even in Lent, when we always say the rosary out loud in the dining room every night, Gene himself said to me the day after Ash Wednesday, 'If you want to say the rosary at noon, Mammy, before I go out, instead of at night when I can't be here, we'll do it.'

"God will see that Gene's happy tonight, won't he, after Gene said that?" the mother asked as she walked out into the hallway with her black-robed daughters grouped behind her. "I know He will," she said, "and I'll—" She stopped, with an arm resting on the banister to support her. "I—I know I promised you girls," said Gene's mother, "that I'd try not to cry any more, but I can't help it." And she turned toward the wall and covered her face with her apron.

The Death of Henry Spencer
Ben Hecht—*Chicago Daily News*—8/1/1914

A hot summer afternoon was ending in the small town of Wheaton, Illinois. The thermometer outside Crowley's Drugstore registered ninety-two degrees. The sun blazed as it slid down a sky, white and smooth as a bed sheet.

Shirt-sleeved, without collar and tie, fanning themselves and mopping their faces with large handkerchiefs, the townspeople dreamed of evening shadows and a prairie wind. Merchants sat in the awning shade of their empty stores. They dozed, gossiped and read the Wheaton *Daily Journal*. There was always news of interest to home folks in the *Journal*, but on this day the editor seemed to have lost his native bearings. The front page was full of tidings that meant nothing to Wheaton. The German Kaiser was acting up again, and Britishers in striped pants were full of alarms—dim and faraway matters, these, to offer Wheaton, Illinois, on a blistering summer day.

The merchants idled, and housewives were busy with suppers in houses that looked as if they had been abandoned. The deserted streets were full of glare and silence. Only such things were moving as make no noises—bugs and butterflies, sparrows, robins and orioles, the heavy leaves of the maple trees changing positions, and a cat that had remembered something.

I entered the Wheaton jail, and the sheriff recognized me and was pleased to see me.

"Go right on upstairs," he said and then made a joke. "He's still there."

The sheriff's assistant led me to a large cell and opened its barred door. Three people were inside. A man and a woman were singing hymns, accompanied by a melodeon which the man was pumping. Another man, in shirt sleeves, tennis shoes and gray flannel trousers, was listening with a tender look on his square blond face. I knew the listener. His name was Henry Spencer, and he was going to be hanged the next morning between six and nine o'clock.

When the music had ended Spencer introduced me to the hymn singers.

"I want you to meet my spiritual brother and sister, Mr. and Miss MacAuslin," he said. The MacAuslins beamed. They looked alike, lean, short, reddish-haired and a little witless.

"My brother and sister in God." Spencer beamed back at them. "I'm very glad to see you. Sit down. Your friend Wallace Smith interviewed me this morning. He got here ahead of you, evidently. How have you been feeling?"

"Fine," I said.

"It's a very hot day," said Spencer. "I imagine this is about the coolest place in town."

He chatted on and I listened, fascinated by a new voice he seemed to have acquired since I had covered his trial a few weeks before. At that time Spencer had spoken in a half-cockney voice, coarse, sneering and illiterate. He was quite the grammatical gentleman now, and like his two other visitors he seemed idiotically cheerful.

"The sheriff kindly sent me a pitcher of ice-cold lemonade," he said. "Would you care for some?"

I took a glass and marveled at Spencer as I drank. This was the worst murderer I had ever yet encountered, a sly, humanless killer.

He had come to Wheaton and sniffed at the town like a wolf looking for easy and harmless quarry. He had found what he looked for—a lonely, aging woman with a bank account. Her name was Allison Rexroat. She was a spinster who went to lectures and studied dancing. Spencer wooed and seduced her and filled her life with matters of which she had foolishly dreamed in all her lonely years—sex and love. He was a juicy fellow with a catlike body, thick in neck and ankles and with large, fluttery hands. Miss Rexroat sinned with him and bought herself new clothes for the wedding he promised. She gave him her suddenly crazed heart and inexpert body and lastly her bank account.

A week after her money had been put in Spencer's name, he took her on a picnic in the woods beyond Wheaton. After wading in the creek and eating the picnic lunch Miss Allison had prepared with doting hands, Spencer insisted that his sweetheart lie down under a bush and allow him to enjoy her sexually. Miss Rexroat lay on her back, her eyes closed, her heart beating with sin and trusting love. Spencer approached her and cracked her skull with a hammer he had brought along for this purpose. He continued to pound her head until it was well bashed. He had also brought to the picnic a small shovel. He dug a grave with this, and after removing two diamond rings from his sweetheart's fingers, he buried her in it.

The next morning Spencer drew out Miss Rexroat's savings, now in his name. He was waiting for a train to take him out of Wheaton and to fresh hunting grounds when the banker and sheriff of Wheaton arrived at the depot. The banker had known Miss Rexroat all her life. He did not believe she would leave Wheaton, as Spencer had said she was doing, without saying good-bye to him.

Spencer was arrested. Miss Rexroat's two diamond rings were found in his pocket. A farmer had seen them entering the woods—carrying a picnic basket. After several days of search, Miss Rexroat's fresh grave was discovered and her body dug up. There was the question, then, of the murder weapon. Spencer roared and cursed for a week that he was an innocent man and the victim of diabolical coincidences. The sheriff's assistant finally lost his temper, listening to the prisoner's stupid denials and contradictory statements, and hit Spencer in the mouth. At the sight of blood dripping from his broken teeth, Spencer became pale and fearful. This man who had smashed a live head into a pulp with a hammer was terrified of pain. To avoid a second blow, he confessed, and there was one detail in his blurted-out confession which he could not undo in his desperate court battle a few weeks later. In the presence of witnesses Spencer told where he had buried the murder weapon, and a half-dozen men went with him to the spot he named and dug up the blood-, hair- and flesh-caked hammer.

The confession offered in court by the state had been beaten out of him, Spencer's lawyers proved to the jury. And Spencer on the witness stand had denied everything, cursing his tormentors and oafishly crying out his innocence.

The evidence of the hammer brought him a death sentence, however, and he was returned to his cell to wait execution on an August morning. This had happened in July. I had left a surly Spencer, still cursing the world, and its sheriff and jury. This happy fellow pouring me a second glass of lemonade and smiling gently at me was, in truth, a thing to marvel at. Not only his voice but his soul had changed.

"I can see how surprised you are," he said. "But I am glad you are not sneering as your friend Wallace did this morning. He got angry when I tried to tell him about certain things and said to me, 'Cut out the act.'"

"What were you trying to tell him?" I asked.

"About God," said Spencer. The MacAuslins nodded like two happy children in a nursery. "And how my brother and sister brought me to him."

"Have you admitted the killing?" I asked.

"That's not important anymore," said Spencer. "I was a sinner. A black sinner. I did evil. Evil was in me. Now it's gone."

"Did you kill Miss Rexroat?" I asked.

The MacAuslins kneeled in the hot cell and began to pray. Spencer joined them on his knees and prayed with them. Then he stood up, dusted his new flannel trousers and said, "Yes, I killed her. I have no secrets from God. He knows me. I am a brand snatched from the burning. I have repented. My soul is washed of all wickedness. God can look into it and see there is nothing evil left. That's why He will let me into Heaven. Because there is not a single lie in me—only truth."

"God forgives those who come to Him with the truth," said one of the little MacAuslins. "Sinners and liars are barred from His grace."

"I'm washed clean," said Spencer and began in a soft voice to tell me the story of his evil doing. He described a picnic, the lovemaking, the vicious preparations of hammer and shovel and the ugly killing.

"I'm talking to you and to God," he said. "He listens to me and hears every world just as plain as you do."

I stayed another hour while the MacAuslins played their melodeon and sang more hymns. I asked them questions about Spencer, but they were like children too full of some mysterious joy to talk. They could only beam, sing and pray. They had been with Spencer for ten days and ten nights, filling the death cell with hymns, psalms and incantations.

I sat marveling now not only at Spencer but at the miracle of religion. The talk of divine grace and divine forgiveness was meaningless to me. Yet it had worked a miracle. Faith in God had altered a man's soul, diction and vocabulary, drained his nerves of panic and given him a serene face for death.

At dinner in the Wheaton Hotel I talked with Wallace about this miracle, and our friendship felt a strain. We were for the first time since we had met of different minds.

Spencer, said Wallace, was a fraud. His whole mumbo jumbo about God and repentance was an act. The man's soul was unchanged and as sly and rotten as ever.

"The sonofabitch," said Wallace, "is providing himself with his own hop. He's scared pissless and he's found something that he thinks will keep his knees from buckling when he starts up the gallows' steps. There's no faith or repentance involved."

"I think there is," I said. "Montaigne writes that philosophy prepares a man for dying as well as living. Religion is a philosophy of an emotional sort. And its history is full of stories about people who have gone to their deaths exalted by something they called God in their hearts."

"Not hammer killers," said Wallace. "Our boy is a murderer and if he wasn't hanged tomorrow he would go on being a murderer. He'd forget all about God and go after another spinster with another hammer. He's picked up religion out of terror."

"Don't most people?" I asked. "I'm only saying that a belief in God has changed a man vitally. He not only talks different, he looks different. He's got a vision in him."

"And a cup of coffee," said Wallace coldly. "I'm only two years older than you and I shouldn't know so much more than you. Makes me feel like I had a long white beard, talking to you." He looked at me queerly and added, "Nothing can change a man. It's all fake. You are what you are. And you can only pretend to be something else. Henry's a rat and he'll die like a rat. I'll give you three to one on it."

We walked through the summer night to the sheriff's house adjoining the jail. We wanted his opinion on Spencer's new soul. But the sheriff had gone to bed early and left word that no one was to disturb him.

"Another frightened man," said Wallace. "I talked to him this morning. He was shaking like a mongoose. He's not only never hanged anybody but he's never even seen a hanging. The whole thing is very upsetting to him."

The sheriff's daughter was sitting on the front porch. She was a girl of seventeen. Her young face looked tender and romantic in the moonlight. She seemed almost nude in her thin summer dress through which the white of her breasts glinted. A large coil of rope was at her feet. She held one end of it in her hands and was busy rubbing Vaseline in its fibers.

"It's the rope they're going to hang Henry with," she said, "and my pa said it'll work better if it's softened up."

"Doesn't that upset you?" I asked. "Fixing up a hanging rope?" I looked at her intent face. "Come on, we'll take a walk," I added.

"I got to finish this."

"I should think your pa would have gotten somebody else to grease it."

"I wouldn't let him," the girl smiled. "He isn't going to let me see the hanging, so I said, anyway, I ought to have some fun out of it. I mean, excitement."

I picked up the rope to examine it.

"You're doing a good job," I said.

The girl frowned. "If you'd lived in Wheaton all your life," she said, "maybe you wouldn't stand there looking so sarcastic. And please go away. I don't want to be bothered."

We left the girl and the hanging rope and walked toward the stockade that had been built on the edge of the town for the execution. The night was thick and without movement. No prairie wind had come. Bugs chirped and made little spatters of sound as they leaped in the shadows. The music of the melodeon rose thinly, pensively, persistently. Frogs grunted. A dog bayed. The heat stirred sweet odors from the earth, its bushes, grass and trees. Overhead the sky sparkled with starlight and billowed with infinity. I wondered that a night could seem so beautiful that promised death in the morning. When I mentioned this to Wallace, he said, "People die all the time. Very nice people. And everything stays just as beautiful."

There were a dozen reporters already in the stockade. They were sitting at the moonlit press table, drinking. Most of them were from Chicago.

I drank and looked admiringly at the stockade. It was almost a Colosseum. Its fence rose fifteen feet in the air. Fifty rows of empty picnic benches faced the gallows. And this, too, was an astonishing structure. It was twice as high as any gallows I had ever seen. The gallows' platform was some thirty feet above the ground. A dangerous-looking, unbroken flight of small steps led up to it.

"Graft," said the Wheaton *Journal* reporter. "This whole hanging is shot through with graft and corruption. Here's a story for you fellas. I can't print it because my editor's a pal of the sheriff. They've got something on each other. But you fellas can spill it. The sheriff's running for re-election next month. That's why this stockade is five times as big as it ought to be. He's given out tickets to every political worker in the country—and he had to make it big enough to hold them all. Some of them got as many as five tickets apiece. Not only that, but the whole stockade is a swindle. The sheriff's brother-in-law owns the Wheaton Lumber Mill. He got the construction job and put in three times more lumber for everything than required. He soaked the county plenty. That's why the gallows is so high up. A guy could get dizzy just standing on it. The stairs, the fence, the gallows—everything is graft."

We drank and told stories of other events we had covered. New booze bottles appeared and were emptied. The smells of a woodland midnight filled the stockade. Owls hooted and a horse neighed from a distant barn. The maple trees towering above the stockade shook with a breeze arrived from the prairie. We lay in the grass in front of the gallows and a reporter named Woody, whom we called Kentuck, produced a pair of dice. We gambled for awhile, but after lighting several boxes of matches to see the dice and denouncing each other as crooks miscalling the numbers rolled, we abandoned the game.

"Here's a game we can play without any daffy cheating," said Wallace. "Let's bet on those gallows' stairs. Everybody put up ten bucks and the winner take all."

"How come?" Kentuck asked.

"We'll bet on which step Spencer's going to trip when he starts up to the gallows in the morning," said Wallace. "Three of us will have to stay out of the betting and be judges."

We looked at the tall flight of gallows' steps with new interest.

"Wallie's right," said Kentuck. "No man alive can walk up those steps without trippin'. They're built too small."

"Spencer won't get farther than the fifth step," said the Wheaton reporter. "He'll go right on his ass."

"Place your bets," said Wallace. "And put them in writing so there'll be no humpty-dumpty arguments afterward."

"Hold your horses," said Kentuck. "Before I put up ten bucks I got a right to have a look in the paddock."

"Look all you want," said Wallace.

"I've had a little liquor," said Kentuck, "but I'm no dizzier than Henry will be when he starts climbing those steps in the morning. So I'll just check."

Kentuck started briskly up the stairs to the gallows' platform. A third of the way up his foot slipped.

"Never seen such stairs," said Kentuck, "a man could break his neck easy on them. I'll take steps twenty to twenty-five. Here's my ten dollars."

Seven other reporters entered the "stair pool." We took turns running up the steps to see how far we could go before tripping. I went the farthest, coming within five feet of the gallows before missing a step and almost toppling to the ground. I bet on the last five steps.

The seventy dollars were handed to three reporters who, as judges in the morning, would note without prejudice on which step the murderer of Allison Rexroat came a cropper on his way to the dangling rope.

The night, full of stars and silence, moved toward the dawn.

Sweet night in the shadow of death, night of crickets chirping and a clover-smelling breeze, night of heedless youth and bawdy tales, of young breasts glinting over a hanging rope, of a darkness full of little things—starlight and owls and weather reports and a melodeon playing for the salvation of a man, and haphazard human doings eerie and unpolitical and with the sap of life in them—that night is gone. And none like it was ever to be in my time again. For on this August, 1914, night, an innocence was departing the world.

Iowa Village Waits All Night for Glimpse of Funeral Train
LORENA A. HICKOK—*Minneapolis Tribune*—8/7/1923

HONEY CREEK, IOWA—Hurling itself into the dawn at 50 miles an hour, the President's funeral train roared past Honey Creek at 4 a.m. today.

A blurred, agonizing glimpse into the dimly lighted observation car heaped to the ceiling with wreaths and flowers was all that Honey Creek got

—and for this her 76 inhabitants had shivered on the dreary station platform for hours.

But in the words of H. L. Ham, station agent, postmaster and notary public, as he stared dazedly after the red taillights dwindling away in the shadows, "Well, it was worth it, wasn't it?"

It was worth it. The long moaning whistle around the bend—the blinding shaft of light down the glittering rails—the roar and wind and trembling of the earth—the breathless wait for the rear car—the flashing vision of wreaths and flags and rigid figures in khaki—the red taillights vanishing like pin points in the dark—yes, it was worth waiting for.

There was no pomp or ceremony in Honey Creek's tribute to the nation's dead leader. No lines of veterans in uniform, no flowers, no spoken prayers. Honey Creek is not given to fluency and high-sounding phrases.

People went down to see that train for two reasons—to show their respect for the President of the United States and to take their children. In Honey Creek it was deemed highly important that the children should see that train, so that they might tell their children and their children's children.

And so it was that fathers, who had served in the nation's armies during the world war, held their little babies high over their shoulders as the train leaped past Honey Creek this morning. And small boys in overalls gazed in wonder from the top of the fence adjoining the station. The chief concern of the adults was in seeing to it that the children got a good view of the train.

Honey Creek, Iowa, used to be on the Lincoln highway until they moved the highway. Until a year or two ago, it was known from coast to coast among automobile tourists as "The place where you strike that awful hill." Finally, to get away from the hill, they moved the highway out of Honey Creek—and now Honey Creek is slowly dying.

"It used to have a population of 90 when the highway went through here," Fremont Hansen, the garage owner, said last night. "But now—I guess it's not much over 75."

"Before they moved the highway we had two stores and a bank and a Commercial club. But one of the stores burned down, and the bank went out of business, and the Commercial club busted up. So Honey Creek isn't much of a town any more."

It is a straggling village, Honey Creek is—houses scattered about at the bases of the wide sweeping hills that mark the boundaries of the Missouri valley. A garage, a filling station, one store—most of the people are farmers. There isn't any mayor, or council.

"Oh, we manage to worry along without much government." One of the inhabitants remarked last night.

Wherefore Honey Creek's reception of the President's funeral train was bound to be informal. At dusk last night, the town's telephone operator called everybody up and passed out the information that the train would pass Honey Creek at 3 o'clock in the morning. That was all the preparation that preceded Honey Creek's demonstration.

Sitting on their porches, the residents talked it over, porch to porch.

"Well, a thing like this won't happen to Honey Creek again in 100 years," said H. French, who was president of the bank that went out of business.

"It will be something for our children to tell their grandchildren about, all right."

"Sure, I'm going down," announced Mace Hansen, who operated the filling station and who served overseas in the world war. "The President of the United States has got coming to him all the respect I can pay him, hasn't he?"

Alarm clocks were set for 1:45 a.m. One woman announced she would ring her dinner bell to wake up the neighborhood. Dr. J. W. Frazier, physician, farmer and justice of the peace, who lives across the road from the station, said he guessed he would sit up and read. "Might as well," he said. "For I don't think I'd get much sleep anyhow."

I stayed at the home of Mr. French, the former banker. It was agreed that we were to get up at 1:45 a.m. At 1:15 a.m. Mr. and Mrs. French and their two small boys and I were en route to the station.

"Did you sleep?" was the query with which each newcomer was greeted.

"Not much," was the answer over and over. "Every time I heard a train I'd jump out of bed."

Incidentally, Honey Creek is on the main line of the Chicago & North Western railway across Iowa, and 60 trains a day pass through there—most of them, it would seem, in the night.

By 2:30 a.m. the whole population of Honey Creek apparently was out on that station platform, or sitting in cars parked below. There was a great play of pocket flashlights, much tramping up and down and hunting for seats. In low, queerly hushed voices, the people discussed the time, crops, the time, their children, the time again, the probable size of the crowd in Omaha, and again the time.

The song of the crickets from Dr. Frazier's cornfield, on the other side of the tracks, made a sort of orchestral background for the conversation.

At 3 a.m. Mr. Ham came out of the ticket office and announced that the train was an hour late. There had been an accident somewhere over in Nebraska—an accident by which the train would certainly have gone in the ditch had it been traveling rapidly.

"Oh, what a mess that would be—with Pershing and Hoover and all those big fellows aboard," groaned Mace Hansen.

The talk drifted to Mrs. Harding. "They say she's left pretty well fixed," some one remarked. "The paper said he left near a million dollars." "I know," Mrs. French interrupted. "But think how lonely she'll be, how she'd rather have him back than a hundred million dollars."

"If only she had some sons or daughters to be with her," another woman sighed, running her fingers through her little boy's shock of yellow hair.

At 3:45 a light came around the bend—the pilot train, a locomotive, day coach and observation car—plunged past the crowd and on into the darkness.

Honey Creek climbed out of its Fords and got in line on the station platform. Two fathers with babies were given places in the front rank. The small boys hopped up on top of the fence. Miss Agnes Young, gray-haired spinster and owner of a large farm at Honey Creek, climbed up on her stepladder which she had carried half a mile to the station, slipping and sliding over muddy roads on foot in the dark.

A light shining up behind the trees around the bend, a mile away. That long, moaning whistle—

"Here she comes!" shrieked a small boy from his post on the signal tower.

The blinding shaft of light down the glittering rails—

"Don't look at it, Ward—it'll blind you!"

Again the whistle, imperious now, deafening—

"Now—watch for the last car, Junior—that lighted one—way back."

Roar and wind and trembling earth. A breathless, agonizing wait of that last car—

There it is! Yes, but dimly lighted. Now, look—quick—wreaths, flowers, a huge American flag. Swift realization that the casket must lie beneath that flag. A frenzied search for the guards. Red tail lights half a mile down the track—

"Well, it was worth it, wasn't it?"

"It was."

Bullfighting Is Not a Sport—It is a Tragedy
ERNEST HEMINGWAY—*Toronto Star*—10/20/1923

It was spring in Paris and everything looked just a little too beautiful. Mike and I decided to go to Spain. Strater drew us a fine map of Spain on the back of the menu of the Strix restaurant. On the same menu he wrote the name of a restaurant in Madrid where the specialty is young suckling pig roast, the name of a pension on the Via San Jerónimó where the bullfighters live, and sketched a plan showing where the Grecos are hung in the Prado.

Fully equipped with this menu and our old clothes, we started for Spain. We had one objective—to see bullfights.

We left Paris one morning and got off the train at Madrid the next afternoon, we saw our first bullfight at 4:30 that afternoon. It took about two hours to get tickets. We finally got them from scalpers for twenty-five pesetas apiece. The bull ring was entirely sold out. We had barrera seats. These the scalper explained in Spanish and broken French were the first row of the ringside, directly under the royal box, and immediately opposite where the bulls would come out.

We asked him if he didn't have any less distinguished seats for somewhere around twelve pesetas for the two tickets, but he was sold out. So we paid the fifty pesetas for the two tickets, and with the tickets in our pockets sat out on the sidewalk in front of a big café near the Puerta del Sol. It was very exciting, sitting out in front of a café your first day in Spain with a ticket in your pocket that meant that rain or shine you were going to see a bullfight in an hour and a half. In fact, it was so exciting that we started out for the bull ring on the outskirts of the city in about half an hour.

The bull ring or Plaza de Toros was a big, tawny brick amphitheater standing at the end of the street in an open field. The yellow and red Spanish flag was floating over it. Carriages were driving up and people getting out of buses. There was a great crowd of beggars around the entrance. Men were selling water out of big terra-cotta water bottles. Kids sold fans, canes, roasted salted almonds in paper spills, fruit and slabs of ice cream. The crowd was gay and cheerful but all intent on pushing toward the entrance. Mounted civil guards with patent leather cocked hats and carbines slung over their backs sat their horses like statues, and the crowd flowed through.

Inside they all stood around the bull ring, talking and looking up in the grandstand at the girls in the boxes. Some of the men had field glasses in order to look better. We found our seats and the crowd began to leave the ring and get into the rows of concrete seats. The ring was circular—that sounds foolish, but a boxing ring is square—with a sand floor. Around it was a red board fence—just high enough for a man to be able to vault over it. Between the board fence, which is called the barrera, and the first row of seats ran a narrow alleyway. Then came the seats which were just like a football stadium except that around the top ran a double circle of boxes.

Every seat in the amphitheater was full. The arena was cleared. Then on the far side of the arena out of the crowd, four heralds in medieval costume stood up and blew a blast on their trumpets. The band crashed out, and from the entrance on the far side of the ring four horsemen in black velvet with ruffs around their necks rode out into the white glare of the arena. The people on the sunny side were baking in the heat and fanning themselves. The whole sol side was a flicker of fans.

Behind the four horsemen came the procession of the bullfighters. They had been all formed in ranks in the entranceway ready to march out, and as the music started they came. In the front rank walked the three espadas or toreros, who would have charge of the killing of the six bulls of the afternoon.

They came walking out in heavily brocaded yellow and black costumes, the familiar "toreador" suit, heavy with gold embroidery, cape, jacket, shirt and collar, knee breeches, pink stockings, and low pumps. Always at bullfights afterwards the incongruity of those pink stockings used to strike me. Just behind the three principals—and after your first bullfight you do not look at their costumes but their faces—marched the teams or cuadrillas. They dressed in the same way but not as gorgeously as the matadors.

Back of the teams ride the picadors. Big, heavy, brown-faced men in wide flat hats, carrying lances like long window poles. They are astride horses that make Spark Plug look as trim and sleek as a King's Plate winner. Back of the pics come the gaily harnessed mule teams and the red-shorted monos or bull ring servants.

The bullfighters march in across the sand to the president's box. They march with easy professional stride, swinging along, not in the least theatrical except for their clothes. They all have the easy grace and slight slouch of the professional athlete. From their faces they might be major league ball players. They salute the president's box and then spread out along the barrera, exchanging their heavy brocaded capes for the fighting capes that have been laid along the red fence by the attendants.

We leaned forward over the barrera. Just below us the three matadors of the afternoon were leaning against the fence talking. One lighted a cigaret. He was a short, clear-skinned gypsy, Gitanillo, in a wonderful gold brocaded jacket, his short pigtail sticking out under his black cocked hat.

"He's not very fancy," a young man in a straw hat, with obviously American shoes, who sat on my left, said.

"But he sure knows bulls that boy. He's a great killer."

"You're an American, aren't you?" asked Mike.

"Sure," the boy grinned. "But I know this gang. That's Gitanillo. You want to watch him. The kid with the chubby face is Chicuelo. They say he doesn't really like bullfighting, but the town's crazy about him. The next to him is Villalta. He's the great one."

I had noticed Villalta. He was straight as a lance and walked like a young wolf. He was talking and smiling at a friend who leaned over the barrera. Upon his tanned cheekbone was a big patch of gauze held on with adhesive tape.

"He got gored last week at Malaga," said the American.

The American, whom later we were to learn to know and love as the Gin Bottle King, because of a great feat of arms performed at an early hour of the morning with a container of Mr. Gordon's celebrated product as his sole weapon in one of the four most dangerous situations I have even seen, said: "The show's going to begin."

Out in the arena the picadors had galloped their decrepit horses around the ring, sitting straight and stiff on their rocking chair saddles. Now all but three had ridden out of the ring. These three were huddled against the red painted fence of the barrera. Their horses backed against the fence, one eye bandaged, their lances at rest.

In rode two of the marshals in the velvet jackets and white ruffs. They galloped up to the president's box, swerved and saluted, doffing their hats and bowing low. From the box an object came hurtling down. One of the marshals caught it in his plumed hat.

"The key to the bull pen," said the Gin Bottle King.

The two horsemen whirled and rode across the arena. One of them tossed the key to a man in torero costume, they both saluted with a wave of their plumed hats, and had gone from the ring. The big gate was shut and bolted. There was no more entrance. The ring was complete.

The crowd had been shouting and yelling. Now it was dead silent. The man with the key stepped toward an iron barred, low, red door and unlocked the great sliding bar. He lifted it and stepped back. The door swung open. The man hid behind it. Inside it was dark.

Then, ducking his head as he came up out of the dark pen, a bull came into the arena. He came out all in a rush, big, black and white, weighing over a ton and moving with a soft gallop. Just as he came out the sun seemed to dazzle him for an instant. He stood as though he were frozen, his great crest of muscle up, firmly planted, his eyes looking around, his horns pointed forward, black and white and sharp as porcupine quills. Then he charged. And as he charged I suddenly saw what the bullfight was all about.

For the bull was absolutely unbelievable. He seemed like some great prehistoric animal, absolutely deadly and absolutely vicious. And he was silent. He charged silently and with a soft galloping rush. When he turned he turned on his four feet like a cat. When he charged the first thing that caught his eye was the picador on one of the wretched horses. The picador dug his spurs into the horse and they galloped away. The bull came on his rush, refused to be shaken off, and in full gallop crashed into the animal from the side, ignored the horse, drove one of his horns high into the thigh of the picador, and tore him, saddle and all, off the horse's back.

The bull went on without pausing to worry the picador lying on the ground. The next picador was sitting on his horse braced to receive the shock of the charge, his lance ready. The bull hit him sideways on, and horse and rider went high up in the air in a kicking mass and fell across the bull's back. As they came down the bull charged into them. The dough-faced kid, Chicuelo, vaulted over the fence, ran toward the bull and flopped his cape into the bull's face. The bull charged the cape and Chicuelo dodged backwards and had the bull clear in the arena.

Without an instant's hesitation the bull charged Chicuelo. The kid stood his ground, simply swung back on his heels and floated his cape like a ballet dancer's skirt into the bull's face as he passed.

"Olé!"—pronounced Oh-Lay!—roared the crowd.

The bull whirled and charged again. Without moving Chicuelo repeated the performance. His legs rigid, just withdrawing his body from the rush of the bull's horns and floating the cape out with that beautiful swing.

Again the crowd roared. The Kid did this seven times. Each time the bull missed him by inches. Each time he gave the bull a free shot at him. Each time the crowd roared. Then he flopped the cape once at the bull at the finish of a pass, swung it around behind him and walked away from the bull to the barrera.

"He's the boy with the cape all right," said the Gin Bottle King. "That swing he did with the cape's called a Veronica."

The chubby faced Kid who did not like bull fighting and had just done the seven wonderful Veronicas was standing against the fence just below us. His face glistened with sweat in the sun but was almost expressionless. His eyes were looking out across the arena where the bull was standing making up his mind to charge a picador. He was studying the bull because a few minutes later it would be his duty to kill him, and once he went out with his thin, red-hilted sword and his piece of red cloth to kill the bull in the final set it would be him or the bull. There are no drawn battles in bull fighting.

I am not going to describe the rest of the afternoon in detail. It was the first bullfight I ever saw, but it was not the best. The best was in the town of Pamplona high up on the hills of Navarre, and came weeks later. Up in Pamplona, where they have held six days of bullfighting each year since 1126 A.D., and where the bulls race through the streets of the town each morning at six o'clock with half the town running ahead of them. Pamplona, where every man and boy in town is an amateur bullfighter and where there is an amateur fight each morning that is attended by 20,000 people in which the amateur fighters are all unarmed and there is a casualty list at least equal to a Dublin election. But Pamplona, with the best bullfight and the wild tale of the amateur fights, comes in the second chapter.

I am not going to apologize for bullfighting. It is a survival of the days of the Roman Coliseum. But is does need some explanation. bullfighting is not a sport. It was never supposed to be. It is a tragedy. A very great tragedy. The tragedy is the death of a bull. It is played in three different acts.

The Gin Bottle King—who, by the way, does not drink gin—told us a lot of this that first night as we sat in the upstairs room of the little restaurant that made a specialty of roast young suckling pig, roasted on an oak plank and served with a mushroom tortilla and vino rojo. The rest we learn later at the bullfighters' pensione in the Via San Jeronimo, where one of the bullfighters had eyes like a rattlesnake.

Much of it we learned in the sixteen fights we saw in different parts of Spain from San Sebastian to Granada.

At any rate bullfighting is not a sport. It is a tragedy, and it symbolizes the struggle between man and the beasts. There are usually six bulls to fight. A fight is called a corrida de toros. Fighting bulls are bred like race horses, some of the oldest breeding establishments being several hundred years old. A good bull is worth $2,000. They are bred for speed, strength and viciousness. In other words a good fighting bull is an absolutely incorrigible bad bull.

bullfighting is an exceedingly dangerous occupation. In sixteen fights I saw there were only two in which there is no one badly hurt. On the other hand it is very remunerative. A popular espada gets $5,000 for his afternoon's work. An unpopular espada though may not get $500. Both run the same risks. It is a good deal like Grand Opera for the really great matadors except they run the chance of being killed every time they cannot hit high C.

No one at any time in the fight can approach the bull except directly from the front. That is where the danger comes. There are also all sorts of compli-cated passes that must be done with the cape, each requiring as much tech nique as a champion billiard player. And underneath it all is the necessity for playing the old tragedy in the absolutely custom bound, law-laid-down way. It must all be done gracefully, seemingly effortlessly and always with dignity. The worst criticism the Spaniards ever make of a bullfighter is that his work is "vulgar."

The three absolute acts of tragedy are the first entry of the bull when the pic-adors receive the shock of his attacks and attempt to protect their horses with their lances. Then the horses go out and the second act is the planting of the banderillos. This is one of the most interesting and difficult parts but among the easiest for a new bullfight fan to appreciate the technique. The banderillos are three-foot, gaily colored darts with a small fish hook prong in the end. The man who is going to plant them walks out into the arena alone with the bull. He lifts the banderillos at arm's length and points them toward the bull. Then he calls

"Toro! Toro!" The bull charges and the banderillero rises his toes, bends in a curve forward and just as the bull is about to hit him drops the darts into the bull's hump just back of his horns.

They must go in evenly, one on each side. They must not be shoved, or thrown or stuck in from the side. This is the first time the bull has been completely baffled, there is the prick of the darts that he cannot escape and there are no horses for him to charge into. But he charges the man again and again and each time he gets a pair of the long banderillos that hang from his hump by their tiny barbs and flop like porcupine quills.

Last is the death of the bull, which is in the hands of the matador who has had charge of the bull since his first attack. Each matador has two bulls in the afternoon. The death of the bull is most formal and can only be brought about in one way, directly from the front by the matador who must receive the bull in full charge and kill him with a sword thrust between the shoulders just back of the neck and between the horns. Before killing the bull he must first do a series of passes with the muleta, a piece of red cloth he carries about the size of a large napkin. With the muleta the torero must show his complete mastery of the bull, must make the bull miss him again and again by inches, before he is allowed to kill him. It is in this phase that most of the fatal accidents occur.

The word "toreador" is obsolete in Spanish and is never used. The torero is usually called an espada or swordsman. He must be proficient in all three acts of the fight. In the first he uses the cape and does veronicas and protects the picadors by taking the bull out and away from them when they are spilled to the ground. In the second act he plants the banderillos. In the third act he masters the bull with the muleta and kills him.

Few toreros excel in all three departments. Some, like young Chicuelo, are unapproachable in their cape work. Others like the late Joselito are wonderful banderilleros. Only a few are great killers. Most of the greatest killers are gypsies.

Battling Siki
WESTBROOK PEGLER—*Chicago Tribune*—12/17/1925

Battling Siki, who tried hard to understand civilization but never quite got the idea, will be trundled out over the roads to Long Island today and buried in the civilized way without a single thump of the tom-tom. A negro minister will commend him to the mercy of the Christian God and negroes will shoulder the casket from the tailboard of the motor hearse at the brink of the hole, but even so there will be nobody there who really understood Siki because the difference was no mere matter of complexion.

In fact, the one person who knew Battling Siki best and loved him as a man loves a friendly but mischievous pet, was a white man, Bob Levy, his fight manager. Siki called him Papa Bob and often assaulted him with moist kisses in the same conciliatory way that a chicken-killing airedale with feathers in its whiskers might slap its master on the cheek with eight inches of sopping tongue.

Siki had heard a lot about the virtues of civilization in a dozen years of exposure to its decorous influence, but in the last minute of his life, when he fell in a dirty gutter in Hell's Kitchen, where the lights of Broadway throw deep shadows and churches face speakeasies across the street, civilization must have been a puzzle and a josh to him.

As Siki stumbled over the curb and his dented plug hat bounced away he may have giggled at the irony of the matter, for he had come all the way from the jungle to the haunts of civilization and chivalry to be shot in the back. He couldn't have received a worse deal back home, where they make no great boast of their civilization.

Siki was one who could giggle with his last gasp, too. He laughed right in Paul Berlenbach's face throughout their fight in the old Garden and the harder Paul slugged him the more he seemed to enjoy the joke. It wasn't that laborious, sneering laugh that a suffering fighter uses to pretend that he can't be hurt.

When Siki laughed it wasn't a mere matter of puckering his face. His mouth would gape open till it looked like a satchel with a red lining and you'd find yourself laughing with him.

As Siki got the idea, civilization was something that was supposed to make men do things they didn't want to do and tried to curtail their natural enjoyment of life. Civilization was a good thing in theory, but it didn't work and Siki saw proof that it didn't work.

For one thing, under civilization, if a man stole your woman, or your ox, or your land you were not allowed to go over to that man's house and razor his head off in person. You were supposed to call a cop and maybe, after a long time, the man would be locked up in a cage for a term of months or years. However, it was against the rules of civilization to kill people.

And then civilization fell out with itself and Siki was given a gun with a knife on the end of it and invited to kill everyone he saw wearing a certain kind of uniform.

Under civilization a man was allowed just one wife at a time and by the strict rule he was supposed to be true to her.

But Siki rattled around Paris enough to learn that civilization was, in civilized language, bunk in this respect.

Siki came to the United States and they told him civilization had made a law whereby it was wrong to drink liquor. Siki had heard that civilization laid considerable store by its laws. By orderly obedience to the law did the civilized man show his superiority over the wild man.

And then Siki toured half of the United States and found civilized men everywhere, both white and black, who would sell him liquor and get him stewed contrary to the statutes. He was more often drunk than sober in a civilized land where the law plainly said there shouldn't be any liquor.

Siki went to nightclubs and to the weird squealing of the woodwinds and the muffled thump of tom-toms, the music of civilization, he saw half-naked black-and-tans wiggling and squirming in the dances of an enlightened tribe.

He fought in the ring and when blood showed the civilized crowds came up from their chairs roaring.

So from what he saw of it, Siki frankly didn't get the plot of this business called civilization. The whole thing was too much for the simple mind of a primitive African, who got a late start at the racket.

The End of *The World*
HEYWOOD BROUN—*New York World Telegram*—2/28/1931

I sat and watched a paper die. We waited in the home of a man who once had run it. A flash came over the phone. *The World* was ended.

F.P.A. looked eagerly at a bowl of fruit upon the table and said, "Mr. Swope, where have you been buying your apples?"

The World fired me, and the *Telegram* gave me a job. Now the *Telegram* owns the *World*. This is a fantastic set of chances almost like those which might appear in somebody's dream of revenge. But I never thought much of revenge. I wouldn't give a nickel for this one. If I could, by raising my hand, bring dead papers back to life I'd do so.

Sometimes in this column I have opposed the theories of those who would break up mergers, end chain stores and try the trick of unscrambling large-scale production. I've said that this couldn't be done—that it wasn't even expedient. In the long run the happiness of all of us depends upon increased efficiency and a shorter sum of toil. That's true. I still believe it. I wouldn't weep about a shoe factory or a branch line railroad shutting down.

But newspapers are different. I am a newspaperman. There are many things to be said for this new combination. It is my belief that the Scripps-Howard chain is qualified by its record and its potentialities to carry on the Pulitzer tradition of its liberal journalism. In fact, I'll go further and say that, as far as my personal experience goes, the *Telegram* has been more alert and valiant in its independent attitude than the *World* papers.

Yet I hope, at least, that this may be the end of mergers. The economic pressure for consolidation still continues. A newspaper is, among other things, a business. And, even so, it must be more than that. A lawyer at the hearing before Surrogate Foley expressed amazement that a paper which had lost almost $2,000,000 within a year could command any of that intangible value known as "good will." He was reasoning from the basis upon which fish are canned and wire wheels turned out.

A newspaper is a rule unto itself. It has a soul for salvation or damnation. I was pleased to hear much said about intangibles in all accounts of the preliminary negotiations leading up to the present merger. I was glad that for once the emphasis was taken away from mere machinery. The fact of presses and linotype equipment was never stressed in the proceedings. This didn't count. The intangibles of the newspaper are the men and women who make it.

First in America, and now in a frenzied form in Russia, there grows a cult which bows and bangs its head upon the floor in worship of the machine. In some calculations man is no more than a device to pull upon a gadget. But here, at last, there was talk of millions, and checks in huge amounts were passed—not for apparatus, moving belts and intricate mechanism. This was a deal for a name and for some of the people who contributed to the making of the name.

Since my feeling is strong that a newspaper can neither rise nor fall beyond or below its staff, I was stirred by the notion—the dream—that *World* men might take over the *World*. I realize, as they do now, the difficulties which lay in the path of any such plan. I'll readily admit that 1,000 to 1 would be a generous price against any such undertaking. But we are, or ought to be, lovers of long shots. There's nothing particularly stirring when the favorite coasts home in front. Although the newspaper crowd didn't put their project over, it isn't fair to call this miss plain failure.

For almost the first time in my life I watched reporters animated by a group consciousness. Newspapermen are blandly and, I think, blindly individualistic. Once I was president of a press writers' union. There were four members. The three others were the secretary, the vice-president and the treasurer. The treasurer never had much responsibility. Nobody would join us, because the average reporter carried in his knapsack the baton of a managing editor, or even the dim hope of being some day a dramatic critic. What did he want with organization? He stood on two feet—a single unit.

But for a time down in the *World* office there was the excitement, the hip-hop-hooray—call it even the hysteria—of mob movement, of people rubbing shoulders and saying, "We are in this boat together."

One of the things which would have made the fruition of the plan extremely difficult is the fact that a paper lives or dies by personality. When forty or fifty are banded together they must select a single one to be the leader and articulate representative. Still, in any dream of a cooperative commonwealth I've always had the feeling that newspapers most of all were fit subjects for some sort of socialization. I've never known even the most obscure reporter who didn't think he knew more about running a paper than the man who owned it. I've always felt that way myself. And once I was right.

The curious thing concerning the death of the *World* was the manner in which it became animate just before the final rattle within its throat. Within the last two or three years there must have been times in which the morale of the staff was low. Last night I went late to see the men I knew and had worked with long ago—that is, two years, or maybe three years, which is a long span in the life of any roving and rebellious columnist. I never found the paper pounding and pulsing quite so much as it did now—when it was dead.

We sat together in a very vigorous sort of democracy. At first I felt I might be out of place as one who was an ex-*World* man. But by four in the morning we were all "ex." We had ex-managing editor, ex-city editor and dozens of ex-reporters. For the first time within many months it was possible for somebody who covered a district to point the finger of scorn or accusation at somebody who had been his boss and spill his whole mind and emotion. You didn't have to "sir" anybody or say "very good" or "yes" unless you wanted to. Out of a situation which was certainly tragic to many there was at least a glimpse of that heaven in which we may all walk and between harp tunes look up and say with impunity to any passing angel or archangel, "Oh, is that so!"

Naturally, I have both hope and confidence in the new paper. Like John Brown's body, the *World* goes marching on. To heights, I hope. But something is gone. They aren't all marching. Men have dropped out. For them there will be nothing more on any newspaper, and I think of these casualties. I think of a profession which grows efficient and overcrowded. And to those who can no longer make the grade and who stand under the indictment of being not good enough I bow low, I swing my hat, as if it bore a plume, and say:

"Good, bad or indifferent, you have been in it. You belong. Some part of stuff set down on paper was you, and ever will be."

Death in the Dust

JOHN STEINBECK—*San Francisco News*—10/21/1936

[Three years before the publication of *The Grapes of Wrath*, John Steinbeck visited California squatters' camps and filed this dispatch for the *San Francisco News*.]

The squatters' camps are located all over California. Let us see what a typical one is like. It is located on the banks of a river, near an irrigation ditch or on a side road where a spring of water is available. From a distance it looks like a city dump, and well it may, for the city dumps are the sources for the material of which it is built. You can see a litter of dirty rags and scrap iron, of houses built of weeds, of flattened cans or of paper. It is only on close approach that it can be seen that these are homes.

Here is a house built by a family who have tried to maintain a neatness. The house is about 10 feet by 10 feet, and it is built completely of corrugated paper. The roof is peaked, the walls are tacked to a wooden frame. The dirt floor is swept clean, and along the irrigation ditch or in the muddy river the wife of the family scrubs clothes without soap and tries to rinse out the mud in muddy water.

The spirit of this family is not quite broken, for the children, three of them, still have clothes, and the family possesses three old quilts and a soggy, lumpy mattress. But the money so needed for food cannot be used for soap nor for clothes.

With the first rain the carefully built house will slop down into a brown, pulpy mush; in a few months the clothes will fray off the children's bodies, while the lack of nourishing food will subject the whole family to pneumonia when the first cold comes. Five years ago this family had 50 acres of land and $1,000 in the bank. The wife belonged to a sewing circle and the man was a member of the Grange. They raised chickens, pigs, pigeons and vegetables and fruit for their own use; and their land produced the tall corn of the middle west. Now they have nothing.

If the husband hits every harvest without delay and works the maximum time, he may make $400 this year. But if anything happens, if his old car breaks down, if he is late and misses a harvest or two, he will have to feed his whole family on as little as $150. But there is still pride in this family. Wherever they stop they try to put the children in school. It may be that the children will be in a school for as much as a month before they are moved to another locality.

There is more filth here. The tent is full of flies clinging to the apple box that is the dinner table, buzzing about the foul clothes of the children, particularly the baby, who has not been bathed nor cleaned for several days. This family has been on the road longer than the builder of the paper house. There is no toilet here, but there is a clump of willows nearby where human feces lie exposed to the flies—the same flies that are in the tent.

Two weeks ago there was another child, a four-year-old boy. For a few weeks they had noticed that he was kind of lackadaisical, that his eyes had been feverish. They had given him the best place in the bed, between father and mother. But one night he went into convulsions and died, and the next morning the coroner's wagon took him away. It was one step down.

They knew pretty well that it was a diet of fresh fruit, beans and little else that caused his death. He had had no milk for months. With this death there came a change of mind in this family. The father and mother now feel that paralyzed dullness with which the mind protects itself against too much sorrow and too much pain.

Here, in the faces of the husband and his wife, you begin to see an expression you will notice on every face; not worry, but absolute terror of the starvation that crowds in against the borders of the camp. This man has tried to make a toilet by digging a hole in the ground near his house and surrounding it with an old piece of burlap. But he will only do things like that this year. He is a newcomer and his spirit and his decency and his sense of his own dignity have not been quite wiped out. Next year he will be like his next-door neighbor.

This is a family of six; a man, his wife and four children. They live in a tent the color of the ground. Rot has set in on the canvas so that the flaps and the sides hang in tatters and are held together with bits of rusty bailing wire. There is one bed in the family and that is a big tick lying on the ground inside the tent. They have one quilt and a piece of canvas for bedding. The sleeping arrangement is clever. Mother and father lie down together and two children lie between them. Then, heading the other way, the other two children lie, the littler ones.

If the mother and father sleep with their legs spread wide, there is room for the legs of the children. And this father will not be able to make a maximum of $400 a year anymore because he is no longer alert; he isn't quick at piecework, and he is not able to fight clear of the dullness that has settled on him.

The dullness shows in the faces of this family, and in addition there is a sullenness that makes them taciturn. Sometimes they still start the older children off to school, but the ragged little things will not go; they hide themselves in ditches or wander off by themselves until it is time to go back to the tent, because they are scorned in the school. The better-dressed children shout and jeer, the teachers are quite often impatient with these additions to their duties, and the parents of the "nice" children do not want to have disease carriers in the schools.

The father of this family once had a little grocery store and his family lived in back of it so that even the children could wait on the counter. When the drought set in there was no trade for the store anymore. This is the middle class of the squatters' camp. In a few months this family will slip down to the lower class. Dignity is all gone, and spirit has turned to sullen anger before it dies.

The next-door-neighbor family, of man, wife and three children of from three to nine years of age, have built a house by driving willow branches into the ground and wattling weeds, tin, old paper and strips of carpet against them. A few branches are placed over the top to keep out the noonday sun. It would not turn water at all. There is no bed.

Somewhere the family has found a big piece of old carpet. It is on the ground. To go to bed the members of the family lie on the ground and fold the carpet up over them.

The three-year-old child has a gunnysack tied about his middle for clothing. He has the swollen belly caused by malnutrition. He sits on the ground in the sun in front of the house, and the little black fruit flies buzz in circles and land on his closed eyes and crawl up his nose until he weakly brushes them away. They try to get at the mucus in the eye corners. This child seems to have the reactions of a baby much younger. The first year he had a little milk, but he has had none since. He will die in a very short time.

The older children may survive. Four nights ago the mother had a baby in the tent, on the dirt carpet. It was born dead, which was just as well because she could not have fed it at the breast; her own diet will not produce milk. After it was born and she had seen that it was dead, the mother rolled over and lay still for two days. She is up today, tottering around. The last baby, born less than a year ago, lived a week.

This woman's eyes have the glazed, faraway look of a sleepwalker's eyes. She does not wash clothes anymore. The drive that makes for cleanliness has been drained out of her and she hasn't the energy. The husband was a sharecropper once, but he couldn't make it go. Now he has lost even the desire to talk. He will not look directly at you, for that requires will, and will needs strength. He is a bad fieldworker for the same reason.

It takes him a long time to make up his mind, so he is always late in moving, and late in arriving in the fields. His top wage, when he can find work now, which isn't often, is $1 a day. The children do not even go to the willow clump anymore. They squat where they are and kick a little dirt. The father is vaguely aware that there is a culture of hookworm, in the mud along the riverbank. He knows the children will get it on their bare feet. But he hasn't the will nor the energy to resist. Too many things have happened to him.

This is the lower class of the camp. This is what the man in the tent will be in six months; what the man in the paper house with its peaked roof will be in a year, after his house has washed down and his children have sickened or died, after the loss of dignity and spirit have cut him down to a kind of subhumanity.

Helpful strangers are not well received in this camp. The local sheriff makes a raid now and then for a wanted man, and if there is labor trouble the vigilantes may burn the poor houses. Social workers have taken case histories. They are filed and open for inspection. These families have been questioned over and over about their origins, number of children living and dead.

The information is taken down and filed. That is that. It has been done so often, and so little has come of it. And there is another way for them to get attention. Let an epidemic break out, say typhoid or scarlet fever, and the county doctor will come to the camp and hurry the infected cases to the pesthouse. But malnutrition is not infectious, nor is dysentery, which is almost the rule among the children.

The county hospital has no room for measles, mumps, whooping cough; and yet these are often deadly to hunger-weakened children. And although we hear much about the free clinics for the poor, these people do not know how to get the aid and they do not get it. Also, since most of their dealings with authority are painful to them, they prefer not to take the chance. This is the squatters' camp. Some are a little better, some much worse. I have described some typical families. In some of the camps there are as many as 300 families like these. Some are so far from water that it must be bought at five cents a bucket. And if these men steal, if there is developing among them a suspicion and hatred of well-dressed, satisfied people, the reason is not to be sought in their origin nor in any tendency to weakness in their character.

Barcelona Bombing
HERBERT L. MATTHEWS—*The New York Times*—3/18/1938

Barcelona has lived through twelve air raids in less than twenty-four hours, and the city is shaken and terror-struck. Human beings have seldom had to suffer as these people are suffering under General Francisco Franco's determined effort to break their spirit and induce their government to yield.

I have just come back from the principal morgue, which is at the Clinical Hospital, and there I counted 328 dead lying side by side. Those were more or less whole bodies. Then there are the others in hospitals and, above all, those who lie in the ruins of dozens of buildings and whose bodies never will be recovered.

The destruction is in one sense haphazard, for the bombs are dropped anywhere at all, without any attempt at specific objectives. However, there is an obvious plan, that every part of the city, from the richest to the poorest, shall get its full measure of tragedy.

Spaniards are meeting this trial—and it is the greatest that their people have had to bear in the whole war—with the stoicism and the dignity of their race, but they are only human, and this is terribly hard to bear. Foreigners are deserting their hotels for the frontier as fast as they can get conveyance, for there is a genuine sense of impending disaster here among those who have escaped so far.

One sees such occurrences as a British newspaperman giving his wife some money in case "something silly happens." A chambermaid said to me this morning: "We are all going to be killed—all."

A clerk at a drugstore sighed as he handed over some headache medicine. "Oh, for a plane to fly to France," he said. "I don't want to die."

7:40, 10:25, 1:55—those were tragic moments during the day. It was not necessary to send many planes each time. Fearful damage done in the last-mentioned raid required only five heavy bombers.

The account of what happened today is an unmitigated succession of horrors, and one feels helpless trying to convey the horror of all this in cold print, which people read and throw away.

One comes back from the scenes dazed: men, women, and children buried alive, screaming in the wreckage of their houses like trapped animals. *I have never seen so many weeping women.*

This bombing is meant to strike terror, demoralize the rear guard, and weaken resistance, because human beings are not built to withstand such horror. It is true they are stricken by terror, all right—terror that freezes the blood and makes one either hysterical or on the verge of hysteria. But then, too, one would not be human if it did not cause rage—deep, burning rage. These people would like to return the compliment.

A tram was wrecked and everyone in it killed or wounded. A truck was still burning, and something black that had been a human being had just been taken out. And there was the noise—ambulances dashing up with whistles blowing, women screaming and struggling hysterically, men shouting. Up the block a house was burning fiercely.

And all around, everywhere we went, were wrecked houses, dead and wounded, and those intangibles of fear, horror, and fury.

I watched them take two wounded persons from a building in the first bombing this morning. Both had been completely buried. A woman was screaming so weakly that we thought she was a child until they extricated her limp body. She seemed dead then, but they rushed her away to a hospital.

The other was a fifteen-year-old boy. By some miracle he had not been crushed, although I could see from his hair down to his bare feet he had been completely buried. His body did not seem to be hurt, but something else was, for he could not control his muscles—the twitching of his face or shuddering.

There are those freakish things which happen to intensify the horror. There is that house where nothing remains on the fifth floor except some clothes hanging on a rack. In another place a corner of the kitchen has somehow escaped, and we could see that the housewife had not had time to wash the dishes. Once a funeral passed along a street where bombs had fallen. There could have been no fitter symbol.

But life must go on. They have been repairing car tracks and clearing wreckage. After each raid they do it. Then they wait for the next.

It is surely the most savage and most ruthless punishment any modern city has taken.

The raid at 1:55 this afternoon left Barcelona shaking under the strain.

This writer was in a restaurant, eating lunch. All of us got up hastily to dash toward the back as the building shook, and I watched in amazement as the windows bent inward under the strain without breaking.

One takes what humor one can out of this tragedy; otherwise it would be hard to remain sane. For my own part I did not find it amusing to see a great hulking fellow who was eating with his girl jump up and beat her to the kitchen by three strides. Another thing, at which everybody laughs ruefully today, is the way everybody jumps at any unusual noise—the horns of cars that sound siren-like, the banging of doors, the roar of automobile motors. I even saw a cat jump as if it had an electric shock when a shopkeeper suddenly lowered his blinds.

There is one remark I heard this afternoon that sticks, for it was not said in jest:

"It may not be the end of the war, but it feels like the end of the world!"

Success
WESTBROOK PEGLER—Scripps Howard—11/1938

There was a gentle, kind old man stopping at the inn on the shore of the Gulf of Mexico a few days ago who somehow looked familiar and turned out to be Harry Daugherty, the Attorney General and tough guy of the Warren G. Harding Presidency. Time had changed Mr. Daugherty. He was seventy-six years old now and softened up by the blows of personal and political tragedy. His wife had died after twenty-eight years of invalidism; his son, Draper, the pride and hope of his younger days, had died some years ago, and of course the smash and scandal of the Harding administration had left scars even on the cast-iron hide of a man who was more furiously hated by more personal enemies, I suppose, than any other American since Thad Stevens.

I once was assigned to follow Mr. Daugherty to Miami and wherever else he might go at a time when there was some thought that he might jump the country and hole up in some banana port to avoid examination as a witness in certain phases of the Ohio regime in Washington.

Knowing that Mrs. Daugherty was very sick, and wanting not to be a nuisance, I proposed to her husband after several days' surveillance that we make a deal. I was to let him alone and he promised to tell me in good time when he was leaving and where he was going. A week later he telephoned me at my room in Miami that he was going back to Washington that night, and that was all there was to it.

But the old man chuckled as we sat in the dark on the front porch at the thought of a reporter trailing an Attorney General of the United States who had William J. Burns and his department fly cops doing the same to many worthy citizens. Mr. Daugherty had J. Edgar Hoover, too, and Gaston Means, the foulest crook, at a rough estimate, that this country has ever produced.

Mr. Daugherty has been blind in one eye and deaf in one ear for many years, and now his good eye and ear are none too good, but good enough, at that, says he, to see and hear the little good that there is in the world. He lives almost altogether in the past now, in the company of men who have died since the Ohio crowd went whooping into Washington with Prohibition and Wayne Wheeler.

In his time he ripped and slashed for power and came on to be the personal boss of a President of the United States, so it was a little comic that night when the pretty young mother with the little boy planned to go to the movies and the old-time tyrant told her to run right along and not worry, for he, Harry Daugherty, personally would sit up in the rocker in the dark at the foot of the little boy's bed and watch over him.

I mean no wrong to Mr. Daugherty when I say that irresistibly I was reminded of Damon Runyon's story of the retired safe blower and the kid, called "Butch Minds the Baby." Mr. Daugherty said the little boy looked just like his boy Draper at the same age, and that he would like to sit in the dark and rock and cover him if he stirred or get him a drink—or anything.

Next day Karl Bickel came over—Bickel, the ex-president of the United Press, who battled around the world for years and years and clawed his way to the top in tough competition, and then suddenly chucked it to retire to a drowsy, sunny little town 'way down the Florida Gulf Coast and putter in little interests such as the Cabana Club and Doc Halton's Free Clinic for the sallow children of the pure Anglo-Saxon backwoods crackers.

It costs $5 overhead to detach a cracker child from his or her adenoids and tonsils and free the patient of hookworm, and the doctor, whose services are tossed in free, is now working on his last batch in the entire county, a group of twenty.

Mr. Daugherty and Mr. Bickel sometimes sat in the sun, two retired guys who had been so fierce and fast in action so short a time ago, talking like Noah and the hero of the Johnstown flood, of times gone past. And there was a man in the placid little community who went about leading a soft-eyed gentle old greyhound on a leash.

"Nice dog you have there," Mr. Bickel said. "Is he a racing dog?"

"He was," the man said. "He was a racing dog. His name is Smiles. He was a very good, fast dog, but one night he caught the rabbit. After that they lose interest. They discover that the thing they have been chasing so hard is just a phony, and they just lie down in the box and watch the other dogs run, like saying, 'Go ahead and run yourselves ragged for a mess of hair and sawdust!'"

Both Mr. Daugherty and Mr. Bickel took a liking to Smiles, and he would stretch out in some shady spot, sigh deeply and go to sleep.

Reflections on Gandhi
WALTER LIPPMANN—*New York Herald Tribune*—2/3/1948

In the life and death of Mahatma Gandhi we have seen reenacted in our time the supreme drama of humanity. Gandhi was a political leader and he was a seer, and perhaps never before on so grand a scale has anyone sought to shape the course of events in the world as it is by the example of a spirit which was not of the world as it is.

Gandhi was, as St. Paul said, transformed in the renewing state of mind, he was not "conformed to this world." Yet he sought to govern turbulent masses of men who were still very much conformed to this world, and have not been transformed. He died by violence as he was staking his life in order to set the example of non-violence.

Thus he posed again the perennial question of how the insight of the seers and saints is related to the work of legislators, rulers, and statesmen. That they are in conflict is only too plain, and yet it is impossible to admit, as Gandhi refused to admit, that the conflict can never be resolved. For it is necessary to govern mankind and it is necessary to transform men.

Perhaps we may say that the insight of the governors of men is, as it were, horizontal: They act in the present, with beings as they are, with the knowledge they possess, with what they can now understand, with the mixture of their passions and desires and instincts. They must work with concrete and with the plainly and generally intelligible things.

The insight of the seers, on the contrary, is vertical: They deal, however wide their appeal, with each person potentially, as he might be transformed, renewed and regenerated. And because they appeal to experience which men have not yet had, with things that are not at hand and are out of their immediate reach, with the invisible and the unattained, they speak and act, as Gandhi did, obscurely, appealing to the imagination by symbolic evocation and subtle example.

The ideals of human life which the seers teach—nonresistance, humility, and poverty and chastity—have never been and can never be the laws of a secular society. Chastity, consistently and versally pursued, would plunge it into misery and disease. Humility and nonresistance, if they were the rule, would mean the triumph of predatory force.

Is it possible that the greatest seers and teachers did not know this, and that what they enjoined upon men was a kind of suicide and self-annihilation? Obviously not. Their wisdom was not naïve, and it can be understood if we approach it not as the rules of conduct but as an insight into the economy and the order and quality of the passions.

At the summit of their wisdom what they teach is, I think, not how in the practical issues of daily life men in society can and should behave but to what ultimate values they should give their allegiance. Thus the injunction to render unto Caesar the things that are Caesar's is not a definite political principle which can be applied to define the relation of Church and State. It is an injunction as to where men shall have their ultimate obligations, that in rendering to Caesar the things that are Caesar's, they should not give to Caesar their ultimate loyalty, but should reserve it.

In the same manner, to have humility is to have, in the last reaches of conviction, a saving doubt. To embrace poverty is to be without possessiveness and a total attachment to things and to honors. To be nonresistant is to be at last noncompetitive.

What the seer points toward is best described in the language of St. Paul as the creation of the new man. "And that ye put on the new man, after which God is created in righteousness and true holiness." What is this new man? He is the man who has been renewed and is "no longer under a schoolmaster," whose passions have been altered, as Gandhi sought to alter the passions of his countrymen, so that they need no discipline from without because they have been transformed from within. Such regenerated men can, as Confucius said, follow what their hearts desire without transgressing what is right. They are "led of the spirit" in the Pauline language, and therefore they "are not under the law."

It is not for such men as them that governments are instituted and laws enacted and enforced. These are for the old Adam. It is for the aggressive, possessive, carnal appetites of the old Adam that there are punishments and rewards, and for his violence a superior force.

It is only for the regenerate man, whose passions have been transformed, that the discipline of the law and of power are no longer needed, nor any incentive or reward beyond the exquisite and exhilarating wholesomeness and unity and freedom of his own passions.

The Sorehead
MURRAY KEMPTON—*New York Post*—11/6/1952

The sun was shining, just as it always does, yesterday morning; the elevator operators, the charwomen and the waiters went about their business at the Hotel Commodore with no visible signs of enchantment.

Downstairs at Eisenhower's headquarters, they moved in silence and slow time, still prisoners of the dream. The mimeograph machine ground forth the itinerary of the General's newest flight; reading it, there was a moment when you were hearing again the marching orders of the crusade, but this was only the winner going off to play golf on a ten-day pass.

The sun was shining, and it was the same 42d Street; the taxi drivers growled the old fraternal obscenities at one another. Nothing had changed; nothing ever will, I suppose. There was no surface sign that this was the end of the world. But for my money, it was the end of world; and neither sun nor the amenities is going to trap me into saying something pleasant about it.

The knuckleheads have beaten the eggheads. You're not going to catch this baby jumping over the net and extending his hand to the winner. Would Colonel McCormick extend his hand to me?

The difference between me and the General is that I may be just and I may be fair, but I sure ain't friendly. David Dubinsky can go ahead and call up Winthrop Aldrich any time he chooses.

The Republicans were sitting in the Commodore celebrating their deliverance Tuesday night. One of the attendants came in and asked whether a Dr. Hartman was in the house. "Oh, Harry needs a doctor tonight, oh, Harry needs a doctor," some wit sang out again and again in one long croon of hate. The man sitting at my right hand said in tones of the philosopher that, after all, these people had been losing for twenty years and they deserve a chance to win.

What is this, Ebbets Field? The Republicans haven't deserved to win since

Lincoln and they don't deserve to win this one. The only justification for their quadrennial assault on truth and reason was the kind of excuse people used to give for holding debutante parties during the depression; it gave employment to a lot of people. But it was one thing to put up with a campaign proposed by B.B.D. & O. and something else again to have it win.

I suppose the woman with the diamond latticework who was pointed out to me as Mrs. Alfred Gwynne Vanderbilt has been losing for twenty years, and I've been winning. Man and boy, I've been loosing since birth, and the only time I've ever won has been with the Democrats. Couldn't George Sokolsky and Fred Waring at least leave me that.

I've been a Giant fan since 1930—four miserable pennants. When a ball player breaks his ankle, it has to be Monte Irvin. When a pitcher shows up with a back ailment defying medical science, it has to be Sal Maglie. Why does it always have to be my team?

During the war, I had a brief, tenuous relationship with an outfit called the 38th Division. Its nickname was the Cyclone Division because it had swept through the enemies of freedom. Of course not. They called it the Cyclone Division because all its tents got blown down on maneuvers. That's how it is with my team every time. I can't even persuade my kinds to be Republicans to escape the family curse.

There are those who say at least Adlai Stevenson was right, and we have the satisfaction of knowing we lost a good cause. I think it would be a little better to know you'd lost in a bad cause. The notion that you deserved to win and didn't may bring some lonely gratification to the noble of spirit; for me, it makes the whole thing twice as bad.

I should have spent election night with Tallulah Bankhead croaking curses upon the electorate, with Joe Bushkin playing a little blues through the smoke behind. That would have been the way to go out—not watching some idiot girl with a dress imprinted with her affection for Ike in five different languages waving a microphone around the Commodore. The sun yesterday may have shined on the just and the unjust.

It didn't shine on me, Mac; it didn't shine on me.

La Nacha, Dirty Dope Queen of the Border
Ruben Salazar—*El Paso Herald-Post*—8/17/1955

La Nacha is the Dope Queen of the Border. She is big stuff. But she will sell you one "papel" (paper) of heroin just like any "pusher" on a street corner.

If you aren't too far gone, the dirty-looking stuff in the folded paper is good for two shots. But that's true only for those who are beginning.

A dope addict, whom I will call "Hypo," buys the $10 size. It has more than the two of the $5 papers, Hypo said. One lasts him a day—most days.

HE MET THE QUEEN

La Nacha—right name Ignacia Jasso—lives in a good house in a bad neighborhood. She's fat, dark, cynical and around 60. She deals out misery from her comfortable home.

She sells usually what is called a "dirty load," which is one that is not white as heroin should be, but a dirty, dusty color.

Her prices are in American money. She does business with many American addicts. She's as casual about it as if she were selling tortillas.

Hypo took me to La Nacha's home and introduced me to the dope queen.

I visited her twice. The first time Hypo and I bought a $5 paper of heroin. The second time we bought the large economy $10 size.

The papers contained dope all right. I saw Hypo, an El Paso married man of 24 whose 19-year-old wife has a three-month-old baby, inject himself with the "carga" (load).

HE'S GOT TO HAVE IT

Hypo, who says he wants to be cured, cannot live without heroin. It costs him about $10 a day—or hours of excruciating pain. Hypo prefers heroin to pain and gets the $10 a day any way he can. He sold all his furniture for heroin. He was evicted from his apartment for not paying rent. He has stolen, borrowed and now has given me his story for $15 which he spent on heroin.

Hypo and I went to visit La Nacha in the afternoon. We parked the car a few blocks from her house. She lives in Bellavista district, which means "Beautiful View." It is far from beautiful. The streets are unpaved and most of the houses are adobe. Naked kids were running about the streets.

We turned on Mercuro Alley and walked toward La Nacha's house, which is on the corner of the alley and Violetas (Violets) Street. Hers is the only decent-looking house in the neighborhood. It is yellow and has fancy iron grillwork on the windows.

SHE HAS A TV SET

Hypo and I walked through the nicely kept green patio.

Inside, the house has all the conveniences of a modern home: gas, stove, nice living room furniture, TV and a saint's statue on the wall.

I had been to Hypo's El Paso apartment and couldn't help thinking about his bare rooms after he had sold the furniture for heroin. The last time I had been at Hypo's apartment, I had seen the baby on the floor on a blanket and

Hypo's wife sitting in a corner watching the baby. There was a sad, vacant look in her eyes.

Once inside the house, which Hypo knows so well that he doesn't even bother to knock, we met Nacha's daughter. She was sitting on a bed talking to another woman. Hypo told her he was going away and wanted to introduce me so I could buy the stuff myself.

"You'll have to ask Mother," Nacha's daughter said.

Then I was introduced to Nacha's son. He is heavyset, wears a mustache and had on an expensive watch.

I noticed a stool nearby which had white strips of paper neatly arranged on top.

She Looked Him Over

Then La Nacha came in. I remembered Hypo's advice that I should be polite to her. She gave me the once-over, I was introduced. She sat in front of the stool and started working the strips. They were the heroin papers.

Hypo told La Nacha that I was a musician working in a dance hall in El Paso and wanted to start buying "loads."

La Nacha glanced at my arms. Hypo explained that I wasn't a "mainliner." That I just liked to "jornear"—breathe the heroin. A "mainliner" is one who injects himself with a hypodermic needle.

La Nacha said, "All right, any time."

"At night we sell it across the street," La Nacha's daughter said.

Hypo asked La Nacha for "a nickel's worth." She handed me a paper of heroin. (She wanted to know if I would handle the stuff, Hypo told me later.) Hypo gave her $5 and we left.

Quicker and Better

After we bought the load we went to a cheap hotel in Juarez. There I saw Hypo, who is a "mainliner," inject himself with heroin.

"You feel better quicker that way," Hypo said.

"Mainliners" need a cup of water, a syringe with a needle, an eye dropper, a bottle cap and the expensive heroin to make them feel, in Hypo's word, "normal."

"A man who is hooked (that is, one who has the habit bad) never feels normal unless he's had at least two shots a day," Hypo said.

I watched Hypo go through the process of injecting himself with heroin. First he carefully placed half a paper of heroin in the bottle cap with a knife. Then with an eye dropper he placed a few drops of water in the cap. He took a match and placed it underneath the cap while holding it with the other hand. After it was heated Hypo dropped a tiny ball of cotton in the cap. "This is so the hypodermic can suck all the heroin out the cap," Hypo explained. The cotton works like a filter.

WILD EYES GLEAM

Hypo then placed the hypodermic syringe in the cap and the brownish substance could be seen running up into the syringe.

Hypo's wild eyes gleamed with excitement.

Hypo crouched on the floor balanced on the front of his shoes. He injected the heroin in his vein. His vein was swollen from so many punctures.

Almost as soon as the heroin had gone into his vein he started rocking back and forth. I asked him how he felt.

"Muy suave, ese," he said. "Real good."

Before long he passed out. His stomach sounded like a washing machine. He snored loudly and uncomfortably. I tried to wake him. I couldn't. So I went home.

TOOK AN OVERDOSE

Later he explained that he had taken an overdose.

"The load was real clean and I misjudged the amount I should have taken," Hypo said. "I could have died."

The second time I saw Hypo we must have bought a load not as clean or he judged the right amount. For the reaction was much different.

Before he injected himself he looked worse than I had ever seen him. His eyes looked like two huge buttons. He complained of pains all over his body. Hypo couldn't even hold a cigarette because of his shaking hands.

We went to La Nacha's and bought some heroin. We only stayed a minute. Hypo needed to be "cured" quick.

After he injected himself this time he actually looked better than before, talked better and acted better. He was only half dead—instead of three quarters.

He stopped shaking. He smoked almost calmly and was talkative. "I've got to quit this habit," he said. "For my little daughter's sake. I love her very much. God, I wish I could stop it."

I, too, hope he can.

Obit on the Dodgers
DICK YOUNG—*New York Daily News*—10/9/1957

[After the 1957 season, the owner of the Brooklyn Dodgers—Walter O'Malley—announced his decision to move the team from its historic home to Los Angeles.]

This is called an obit, which is short for obituary. An obit tells of a person who has died, how he lived, and of those who live after him. This is the obit of the Brooklyn Dodgers.

Preliminary diagnosis indicates that the cause of death was an acute case of greed, followed by severe political complications. Just a year ago, the Brooklyn ball club appeared extremely healthy. It had made almost a half million dollars for the fiscal period, more than any other big league team. Its president, Walter O'Malley, boasted that all debts had been cleared, and that the club was in the most solvent condition of its life, with real estate assets of about $5 million.

O'Malley contends that an unhealthy environment, not greed, led to the demise of the Dodgers in Brooklyn. He points out that he became aware of this condition as long ago as 1947, when he began looking around for a new park to replace Ebbets Fields, capacity 32,000.

At first, O'Malley believed the old plant could be remodeled, or at least torn down and replaced at the same site. But, after consultation with such a prominent architect as Norman Bel Geddes, and the perusal of numerous blueprints and plans, O'Malley ruled out such a possibility as unfeasible.

So O'Malley looked around for a new lot where he could build this bright, new, salubrious dwelling for his Dodgers; a dream house, complete with a plastic dome so that the games could be played in spite of foul weather, a plant that could be put to year-round use, for off-season sports and various attractions.

O'Malley suggested to the City of New York that the site of the new Brooklyn Civic Center, right outside the Dodger office windows in Boro Hall, would be ideal for the inclusion of a 50,000 seat stadium—a War Memorial stadium, he proposed.

That was all very patriotic, the City Planning Commission said, but not a stadium; not there. Sorry.

So, O'Malley looked farther, and hit upon the area at Flatbush and Atlantic Avenues—virtually the heart of downtown Brooklyn, where all transit systems intersect, and where the tired Long Island Rail Road limps in at its leisure. O'Malley learned that a vast portion of the neighborhood, which included the congested Ft. Greene market, had been declared a "blighted area" by city planners who had earmarked it for rehabilitation.

Here began one of the most forceful political manipulations in the history of our politically manipulated little town. With O'Malley as the guiding spirit, plans for establishment of a Sports Authority were born. It would be the work of such an Authority to issue bonds and build a stadium with private capital—utilizing the city's condemnation powers to obtain the land.

With O'Malley pushing the issue through his lifelong political contacts, the bill was drafted in Albany, passed overwhelmingly by the City Council, squeezed through the State Legislature by one vote, and ultimately signed into law by Governor Harriman.

At that moment, April 21, 1956, the prospects for a new stadium, and a continuance of Brooklyn baseball were at their highest. Thereafter, everything went downhill. City officials, who had supported the bill originally, in the belief Albany would defeat it, went to work with their subtle sabotage. Appropriations for surveys by the Sports Center Authority were cut to the bone, and O'Malley shook his head knowingly. He was getting the works.

O'Malley, meanwhile, had been engaging in some strange movements of his own. He had leased Roosevelt Stadium, Jersey City, for three years with the announced intention of playing seven or eight games a season there. Later, he sold Ebbets Field for $3,000,000 on a lease-back deal with Marv Kratter. The lease made it possible for O'Malley to remain in Brooklyn, in a pinch, for five years. He had no intention of doing so—it was just insurance against things blowing up at both political ends.

Why was Ebbets Field sold?

Politicians claimed it was an O'Malley squeeze on them. O'Malley claimed it was a manifestation of his good intentions; that he was converting the club's assets into cash so that he might buy Sports Authority bonds and help make the new stadium a reality.

Then, O'Malley moved in a manner that indicated he didn't believe himself. At the start of '57 he visited Los Angeles. Two months later, he announced the purchase of Wrigley Field. Shortly thereafter, Los Angeles officials, headed by Mayor Paulson and County Supervisor Ken Hahn, visited O'Malley at Vero Beach, Fla.

It was there, on March 7, that serious consideration of a move to Los Angeles crystallized in the O'Malley mind. They made grandiose stipulations to the L.A. authorities—and was amazed to hear them say: "We will do it."

From then on, Los Angeles officials bore down hard on the project, while New York's officials quibbled, mouthed sweet nothings, and tried to place the blame elsewhere. With each passing week, it became increasingly apparent the Dodgers were headed west—and, in an election year, the politicians wanted no part of the hot potato.

Bob Moses, park commissioner, made one strong stab for New York. He offered the Dodgers park department land at Flushing Meadow—with a string or two. It wasn't a bad offer—but not as good as L.A.'s.

By now, O'Malley's every move was aimed at the coast. He brought Frisco Mayor George Christopher to dovetail the Giant move to the coast with his own. He, and Stoneham, received permission from the NL owners to transfer franchises.

That was May 28—and since then, O'Malley has toyed with New York authorities, seeming to derive immense satisfaction from seeing them sweat unnecessarily. He was repaying them.

Right to the end, O'Malley wouldn't give a flat, "Yes, I'm moving"—as Stoneham had done. O'Malley was using New York as his saver—using it to drive a harder bargain with L.A.'s negotiator Harold McClellan, and using it in the event L.A.'s city council were to reject the proposition at the last minute.

But L.A., with its mayor whipping the votes into line the way a mayor is expected to, passed the bill—and O'Malley graciously accepted the 300 acres of downtown Los Angeles, whereupon he will graciously build a ball park covering 12 acres.

And the Brooklyn Dodgers dies—the healthiest corpse in sports history. Surviving are millions of fans, and their memories.

The memories of a rich and rollicking history—dating back to Ned Hanlon, the first manager, and skipping delightfully through such characters as Uncle Wilbert Robinson, Casey Stengel, Burleigh Grimes, Leo Durocher, Burt Shotten, Charley Dressen and now Walt Alston. The noisy ones, the demonstrative ones, the shrewd and cagey ones, and the confused ones. They came and they went, but always the incredible happenings remained, the retold screwy stories, the laughs, the snafued games, the laughs, the disappointments, the fights, and the laughs.

And the players: the great ones—Nap Rucker, Zack Wheat, Dazzy Vance, Babe Herman, Dolph Camilli, Whit Wyatt, Dixie Walker; the almost great ones but never quite—like Van Lingle Mungo and Pete Reiser; the modern men who made up the Dodgers' golden era—Duke Snider, Preacher Roe, Hugh Casey—and the man who made history, Jackie Robinson, and the boy who pitched Brooklyn to its only world championship in 1955, Johnny Podres.

And the brass: the conflicts of the brothers McKeever, and the trials of Charley Ebbets; the genuine sentimentality of Dearie Mulvey and the pride of her husband, Jim Mulvey; the explosive achievement of Larry MacPhail, the unpopular but undeniable success of Branch Rickey—and now, Walter O'Malley, who leaves Brooklyn a rich man and a despised man.

There Is No News from Auschwitz
A. M. ROSENTHAL—*The New York Times*—8/31/1958

BRZEZINKA, POLAND—The most terrible thing of all, somehow, was that at Brzezinka the sun was bright and warm, the rows of graceful poplars were lovely to look upon, and on the grass near the gates children played.

It all seemed frighteningly wrong, as in a nightmare, that at Brzezinka the sun should ever shine or that there should be light and greenness and the sound of young laughter. It would be fitting if at Brzezinka the sun never shone and the grass withered, because this is a place of unutterable terror.

And yet every day, from all over the world, people come to Brzezinka, quite possibly the most grisly tourist center on earth. They come for a variety of reasons—to see if it could really have been true, to remind themselves not to forget, to pay homage to the dead by the simple act of looking upon their place of suffering.

Brzezinka is a couple of miles from the better-known southern Polish town of O wi cim. O wi cim has about 12,000 inhabitants, is situated about 171 miles from Warsaw, and lies in a damp, marshy area at the eastern end of the pass called the Moravian Gate. Brzezinka and O wi cim together formed part of that minutely organized factory of torture and death that the Nazis called Konzentrationslager Auschwitz.

By now, fourteen years after the last batch of prisoners was herded naked into the gas chambers by dogs and guards, the story of Auschwitz has been told a great many times. Some of the inmates have written of those memories of which sane men cannot conceive. Rudolf Franz Ferdinand Hoess, the superintendent of the camp, before he was executed wrote his detailed memoirs of mass exterminations and the experiments on living bodies. Four million people died here, the Poles say.

And so there is no news to report about Auschwitz. There is merely the compulsion to write something about it, a compulsion that grows out of a restless feeling that to have visited Auschwitz and then turned away without having said or written anything would somehow be a most grievous act of discourtesy to those who died here.

Brzezinka and O wi cim are very quiet places now; the screams can no longer be heard. The tourist walks silently, quickly at first to get it over with and then, as his mind peoples the barracks and the chambers and the dungeons and flogging posts, he walks draggingly. The guide does not say much either, because there is nothing much for him to say after he has pointed.

For every visitor there is one particular bit of horror that he knows he will never forget. For some it is seeing the rebuilt gas chamber at O wi cim and being told that this is the "small one." For others it is the fact that at Brzezinka, in the ruins of the gas chambers and the crematoria the Germans blew up when they retreated, there are daisies growing.

There are visitors who gaze blankly at the gas chambers and the furnaces because their minds simply cannot encompass them, but stand shivering before the great mounds of human hair behind the plate-glass window or the piles of babies' shoes or the brick cells where men sentenced to death by suffocation were walled up.

One visitor opened his mouth in a silent scream simply at the sight of boxes—great stretches of three-tiered wooden boxes in the women's barracks. They were about six feet wide, about three feet high, and into them from five to ten prisoners were shoved for the night. The guide walks quickly through the barracks. Nothing more to see here.

A brick building where sterilization experiments were carried out on women prisoners. The guide tries the door—it's locked. The visitor is grateful that he does not have to go in, and then flushes with shame.

A long corridor where rows of faces stare from the walls. Thousands of pictures, the photographs of prisoners. They are all dead now, the men and women who stood before the cameras, and they all knew they were to die.

They all stare blank-faced, but one picture, in the middle of a row, seizes the eye and wrenches the mind. A girl, 22 years old, plumply pretty, blond. She is smiling gently, as at a sweet, treasured thought. What was the thought that passed through her young mind and is now her memorial on the wall of the dead at Auschwitz?

Into the suffocation dungeons the visitor is taken for a moment and feels himself strangling. Another visitor goes in, stumbles out, and crosses herself. There is no place to pray in Auschwitz.

The visitors look pleadingly at each other and say to the guide, "Enough."

Archie's Kind of Music
JIMMY CANNON—*New York Post*—1/1959

Someone should tell Archie Moore what he is in his kind of music. Most of that music is laid away with the ragtime professors in the slums of old graveyards where the weeds grow tall as rich people's stones. The music just faded away, time-taken and echoless in the storm of rock 'n' roll, faint as the butt-strangled voices that spoke the hustlers' stories in the sneak-joints in the bad parts of wide-open towns. The piano players were scufflers themselves and a lot had jail time behind them for weak men's crimes.

They were underworld minstrels, speakeasy entertainers calling out the tragedies of their night and explaining the small victories of their breed in the same sad style, as if all the cards were marked and no one could believe a hold card until the last hand was run. They should define Archie Moore and they might get it exactly right because this is one for everybody who has been imprisoned in the solitude of obscurity.

The old piano players, singing those metropolitan lullabies to strays and losers, carrying everybody's torch for their own, would find an anthem for Archie

Moore, the hockshop champion. The important composers wouldn't be simple enough. They would allow their craft to dominate them and mislay it in the techniques of their form. I once heard an old man in a bust-out joint in Kansas City whisper the anguish of a safecracker doing a bread and water bit in an Australian prison far from his girl. The words have slipped out of memory now. The tune's gone, as that crib on 12th Street must be, as the old piano player certainly is. But if they would find him and sit him down on his stool, loosen him up with a few balls, I'm sure he'd reach back and handle Archie Moore's case with a song.

I'm not the guy to tell it because this shouldn't be played on a typewriter. The violins shouldn't be in on it and it doesn't need horns or a muggled-up drummer busting out with a solo until his sticks bust. It's not a dance hall ballad either or one out of the pits of theaters and television would spoil it with tux-wearing sidemen cutting out for the suburbs in station wagons when the program's over. The beat generation, let them get lost forever. They celebrate all the aimless roads men take and Archie followed the hard way to Montreal, through all the tough towns. It has to be an old professor, pawn-wise, or it will be no one at all.

They'd get it in, all right, the whole package of it, all the misery, all the sickness of despair, all the short-money pain, all the dirty deuces in all the bottom-dealt decks. They didn't fade anyone with epics about statesmen or world-bossers, or those Broadway jingles about tea for two and that rainbow that comes after every shower. They sang the blues as men alone knew them and how luck maimed them or the law tripped them or how they were hooked on junk or horses or dropped a duke to rum. They would get in Tasmania, too. They wouldn't neglect Tasmania because odd names appealed to the historians of city nights who sang their concerts to guys who could understand the songs.

The fight mob gave many a fin to professors for those old songs. When I first covered them, we generally finished up in those clubs which usually weren't clubs at all but the backrooms of stores with a bar and a piano and a professor to work on it. The greatest of these was Tommy Lyman, who gave his recitals in the big towns. The guys I mean never made it to New York or Chicago or San Francisco, but they never stopped dreaming about getting there.

***

Start it in St. Louis where the blues are old, professor, and move it around away from the big river and across the land, back and forth, bus riding, daycoach napping, flophouse sleeping, and suggest the gladness of the kid fighting on top in the small clubs. It was plain that this was a great fighter, Archie Moore, getting small touches and joyous because he was learning his trade and being paid for his apprenticeship. Not much but up ahead was the money and didn't he take out Deacon Logan in three to win the championship of Missouri?

Nellie Bly was a pioneering investigative reporter and perhaps the most famous journalist of her time, giving rise to board games and Broadway plays.

"A newspaper reporter, in those remote days," H.L. Mencken wrote in his memoir, "had a grand and gaudy time of it, with no call to envy any man."

Will Rogers was a nationally syndicated humor columnist, cowboy philosopher and movie star beloved for his "cool mind and warm heart."

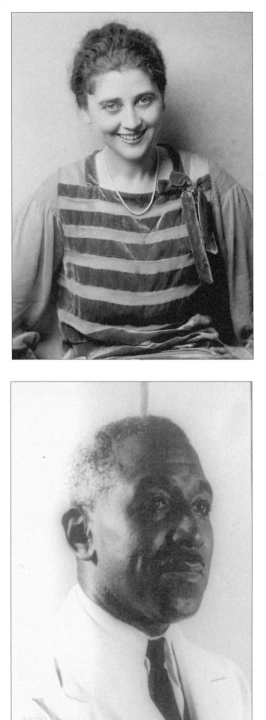

Maurine Dallas Watkins's Jazz Age writing for *Chicago Tribune* supplied enough material for a lifetime, inspiring the musical and film *Chicago* decades later.

"The dean of American sportswriters," Grantland Rice helped the sports column evolve by adopting a literary style and became a star in his own right. "A wise man makes his own decisions," Rice wrote. "An ignorant man follows the public opinion."

George S. Schuyler was a groundbreaking African-American conservative columnist for the *Pittsburgh Courier*. H.L. Mencken called Schuyler "the most competent editorial writer now in practice in this great free republic."

Called the "First Lady of American Journalism,"
Dorothy Thompson helped define the 1930s and
1940s. "Only when we are no longer afraid," she
wrote, "do we begin to live."

A founder of the Newspaper Guild, Heywood
Broun's outsized talents allowed him to tackle
subjects ranging from politics to art to sports
to war.

"Westbrook Pegler's place as the great
dissenter for the common man is unchallenged,"
declared *Time* magazine in 1938. Three years
later, Pegler became the first columnist to win
a Pulitzer Prize for reporting by uncovering
criminal racketeering in labor unions.

Marguerite Higgins was the first woman to win the Pulitzer Prize for war correspondence. "I wouldn't be here if there were no trouble," she said. "Trouble is news, and gathering news is my job."

The G.I. Journalist, Ernie Pyle (*center*) remains the patron saint of war columnists. After his death in combat, President Truman said he "told the story of the American fighting man as the American fighting men wanted it told."

One Dead, 40 Hurt in East L.A. Riot

Times Columnist Ruben Salazar Killed by Bullet

BY CHARLES T. POWERS
and JEFF PERLMAN
Times Staff Writers

An East Los Angeles parade and rally that attracted about 20,000 persons to demonstrate Mexican-American opposition to the war in Southeast Asia erupted into a riot Saturday, claiming the life of one of the city's leading spokesmen for Chicano rights.

The dead man was Ruben Salazar.

Ruben Salazar, the first Latino columnist employed by the *Los Angeles Times*, was killed by a police tear gas canister during a riot in the summer of 1970. He is one of five journalists honored on a U.S. postage stamp.

"Murray Kempton is the greatest of all living newspapermen," wrote the *New Yorker*'s David Remnick in 1994. "He is a moralist who does not preach; an artist who reports."

"If there is a common thread in William F. Buckley's writings," fellow conservative columnist George Will wrote, "it is the compatibility of seriousness, even occasional indignation, with an unfailing sense of merriment about the pleasures of intellectual combat."

For over seventy-five years, Shirley Povich wrote his celebrated sports column for *The Washington Post*. Seen here in the Yankee dugout between Joe DiMaggio and Yogi Berra, Povich told colleagues his formula for success: "I write what I like to read."

Eugene Patterson wrote a column for the *Atlanta Constitution* while also serving as its editor-in-chief in the 1960s. A pro-civil rights conscience in the segregated South, he is seen here (*at podium*), far left, speaking at a conference with Dr. Martin Luther King.

The archetypal newspaper columnist, Jimmy Breslin's favorite subject is his hometown, New York: "The city that I love and hate both equally."

"Show me somebody who is always smiling, always cheerful, always optimistic," said Chicago's legendary Mike Royko, "and I will show you somebody who hasn't the faintest idea what the hell is really going on."

Dave Barry says he worked seven days a week to make his column sound like he "dashed it off while carpet-chewing drunk"—and won a Pulitzer in the process.

The preeminent chronicler of Casino-land, John L. Smith's columns for the *Las Vegas Review-Journal* involve "aging boxers, two-bit mobsters, bookmakers, loan-sharks and wait-resses at Denny's—preferably a combination of two or more."

Washington Post columnist Colbert King is embraced by colleague E.J. Dionne after winning the Pulitzer Prize in 2003 for "against-the-grain columns that speak to people in power with ferocity and wisdom."

But his reputation swindled Archie Moore out of his rewards. He knew too much about fighting. They ducked him and ran out on him and Missouri is a fine place to be champion of, but the world is the true champion's field. There were some good scores and Ezzard Charles was too much for him, but the good ones hid from him. Managers didn't want their prospects laid out. So Archie Moore fought in places such as Montevideo and Cordoba, North Adams, Massachusetts, Adelaide and Tasmania. He grew old on the road and anyplace where they would pay to see him he called his hometown and stayed until he ran out of opponents.

All the while, Archie Moore knew he was a great fighter and he held on to that and never let it go. Punks got rich fighting in the Garden during the war. And Archie Moore, a light-heavyweight, was tipping over 200-pound assassins for moving-around money. Preliminary boys made as much as he did. The professors would know all about this. You hear a lot of this, told by different men in various ways, in curfew-cheating saloons.

They'd sing the late-coming happiness in there, too, beating Joey Maxim and Bobo Olson, getting the shots in the senility of his athletic career. They wouldn't miss the laughs then and the pictures in the newspapers and being represented by a lawyer who became the governor of Ohio. They would really dig in on that cold night's work in Montreal a couple of weeks ago when he was down three times in the first round, again in the fifth and got up to knock out Yvon Durelle.

Final Returns, Final Night
MURRAY KEMPTON—*New York Post*—9/8/1961

[Known as the last boss of New York City's Tammany Hall political machine, Carmine DeSapio was defeated by Greenwich Village Reform Democrats in a local election for district leader, provoking this surprisingly sympathetic profile.]

Carmine DeSapio came to rest a little while last night at the Fifth Avenue Hotel, an hour before the polls closed.

Someone had chalked on the blackboard that "Now Is the Time" and "This is D-Day" and "What Can You Do for Him?" Mrs. DeSapio was still working the phones; DeSapio sat at a long table, detached from pain or blame or rancor, and said that there were so many conflicting views of what a big vote meant that an outsider could not possibly make an estimate.

"Some of them say try for a light vote, some say try for a heavy one." The Village, he observed, was so quiet; a visitor, searching for consolation, said that he had heard a shout when Roger Maris hit a home run just now. Carmine DeSapio smiled politely. With all his other troubles, can he be a Ruth man too?

He doodled with his pen. He doodled the initials "V. I. D." and scratched them over. The visitor asked how big the vote was, and Carmine DeSapio rose, with the grace that will never leave him in life, and said he would find out. He called. "What do you hear around?" he asked into the phone. He came and said that up at the Biltmore they said it would be close to a million and what did that mean? The visitor said they must be crazy.

AT THE SCHOOLHOUSE

It was time for him to go, a field marshal on a lonely patrol in the enemy country. He said he would try the South Village; there had been complaints about the machines there. He came to the Little Red Schoolhouse; the line out to the door looked like a convention of folk singers. He went inside; there was a sense that, although he is a man too polite ever to suggest it, he did not want the company on this pilgrimage. He was there a long time. The visitor moved in to find him; DeSapio was standing by himself on the side watching the enemy challenge every vote. He clapped his hands once and said: "Come on; these people have to vote."

The tables rustled and stirred a moment with the habit of discipline; then they went back to their slow quarrel, the illusion of authority having passed. Carmine DeSapio walked out past the long line of assassins, stopping now and again to shake the hand of a middle-aged man with a necktie. "How are you; it's nice to see you." Most of the line—insurgents don't wear neckties in public— would not look at him; the visitor remembered the old rule about juries and the defendants they cannot bear to look upon.

Carmine DeSapio smiled and said that he supposed it was time to go and get the results.

Tamawa was as chaste as ever, and as ever a dedicated citadel of respectable upper mobility. The captains were not back yet; their ladies sat in a row on the side; Tamawa has always had the good old rule about the silence of women in church. There was a long table for taking returns; DeSapio went to a cubicle at the side of the room, which began to fill, horridly silent; every now and again a man would come in with his bundle of tally sheets and hand it over to the captain as if it were a secret document. The attendant would look at it, check the election district and send it back to the cubicle.

"EVERYBODY CAN'T WIN"

A half hour went that way. There was by now a crowd of the sort that shows up at disasters. DeSapio came out to talk on the radio. The smile on the face of the tiger was a wound. Downtown the police reported Lanigan leading by a thousand votes; DeSapio said his figures showed him slightly behind. He was asked about the mayoralty. "I really don't know," he answered, "I haven't had an opportunity to talk to any of the county chairmen."

By eleven fifteen he came out holding the tally sheets. He said that he was behind 5,210 to 4,093 with five electoral districts missing. "I wouldn't say at this stage Lanigan is the victor. The results in the city are not encouraging."

"Has everybody got the figures?" he asked. It was the tone of a host searching for the last lonely guest whose glass is running dry. He went back to the cubicle. His people stayed; when he came back to dismiss them, they applauded.

"I can't tell you how grateful I am. We're not going to close the club. Things will adjust themselves as we go along. That's the democratic form of government. Nobody likes to lose but everybody can't win."

I sometimes think if Carmine DeSapio were running against Lucifer he would consider it ungentlemanly to mention that little trouble in heaven.

"It's not easy for me, but try to accept it as graciously as you possibly can." He stopped; the wistful, disembodied smile played on. "I know you are going to say that fellow DeSapio is too soft; he wants to forgive everybody."

This was too much for even the habitual docility of the ladies along the wall. "You are, you are," they cried.

"Let me please once again say from the bottom of my heart," Carmine De-Sapio began again. "We tried and we lost. Don't let's get sick about it."

He adjourned them and loyally they went home.

Carmine DeSapio's father was waiting patiently and without rancor, twisting a discarded tally sheet in his old longshoreman's hands. What must it be to raise a son who believes in every virtue in the book and see him defiled and brought down like this? The DeSapios keep such reflections in private. Carmine DeSapio began introducing the stray guests to his father, the distant relative who is the rock of all occasions of family sorrow, welcoming the stranger, consoling the mourner.

He had to go back to the Fifth Avenue Hotel, the command post for the genteel among his supporters. There were perhaps ten persons who had risen in the world with him; there was a piano and a lady wondering whether anyone could play it so that we could sing "East Side, West Side."

No one felt like playing and Carmine DeSapio rose and talked interminably about not being indispensable and not being immortal and about being very sorry if I have let you down; I'll call you in a day or two and we'll have a little party and a little celebration in the climate of friendship that's endured for many years.

There was nothing to do then but wait for Mike Prendergast, the state chairman, who came to say that he was proud to have his picture taken with Carmine DeSapio. It was then one o'clock; Sydney Baron said that Carmine was tired and hadn't eaten and someone should get him a sandwich. Carmine DeSapio roused himself as though he had lost his manners, and said he was sorry, they must be hungry; could he get them a sandwich?

That way his visitor left him and walked into the streets and noticed that there were no slums any more, and no landlords, and the Age of Pericles had begun because we were rid of Carmine DeSapio. One had to walk carefully to avoid being stabbed by the lilies bursting in the pavements. I wish the reformers luck—with less Christian sincerity than Carmine DeSapio does. I will be a long time forgiving them this one.

Kennedy Assassinated
MERRIMAN SMITH—UPI—11/23/1963

It was a balmy, sunny noon as we motored through downtown Dallas behind President Kennedy. The procession cleared the center of the business district and turned into a handsome highway that wound through what appeared to be a park.

I was riding in the so-called White House press "pool" car, a telephone company vehicle equipped with a mobile radio-telephone. I was in the front seat between a driver from the telephone company and Malcolm Kilduff, acting White House press secretary for the President's Texas tour. Three other pool reporters were wedged in the back seat.

Suddenly we heard three loud, almost painfully loud cracks. The first sounded as if it might have been a large firecracker. But the second and third blasts were unmistakable. Gunfire.

The President's car, possibly as much as 150 or 200 yards ahead; seemed to falter briefly. We saw a flurry of activity in the secret service follow-up car behind the chief executive's bubble-top limousine.

Next in line was the car bearing Vice-President Lyndon B. Johnson. Behind that, another follow-up car bearing agents assigned to the vice-president's protection. We were behind that car.

Our car stood still for probably only a few seconds, but it seemed like a lifetime. One sees history explode before one's eyes and, for even the most trained observer, there is a limit to what one can comprehend.

I looked ahead at the President's car but could not see him or his companion, Gov. John Connally. Both had been riding on the right side of the limousine. I thought I saw a flash of pink that would have been Mrs. Jacqueline Kennedy.

Everybody in our car began shouting at the driver to pull up closer to the President's car. But at this moment, we saw the big bubbletop and a motorcycle escort roar away at high speed.

We screamed at our driver, "get going, get going." We careened around the Johnson car and its escort and set out down the highway, barely able to keep in sight of the President's car and the accompanying secret service car.

They vanished around a curve. When we cleared the same curve, we could see where they were heading—Parkland Hospital. We spilled out of the pool car as it entered the hospital driveway.

I ran to the side of the bubbletop.

The President was face down on the back seat. Mrs. Kennedy made a cradle of her arms around the President's head and bent over him as if she were whispering to him.

Gov. Connally was on his back on the floor of the car, his head and shoulders resting on the arms of his wife, Nellie, who shook with dry sobs. Blood oozed from the front of the governor's suit. I could not see the President's wound. But I could see blood spattered around the interior of the rear seat and a dark stain spreading down the right side of the President's dark gray suit.

From the telephone car, I had radioed the Dallas UPI Bureau that three shots had been fired at the Kennedy motorcade.

Clint Hill, the secret service agent in charge of the detail assigned to Mrs. Kennedy, was leaning over into the rear of the car.

"How badly was he hit, Clint?" I asked.

"He's dead," Hill replied curtly.

Malcolm X: The Fruit of Islam
MURRAY KEMPTON—*New York Post*—2/23/1965

And now that Malcolm X is dead, it is odd how sad some of us who knew him find ourselves and how pitiful, for all his dignity, he seems to have been all through our memory.

We knew him first and best as the preacher of the eternal separation of black and white; there is a theory that near the end he was struggling unevenly towards some idea of community. But I do not think he changed much with time; he lived with America for thirty-nine years and, whether from love or hate, I should doubt he really knew until the day he died.

Yet he was always a man of Harlem; he never entered white New York, except as ambassador from an independent, hostile nation. Never, that is, except the last night of his life, when he came to us as a refugee. He spent Saturday night at the New York Hilton because he did not feel safe in Harlem. That night he was a fugitive from black men; his dignity must have commanded him to go back among them Sunday and now he is dead.

Until the end, Malcolm X preached that Negroes must arm themselves against us, the enemy. And now he has been assassinated by armed Negroes at a meeting from which white people were barred.

It was his conviction that his father had been murdered by white men and thrown under a streetcar. Now his widow will have someday to explain to her youngest daughter Lomumbah that her father was shot down by Negroes.

The journalists always suspected that he was their creation, and in a way he was. He had both an exotic presence and considerable native wit; he came to New York at a time when he perfectly suited the demands of electronic journalism. There have been very few public men whose message fit so snug and yet so lively into a two-minute segment of a news broadcast.

The gift would have made him notorious under any circumstances; but he had something else. I do not know a Negro so completely adjusted that some part of him did not respond to what Malcolm X was saying, just as I do not know a Negro so entirely alienated that some part of him does not respond to what Martin Luther King, Jr. is saying. Just by his insistence, Malcolm X created himself a nation to which every Negro owed a small allegiance. As Jimmy Jicks said yesterday, this *was* an assassination, for Mr. Malcolm was a head of state.

And yet he had a strange, trusting side. The longest I ever talked to him was in Miami the night before the Cassius Clay-Sonny Liston fight where Mr. Malcolm had gone to Clay's spiritual prop. I remember his saying that, if you found a good white man, he was usually a Southerner, and how innocent that notion seemed to me as a hybrid Southerner. I tried to disabuse him and failed, and then the subject turned to Cassius and I said I hoped he wouldn't be immobilized by fear of Liston.

"To be a Muslim," Malcolm X replied, "is to know no fear."

And there he seemed to me correct, insofar as any white man can judge whether a Negro is correct about other Negroes; there was a quietness, a containment and a dignity about the young men around him that made you believe that Mr. Malcolm and they have been given a community and rescued from fear.

He lost the community when he was expelled from the Nation of Islam and it must have taken an immense amount of character to carry on as well as he did. Now what can we believe but that he was killed by young men very like the ones who used to surround him, and whom he had helped liberate from fear?

I do not think that, until now, I have ever really known what a terrible thing a ghetto is.

The Stone's at the Bottom of the Hill
JACK NEWFIELD—*Village Voice*—6/13/1968

LOS ANGELES—It was a little before midnight, a half hour before he was to be assassinated as he reached out to grasp the workingman's hand of a $75-a-week Mexican busboy in the bowels of the Ambassador Hotel.

Robert Kennedy was holding a victory cigar in his swollen and stubby fingers, and squatting on the floor of room 511. His famous political and intellectual supporters were in the room with him. The awful little pornographers of power were there too. And so were the special people, the victims and rebels Robert Kennedy identified with. Doris Huerta of the grape strike was there, and Charles Evers, and John Lewis, who once led SNCC, and Budd Schulberg, who runs a writers' workshop in Watts. And Pete Hamill and Jimmy Breslin, two gut journalists who never went to college, but who Kennedy sensed know more about America than the erudite pundits.

In this last hour, Kennedy seemed the most zestful and most inwardly serene I had seen him since Lyndon Johnson withdrew from the race. When that had happened Kennedy became troubled and confused. He had lost his enemy and his issue—the war—and he acted like a lost soul, even as he won in Indiana. He seemed, suddenly, not to know who he was.

Defeat in Oregon, and physical exhaustion in California, had gutted his spirit even more. On Sunday he seemed somber and withdrawn as he looked blankly out the window of his 727 Electra campaign jet. Normally Kennedy would gossip and joke with me on a campaign trip. But on Sunday all he said was that he hoped Al Lowenstein, who was supporting McCarthy, would win his congressional primary fight on Long Island. Then he turned his worn-out face to the breathtaking landscape of California.

On Monday he was drained, and his speeches flat, and he got sick to the stomach in the middle of his final campaign speech in San Diego. The press whispered about a premonition of defeat.

But now, just before midnight, he seemed to be discovering his natural rhythm again, finally to feel liberated from gloom, fatalism, and yes, guilt over not running earlier, and somehow betraying the young he so wanted to lead.

He had won Humphrey's native state of South Dakota and in California. The Indians and the Mexicans and the Negroes ("my people") had given him his margin of triumph. The turnout of voters in supposedly fragmented, apathetic Watts was higher than in educated, affluent Beverly Hills. Key supporters and aides of Eugene McCarthy had told Richard Goodwin earlier in the night they might now come over to Kennedy's campaign. He had come back from defeat, and won his own. Robert Kennedy, who was always more Boston than Camelot, once again found the two things he always needed: a cause—the dispossessed—and a clear enemy.

"I am going to chase Hubert Humphrey's ass all over America," he said. "I'm going to chase his ass into every precinct. Wherever he goes, I'm going to go."

Then he went downstairs carrying his notes for a speech that would attack war and violence.

I spent the death watch in Kennedy's hotel room, watching television, and answering the grieving and bereft phone calls from as far away as London. About twenty people spent the night there, spread out among five or six rooms on the fifth floor. Occasionally a sob or shriek came out of one of the rooms. We drank all the liquor there was, but nobody got drunk.

At about 4 a.m. Adam Walinsky called from the Hospital of the Good Samaritan to mumble that the outlook was bleak. Then a tape of a speech Kennedy gave at Berkeley attacking poverty and racism flashed on, and I finally broke down. As I wept, two crew-cut employees of the Los Angeles telephone company came into the room, and mechanically began to remove the special telephones that had been installed for the evening, direct lines to the ballroom, and phones used to call South Dakota and Washington. They acted as if nothing was happening, just casually pulling the wires out of the wall, and coiling them around the phones.

In another room in the suite John Lewis, who had campaigned around the hostile, middle-class Jews in California, sat on the arm of a chair, tears in his eyes, and mumbling to himself, "Why, why, why?" John Barlow Martin, his gaunt, Modigliani-like face the color of chalk, said to no one in particular, "Bomb America. Make Coca-Cola someplace else."

Again and again the television played the drama. Kennedy's last speech, the ballsy challenge to Humphrey, the attack on the war, the jibe at Yorty, and the last awkward victory sign with his two fingers. The moan that broke across the ballroom like a wave. Men and women weeping, praying, pounding the floor.

Blair Clark, McCathy's campaign manager, the columnist Mary McGrory, who loved Bobby almost as much as she loved Gene, came, offered condolences, fought to hold back tears, and left, reeling like sleepwalkers.

At 5:30 a.m., I went downstairs to help pick up Ed Guthman at the hospital. Outside the Ambassador Hotel sat Charles Evers, Medgar's brother. "God, they kill our friends and they kill our leaders," he said. Outside the hospital the press and a few hippies prayed.

Guthman's face said everything. Jimmy Breslin and George Plimpton left the hospital at the same time, and their faces also said that Kennedy's brain was already dead, and only his street fighter's heart kept him technically alive.

Wednesday morning I wandered around the ugly hotel. Scavengers were stealing mementos—campaign hats, banners, posters—from the ballroom.

Now he rests next to his brother, and feelings of rage mingle with a few random personal memories of a soulful man the world thought was ruthless.

Rage at the professional Bobby haters. Not just Joe Resnick or Drew Pearson, but all those Reform Democrats and liberal columnists who made hating Bobby so respectable, and even fashionable.

Rage at politicians who now urge passage of the crime bill with its gun-control clause as a "memorial" to Kennedy, even though Kennedy, in life, opposed that legislation because of its provisions for wiretapping and denial of rights to defendants.

Rage at a man like Sam Yorty, who had the Los Angeles police give a traffic ticket to the entire Kennedy motorcade last week, who began red-baiting before Kennedy's heart stopped beating, and who had crashed the funeral, and refused to leave even after being asked by Jack English.

Rage at men like Archbishop Cooke and Eric Hoffer who say America should feel no national guilt, because the assassin was a Jordanian nationalist. Rage at those eulogizers who never mention the violence of Vietnam, Mississippi or Texas. Rage at men who cannot face the fact that the truest symbol of America is that lonesome plane from Los Angeles that carried the widows of John Kennedy, Robert Kennedy, and Martin Luther King.

But a few memories linger too.

Kennedy quietly reading the Old Testament as a private gesture of irreverence all through the three-hour funeral mass for Cardinal Spellman. Kennedy sitting in his Manhattan apartment and reading me a poem from Emerson. Kennedy visiting a migrant worker camp near Buffalo, and walking past the manager who held a gun, and into a rotting trailer that was a home for ten migrants. Kennedy pausing while campaigning in Brooklyn in front of a small girl with glasses and suddenly saying, "My little girl wears glasses too. And I love her very much." Kennedy visiting a hospital for retarded children in Westchester last January, and impulsively taking sixteen patients for a ride to buy ice cream, while doctors and aides panicked.

If I had written these things two weeks ago, *The Voice* would have been deluged with letters calling me a whore. Now such anecdotes fill the papers and the networks, and no one doubts them.

When he sent a plane to take Martin Luther King's widow to Memphis, people called it a cheap political gimmick. Two weeks ago I described him being called out of a shower in Indianapolis, and quipping as he groped for the phone, "Make way for the future leader of the Free World." I got a letter saying that proved his arrogance.

Robert Kennedy was not a saint. He was a politician who could talk about law and order in Indiana.

But anyone who rode on his funeral train last Saturday, and looked out at the rows of wounded black faces that lined the poor side of the tracks, knew what might have been. The stone is once again at the bottom of the hill and we are alone.

P.F.C. Gibson Comes Home
JOHN FETTERMAN—*Louisville Times*—7/1968

It was late on a Wednesday night and most of the people were asleep in Hindman, the county seat of Knott County, when the body of Private First Class James Thurman (Little Duck) Gibson came home from Vietnam.

It was hot. But as the gray hearse arrived bearing the gray Army coffin, a summer rain began to fall. The fat raindrops glistened on the polished hearse and steamed on the street. Hindman was dark and silent. In the distance down the town's main street the red sign on the Square Deal Motor Co. flashed on and off.

Private Gibson's body had been flown from Oakland, Calif., to Cincinnati and was accompanied by Army Staff Sgt. Raymond A. Ritter, assigned to escort it home. The body was picked up in Cincinnati by John Everage, a partner in the local funeral home, and from that point on it was in the care of people who had known the 24-year-old soldier all his life.

At Hindman, the coffin was lifted out while Sgt. Ritter, who wore a black mourning band on his arm, snapped a salute. One funeral home employee whispered to another: "It's Little Duck. They brought him back."

Most of his life he had been called Little Duck—for so long that many people who knew him well had to pause and reflect to recall his full name.

By Thursday morning there were few people who did not know that Little Duck was home—or almost home. During the morning the family came; his older brother, Herschel, whom they call Big Duck; his sister Betty Jo; and his wife Carolyn.

They stood over the glass-shielded body and let their tears fall upon the glass, and people spoke softly in the filling station next door and on the streets outside.

The soldier's parents, Mr. and Mrs. Norman Gibson, waited at home, a neat white house up the hollow which shelters Flax Patch Creek, several miles away. Mrs. Gibson had been ill for months, and the family did not let her take the trip to Hindman. Later in the morning, they took Little Duck home.

Sweltering heat choked the hills and valleys as Little Duck was placed back in the hearse and taken home. The cortege had been joined by Maj. Lyle Halde-man, a survival assistance officer, sent, like Sgt. Ritter, to assist the family. It was a long, slow trip—over a high ridge to the south, along Irishman Creek and past the small community of Amburgey.

At Amburgey, the people stood in the sun, women wept and men removed their hats as the hearse went past. Mrs. Nora Amburgey, the postmistress, low-ered the flag of the tiny fourth-class post office to half-mast and said, "We all thought a lot of Little Duck."

At the point where Flax Patch Creek empties into Irishman Creek, the hearse turned, crossed a small wooden bridge and drove the final mile up Flax Patch Creek to the Gibson home. The parents and other relatives waited in a darkened, silent home.

As the coffin was lifted upon the front porch and through the door into the front living room, the silence was broken by cries of grief. The sounds of anguish swelled and rolled along the hollow. Little Duck was home.

All afternoon and all night they came, some walking, some driving up the dusty road in cars and trucks. They brought flowers and food until the living room was filled with floral tributes and the kitchen was crammed with food. The people filled the house and yard. They talked in small groups, and members of the family clasped to each other in grief.

They went, time and time again, to look down into the coffin and weep.

The mother, a sweet-faced mountain woman, her gray hair brushed back and fastened behind her head, forced back the pangs of her illness and moved, as in a trance, among the crowd as she said:

"His will will be done no matter what we say or do."

The father, a tall, tanned man, his eyes wide and red from weeping, said:

"He didn't want to go to the Army, but he knew it was the right thing to do; so he did his best. He gave all he had. I'm as proud of him as I can be. Now they bring him home like this."

Around midnight the rain returned and the mourners gathered in the house, on the porch and backed against the side of the house under the eaves.

The father talked softly of his son.

"I suppose you wonder why we called him Little Duck. Well, when the boys were little they would go over and play in the creek every chance they got. Somebody said they were like ducks.

"Ever since then Herschel was 'Big Duck' and James was 'Little Duck.'

"You worked hard all your life to raise your family. I worked in a 32-inch seam of coal, on my hands and knees, loading coal to give my family what I could.

"There was never a closer family. Little Duck was born here in this house and never wanted to leave."

Other mourners stepped up to volunteer tributes to Little Duck.

"He never was one to drink and run up and down the road at night."

"He took care of his family. He was a good boy."

Little Duck was a big boy. He was 6 feet 5½ inches tall and weighed 205 pounds. His size led him to the basketball team at Combs High School where he met and courted the girl he married last January.

Little Duck was home recently on furlough. Within a month after he went down Flax Patch Creek to return to the Army, he was back home to be buried. He had been married six months, a soldier for seven.

The Army said he was hit by mortar fragments near Saigon, but there were few details of his death.

The father, there in the stillness of the early morning, was remembering the day his son went back to the Army.

"He had walked around the place, looking at everything. He told me, 'Lord it's good to be home.'

"Then he went down the road. He said, 'Daddy, take care of yourself and don't work too hard.'

"He said, 'I'll be seeing you,' but he can't see me now."

An elderly man, walking with great dignity, approached and said, "Nobody can ever say anything against Little Duck. He was as good a boy as you'll ever see."

Inside the living room, the air heavy with the scent of flowers, Little Duck's mother sat with her son and her grief.

Her hand went out gently, as to comfort a stranger, and she talked as though to her self.

"Why my boy? Why my baby?"

She looked toward the casket, draped in an American flag, and when she turned back she said:

"You'll never know what a flag means until you see one on your own boy."

Then she went back to weep over the casket.

On Friday afternoon Little Duck was taken over to the Providence Regular Baptist Church and placed behind the pulpit. All that night the church lights burned and the people stayed and prayed. The parents spent the night at the church.

"This is his last night," Little Duck's mother explained.

The funeral was at 10 o'clock Saturday morning, and the people began to arrive early. They came from the dozens of hollows and small communities in Letcher, Knot and Perry counties. Some came back from other states. They filled the pews and then filled the aisle with folding chairs. Those who could not crowd inside gathered outside the door or listened beneath the windows.

The sermon was delivered by the Rev. Archie Everage, pastor at Montgomery Baptist Church, which is on Montgomery Creek near Hindman. On the last Sunday that he was home alive, Little Duck attended services there.

The service began with a solo, "Beneath the Sunset," sung by a young girl with a clear bell-like voice; then there were hymns from the church choir.

Mr. Everage, who had been a friend of Little Duck, had difficulty in keeping his voice from breaking as he got into his final tribute. He spoke of the honor Little Duck had brought to his family, his courage and his dedication. He spoke of Little Duck, "following the colors of his country." He said Little Duck died "for a cause for which many of our forefathers fought and died."

The phrase touched off a fresh wail of sobs to fill the church. Many mountain people take great pride in their men who "follow the colors." It is a tradition that goes back to October 1780, when a lightly regarded band of mountaineers handed disciplined British troops a historic defeat at Kings Mountain, South Carolina, and turned the tide of the Revolutionary War.

Shortly before Little Duck was hit in Vietnam, he had written two letters intended for his wife. Actually the soldier was writing a part of his own funeral. Mr. Everage read from one letter:

Honey, they put me in a company right down on the Delta. From what everybody says that is a rough place, but I've been praying hard for the Lord to help me and take care of me so really I'm not too scared or worried. I think if He wants it to be my time to go that I'm prepared for it. Honey, you don't know really when you are going to face something like this, but I want you to be a good girl and try to live a good life. For if I had things to do over I would have already been prepared for something like this. I guess you are wondering why I'm telling you this, but you don't know how hard it's been on me in just a short time. But listen here, if anything happens to me, all I want is for you to live right, and then I'll get to see you again.

And from another letter:

Honey, listen, if anything happens to me I want you to know that I love you very very much and I want you to keep seeing my family the rest of their lives and I want you to know you are a wonderful wife and that I'm very proud of you. If anything happens I want Big Duck and Betty Jo to know I loved them very much. If anything happens also tell them not to worry, that I'm prepared for it.

The service lasted two hours and ended only after scores of people, of all ages, filed past the coffin.

Then they took Little Duck to Resthaven Cemetery up on a hill in Perry County. The Army provided six pallbearers, five of whom had served in Vietnam. There was a seven-man firing squad to fire the traditional three volleys over the grave and a bugle to sound taps.

The pallbearers, crisp and polished in summer tans, folded the flag from the coffin and Sgt. Ritter handed it to the young widow, who had wept so much, but spoken so little, during the past three days.

Then the soldier's widow knelt beside the casket and said softly, "Oh, Little Duck."

Then they buried Little Duck beneath a bit of the land he died for.

The Cubs and Conservatism
GEORGE WILL—*Washington Post*—3/21/1974

A reader demands to know how I contracted the infectious conservatism for which he plans to horsewhip me. So if you have tears, prepare to shed them now as I reveal how my gloomy temperament received its conservative warp from early and prolonged experience to the Chicago Cubs.

The differences between conservatives and liberals are as much a matter of temperament as ideas. Liberals are temperamentally inclined to see the world as a harmonious carnival of sweetness and light, where goodwill prevails, good intentions are rewarded, the race is to the swift and a benevolent Nature arranges a favorable balance of pleasure over pain. Conservatives (and Cub fans) know better.

Conservatives know the world is a dark and forbidding place where most new knowledge is false, most improvements are for the worse, the battle is not to the strong, nor riches to men of understanding and an unscrupulous Providence consigns innocents to suffering. I learned this early.

Out in central Illinois, where men are men and I am native, in 1948, at age seven, I made a mad, fateful blunder. I fell ankle over elbows in love with the Cubs. Barely advanced beyond the bib-and-cradle stage, I plighted my troth to a baseball team destined to dash the cup of life's joy from my lips.

Spring, Earth's renewal, a season of hope for the rest of mankind, became for me an experience comparable to being slapped around the mouth with a damp carp. Summer was like being bashed across the bridge of the nose with a crowbar—ninety times. My youth was like one long rainy Monday in Bayonne, New Jersey.

Each year the Cubs charged onto the field to challenge the theory that there are limits to the changes one can ring on pure incompetence. By mid-April, when other kids' teams were girding for Homeric battles at the top of the league, my heroes had wilted like salted slugs and begun their gadarene descent to the bottom. By September they had set a mark for ineptness at which others—but not next year's Cubs—would shoot in vain.

Every litter must have its runt, but my Cubs were almost all runts. Topps baseball gum cards always struggled to say something nice about each player. All they could say about the Cubs' infielder Eddie Miksis is that in 1951 he was tenth in the league in stolen bases, with eleven.

Like the boy who stood on the burning deck whence all but he had fled, I was loyal. And the downward trajectory of my life was set.

In 1949 I reported for Little League, the teams sponsored by local merchants. My friends played for teams like Rasmussen Masonry Braves and Kuhn's Department Store Cubs. Their team colors were bright red and vivid blue. I was a very late draft choice of the Mittendorf Funeral Home Panthers. Our color was black. An eight-year-old could not face these fires without being singed, unless he had the crust of an armadillo, and how many eight-year-olds do?

Of the sixteen teams that existed in 1949, all have since won league championships—all but the Cubs. And which of the old National League teams was first to finish in tenth place behind even the expansion teams? Don't ask. Since 1949 the Cubs have lost more than 2,200 games. That's more than 6,000 hours of losing baseball. They never made me like losing, but they gave me superb training for 1964 when I cast my first vote for president, for Barry Goldwater.

My cruel addiction continued. In 1964 I chose to do three years of graduate study at Princeton because Princeton is midway between Philadelphia and New York—two National League cities. All I remember about my wedding day in 1967 is that the Cubs dropped a doubleheader.

But the gentleman with the horse-whip should stay his hand. I share his fervent desire that I should quit writing about politics. I still hope to reverse the career pattern of James Reston, who began working in baseball but has sunk to writing a political column (for *The New York Times*). I hope to rise as far as he has fallen. I want to be a baseball writer when I grow up.

We Should All Be Dead Today
RICH HEILAND—*Xenia Daily Gazette*—4/4/1974

I will cry a hundred years from now, no matter how many memories come and go, when I think of what this wind did to my city and its people.

Yes, my city, now more than ever, though I have absolutely nothing left to show for my existence here except the most important thing of all—life. My life, the lives of my children, and my wife.

We should all be dead today as, sadly, too many are. But we are alive and we will be back, and we will survive, as will my city, our city, your city.

It was terror, a time when people, myself included, did things that today will make us vomit and tremble when we recall them.

Something funny hit me moments before the tornado struck yesterday, something funny that made me call my wife and tell her to lie down in the only protected part of our Arrowhead home only 75 yards from the shell that was Warner Junior High School.

Not more than 10 seconds later, we heard a sheriff's deputy scream over his radio, "Twister by the bypass and 42." For some reason (we had just told each other we'd never do something like that) Randy Blackaby and I grabbed a camera and ran down Second Street to his car.

We thought the twister was on the edge of town. My God, how wrong we were! At the Five Points intersection, I got out of the car and looked almost straight up at the funnel, swirling with dead birds and debris as it neared St. Brigid Church, which it ripped and killed like a demon that had waited 2,000 years for a victory.

We got back to the car, the roar around us, and escaped the path of the funnel somehow. Our first thoughts were to be newsmen, find out what happened and fast. I copped out, failed, I guess.

As soon as we got near Cincinnati Avenue, I knew. It had hit my house. There was no way it could have missed. We circled around on the bypass, trying to get to Arrowhead. No luck.

I finally found a boy, the son of Tom McCatherine, our associate editor, to show me a short cut behind Warner Junior High.

When I rounded the corner, I just thought, "No, God, no. Don't go any farther, remember them like they were."

The house was destroyed. A couple of walls were standing, the rest had caved in. No one could have lived through it. But, like a ray of sunshine out of the most terrible sky to ever cover Xenia, came my wife's voice, and I never knew how much I loved her and my six-week-old son and five-year-old daughter, who were untouched.

Our only casuality was the family Doberman Pinscher, a gentle dog named Baron who I think escaped. I pray someone will return him to us.

After I rushed the family down to my parents' home in Wilmington, I came back to begin an all-night grind with hundreds of other people trying to help.

There were moments of beauty in terms of sacrifice:

—Men straining to lift fallen timbers off bodies that might still have life in them.

—Bob Stewart, Xenia's city manager, with only half a city, taking charge of a massive rescue and cleanup operation, and not knowing until early morning if his family were alive or dead.

—Gene's Corner, throwing open its doors and coffeehouse to anyone who needed a warm drink and a doughnut.

By the time the sun came up, it was apparent what the wind had done, and I hate it for that. But we are alive, most of us, although many of us are homeless and must now dig through the wreckage of our dreams for bits of furniture, mementos such as a family photo album.

And dig we will. And survive we will, dammit.

Dies the Victim, Dies the City
JIMMY BRESLIN—*New York Daily News*—11/1976

They were walking alone in the empty gray afternoon, three of them, Allen Burnett, Aaron Freeman, and Billy Mabry, Burnett the eldest at 17, walking up Bedford Avenue in Brooklyn and singing out Mohammed Ali rhymes into the chill air. As he reached the corner of Kosciusko Street, it was Allen Burnett's turn to give his Ali rhyme: "AJB is the latest. And he is the greatest."

"Who is AJB?" one of them said.

"Allen J. Burnett." They were laughing at this as they turned the corner onto Kosciusko Street. The three wore coats against the cold. Burnett was in a brown trench coat; Freeman, a three-quarter burgundy leather; and Mabry, a three-quarter beige corduroy with a fox collar. A white paint stain was on the bottom at the back of Mabry's coat. Mabry, walking on the outside, was suddenly shoved forward.

"Keep on walking straight," somebody behind him said.

Billy Mabry turned his head. Behind him was this little guy of maybe 18, wearing a red sweater, dark pants, and black gun. Aaron Freeman, walking next to Mabry, says he saw two others besides the gunman. The three boys kept walking, although Mabry thought the guy in the red sweater had a play gun.

"Give me the money."

"I don't have any money," Allen Burnett said.

The guy with the gun shot Allen Burnett in the back of the head. Burnett pitched into the wall of an apartment house and went down on his back, dead.

The gunman stood with Allen Burnett's body at his feet and said now he wanted coats. Billy Mabry handed back the corduroy with the paint stain. Freeman took off his burgundy leather. The gunman told the two boys to start running. "You don't look back!" Billy Mabry and Aaron Freeman run up Kosciusko Street, past charred buildings with tin nailed over the windows expecting to be shot in the back. People came onto the street and the guy in the red sweater waved his gun at them. The people dived into doorways. He stuffed the gun into his belt and ran up Bedford Avenue, ran away with his new coats. Some saw one other young guy with him. Others saw two.

It was another of last week's murders that went almost unnoticed. Allen Burnett was young. People in the city were concentrating all week on the murders of elderly people. Next week you can dwell on murders of the young, and then the killing of the old won't seem as important.

Allen Burnett's murder went into the hands of the Thirteenth Homicide Squad, situated on the second floor of a new police building on Utica Avenue. The outdoor payphone in front of the precinct house has been ripped out. The lunchette across the street is empty and fire-blackened. At first, a detective upstairs felt the interest was in a man who had just beaten his 22-month-old child to death with a rotting crop. That was unusual. Allen Burnett was just another homicide. Assured that Burnett was the subject, the detective pointed to Harold Ruger, who sat at a desk going through a new manila folder with Burnett's name on it. Ruger is a blue-eyed man with wavy dark brown hair that is white at the temples. The 24 years he has spent on the job have left him with a melancholy face and a soft voice underlined with pleasant sarcasm: "They got two coats. Helluva way to go shopping. Looks like there was three of them. That leaves one guy out there without a coat. I'll look now for somebody who gets taken off for a coat tonight, tomorrow night, the next few days."

In a city that seems virtually ungoverned, Harold Ruger forms the only municipal presence with any relationship to what is happening on the streets where people live. Politicians attend dinners at hotels with contractors. Bankers discussed interest rates at lunch. Harold Ruger goes into a manila folder on his desk and takes out a picture of Allen Burnett, a young face covered with blood staring from a morgue table. In Allen Burnett's hand there is a piece of the veins of the City of New York.

Dies the victim, dies the city. Nobody flees New York because of accounting malpractice. People run from murder and fire. Those who remain express their fear in words of anger.

"Kill him for nothing, that's life—that's what it is today," his sister Sadie was saying. A large impressive family had gathered in the neat frame house at 30 Van Buren Street. "He was going into the Army in January and they kill him for nothing. That's the leniency of the law. Without capital punishment they do what they want. There's no respect for human life."

Horace Jones, an uncle, said, "The bleeding hearts years ago cut out the electric chair. When the only way to stop all this is by having the electric chair."

"We looked at mug shots all last night," Sadie said. "None of them was under 16. If the boy who shot Allen is under 16, there won't be any picture of him. How do you find him if he's under 16? Minors should get treated the same as everybody else. Equal treatment."

"Electric chair for anybody who kills, don't talk to me about ages," Horace Jones said.

The dead boy's mother, Lillian Burnett, sat with her head down and her hands folded in her lap.

"Do you think there should be an electric chair?" she was asked.

"I sure do," she said, eyes closed, head nodding. "Won't bring back my son, but I sure do want it. They tied up three old women and killed them. If they had the electric chair I believe they would rob the three women, but I don't believe they'd kill them."

The funeral was held two days later at the Brown Memorial Baptist Church on Washington Avenue. A crowd of 300 of Allen Burnett's family and friends walked two by two into church. Walked erectly, solemnly, with the special dignity of those to whom suffering is a bitter familiarity. Seeing them, workmen in the street shut off pneumatic drills. Inside the church the light coming through the doorway gleamed on the dark, polished wood of the benches. The doors were closed, an organ sounded, and the people faced the brutality of a funeral service; a baby cried, a woman rocked and screamed, a boy sobbed, a woman fainted, heads were cradled in arms. The mother screamed through a black veil, "My baby's gone!"

An aunt, Mabel Mabry, walked out of the church with lips trembling and arms hugging her shaking body. "My little nephew's dead," she said loudly. "They find the ones who killed him. I'm telling you, they got to kill them too, for my nephew."

The city government, Harold Ruger, just wants to find the killer. Ruger was not at the funeral. "I got stuck in an 80-floor elevator," he said when he came to work yesterday. "I was going around seeing people. We'll leave the number, maybe they'll call us. That's how it happens a lot. They call." He nodded toward a younger detective at the next desk. "He had one, an old man killed by a kid. Information came on a phone call, isn't that right, Al?"

"Stabbed eight times, skull fractured," the younger detective said.

Harold Ruger said, "What does it look like you have? Nothing. And he gets a phone call. See what I mean? The answer is out there and it will come." His finger tapped the file he was keeping on the murder of Allen Burnett.

Civility and Madness
VERMONT ROYSTER—*Wall Street Journal*—5/30/1979

If there were one word that could encompass such a man it would be civility. If there were one word that could describe the manner of his murder it would be madness.

Charles Frankel was best known to the general public through his television series that traced mankind's journey over the centuries in pursuit of liberty. It was, as Dr. Frankel showed us, a journey not yet ended.

If we have come close to finding it in our own country, and have it at least as a grail devoutly to be sought, we need only look around us to see how far beyond hope the dream of liberty lies for so many of the people of our earth. That is brought home to us every day in the news of the world.

But it was not only the pursuit of liberty that Charles Frankel preached, though he did that superbly. He was a philosopher as well as a historian, a teacher of both in classrooms, in books and wherever he could gather a few who would listen; then he would tire the sun with talking and send it down to bed.

Indeed I suspect that, to him, liberty was as much a means to an end as a thing desirable in itself. He knew that liberty by itself can be abused, turning into an anarchy as oppressive as tyranny. What he sought from liberty was the freeing of the human spirit because he believed, above all else, in the dream of civilized man.

Civility and madness. They met one night in the quiet village of Bedford Hills, N.Y. There some person or persons—made, as Charles would put it, in the image of God—went on a wanton spree of violence. They broke into two houses and killed all the occupants of each. Among the dead were Charles and Helen Frankel.

You will search in vain for a motive. The intruders were not professional burglars. They killed first, slipping quietly into bedrooms to put bullets in the heads of their sleeping victims. When they afterwards ransacked the houses it was in aimless fashion, leaving fingerprints everywhere. Much of what they took they left in their stolen car, casually abandoned later in Brooklyn.

Nor were they of the familiar breed of terrorists bent on vengeance or, in the fashion of our times, on spreading fear to make some political point. There was no connection between the two houses, other than proximity; they were simply chosen at random. All the available evidence suggests the murderers did not even know whom they had killed until, perchance, they read about it in the morning paper or heard it on the TV news.

Madness, then, seems the only word for it. The police say the killers were either psychopaths or junked up on dope, killing in a frenzy, shooting some of their unknown victims many times.

What is one to say about such madness? There is a temptation to think this kind of madness endemic to our times, something spawned by these times alone, a sign of a breakdown in our culture, one more manifestation of our moral degeneration. After all there have been other such senseless killings, a man in a college tower or in a shopping center shooting randomly at strangers.

Charles Frankel the historian would not, I think, have succumbed to that temptation. He knew madness and killing have never been strangers to our species, any more than oppression, tyranny, avowed terrorism or the vengeance of revolutionists. Iran's is not the first revolution to devour itself in bloody slaughter. Man's inhumanity and madness are a recurrent cancer on our species.

There is also, I must confess, a temptation to weep the more at the tragic irony that in this case the random victim should be one who believed so much in the ability of man to overcome his barbarism and madness. He had a deep and abiding faith in the rationality of man, in the power of civility in discourse and disagreement.

Yet Charles Frankel the philosopher would have known that there was as much tragedy in the death of his neighbors as in his own, for all that he was famous and they were not. And he would not, or so I think, even in death lose his faith in the worth of man's struggle to, someday, civilize himself.

To believe in the ultimate goodness of man, he once wrote, "is not to say that men's good deeds outnumber their evil deeds, or that benevolence is a stronger disposition in man than malice." His faith, rather, was to keep looking for cures to the human ailments that lead to evil "and of refusing to take No for an answer."

He himself would never accept such an answer. In what were to be his last days he was the moving spirit in founding The National Humanities Center, a place where scholars can gather seeking new light on the human condition. In his vision their searches will not be alone for knowledge about the physical universe in which we live but for something equally and perhaps more important, an understanding of what we are as a human species and of our relation to each other and to that universe.

It is there that Charles Frankel built his own monument. For he built well and what he began will endure. Those whom he brought together with his visions will see to it that the vision is not lost.

So much, then, for the public place of Charles Frankel, historian and philosopher. But there is one more thing to be said. Most of us who knew him had not his gift for civility in all things. To have lost in such a manner a good and gentle friend makes us think how thin is that veneer called civilization, and we can only cry out in helpless anger at the madness in man that will not be exorcised.

Thanks to All of You
MIKE ROYKO—*Chicago Sun-Times*—10/5/1979

It helps very much to have friends, including so many whom I've never met.

Many of you have written to me, offering words of comfort, saying you want to help share the grief in the loss of my wife, Carol.

I can't even try to tell you how moved I've been, and I wish I could take your hands and thank each of you personally.

Others have called to ask when I'll be coming back to work. I don't know when. It's not the kind of job that should be done without full enthusiasm and energy. And I regret that I don't have much of either right now.

So I'm going to take a little more time off. There are practical matters I have to take care of. I want to spend time with my sons. And I can use some hours just to think and remember.

Some friends have told me that the less I look to the past the better. Maybe. But I just don't know how to close my mind's door on 25 years. That was our next anniversary, November.

Actually, it was much longer than that. We met when she was 6 and I was 9. Same neighborhood street. Same grammar school. So if you ever have a 9-year-old son who says he is in love, don't laugh at him. It can happen.

People who saw her picture in this paper have told me how beautiful she appeared to be. Yes, she was. As a young man I puffed up with pride when we went out somewhere and heads turned, as they always did.

But later, when heads were still turning, I took more pride in her inner beauty. If there was a shy person at a gathering, that's whom she'd be talking to, and soon that person would be bubbling. If people felt clumsy, homely and not worth much, she made them feel good about themselves. If someone was old and felt alone, she made them feel loved and needed. None of it was put on. That was the way she was.

I could go on, but it's too personal. And I'm afraid that it hurts. Simply put, she was the best person I ever knew. And while the phrase "his better half" is a cliche, with us it was a truth.

Anyway, I'll be back. And soon, I hope, because I miss you, too, my friends. In the meantime, do her and me a favor. If there's someone you love but haven't said so in a while, say it now. Always, always, say it now.

John Lennon: It's the Promise That's Gone
ELLEN GOODMAN—*Boston Globe*—12/9/1980

I had seen his face only last Sunday: he and the other three looking out from the 1960s buttons and posters. The four were all encased in glass, like cameos of Queen Victoria. They were captured in a Beatles Booth at an antique show.

It startled me then to see the Beatles sold as something old. But it is always surprising when our youth becomes a collector's item.

On Tuesday, I saw his face again, on the front page. John Lennon, the most complex of the Beatles, had been shot dead by a loony, a cuckoo, a nutcake—the New York police used all the familiar words, including "allegedly." The killer apparently was some crazed cousin to all the crackpots and criminals who can buy guns as easily as Christmas trees. Amen to that.

But the Lennon I'll miss isn't the brilliant Beatle of the sixties with his hair "rebelliously" grown below his ears. That John Lennon exists on my records. The man I'll miss is the one I just met again, the man of the eighties, moving in new ways, making new sounds. Five bullets wiped out this father, husband, musician . . . human work in progress.

I am more a member of the Beatles' generation than the fans' generation. So I was moved by the emergence of John Lennon at forty.

It was good to see him sell Promise at Forty. Not depressions, not complacency, not mania, but Promise. "It's quite possible," he said, "to do anything."

The new record he made with his wife, Yoko Ono, *Double Fantasy*, was the work of a survivor. "You have to give thanks to God or whatever is up there (for) the fact that we all survived—survived Vietnam or Watergate, the tremendous upheaval of the whole world," he said in an ironic prelude to his death.

But it wasn't just the decades he'd survived. He'd overcome something else: other people's expectations.

John Lennon got lost for a time, wandering in the body of The Famous John Lennon. He became so public a person that his life became a role he was playing. Other people were the directors.

There were the fans who expected him to be a Beatle Forever, until he ended up singing "I Wanna Hold Your Hand" in Las Vegas nightclubs. There were the business managers who wanted him to be their product. "I was a machine," he said, "that was supposed to produce so much creative something and give it out periodically for approval to justify my existence on earth."

There were even people who expected him to self-destruct like Dylan Thomas or the rock stars with needle tracks up their arms. "I'd just naively accepted the idea," he said, "that an artist had to self-destruct in order to create."

He survived all these expectations by getting better, saner, older. In 1975, he jumped into his private life as if it were a lifeboat. His fans called it seclusion. He called it becoming a "househusband." But he got in touch with the routines that root all of us, with daily-ness. He took care of his child, instead of being taken care of like a child. He let himself go into his new rhythms.

Five years later, this fall, he and his wife came out with music and words. He talked about men and women "Starting Over," about balancing family and work, about growing up.

"Is it possible to have a life centered around a family and a child and still be an artist?" he asked one reporter. "When I look at the relative importance of what life is about, I can't quite convince myself that making a record or having a career is more important or even as important as my child, or any child," he told another.

The man changed, and typically refused to apologize or simplify it. "The attitude is that when you change when you get older there's something wrong with that. Whatever changes I'm going through because I'm forty I'm thankful for, because they give me some insight into the madness I've been living all myself."

In a way he was talking to and for his own generation. "I'm saying, 'Here I am now, how are you? How's our relationship going? Did you get through it all? Wasn't the 70s a drag, you know? Well, here we are, let's make the Eighties great because it's up to us to make what we can of it.'"

John Lennon of the sixties survived so much—even pessimism—only to get murdered. He made a life late and died early.

Did his murderer aim for the Sixties' Superstar, the Beatle, the face under glass? What craziness and waste. You can't kill what a man has already done. You can only kill what might have come next.

The antique John Lennon had already been preserved. Dammit, it's the promise that's gone.

Beyond Politics
JIMMY BRESLIN—*New York Daily News*—1/21/1981

Know that the day belongs to Pamela Mayo, whose husband, an air force sergeant, died in the desert in Iran last April. In the recording of the 444 days of the hostages in Iran, in tales of spies and clerks, of political fakery and national will, of honor and dishonor, the purity of her husband's act places him above all. He died trying to rescue other human beings.

On morning television yesterday, each mention of the hostages would cause one of Pam Mayo's kids to call out and the others in the family of four boys and a mother to run through the house to the set.

"The reason that it's so important to us is that maybe it won't be over for us until it's over for them," Pam Mayo, who is thirty-one, was saying. Her husband, Joel Mayo, who was known as Buck, was an in-flight engineer on C-130 transports. In Iran, age thirty-four, he died in the darkness when a helicopter crashed into a C-130.

She lives as a stranger in the town where she was born, Harrisville, Michigan. In the morning, as she heard discussions on television about the difficulties the hostages could have in becoming used to having families around them again, she thought of the day in 1966 when she met her husband. She was eighteen and in high school and a girlfriend brought him into her mother's kitchen in Harrisville. He was an airman, assigned to the base fire department at Wurtsmith Air Force Base at Oscoda, Michigan. He was Irish and Indian from Florida and she was Yugoslavian from the forestland of upper Michigan. They were married and began thirteen and a half years of living on air bases.

And she remembered the last time she saw him. It was a spring night at Fort Walton Beach, Florida, and he was leaving for temporary duty that he would not talk about. Many weeks before that, FBI agents suddenly started interviewing his family and friends because, they said, Buck was being given a "top secret" security clearance. Once that happened, his wife never asked him about his military work.

Usually, when Buck was going away, he spent the last hours teasing his wife or working on something around the house. Varnish a table, fix a bike, tighten a doorknob. This time, last April, Buck Mayo was listless and said nothing. It was the first time, his wife said to herself, that he ever had seemed reluctant to go anyplace with his squadron.

They had his favorite dinner, pork chops. During it, he said nothing. After dinner, she had the young kids in the tub and he came in and said good-bye to them. She walked him out to the carport, and he stood by their 1969 station wagon.

"No sense you coming," he said. "I'll drive over to the squadron and leave the car locked in the parking lot. Get somebody to drive you over in the morning and pick it up."

"Well, I don't want to haul the kids out of the bathtub," she said.

"That's what I mean," he said.

There was no reason to ask him where he was going. She was a military wife and she knew that she was supposed to say nothing. At the same time, it was plain that it was Iran. The only way to snatch the hostages was by air.

Buck kissed her good-bye. During the kiss, the notion ran through her that he would die. The kiss in front of the 1969 car became one of the horrible moments of her life.

And then he was gone, and she changed her life. Television news was not allowed in the house. The kids put on cartoons, or old horror movies, but she wanted no news reports as she walked about her house.

On April 25, she and her children slept through the night while the ones who determined her life sat by phones in the White House.

That there were hostages in the first place was President Carter's fault. He had allowed people with personal interests—John McCloy, Henry Kissinger, and David Rockefeller—-to cause him to place his caution aside and allow the shah of Iran to enter a hospital in New York. Tehran erupted, and the hostages were taken. At first, in his reelection campaign, Carter found that the country's willingness to support a president in time of trouble was an asset in Democratic primaries. But then Carter lost five of seven primaries and caucuses and the issue of the hostages became an ominous one.

At the same time, it was intolerable that they were being held, and people of the nation, particularly those who were older, increasingly called for America to stand up to these screaming Iranians they watched each night on television.

"This country needs a win," one of Carter's people said one day. And now, on April 25, cynical politics and patriotism were mingled, and as the Mayo family slept in Florida, the father landed in the desert in Iran on the raid that was designed to get back hostages, bring America to its feet, as if for a great football touchdown, and insure a president's reelection.

When Pam Mayo woke up in the morning, one of the kids called from the bedroom, "They tried to rescue the hostages last night. It didn't work."

Now, Pam Mayo told herself, we'll see if you know how to keep yourself under control. She said nothing and got the kids off for school and then went to her job as lunchroom cashier at the grammar school. When she came in, the woman in charge, Brunelle, said, "Have you heard the news?"

"Yes," Pam said.

"Are you going to be all right?" Brunelle asked.

"As long as the other girls can forget trying to be television news announcers and talk about the weather," Pam said.

Brunelle laughed and went to her office. Pam sat in the cafeteria kitchen and had coffee. Her husband, she told herself, was dead.

A few minutes later, Brunelle came into the cafeteria. "Pam, could you come with me for a minute?" she said.

Pam put down the coffee and followed the woman into the office. Inside were a doctor, a priest, the base commander, and a sergeant and his wife.

"You didn't have to come," Pam Mayo told the doctor.

Then they told her what she had known from the moment Buck Mayo kissed her good-bye.

And today, the nation celebrates its hostages; it examines them and pampers them and exults, and President Carter leaves office with his engineer's determination intact; he had taken this problem and finally solved it. And Pam Mayo and her children, who gave the most, sit in front of a television set in Michigan and cheer.

"When I came back here, people didn't know how to take me," she was saying. "I was alone. I wasn't divorced or embittered by my husband. And they had seen me on television. This is a small town up here. It's just like a Southern town without an accent. I've been away for over thirteen years. Everything is taking a lot of time. Now it might be a little different. It's over for the hostages and now it's over for me. I can begin the rest of my life."

She never understood the politics of Iran. Last fall in Michigan, she forgot to register and did not vote in the November election. She doesn't want anybody tormenting her with the idea that her husband might have died because of a political campaign. All she knows is that he died as a hero of his country and today, the day that belongs to her, we celebrate his heroism.

A Child Wrestles with His Dog's Death
PETE DEXTER—*Philadelphia Daily News*—2/13/1981

The year I turned five my family moved to Milledgeville, a little town in central Georgia, where my father taught physics at the military college.

Our house was on a red clay road, next to a pine woods and a sawmill. The plums came off the trees hot from the sun, and I had a cocker spaniel puppy that followed me everywhere I went. Nobody wore shoes all summer long, except to Sunday school.

The puppy was almost grown when he was killed. A city garbage truck hit him and left him where he stopped rolling, beside the road on a hill half a mile from the house. I heard about it from a kid named Kenny Durkin, who was the kind of kid who would spend half the afternoon looking for you to be the one to tell you your dog was dead.

He is probably working for a newspaper now.

Anyway, Kenny found me down at the sawmill, walking around the inside edge of a round cement building where they burned scrap wood. The building had a clay floor, dug out into pit, and if you fell off the edge, that's where you ended up, in there burning with the wood.

I went there once or twice a week and waited for the watchman to chase me out. I wanted to see it when he fell off the edge.

Kenny Durkin stuck his head into the open door and yelled at me. "Peedah," he said, "the city truck done run over your dog and he's dead."

We ran from the sawmill to the hill where the city truck had left my dog, stopping every now and then for Kenny Durkin to get his breath.

By the time we got to the place on the hill, the sun had baked one side of the dog's coat so hot you could hardly touch him. The flies were all over his ear and eyes, and I brushed them away and picked him up. He had never seemed so heavy before.

I carried the puppy up the hill, stumbling under the weight. I fell in some stones, and he rolled into the ditch. I pulled him out by a leg, and there was a trail of blood and bubbles where his mouth had slid along the ground.

It was cool in the ditch and I thought about leaving him there, but there was something worse in that than in what had already happened.

I picked him up and started for home again. I moved him from one side to the other, trying to get rid of the ache in my muscles. But the ache got worse and worse and the next time I fell I couldn't pick him up again, so I dragged him home by the leg.

And I was crying as much from the ache as for the dog.

A neighbor woman came out from behind her screen door and told me to leave the puppy out in the street. "Come on in and have some ice tea," she said. "Your daddy'll be by directly."

But I was dizzy from the heat, watching my feet move, one in front of the other against the red Georgia dirt, and I didn't answer.

And a long time went by before I got the puppy home.

I remembered all that last week. I was driving some back roads near Elmer, New Jersey, when I came on a kid carrying a dead dog.

He was older than I had been—he might have been nine or ten—but you don't pick the times you grow up, they pick you. The dog was a mongrel, maybe thirty-five pounds, and the kid was trying to balance it in front of him on the frame of his bicycle.

He'd pedal a few yards, then the handle bars would get away from him. He'd reach up to steady himself and the dog would fall off onto the road. I stopped the car behind him and asked what had happened.

"She got run over," he said. The dog was lying at his feet and the boy couldn't control his voice any more than the handle bars. Everything was falling apart all at once.

I said, "I can help you get her home."

He said, "I can do it." He picked up the dog and lay her across the bicycle. The eyes swung in the air. The boy got back on the bicycle and tried again, the dog fell off again. "Oh, Goldie," he said.

Then the kid laid his dog across the bicycle, held her there with one hand and began to walk toward a red and white farmhouse a long ways down the road. From the back you could see him crying. Maybe if I'd asked him again he would have let me drive him home.

But, then, maybe after the dog was buried, getting her home by himself would be all he would have to take her place.

Ireland's Rage: Sands' Mourners Will Not Be Pacified

RICHARD BEN CRAMER—*Philadelphia Inquirer*—5/10/1981

BELFAST, NORTHERN IRELAND—In a grimy gray drizzle, under ragged black flags that lifted and waved balefully in the fitful air; to the wail of a single piper, on streets through charred and blasted brick spray-painted with slogans of hate; by silent tens of thousands, past fathers holding sons face-forward that they might remember the day, past mothers rocking and shielding prams that held tomorrow's fighters, past old men who blew their rheumy red noses and remembered their own days of rage . . . Bobby Sands was carried Thursday to a grave of raw Ulster mud.

It was the largest spectacle Belfast ever saw. There was no way to count the crowd that started as a file 10 abreast and a half-mile long, then grew with every passing block to a surging, spreading flood that washed up and broke, finally, amidst the drizzle-darkened stones of a rundown graveyard.

In some ways it was the scariest. For in the faces that lined the route, among the thousands who formed the cortege, there was none of the grief that passes and cleanses with a rush of hot tears; there was not the anger that can suddenly spark fiery riots and just as suddenly vanish. There was instead a grim, lingering rage, a quiet, determined, smouldering smite; these mourners will not be pacified.

At the head of the long procession, ahead of the coffin, ahead even of the marshalls who cleared the way, a quiet man named Liam Rice, 66, walked the three-mile route. He had walked a hundred funerals, fought for years with the IRA; he had been wounded by a soldier's bullet and lived to fight again; he had been jailed, beaten and held naked in a solitary cell, and been freed to fight again; he had joined a hunger strike and watched his friend, Sean McCaughey, die from self-inflicted starvation 35 years ago.

"It's been going on a long time. Yes, a long time," said Rice as he turned to gaze at the endless mass of mankind behind him. "I could tell you of my time. The ones my age remember. No, but I can tell you, now: There's never been a feeling like this."

* * *

Saint Luke's, in the housing project of Twinbrook, southwest of Belfast, was not meant for crowds. The church is a spare, brick octagon with eight blond wood beams sweeping up from the joints of the walls to the modest dome. Bobby Sands' coffin stood at the base of the altar.

In the pews, people were shoulder to shoulder. In the aisles, they stood with their faces half a foot from the next person's back. There were thousands who could not get in.

Father Liam Mullan's voice cut briskly through the heavy air. He wasted no time. He minced no words.

"We are here to help Bobby Sands' soul, and as we help Bobby today, let us pray for all the people who have died in our country since 1969 because of violence."

Mullan made it a Mass of peace. He never asked for prayers for Sands without adding another plea: for the souls of two men who died in Belfast the day before in the spurt of violence that heralded this Mass.

"Love one another today by striving for peace, for restraint, for moderation and for an end of violence. . . ."

Mullan, 63, a priest for 38 years, did not try anything fancy. His remarks were short and clear. The sermon on the mount provided his theme. He did not glorify Bobby Sands but commended the Sands family for their courage and faith.

He knew where his duty lay. Pope John Paul II, the "bishop of bishops," had spelled out the message of peace in Ireland in a visit almost two years ago. "And we can hardly be called Catholic," Mullan said, "if we do not believe in the counsel of our bishops. . . ."

Perhaps he also knew fancy words would not alter anything. Perhaps he knew that the crucifix he had laid on Sands' coffin would be replaced, just outside the church door, with the Irish tricolor flag and a commando's gloves and beret. He knew, perhaps, that he could offer Holy Communion to a fraction of the 1,200 who had packed the church, while just outside the doors, 5,000 who could not get in were staring, fascinated at seven hooded IRA men drawn up as an honor guard.

He knew, perhaps, after 22 years in Belfast, that the lesson of peace—respectfully received amid stifled coughing and shushing of babies in church—might not carry far on the glitter glass–strewn, bitter bomb-blown streets.

"It's two different things," said Marie Lyons, a steel-gray woman who stood outside the church in the green tunic and cocked ranger hat of the Clann Na Ngael, the women's wing of the IRA. "Our funerals are always quiet. We have respect for the dead. But when our dead is buried, then we'll see how quiet it is, please God!"

Oh, it was deathly quiet on that long march Thursday while the rain damped the footfalls and the faithful said not a word.

Even the disrespectful clatter of army helicopters continuously circling above could not break the grim stillness on the street.

The marshalls murmured their commands. The Dalmers carrying the coffin and two carloads of family—Sands' mother and sister, his 7-year-old son, Gerard, his cousin, a nun, Sister Bernadette, who read the Gospels at the funeral Mass—purred in a silent idle at the head of the file.

Astride the lead car, the IRA honor guard marched in two noiseless rows. Here was muteness intensified; their hoods hid all expression and lent with round, unblinking eyeholes a horrifying android stare.

Then, a rank of gray silent men, the Republican Burial Society, who tend the IRA cemetery and add to events of this sort a careful competence with death.

Then, hundreds of women, carrying before them hundreds of wreaths, the front row with four identical arrangements contrived in the shape of an "H." These conjured the H-block prisons at Maze, where Bobby Sands died and where his friends and fellows are still refusing food.

Then, the mourners, stretched in a solid file so massive and, when seen from a distance, so still it might have been paint on the street. The pace was slow and halting. Each block had to be cleared ahead. Each block yielding new marchers who lengthened the line.

And yet it was silent.

Near the midpoint of the route, an IRA squad bearing rifles materialized near the hearse. Without haste, without any apparent fear, they fired three volleys in salute. Then they and their illegal guns melted back into the crowd.

When the column squeezed into a curve around a Protestant neighborhood which the policy and army blocked off with huge, portable metal and canvas screens, there was no jostling, just tens of thousands waiting patiently in the rain.

When spray paint on the walls of that neighborhood screamed "F— the IRA hoods," there were no screams in reply.

To be sure, the detour and the insults were noticed. "That's one little bit of Loyalist territory the route goes through—a couple hundred yards," muttered Willie John McCurry, one of the burial society men. "And they're divertin' the whole funeral. That shows you who's the first-class and who's the second class."

But he, too, had caught the mood of the march. There would be no unruly display.

"Aye, it's determination we're showin'—to finish the job this time."

The Anderson and Falls Roads took the march into the IRA's breeding ground. Here, the scarred walls were spray-painted "F— the British." And "Smash the H-blocks." Here, the mesh-clad windows displayed pictures of Bobby Sands—chubby and scruffy and smiling at the camera, not the wasted little frame in the coffin ahead. Still, there was no loosening of control. Still, the marshalls murmured the procession along. Still the crowds watched, grim and quiet.

At the gates of the Milltown cemetery, the column paused while the marshalls linked arms to hold the crowds away from the arrow passage. The mourners closest to the gates knelt and, as if on command, recited the rosary as the Daimiers and the faceless honor guard squeezed onto the cemetery grounds.

At the window of one of the limousines, Rosaleen Sands, Bobby's mother, gripped her haggard face with one hand, as if, physically, to hold in the pain, to keep control, just a bit longer.

Slowly, the cortege moved up the graveyard's main path. On either side mourners flooded in toward the grave sight, picking their way among tombstones in high, untended grass. From the main path, with thousands moving along on either side, it seemed as if the mourners stood still while the graves of Ulster's Catholic dead floated by in a supernatural review.

Liam Rice, the IRA veteran, stood near the old monument to Republican volunteers and watched the crowd moving through the tall grass in the late afternoon mist.

"It will have its reaction, you know. It has its reaction in Ireland."

His friend, Patrick O'Neill, who served time in jail with Rice, said, solemnly, "How soon?"

"Here, England will have to give up and pull out," Rice said. "That's the only thing that faces them now." He added, without emotion: "It could be that they'll let the other ones (hunger strikers) die, too."

O'Neill wiped his damp nose. "If they die," he said, "there'll be many to fill their places. There's 70 volunteers at the moment."

Rice nodded and said: "Aye, plenty."

A Night to Be Jolly
JIMMY BRESLIN—*New York Daily News*—12/25/1981

Any place with a bar in it yesterday was packed. They were shaking hands and kissing each other and then taking a drink whether they wanted one or not because everybody drinks before he goes home on Christmas Eve.

Ida Ryan was catching them on the other end, when they came off the train at the el station at Broadway and 31st Street, out in Astoria.

She sat and watched them as they came down the stairs, walking quickly, the whisky showing in their faces, saying, "Merry Christmas," and, "Have a good holiday," to each other as they started for home.

One of them came up to the change window, a dollar bill in the hand under the packages.

"Could I get change for the bus?" he said.

Ida took the bill and pushed silver through the window and the hand fumbled from under the packages and picked it up.

"You know, this must be an awful tough night for you to work," the guy said, because he thought that was good to say to somebody working on Christmas Eve.

"Uh huh," Ida said. "Merry Christmas."

She said it automatically, but she was looking down, arranging her change and tokens. It was Christmas for everybody else last night, but to Ida Ryan it was just an eight-hour shift in a change booth.

Her husband, Jimmy Ryan, is in a cell in Attica State Prison. Her son, James Jr., is eighteen and is in the narcotics ward at Manhattan General Hospital. The boy was in grammar school, with report cards that showed honor marks, when the father was sent away in 1957. From then on, the boy slipped in school, and a year ago he came home with his eyes glazed from taking goofballs. Nobody could get him off the habit.

The daughter, Helen, is twelve and Ida has her living with a sister on Long Island now because she can't do much for her at home. A couple of years ago Helen began to have trouble hearing out of the right ear. The condition persisted until the ear went dead altogether. Then the left ear began to go. The doctors look at the ears and say nothing can be done.

"What am I going to do?" Ida said. "Something happens and I guess everybody has to pay for it. Now I have my father down. He's a job all by himself."

"The father? What happened to him?"

"He lost a leg a year ago. Then he had a stroke, and now he's just a patient in bed. He's another patient. That's all we have is patients."

Jimmy Ryan was a first-grade detective in New York. In 1957 he was sentenced to 7½ to 15 years and 2½ to 5 years for burglaries and holdups. He was also hit with a 4-year federal sentence for handling counterfeit money. He was no bargain when they put him away. Gambling had him over his head with money, and he took his gun and instead of protecting people with it he turned it on them. He knew it better than anybody else when he went away: he rated everything he got.

Then, a year ago, Ida Ryan came into the visiting room at Attica and she spoke over a table to her husband and told him that his son was on junk.

"I'll get him, I'll chain him to the bed," Jimmy said. "Let me get my hands on this kid."

"You can't," Ida said. "That's the trouble. You can't do a thing to him. You're here and he's on the street."

Then a guard stepped up and pounded his club on the table. "Time's up," the guard said.

He was locked in his cell for the night at 3:45 p.m. yesterday, just a few minutes after Ida started work in the change booth and all the people came down the stairs with their packages and the whisky in them and saying, "Merry Christmas" to each other.

The stories today are all about Tiny Tim and fat men seeing hungry faces in the windows and stepping out to give them something to eat, and there always is warmth and hope in them, which is why they are fables you tell at Christmas.

She smiled. "Hope, what kind of hope have I got? He's got years to go and his son and daughter are falling into pieces. He comes up for parole in November; if he could get paroled he could start on the federal sentence. But he may not even get paroled this time. I don't know. I just wish I could see a little light. If somebody would come and tell me tonight that I have a chance, that I can see some light, then it would be different. I could hope. Now I just have to sit here and make change."

At a few minutes before midnight somebody came to relieve her and she walked out of the booth and went downstairs to the street and walked up to Saint Rita's for midnight mass.

"I have to make it," she said. "I have more things to talk about in there than anybody else."

Homeboys and Heroes
FRANK DEL OLMO—*Los Angeles Times*—7/30/1987

This is my last column for a while. My plan was to go back to my old neighborhood in Pacoima and write about the place. It's a run-down part of town, but it's getting more positive attention these days than it usually does, because it was also home to Ritchie Valens, a Chicano rock 'n roll idol whose brief stardom is the subject of a new movie.

That film, *La Bamba*, named after a hit record that Valens made by adapting a Mexican folk tune to a '50s rock beat, appears to be a mainstream success. Even if it isn't, it will be eagerly devoured by Latino audiences, ever hungry for entertainment that positively portrays their community or features Latino heroes and role models.

Valens, whose real name was Richard Valenzuela, was only 17 when he died in 1959 in an airplane crash that also killed Buddy Holly, another rising young rock star. As with many public figures who die young, the lingering interest in

Valens' life stems not just from what he achieved; we wonder what might have been had he lived.

So, after seeing the movie, I thought that I'd return to the old barrio and write something about the homeboy who made good and maybe even some upbeat things about Pacoima itself.

But then they killed Alejandro Salazar.

Alejandro was only 10 when he died last week, hit by a stray bullet fired by a gang member. As I read news accounts of the incident, I could see it precisely.

Alejandro was walking home from Pacoima Recreation Center, the city park where I played every day as a child. It's right across the street from San Fernando Gardens, the housing project where I grew up and where Alejandro lived with his parents, a sister and a brother.

He was standing just outside the park fence, a few yards down from Pacoima Elementary School, where he was in fourth grade. Across the street is Guardian Angel, the Roman Catholic parish school. I attended both as a youngster.

Alejandro's friends said that he was trying to come up with enough change to buy an ice cream from a street vendor when a scuffle broke out between a local Latino punk who deals drugs and some would-be customers, who were black. Also nearby were members of a street gang that have claimed the housing project as their turf. Seeing a homeboy hassled by blacks, one of the gang members pulled a gun and started spraying shots about wildly. Alejandro fell to the ground, blood spurting from his head. He died in a hospital a few hours later.

Alejandro Salazar was the seventh child to be killed or wounded by stray gang bullets this month in the Los Angeles area.

The homeboys are being quiet about it. "They're going around with their heads low right now," according to Manuel Velasquez, a local gang worker. "But I wonder how long it will last."

Velasquez has good reason to be dubious. For six years he has been a street worker for the Community Youth Gang Services Project, the county agency that tries to intervene to stop gang violence before it happens. He's a courageous, caring young man, but he knows the gang mentality all too well.

Chilling as it sounds, the cretins who contributed to Alejandro's death are trying to rationalize what happened.

"Now that one of their friends has been arrested," Velasquez told me, "some of them are saying it wasn't his fault, but the blacks' [fault] for buying drugs, or the guy who was dealing."

Right, fellas. You were just defending the barrio against interlopers. What asinine, macho stupidity!

I remember . . .

Growing up in Pacoima 30 years ago, I was supposed to hate guys from San Fernando just because they were from San Fer and I was from Pacas. It makes no more sense now than it did then. And I don't know what makes me angrier about it—the fact that such a backward mentality is still there after all these years, or the fact that Chicanos like me who grew up in places like Pacoima, but moved away, haven't done more to help snuff it out.

Oh, I know all the reasons youth gangs exist—poverty and unemployment, fed by racism and discrimination. I try to struggle against those problems whenever I can, and maybe someday we'll have them licked. But, damn it, in the meantime we must do more to protect innocents like Alejandro Salazar.

More gang workers like Velasquez would sure help. Right now he and the important program that he works for don't get nearly enough money. The gang project's budget is so tight that Velasquez and one other street worker must cover the entire San Fernando Valley, keeping track of more than 80 gangs—a dozen in Pacoima alone. And you can multiply his problems by the hundreds in South-Central Los Angeles and East L.A., in Santa Ana and Riverside.

I'm grateful that people like Velasquez are out there trying to keep a lid on the insanity that lurks on some of our meaner streets. If we need either role models or unsung heroes, there they are, right under our noses. But we don't do nearly enough to help them control the punks like the one who killed Alejandro. As long as there are losers like that around, the many winners that the Latino barrios produce will never get the attention that they deserve.

Alejandro Salazar was just an average student, according to the staff at Pacoima Elementary School—but he was also a popular kid who "had everything going for him," in the words of Principal Robert Owens. He might not have been another Albert Einstein, but maybe he could have been another Ritchie Valens. And until those of us who presume to lead, or speak for, the Latino community do more to abolish gangs, the achievements of Chicanos like Valens will seem shallow in the eyes of society at large.

Echoes of Grief "in the Line of Duty"
MIKE BARNICLE—*Boston Globe*—2/20/1993

At 7:15 last night, a doctor, Alasdair Conn, his face grim with bad news only growing worse, walked across the emergency room of Massachusetts General Hospital and knocked on a door where the family of Thomas Rose, a 42-year-old Boston cop shot hours earlier, sat together waiting for medical updates. Rose had arrived at the hospital about 4:30 in the afternoon with a bullet lodged in his right side and one in his arm and was immediately rushed into surgery, given

30 units of blood, his whole life now in the hands of Susan Briggs, a spectacular surgeon looking for one more miracle.

"I'm afraid he's not doing well," Conn told the family. "We're having trouble with his blood pressure. He's more critical now than when we first saw him. As soon as I have anything further, I'll let you know."

Inside the small room were Rose's mother, Nora; two of his children, Tommy and a daughter Kelly; his girlfriend Jean; his sister Peggy, and one of his brothers, Eddie, a Boston firefighter assigned to Ladder 21.

When Conn finished, Tommy Rose Jr. pounded the plaster wall and the noise reverberated through the emergency room. His daughter began to cry. His sister screamed, "His own gun. He was shot with his own gun."

Rose was assigned to the Area A station. Around 4 p.m. he was taking a prisoner by the name of Terrell Muhammad to a phone to make a call. Suddenly, Muhammad bolted for the door and Rose lunged for him, the two men struggling on the floor. The prisoner got hold of the cop's gun and four shots were fired, one of them doing great damage to Rose's liver.

The shots echoed through the police station. Joe O'Malley, 26 years on the job, raced across the lobby and grabbed Muhammad, removing the weapon from a man who had just been arrested for larceny two hours before.

Muhammad, who uses several aliases, was arrested in Dorchester on May 27, 1986, for murder. In September 1988, he pleaded down to manslaughter and received a 6- to 10-year jail term. By Friday afternoon, the system had kicked him back and he was on Washington Street in Boston.

Now Dr. Briggs was in the operating room along with Dr. Burt Enos and several other surgeons. In the hospital lobby, a crew of police officers waited, in great frustration, to give blood or an ear of sympathy to a waiting family.

At 7:35, Dr. Conn came walking back through the lobby. He was followed by Dr. Briggs and Dr. Enos, blood spattered on the cuffs and sleeves of their hospital greens.

The door to the waiting room was held open. Father Tom Riley, a police chaplain, walked in ahead of the surgeons and stood bolt-straight as Conn began, "I'm sorry . . ."

The eternal and familiar wail of grief filled the halls and spilled out into the parking lot where a cold wind whipped the TV crews waiting with their lights and constant demand. The dead policeman's son and daughter shook with grief and tears. His mother said, "Oh my God, they've killed my boy."

Tommy Rose's brother Eddie grabbed his nephew Tommy and held him as if he were trying to squeeze all of his dead brother's life back into the boy's body. But the boy, dressed in the uniform of youth—gray sweatshirt and blue pants, simply shook with sorrow and said, "Dad . . . Dad . . . Don't be dead, Dad. Please don't be dead."

Now, the official ritual of municipal loss began: The mayor, Ray Flynn, and the police commissioner, Mickey Roache, his face a straight line of pain, met with the Roses. All the waiting cops, their assistance rendered useless by a single moment of violence, wandered, almost aimlessly, in the hallways while detectives from the homicide unit went briskly and efficiently about their work.

In the city outside, the Friday night lights flickered as if nothing much had happened. Of course, the police force has taken a public pounding for many months now but, with a patrolman dead on a table, the job description again came to public notice: To serve, protect and, sometimes, even die for a city and its citizens.

So it was that at 8:40 last night, a dispatcher sitting in the turret at headquarters tapped the key and said over police radios citywide: "To all units, please be notified that Patrolman Thomas F. Rose died tonight at 20:40 hours, in the line of duty."

Amid Destruction, City's Heroes Robbed of Chance to Save Lives
MICHAEL DALY—*New York Daily News*—9/12/2001

One after another they pitched themselves from the remaining tower, choosing certain death over the blazing horror above.

As each dark figure plummeted, a lone human life seemed more enormous than all the destruction.

They invariably extended their arms and legs and they always seemed to land on their backs with a boom the living will never forget. One woman hit a building sign and ceased to resemble a woman at all.

Then, just as you had watched yet another person take the fatal leap, the second tower began to collapse. Your mind registered debris exploding out from all sides, and then you were running along with firefighters and cops and paramedics.

"We're still too close!" a cop cried out.

You looked back and now saw only an impossibly big cloud broiling toward you. You ran on, trying to figure how many blocks long the tower was, realizing you would surely die if it fell your way like some huge tree.

Then the cloud caught up with you and you waited to be struck by something. There was only choking, blinding ash, and you scrambled on until the air began to clear.

You looked back and realized that the second tower must have pancaked almost straight down. The whole area was covered under a thick gray powder. You saw strips of window glazing hanging from a pair of trees.

REMNANTS OF LIFE

Bits of paper blew around your ankles, and you were puzzled until you retrieved a charred financial form and saw the words, "Attn: R Damani 98th Fl. 1 World Trade Center."

Your eyes then chanced on a photo blown from its frame of a smiling girl of about 8 years old wearing a white turtleneck with a shamrock on the collar. Beside that was a shredded picture of a group smiling in front of a swimming pool. The American flag was fluttering behind them.

"How many people died back there?" a firefighter from Engine 353 asked. "How many people were lost?"

A firefighter paused to examine a check from the Sumitomo Marine Claims Services of Suite 9035, 1 World Trade Center. He read aloud the amount with a hollow tone that said this was one day in the financial capital of the world when money meant absolutely nothing.

"A hundred and seven thousand dollars," he said.

A mass of dollar bills was strewn in the ash nearby, but nobody touched them as the firefighters and cops trudged toward the skeletal remains of the two towers. They had only axes and steel bars and a single hose run from a fireboat in the river.

"We're going to regroup," a voice said over the fire radio.

A few stories of the second tower's facade were visible, but otherwise there was just a smoking heap. You thought of all those trapped inside who had not leaped.

You also thought of the very best people you knew, particular firefighters and cops who always seemed to be among the first to rush into danger. You chanced into a chief, who told you that one person dear to everyone in the Fire Department was definitely dead. Two others were missing, one as dear to you as a brother, the other one of the world's leading experts in addressing the aftermath of a terrorist attack.

Back on West St., everybody jumped when the gas tanks of cars in a parking garage began to explode. A firefighter's air tank popped and skidded crazily on the ground. A whole stack of air tanks lay with their out-of-air alarms going off. A bloody-faced firefighter named Jimmy Grillo borrowed a cell phone and managed to get through to home.

"I'm alive," he said. "See you later."

Retired Firefighter Kevin Horan, now fire safety director at the World Trade Center, came up with his head bandaged and his arm in a sling.

"I just saw pieces of bodies," he said.

Horan set off in search of his old unit, Ladder 3. You knew two of the company, and the day held no more beautiful sight than one of them standing unhurt on Liberty St. Your heart sank when he told you the other man had been on the 50th floor when the tower went down. You again looked at the rubble and remembered when you last saw your friend, the two of you laughing and joking as you marched to a communion breakfast.

The missing & the dead

A squad of ash-covered firefighters now trooped past, saying they hoped to help rescue people from Ladder 6 and Engine 39.

"They're trapped, but we're in communication with them," one of the firefighters said.

On Albany St., a group of EMS paramedics manned a triage area. Paramedic Timothy Keller had managed to pull an injured firefighter from the falling debris but was losing hope for his captain.

"She was 10 feet behind me, trying to get the other people to cover," he said.

A voice then came over the radio announcing that 7 World Trade Center was in danger of collapse.

"We're going to move everybody off the pile," the voice said. "We're stopping the operation."

Back on West St., some police officers saw a gun and then a second gun lying in the ashes. They picked up a piece of medal and found a dead Port Authority officer underneath.

A firefighter named Craig Monahan had already scrambled under a collapsed passageway and on into the rubble pile in search of the rest of Ladder 5. He rushed to the scene from home along with two of his comrades, and just before the collapse he had gone over to move the company's truck so a chief could get down from a ledge.

"Now they're gone," he said.

A big firefighter came up to Monahan.

"Were they in the building?" the firefighter asked.

"Yes," Monahan said.

The firefighter hugged Monahan.

"You sure you're okay?" the firefighter asked.

"Yeah," Monahan said.

And then he walked back through the ashes to where so many of our very finest people were last seen.

Amid the Ruins, a Separate Peace
STEVE LOPEZ—*Los Angeles Times*—9/15/2001

Midnight came and went, and Manhattan couldn't sleep.

"Look at this. Just look at this," Vincent Bury said as he aimed his yellow cab toward the smoke. "That used to be a beautiful view of the towers, but I'm going to tell you something. You see all these people out here? Everybody helping out in whatever way they can? They tried to break us up, but this city's never been more unified."

Vincent Bury drove slower than any cabby has ever driven in New York, loving his wounded city. The heavens thundered with an advancing storm, and flashes of lightning illuminated American flags that hung from fire escapes.

A few poor souls wandered the streets like ghosts, photos of missing loved ones taped to shirts or strung around their necks. They were consoled by people they did not know and would never see again.

"Look at this," Vincent Bury said again, his heart full.

He turned a corner at 15th Street and 11th Avenue to find a group of teenagers cheering. "Thank you Thank you Thank you," said the signs they held. They were spending the night at the intersection to greet rescue workers who came up for air after digging with their hands for hours. Digging for miracles. Ambulances lined the streets, waiting for a call.

On a normal night, Vincent Bury would have been driven off the road by angry motorists leaning on horns. But they passed politely, letting him mourn in his own time. He calls himself the last white native New York cabby, and he is different in another way too. Instead of ramming fenders and bumpers, like you're supposed to do to let off steam, he meditates.

"The inner self never dies," he said, and he was sure something good was going to come of this tragedy.

"Where to now?" he asked.

"A Hundredth and Riverside. The fireman's memorial."

Bury parked on Riverside and got out of the car with a camera. He said that in his 49 years, he had never seen the fireman's memorial and its twin statues of Courage and Duty. He wanted to take the memory home to Brooklyn with him.

A little earlier in the evening, an advertising man named John Avery had left his Upper West Side apartment to walk his poodle Gracie. Avery had been in a state of shock over the attack on New York, but the shock was becoming sadness and anger. A co-worker lost her husband in one of the towers, and it was hitting Avery in a way it hadn't until then.

He was thinking, too, about the estimated 300 firefighters believed to have died under the rubble of what used to be an American symbol.

Three hundred.

Avery walked two blocks to the memorial that has stood since 1913. Firefighters never hesitate, he was thinking as Gracie tugged on the leash. They take chances with their own lives to save others, and there is a striking gallantry about them. The bravery, the bond, the cut of the uniform.

On this night, candles had been left at the memorial, and they flickered in the breeze of the coming storm. Bouquets were laid about, and some well-wishers had written anonymous notes of thanks and sympathy.

"The whole world is a very narrow bridge," said one. "Words can not express our sorrow," said another.

Avery's eyes filled, and anger floated just beneath the sadness. President Bush and the rest of America have to have the guts to root out terrorists wherever they are, he said, his voice deepening.

"We must go after the terrorists and anyone who harbors or finances them. It's not about revenge; it's about protection. If we don't do it, this can happen again. But if it's about revenge, we've sunk to the morality of the terrorists."

The storm had moved across the Hudson, bringing with it a drenching rain that sent John Avery and Gracie the poodle home.

Vincent Bury took a picture of the memorial, which has the following inscription:

"To the men of the fire department of the city of New York, who died at the call of duty. Soldiers in a war that never ends."

Vincent Bury drove away at funeral speed, in touch with both the living and the dead. It rained like everyone was crying all at once, and it seemed to me that New York had never been more beautiful.

Going So Fast . . . Gone Too Soon
MITCH ALBOM—*Detroit Free Press*—12/22/2004

How could they go that fast? You turn your vehicle at the blinking yellow light and you come off Northline Road to Murray Street, a straight line of asphalt into a working-class neighborhood. How could they go that fast? On this street? A dusting of snow covers the yards. It is dark and quiet and cold, early evening, about the time when families wash the dinner dishes, about the time when the TV sets go on, about the time when two young men, who grew up here in Taylor and were top hockey prospects, left a high school basketball game, headed for practice and decided, for some reason, to turn a black Chevy Blazer onto this road to nowhere.

How could they go that fast?

You do what the driver did.

You hit the gas.

You accelerate past the first low house with the dark shingle roof—10 m.p.h.—past an empty lot of frozen grass—20 m.p.h.—already you feel as if you are going too fast for this narrow street, past the telephone poles and the candy canes on a lawn—30 m.p.h.—you are over the speed limit now and the mailboxes are whizzing past, and so is the house with the covered white porch—40 m.p.h.—too fast, your instincts tell you, too close to the curb, what if a car is parked in the street?—45 m.p.h.—a blur of a fence, a trash can, a Santa Claus—too fast! What if someone steps out?—you hit your brake because your instinct for danger has taken over, but that instinct never kicked in that night, the Blazer kept accelerating—60, 70, 80 m.p.h.—clipping a mailbox, just missing a car, flying down the road, which curved sharply to the right, but when that road curved the Blazer did not, it kept zooming straight like a ground-based missile, no skid marks, no stopping, perhaps as fast as—85 m.p.h.—over the curb, over the lawn, sideswiping a tree and plowing into a yellow brick ranch house where a mother and her baby were about to step into the living room.

And someone was about to die.

BAM! As if a bomb went off, an eruption of glass, bricks, wood, drywall, furniture, lights, tables, shards and shreds and dust and destruction. The electricity blew out, and in the darkness the mother and baby were knocked to the floor, even as the Blazer mowed through the house, through what used to be the living room and the dining room, what used to be the halls and the shelves, what used to be the clocks and the furniture, pulverizing the rear wall and stopping only when the hood protruded two feet onto the deck, as if taking a peek at the backyard.

In the sudden silence, the driver of the car, 17-year-old Rodney Stewart, was amazingly still alive, reportedly moaning, refusing help, at one point actually trying to start the car as if to pull away. The mother, 23-year-old Rachel Nicita, and her 18-month-old son, Angelo, were alive, too, though shaken up, having missed certain death by a few seconds and feet. They were all, as witnesses whispered, "so lucky."

But there was one more.

The passenger, 18-year-old Shane Simmons, a smooth-skating forward with blond-streaked hair and a fetching smile, was in the front seat of that Blazer, as lifeless as the wreck that had delivered his destruction.

He was not so lucky.

How could he go so fast? From childhood, speed was part of Shane Simmons' world. He put on skates when he was 3 years old, and the folks at Southgate Ice Arena gave him a chair. "Here, hold onto this and push," they said. He didn't need it. By the end of the day, Shane was skating on his own. So fast!

By the time he was 5, he was playing hockey, zooming past the other Downriver kids his age. By the time he was 9, he had played all over Canada. By the time he was a teenager, he was a promising forward, traveling to Europe and Russia, playing in tournaments and turning heads. He played for Viktor Fedorov, Sergei's father, on the Belle Tire teams. Everyone talked about his professional promise.

"He was phenomenal," says Larry DePalma, coach of the Detroit Trackers. "He could see the entire ice, he had unbelievable hands and was such a graceful skater. He was NHL potential for sure."

So Shane's family—father, Tim; mother, Debbie, sisters Summer and Shannon—did what hockey families do; they sacrificed. They lived around his life. They worked around his schedule. They sold pizza kits, bowling nights and lottery tickets to raise money for Shane's trips and equipment.

"We were the best fund-raisers," Tim says, "because we were the poorest family on the team."

They pooled their vacations; they went where Shane went. They got up ridiculously early and came home ridiculously late, always driving back from some rink, some game, some tournament. When Shane moved up a level, they felt as if they had moved up, too. When Shane won an MVP award, they felt as if they had shared in it. When Shane scored a goal, made a deft move on the ice or was glowingly touted—like the scouting service that wrote "Shane has all the tools to be an NHL player, and could be one of the most skilled players in the United States"—they glowed a little, too.

Maybe if Shane had been more selfish, they wouldn't have embraced all this sacrifice. But the kid embraced them back, from the time he was a tyke to his fully grown 6-foot-1, 170-pound frame. He loved his family, he loved hanging around the house, he loved challenging his father to a pizza-eating contest or taking his grandfather to the movies. He wasn't shy about kissing his parents. He never held back a hug.

"His friends would call and want to go out, and he'd say, 'Nah, I'm gonna have family time here,'" his mother recalls. "How many 17- or 18-year-old boys say that?"

In his senior year at Taylor's Kennedy High, Shane moved to Montana to play Junior A hockey for the Helena Bighorns. The family missed him, but they understood. Part of the journey. Other NHL players did it.

And this past October, when he returned, looking for more ice time with a team in Michigan, they were happy to have him back, happy to see his face. Shane was in the house again, scarfing food, watching TV, knocking around with his sisters.

He had three good weeks of his beloved family time.

And then he was dead.

Why so fast? How could we lose him so fast? The last day of Shane's life gave no clue as to its ending. Debbie, 41, a lab technician with straight chestnut hair and sharp, pretty features, came home from her midnight shift, and Shane wandered downstairs. Debbie asked him about a country song she had heard that she had liked, something by Brooks and Dunn.

"I know that one," Shane said, "It's called 'That's What It's All About.'"

He downloaded it from a computer, and his sister Shannon joined them and they were eating a little breakfast and dancing to the song:

Hey, that's what it's all about

Hey, this is the life

I couldn't live without

A few minutes later, Debbie went to bed.

That morning was the last time she saw her son.

Tim, a 43-year-old printing pressman, came home that evening and raked some leaves into a huge pile so that his youngest child, Summer, could jump into it. They were outside when the black 2002 Chevy Blazer pulled up, Rodney Stewart driving. Shane hopped out to grab some clothes and his hockey equipment. They had a practice that night with the Trackers, a AAA team Shane planned to join.

"Maybe we'll pop up later and watch," Tim said.

"OK," Shane answered.

He waved so long, got in the Blazer and drove away.

As the Simmonses would later learn, Shane and Rodney stopped at Kennedy High to watch part of a girls basketball game. When they left, they took a turn off of Northline onto Murray Street. Why? No one knows why. The road was not en route to practice. The road was not a shortcut. The road, like much of this story, remains a mystery.

Tim knew none of that the night of Oct. 26. He only knew that the hour was growing late, and he put Summer to bed. At 10 o'clock, the phone rang. It was DePalma, the Trackers' coach.

"Hi, Larry, what's up?" Tim said.

"Is Shane around?"

"No, I thought he went to practice."

"Well, he never showed up."

"He was with Rodney."

"Rodney never showed up, either."

Tim was puzzled. He called Shane's cell phone. He got the voice mail, so he hung up. That's not like Shane, messing up like that, Tim thought. He was bothered. His son was too old to be horsing around and missing practices. So he called back again. This time he left a message.

Fifteen minutes later, he got a call back. He thought it was Shane.

It was the police.

Too fast! Too much! Why him? Why now? When Shane's parents learned of their son's death, they were in different places, but their reactions were the same: They fell down. Tim, informed by the police that "there's been a fatality," began to shiver uncontrollably, his body in a frozen spasm, "like it was 30 degrees," he says. Debbie, who was at work, collapsed when she got the phone call. A friend drove her home. She burst from the car and ran past a ditch where Shane used to jump his bicycle. Her daughter Shannon ran to meet her, and Debbie yelled, "Just tell me I'm going to see Shane again!"

Shannon hugged her. Debbie fell to her knees.

Tim went to identify the body. He went to that yellow brick ranch house where Murray Street turns to Emmett Street—that sharp right curve. The house was, as Tim remembers it, "a wreck. Like when a bomb goes off and there's rubble everywhere."

The Blazer, smashed, had Shane's hockey equipment in the back. Neither player had been wearing seat belts. Rodney already had been taken for medical treatment, but Shane's body was still there, out of the vehicle, on the dining room floor, dead from what police told Tim was "extensive damage to the right side of his head." His skull was, essentially, crushed.

Were you able to identify him? Tim is asked.

"From the left side," he says.

Not from the right?

The father shakes his head no.

Why was he going that fast? Rodney Stewart was taken to Heritage Hospital. A Taylor police officer questioned him about the crash. According to the preliminary examination, this is what was said.

Officer: "He asked me, 'What did I hit?'"

And what did you reply?

"I said he hit a house."

And what did he say when you asked him who he was with?

"He said he couldn't recall."

Did he say anything about how the accident happened?

"He stated that they were just driving around."

Did he use the word "they"?

"Yes."

Rodney Stewart, a strapping, dark-haired defenseman—only a senior in high school—had been friends with Shane for several years. Last summer, Rodney joined the Simmons family on a Fourth of July camping trip. He had eaten with them, laughed with them, gone canoeing with them. In the weeks Shane was home before his death, the Simmons family saw Rodney "almost every day," Tim says. They planned to be teammates on the Trackers.

Which is what makes this all so strange. At first, Debbie thought both young men were victims of a terrible accident. She felt sorry for Rodney, and Rodney's mother came over on Halloween, a few days after the crash.

"We sat and talked and cried," Debbie says.

But as details began to emerge, the Simmonses' sympathy chilled. Police discovered that Rodney had been issued a ticket in Dearborn two nights earlier for driving on a lawn and hitting a tree—with the same Chevy Blazer. The initial toxicology report of Rodney's bloodstream showed traces of THC, the primary intoxicant in marijuana, and benzodiazepines, a central nervous system depressant such as you would find in Xanax.

"Then," Debbie Simmons says, "I started to get angry."

Rodney was arrested. He was taken to Wayne County Jail. The prosecutor charged him with second-degree murder, citing the "willful and wanton disregard for the result of one's actions."

The sentence carries a maximum of life in prison.

Communication between the families stopped. There were no more visits. The Simmonses said they received one letter from Rodney but were disappointed that "it didn't explain anything and didn't show much remorse," Tim says.

The families used to see each other at the rink. Now they see each other in court.

"I know (Rodney) didn't try to kill anybody," says Pat Muscat, a Wayne County assistant prosecutor, "but the evidence will show he willfully drove that car ignoring the effects of what that driving would be.

"If you willfully fired a gun into a crowd but had no intent of killing anybody, you're still willfully discharging, ignoring the risks. And it's still a potential second-degree murder."

Rodney's lawyer, Marvin Barnett, insists his client is a victim, too.

"The young man has no memory of the incident," Barnett says. "That was his best friend. This is a tragedy."

As to why Rodney was driving that fast, Barnett says: "The experts could not determine if he was conscious or not."

On Tuesday, a judge lowered Rodney's bond, allowing for his release from jail, provided he remains tethered, essentially housebound, and doesn't drive. The case is scheduled to go to trial next spring. Barnett likely will argue that somehow Rodney passed out, that his foot pressed down on the accelerator and never came up. Is it possible? Is it far-fetched? What did Shane do as it happened? Why were there no skid marks? Why didn't the Blazer swerve before hitting the house? Who knows? Who's to say? The Simmonses want justice for their son, but should it come at the expense of his friend—or must it?

"Have I ever sped before? Yes," Tim says. "Have I ever gone down a side street at 85 miles an hour? No."

"What was his motivation?" Debbie says. "It couldn't have been fun."

"If you're driving a car," Tim says, "it's like carrying a loaded gun. You're responsible for people in that vehicle."

"It's not normal," Debbie says.

"Accidents happen," Tim says, "but this was totally uncalled for."

"It's not normal," Debbie says.

Tim sighs. Then he says what they have been wrestling with for months. "We don't know what was going through his head."

All they do know—all anyone knows right now—is that two young friends will never spend another minute together. And two neighborhood families that once shared the bleachers at hockey games will now share benches on opposite sides of a courtroom.

Hey, that's what it's all about . . .

The funeral home, Risko-Ferguson-Obarzanek in Detroit, made a lovely video to that Brooks and Dunn song, a montage of Shane photos—in various hockey uniforms, in his blue graduation robe, on the couch clowning with his sisters. The service was attended by more people than you could count, family and friends and former teammates from all over the country, including a group from Montana that flew in just for that.

"Some of his friends have gotten tattoos in his memory," Debbie says. "Some have had his number put on their cars . . . "

She smiles at their kindness. But she could barely handle the funeral. She goes to Shane's room sometimes and lies in his bed. Holidays are pretty much a disaster. She tried to have people over for Thanksgiving, but as soon as they came, they were talking and laughing and it began to throb in her head—Wrong! Wrong! Wrong!—and she had to leave.

"It was like, everybody seemed to be OK, like, 'We're going on now.' They could laugh and be happy. But Thanksgiving was Shane's favorite holiday, and I'm not laughing and happy . . . "

She wipes back tears.

"I'm not ready to be OK yet."

Christmas is this weekend. In the Simmons home, it will be shrunk to a minimum. What used to be a three-day holiday feast will be quiet and small now. "We'll hold on to our family and try to get through it," Debbie says.

There are no hockey trips to plan anymore. No hockey clothes that need washing. No Shane to speak about his hockey dreams, his travels, his future. When the crash occurred, it made the TV news. Many people saw the images. What they didn't see is how that vehicle keeps crashing through the lives of the survivors, day after day.

You pull in the drive
And you hit the chair
And the one that you love
Is waiting there
And hey, that's what it's all about
Hey, this is the life
I couldn't live without . . .

It's a wonderful song, but it plays differently now, because they do live without it, they have to, every day. The sisters have to live without their brother, the defendant has to live without his good friend, the mother—who by her own words has "just started getting out of bed"—has to live without her son. And the father, who stands now in the driveway of his Taylor home, hands in his pockets against the winter cold, has to live without the promising athlete, the pizza-eating pal, the hugging child who would have carried on the family name.

"The thing is," Tim Simmons says, "so much of our life was wrapped up around Shane, you know? I mean, all the things we did. The trips we took. And now . . ."

He wants to say more, but he can't find the words. He doesn't need to. A blind man could see it.

On your ride home, you turn again down Murray Street, at a slower pace now, and you look once more at the last things Shane Simmons saw, the modest houses, the mailboxes, the telephone poles, the straight line of asphalt that led to his funeral. You reach the yellow ranch house where it all came crashing down. It is dark. No one inside. The front wall is boarded up now, a huge piece of wood where a picture window once stood.

Let's face it. A hole has been blown through this house, like the hole blown through the Simmons family, like the hole blown through the Stewart family, like the hole blown through the heart of everyone involved. Why so fast? Why them? Why him? The song is wrong. This is what it's all about now, a car that didn't stop and a heartache that never will.

After the Sky Fell
BRADY DENNIS—*St. Petersburg Times*—1/28/2005

The few drivers on this dark, lonely stretch of the Suncoast Parkway in Pasco County pull up to the toll booth, hand their dollars to Lloyd Blair and then speed away. None of them knows why the old man sits here, night after night, working the graveyard shift.

Well, here's why:

Because years ago, on a freezing winter night at a party in Queens, N.Y., he met a woman named Millie.

Because he fell in love with her brown hair and wide eyes and 100-watt smile.

Because they got married, moved to Staten Island, had a son and worked for decades in Manhattan; she as an accountant, he as a banker.

Because it had been their dream to retire to Florida, and so they saved all their lives to make it possible.

Because, just as they began to talk of leaving New York and heading south, she was diagnosed with breast cancer, and they spent their time and money traveling to New Jersey, San Diego and Mexico in search of a cure.

Because, in the end, they came to Florida anyway.

Because they finally bought a house in Spring Hill, although she was too weak that day to get out of the car.

Because she died nine days later on Jan. 5, 2002, a day "the whole sky fell," he says.

Because, after she was gone, he found himself alone and $100,000 in debt.

And so he took a job collecting tolls. The drivers who pass by see a smiling 71-year-old man with blue eyes and a gray mustache who tells each of them, "Have a great night!"

They don't know the rest of Lloyd Blair's story, or that he keeps Millie's picture in his shirt pocket, just under his name tag, just over his heart.

Former Tropicana Owner Still Has Faith After Mob; Corporate Muggings
JOHN L. SMITH—*Las Vegas Sun Review*—2/22/2009

The Peppermill on the Strip was crowded with its usual lunch-hour mix of tourists and locals. Waitresses in tropical print blouses hefted overstuffed dishes and hustled from one table to the next.

The older woman at the table for two drew no attention, which is fine with Mitzi Stauffer Briggs. A little peace amid the boulevard's cacophony: just the way the quietly spiritual woman likes it.

From where Briggs sat it was about a $3 cab ride to the Tropicana, the hotel she once owned. Before she busted out, Briggs was victimized by mob and corporate sharks. She was tricked like a carnival rube and watched her 51 percent stake and $44 million fortune disappear.

Briggs, who studied philosophy and education at Stanford, once owned substantial real estate that included an island in the Bahamas and lavish homes in California and Nevada.

Today, the 79-year-old lives humbly in an apartment not far from her job at the Guardian Angel Cathedral, just off the Strip not far from the Peppermill. She sets up the communion altar for the priests, plans weddings and works in the gift shop. She struggles with her personal finances. Long ago, she used up her reserves helping to care for family, but she does not complain.

Briggs was introduced to the Tropicana in 1975 after learning that casinos netted 20 percent profits.

"Well, it turned out that that wasn't quite the way it was in there," she said, a self-effacing sense of humor emerging.

She wasn't told that profitable casinos had locks on their back doors, verifiable owners of record and a minimum of thievery. The angle-shooters at the Tropicana saw her coming from 100 miles away.

She was befriended by Joseph Agosto, who officially was affiliated with the Folies Bergere but unofficially ran the casino skim for the Kansas City mob. With Briggs under Agosto's charm, her fate was sealed as millions in bad gambling markers went uncollected. The casino's credit book was filled with more fiction than *Jane Eyre*.

Gullible to the end, Briggs denied the undeniable even after FBI agents and Gaming Control Board investigators pulled off a raid in February 1979 that became known as the second "St. Valentine's Day Massacre." The investigation resulted in a solid case of skimming that linked the Civella family in Kansas City to their pals at the Tropicana.

Briggs was so taken in by Agosto that, once his loyalties were revealed and he was jailed, she flew to the prison and asked him if what she'd read in the newspapers was true.

"Mitzi, I couldn't help it. They had a gun to my head," Agosto told her.

She decided to believe him. At the Peppermill three decades later, she still called him "Poor Joe Agosto."

Gradually, Briggs came to the painful realization that she had been a pawn. While she tried to maintain an ethical standard at the Tropicana, millions in bad credit markers went uncollected and small percentage owners used the hotel as their personal playground.

In hindsight she admitted, "We were some kind of unauthorized bank for those people."

But Mitzi Briggs' bruising Las Vegas thrill ride wasn't finished. When she and her fellow investors sold the hotel to Ramada, the result was a corporate mugging that finished off her faltering fortune.

Even after a Nevada court finally forced Ramada's hand, Briggs was cut out of the final Tropicana payday.

Through all that she betrays no bitterness. In fact, her faith seems stronger than ever.

"Without my faith, I would be dead," she said. "I've been very grateful to God that I still have a job and still have the health to work. The only thing I've really got left is my faith."

Her millions didn't guarantee happiness, and losing a fortune hasn't made her miserable. It's helped her appreciate all the good people she met at the Tropicana.

"The people that worked there were my greatest allies," Briggs said. "They were so good to me. They did everything they could. They were trying so hard to make a go of it."

These days, she occasionally meets one of her former employees at church, where locals and tourists gather for Masses that sometimes touch on the fleeting nature of material wealth.

And when someone laments their bad luck at the tables and complains of losing it all in Las Vegas, Mitzi Stauffer Briggs consoles them and tells them she understands.

A Lesson Before Dying
BRETT STEPHENS—*Wall Street Journal*—12/13/2011

Does the manner of our dying count in the final reckoning of how we have lived our lives? Nearly my first assignment at the University of Chicago was to read the Platonic dialogues on the trial and death of Socrates. "Then, holding the cup to his lips, quite readily and cheerfully he drank off the poison." It is the supreme moment in the Western philosophical tradition, when wisdom and courage, resignation and defiance, combine to overcome injustice and, in a sense, death itself.

Would that we could all die as Socrates did. Generally we don't. "The good death has increasingly become a myth," wrote the Yale surgeon and bioethicist Sherwin Nuland in his 1993 prize-winning book *How We Die*. Dying, in Dr.

Nuland's eloquent telling, amounts to "a series of destructive events that involve by their very nature the disintegration of the dying person's humanity." Who can—who would dare—judge a man's worth when his mind and body are being picked bare by disease?

I've been thinking about all this for over a year now as I watched a brain tumor, along with the associated medical interventions, pick away at my father bit by bit. First, an operation to remove the tumor, which erased his right field of vision and took away his ability to read and drive. Next came debilitating bouts of chemo and radiation, along with an agonizing case of shingles. Then avascular necrosis set in, leaving him unable to walk. Later, as the tumor returned, his memory began to slip. Near the end he was almost totally blind, couldn't utter a sentence, couldn't swallow a pill, couldn't hold his food down. Cancer is a heist culminating in murder.

I suppose Dr. Nuland's book should have prepared me for this. I suppose, too, that I should have known what was coming after visiting my aunt as she was dying of brain cancer. My father had been with me on that trip to wish his sister a final happy birthday. His own tumor was diagnosed three weeks later.

But I wasn't prepared. My father, always in excellent shape, had a way of projecting an air of indestructibility. When he phoned to tell me about the diagnosis, it was in a tone suggesting it was only slightly more serious than a fender-bender. The five-year survival rate for his kind of cancer is 4%. I looked that up on the Internet, then persuaded myself that he was surely in the 4%.

"The body has 1,000 lines of ingenious defense," I remember my father telling me as a child, in what must have been one of our first talks about death. And I had believed him, because to me he was the living proof.

To grow up is to understand that the confidence a parent radiates around his children is rarely the confidence the parent feels. I knew my father well enough to know his various fears and insecurities. I knew he had seen his own father die of brain cancer and was intimately familiar with the course of the disease. I knew that, born optimist though he was, he had no faith in an afterlife. My father loved the life he had, lived it fully and well, had no desire to leave it.

All this meant that the diagnosis should have been devastating to him. Yet he never betrayed the slightest sign of fear. Except when his shingles were at their most excruciating, he remained his cheerful, interested, encouraging self. For a while I put this down to his belief that he would somehow beat the cancer, a belief I was eager to share.

Yet my father maintained his usual sangfroid even when it became clear that there would be no getting well. There were no five stages of grief, no bouts of denial, anger, bargaining and depression. About six weeks before the end, when we had brought him to a hospice, I asked if he wouldn't rather be at home. "Given where I am," he replied with a cocked eyebrow, "I am where I am." I was astonished he could even speak. We brought him home anyway.

How did my father maintain his composure in the face of his progressive deterioration? We never spoke about it. I sometimes chalked it up to being born in the 1930s, before the baby boom and the cult of self. He was not a complainer. To bemoan his illness after a life in which the good breaks outnumbered the bad ones would have seemed to him ungrateful. The worst he ever said to me about his cancer was that it was "a bummer."

Yet there was something else at work. The sicker my father got, the more dependent he became on his family, the less he had to give back. What could he offer, except not to sink us into the terror he surely must have felt? So he maintained his usual active and joyful interest in our lives and the lives of his friends and in politics and the movies we watched together. Sticking to the mundane and the lighthearted was his way of being protective with the people he loved. For as long as he could muster his wits, death was not allowed to enter the room.

Throughout his life my father taught me many lessons: about language, history and philosophy; about ethics, loyalty and love. In the end, he taught me that death cannot destroy the dignity of a dignified man.

Charles J. Stephens, 1937–2011. May his memory be for a blessing.

TRIUMPHS

These are stories of the long shot that comes in, struggles against the odds that prove the cynics wrong. It is the reward for hard work, redemption at the end of a rough stretch. It is the hope that keeps us going and aiming for new heights in the belief that we can build a better world.

The most elemental triumph is man's successful effort to change his fate. That's why this section begins with the American invention that changed the world—flight. From an eye-witness account of the Wright Brothers liftoff at Kitty Hawk to Charles Lindbergh's solo flight across the Atlantic two decades later, these dispatches reminds us how revolutionary the daily flights we now take for granted really are. And even these leaps in human innovation seem small in comparison to man landing on the moon, captured by Lacey Fosburgh in *The New York Times*.

Sports provide perhaps the most dependable dose of triumph in our daily lives—whether it is a championship fight or a World Series struggle, boxing and baseball seem particularly adept at inspiring journalists. The turn-of-the-century fights of Jack Dempsey were exhaustively lauded by legendary newspapermen like Grantland Rice. Damon Runyon christened Jim Braddock the "Cinderella Man" inspiring a movie of the same name decades later. When Joe Louis took the heavyweight crown, black America rejoiced, as one of their own was restored to the heavyweight throne and future novelist Richard Wright was there to capture the excitement on the streets of Chicago. Decades later, Red Smith would provide the same treatment for Cassius Clay's defeat of Sonny Liston to claim the world championship at the tender age of twenty-two.

In the arena of America's pastime few columnists have captured a moment of triumph better than Shirley Povich on Don Larson's perfect game in the 1956 World Series. Mike Royko recounting his attendance at Jackie Robinson's debut game in Chicago expresses the triumph of excellence over prejudice, as Wells Twombly does in his posthumous tribute to Roberto Clemente in "Super Hero." The great *Los Angeles Times* scribe Jim Murray honors the sustained effort of Jim Gilliam and the straight-from-Hollywood, walk-on World Series home run by the injured Kirk Gibson.

Mythic narratives of military glory have given way to the reality captured by journalists working on the front lines, but war remains a marker that turns the pages of history. Helen Kirkpatrick surveys the surreal strength of a defiant London the morning after a Blitzkrieg attack during the Battle of Britain. Ernie Pyle, the legendary GI journalist, captures the joy of the liberated City of Light. Dropping the atomic bomb on Japan arguably saved many lives compared to the alternative of a land invasion, and enclosed are different looks at this epochal event: William Laurence reporting from the flight that dropped the bomb over Nagasaki and Homer Bigart reporting on the ground from Hiroshima one month later. Writing in the *Mississippi Delta Democrat*, Hodding Carter Jr. wrote a poignant argument for honoring Japanese-American soldiers in "Go for Broke"—a tribute to the better angels of our nature. And Walter Lippmann captured the moment of victory with words of enduring wisdom in "The Rise of the United States."

The civil rights struggles of our nation have also been marked by moments of triumph that came after the scandal of slavery and the tragedy of segregation. Writing in the *New York Post*, Ted Poston captured a twenty-eight-year-old Martin Luther King wondering what was next after his victory in the Montgomery bus boycott. Less than a decade later, Eugene Patterson instantly recognized the importance of King's "I Have a Dream" speech on the Washington Mall. King himself sent a letter to Patterson, expressing his belief that the column had captured the moment correctly. Decades later, Dorothy Gilliam detailed how echoes of "We Shall Overcome" helped topple the Berlin Wall half a world away.

The triumph of individualism over the ignorance of the mob was often H. L. Mencken's subject, encapsulated here in the near-manifesto "Homo Neanderthalenis." Small victories and moments of defiance are sometimes the triumphs that hit closest to home, such as the New York City commuter who decides to make a Bartleby-esque stand in "The Subway Rebel" or Diane Griego Erwin's tale of a migrant laborer disrespected by a DMV bureaucrat. It is the essence of the generosity of spirit seen in Rick Bragg's story of a washerwoman who gave $150,000 to a local college or Tom Friedman's tribute to his high school journalism teacher. Of course, survival in the face of death is the most basic form of triumph and Jim Dwyer's column about three men who were among the last to escape the destruction of the World Trade Center is a rare inspirational story from that ashen day.

Triumphs provide proof that breaking news can also be good news. Cynicism often passes for wisdom in the newspaper business, but this particular pursuit of happiness propels us to invent and invest and reach beyond the sometimes suffocating status quo that surrounds us.

—JOHN AVLON

Twelve Seconds That Changed the World
H. P. MOORE—*Norfolk Virginian-Pilot*—12/18/1903

[This is the only contemporary newspaper account of the Wright Brothers' first flight at Kitty Hawk, North Carolina. While marking a seminal moment in history, its author relied on eye-witness accounts communicated over telegraph. The resulting dispatch included numerous inaccuracies, most notably the description of the initial flight covering three miles. In fact, it was just a hundred yards and lasted twelve seconds.]

The problem of aerial navigation without the use of a balloon has been solved at last.

Over the sand hills of the North Carolina coast yesterday, near Kittyhawk, two Ohio men proved that they could soar through the air in a flying machine of their own construction, with the power to steer and speed it at will.

This, too, in the face of a wind blowing at the registered velocity of twenty-one miles an hour.

Like a monster bird, the invention hovered above the breakers and circled over the rolling sand hills at the command of its navigator and, after soaring for three miles, it gracefully descended to earth again, and rested lightly upon the spot selected by the man in the car as a suitable landing place.

While the United States government has been spending thousands of dollars in an effort to make practicable the ideas of Professor Langley, of the Smithsonian Institute, Wilbur and Orville Wright, two brothers, natives of Dayton, Ohio, have, quietly, even secretly, perfected their invention and put it to a successful test.

They are not yet ready that the world should know the methods they have adopted in conquering the air, but the *Virginian-Pilot* is able to state authentically the nature of their invention, its principles and its chief dimensions.

The idea of the box kite has been adhered to strictly in the basic formation of the flying machine.

A huge framework of light timbers, thirty-three feet wide, five feet deep, and five feet across the top, forms the machine proper.

This is covered with a tough, but light canvas.

In the center, and suspended just below the bottom plane, is the small gasoline engine which furnished the motive power for the propelling and elevating wheels.

These are two six-bladed propellers, one arranged just below the center of the frame, so gauged as to exert an upward force when in motion, and the other extends horizontally to the rear from the center of the car, furnishing the forward impetus.

Protruding from the center of the car is a huge, fan-shaped rudder of canvas, stretched upon a frame of wood. This rudder is controlled by the navigator and may be moved to each side, raised, or lowered.

Wilbur Wright, the chief inventor of the machine, sat in the operator's car, and when all was ready his brother unfastened the catch which held the invention at the top of the slope.

The big box began to move slowly at first, acquiring velocity as it went, and when halfway down the hundred feet the engine was started.

The propeller in the rear immediately began to revolve at a high rate of speed, and when the end of the incline was reached the machine shot out into space without a perceptible fall.

By this time the elevating propeller was also in motion, and keeping its altitude, the machine slowly began to go higher and higher until it finally soared sixty feet above the ground.

Maintaining this height by the action of the under wheel, the navigator increased the revolutions of the rear propeller, and the forward speed of the huge affair increased until a velocity of eight miles was attained.

All this time the machine headed into a twenty-one-mile wind.

The little crowd of fisherfolk and coast guards, who have been watching the construction of the machine with unconcealed curiosity since September, were amazed.

They endeavored to race over the sand and keep up with the thing in the air, but it soon distanced them and continued its flight alone, save the man in the car.

Steadily it pursued its way, first tacking to port, then to starboard, and then driving straight ahead.

"It is a success," declared Orville Wright to the crowd on the beach after the first mile had been covered.

But the inventor waited. Not until he had accomplished three miles, putting the machine through all sorts of maneuvers en route, was he satisfied.

Then he selected a suitable place to land, and gracefully circling, drew his invention slowly to the earth, where it settled, like some big bird, in the chosen spot.

"Eureka!" he cried, as did the alchemists of old.

The success of the Wright brothers in their invention is the result of three years of hard work. Experiment after experiment has been made and failure resulted, but each experiment had its lesson, and finally, when the two reappeared at Kittyhawk last fall, they felt more confident than ever.

The Dempsey-Willard Fight
GRANTLAND RICE—*New York Tribune*—7/5/1919

Jack Dempsey proved to be the greatest fighting tornado, in a boxing way, the game has ever known, when in nine minutes of actual combat today, he crushed Jess Willard into a shapeless man of gore and battered flesh.

One minute and 58 seconds after the two men had squared away, Dempsey hooked a three-quarter left to the point of Willard's jaw, and the champion sat down heavily with a dazed and foolish look, a simple half-smile crowning a mouth that twitched with pain and bewilderment.

At the count of six, Willard rose slowly to his feet. Less than ten seconds later, another of Dempsey's terrific hooks lifted the human mountain from his tottering base, and once again he crushed the sun-baked canvas with a thud that rolled forth the echo of his doom.

Seven times in that first round Dempsey tore in and lifted the reeling, battered champion off his feet. Six times Willard slowly lifted his weary, broken frame back into position to receive once more a right or a left hook that snapped his bloody head to the back of his wilting spine.

Never in all the history of the ring, dating back to days before all memory, has any champion received the murderous punishment which 245-pound Jess Willard soaked up in that first round and the two rounds that followed.

While Dempsey gave one of the greatest exhibitions of mighty hitting anyone here has ever seen, Willard, in a different way, gave one of the greatest exhibitions of raw and unadulterated gameness. He absorbed enough punishment to kill two ordinary men and only his tremendous vitality and that hack of the bell carried him beyond the first round.

About ten seconds before the bell closed the first round, Willard reeled over toward the right corner, away from Dempsey, and there the Colorado slugger, putting everything he had into a right hook, dropped the champion for the seventh time.

As Willard flopped on the occasion nothing but the bell could have saved him. He sat there dazed, bewildered and helpless—his big, bleeding mouth wide open, his glassy bloodshot eyes staring wearily and witlessly out into space, as a 114-degree sun beat down upon his head and that was rank with perspiration and blood.

The big crowd, seeing Willard's utter helplessness, failed to hear the bell in the wild uproar that followed. Dempsey started to crawl through the ropes as Willard was dragged to his corner, as one might drag a sack of oats. There was no expression on his face except the witless, faraway look that might belong to a simpleton who had just crawled out from under a rock crusher, wondering what it was all about.

While the uproar was at its height Dempsey was hurriedly called back to the ring and the bloodless, pitiless drama went on to the second act.

Twenty seconds after the second round opened Willard was a terrible wreck to behold. His right eye was completely closed, a big blue moon with a fringe of crimson protruding far beyond his face, with a gray, twitching slit where his eye once had been.

Dempsey fought with all the necessary brutality of his craft. With the championship now in plain sight, with the goal of his dreams just at the end of another hook, with all the world before him at twenty-four—lifted from a tramp two years ago to a millionaire's income ahead—he hooked those salvos of rights and lefts, shifting from Willard's mutilated face to his quivering body, with only a few pauses between his deadly blows.

After the first round Willard came back as a game man comes to meet his fate, as sure and as certain as death and the grave. Here and there he handed a few weak, faltering punches that failed to even check Dempsey's rush; but in the main he spent his time glaring helplessly at his opponent out of his one undamaged eye and groping feebly to rest his great bulk upon the lighter man, not to wear him down, but to find a moment's rest from the vast and utter weariness that was beginning to soak through his giant frame, deadening his nerve cells and moving slowly but steadily to his brain.

At the end of the second round there was a question again as to whether Willard would answer the bell. But once again he lifted his bulk to reeling, tottering legs and stood to receive the rush of his successor who, without a moment's delay, started the fountain of gore spurting again as Willard wearily turned his head to spit out clots of blood upon the canvas.

It was easy to see in the middle of the third round that the conqueror of Jack Johnson would never answer another bell. For, in the meanwhile, the right side of his face had swollen to unbelievable proportions. The flesh there had been so badly cut and jabbed and mashed by Dempsey's terrific hitting force that purple blotches began to intermingle with the red.

If you could imagine a thick hamburger steak, painted blue and purple and crimson, plastered to the side of a man's face, you might get some idea of how Willard looked in the middle of that third round. If a six-inch shell had exploded against his right jaw it could hardly have changed his features more.

No dreams came to him of a vanishing title. He knew no anguish of fading glory. With glossy, rolling eye and a foolish, twisted face he reeled along his way to oblivion.

The endless punishment he had received had first deadened his nerve cells and shut off all electricity that runs the human system. The deadening growth had moved to the brain, so that in the closing minutes of the fight he had no sign of intelligence left. He stood or reeled without any sign of comprehension displayed over his face—if you'd care to call something a face that some time before had lost any resemblance to anything human or to anything even belonging to the wild.

The wonder is that his vast system had enough vitality to carry that much punishment and still stay up. For after the first round Dempsey scored no further knockdowns, unless two are so registered where Willard crumpled against the ropes and hung there like a side of beef on display in a butcher shop. No other man could have taken that much punishment and lived.

If there was any pity in the prize ring (which there isn't) it might have found expression here where this man once known as the physical marvel of the ring— this man who five minutes before had stood with a bold and confident look as champion of the world, trained to the day, as fit as he could ever hope to be— now stood as an open target for an opponent nearly fifty pounds lighter and six inches shorter in stature—a target that rocked and swayed under the blistering sun while 50,000 looked on and waited for the coming end.

As time was called for the third round there was no need of Walter Monahan's sponge to announce that Jess had closed his engagement as champion of the world and that Jack Dempsey now wore that crown that had belonged in turn to Sullivan, Corbett, Fitzsimmons, Jeffries, Johnson and Willard.

And Dempsey had proved to be the most spectacular champion of them all.

It had taken Corbett twenty-one rounds to knock out Sullivan. It had taken Fitzsimmons fourteen rounds to drop Corbett. Jeffries had needed eleven rounds to crush Fitz. Johnson travelled fifteen rounds to blog out Jeff, and Johnson lasted twenty-six rounds against Willard. But Dempsey, with the crushing force and the blazing speed, in those punishing hooks, delivered with either fist, needed no such leeway.

Only a matter of a few seconds saved Willard a one-round knockout for, if the bell had known a second's delay, Dempsey would have drawn another one-round verdict to add to his amazing list of one-round affairs.

How Willard ever stayed on his feet after the fusilade of that first round will ever remain one of the mysteries of the game. Doughboys have taken a .45 bullet into their bodies and still rushed forward for one last trench knife blow.

You may recall how Fuzzy-Wuzzy, in Kipling's verse, soaked up British fire and still broke a British square. But here was a man who through the last six minutes of the battle stood up to take an almost countless flurry of punches from a man who had already shown he was the hardest hitter the fighting game had ever known.

It was unbelievable. From less than ten feet away we looked on and refused to credit the vision of our eyes. It looked as if every punch must tear away his head, but in place of this the fountain continued to gush, the features continued to swell, the raw meat continued to pop open in deep slits as the red surf rolled from his shaking pulp-smashed frontispiece.

If Willard had not been in wonderful shape he would have been killed. He surely would never have answered the bell for the second round.

Dempsey left the ring unmarked. He had planted his nerve-killing blow before Willard had ever found opportunity to test the hitting power of his long, tremendous arms. Where was the famous uppercut? No one will ever know, for before the Kansan had a chance to test either, his motive power was paralyzed and he needed every ounce of vitality left to keep him on his feet.

And how this Dempsey can hit! No wonder Carl Morris and Fred Fulton and so many others crumpled up before his blows. When he hit Willard it was exactly the same as if some strong man had swung upon the ex-champion with a heavy hammer. It felt as if raw steel had broken through his skull. He fell before a man who must be able to hit harder than any man who ever lived.

And so, as Willard at thirty-eight passed out, Dempsey at twenty-four becomes champion of the world. The champion boxer—not the champion fighter. For it would be an insult to every doughboy that took his heavy pack through the mules' train to frontline trenches to go over the top at dawn to refer to Dempsey as a fighting man. If he had been a fighting man, he would have been in khaki when at twenty-two he had no other responsibilities in the world except to protect his own hide.

So let us have no illusions about our new heavyweight champion. He is a marvel in the ring, the greatest boxing or the greatest hitting machine even the old timers here have ever seen.

But he isn't the world's champion fighter. Not by a margin of 50,000,000 men who either stood, or were ready to stand the test of cold steel and exploding shell for anything from six cents to a dollar a day.

It would be an insult to every young American who sleeps today from Flanders to Lorraine, and from the Somme to the Argonne, to crown Dempsey with the laurels of fighting courage.

He missed the big chance of his life to prove his own manhood before his own soul—but before that he stands as the ring marvel of the century, a puncher who will be unbeatable as long as he desires to stay off the primrose way and maintain the wonderful vitality of a wonderful human system.

The Subway Rebel
FREDERICK B. EDWARDS—*New York Herald Tribune*—11/20/1924

Benjamin Mehlig, a small man with an office at 132 Fulton Street, who had a habit of leaving the West Side Interborough subway at 157th Street and Broadway every evening at a little before 6 o'clock, set his teeth firmly together yesterday afternoon, looked a squad of subway guards firmly in the eye and started what may become a Movement.

Life in New York is like that. A plain citizen leaves his place of business immersed in conventional affairs. His thoughts are on this or that; his job, income tax, crossword puzzle, the price of a new overcoat, or what he has forgotten that his wife told him to be sure and remember. Then without warning the Fates seize him and hurl him for a loss square in the middle of a revolution, a banditry, a fire or a Movement.

No vast impulses yeasted within the soul of Benjamin Mehlig as he boarded a subway train to Pennsylvania Station at a little after 5 o'clock last night. He wished to go home. A train came along empty, having been run through for the benefit of the midtown rush hour crowds. Benjamin Mehlig was among the surge, wishing merely to go home. He noted that the train was marked Van Cortlandt Park, and Benjamin Mehlig's heart was lifted within him. It was his train and it was empty!

Benjamin Mehlig's moment was at hand. But had some prophet, gifted with vision, whispered into his ear, "Benjamin, you are shortly to achieve something that Napoleon never even thought of attempting," he would have said, "Go away, you nut," or words to that effect.

The ten-car train was quickly filled. Times Square added a quota to the grand 5 o'clock shove. Seventy-second Street decanted merely a handful, and others took their places. Benjamin Mehlig read his Wall Street edition and wondered what was for supper.

At Ninety-sixth Street a guard poked his head into the car and shouted something that sounded to Benjamin Mehlig like "Awsingeackwowshoawlwow!" Benjamin's interest was merely casual until he observed a general restlessness among his fellow passengers.

"What did he say?" asked Benjamin Mehlig, whose great moment was even now upon him.

"He said," a neighbor replied with bitterness, "that we should all change at 103d Street because this train is going to the car barns."

Benjamin Mehlig pondered this for a while. He was not surprised. It had happened to him before. But somehow this time was different. The soul of Benjamin Mehlig was in revolt. He felt filled with fire. He arose in his seat and shouted at the guard. Benjamin Mehlig, the small man of 132 Fulton Street, yelled at a subway guard!

"Hey, you!" said Benjamin Mehlig, "what is this?"

"Yawlsingecawwahbaw," the guard replied, and Benjamin Mehlig said:

"Like hell!"

The guard tottered and caught at the door frame for support. He shook his head, puzzled. It appeared to his bewildered senses that the small Benjamin Mehlig was in revolt. That there was, in fact, a mutiny on board. Yet . . . impossible, surely.

The guard came into the car and addressed Benjamin Mehlig, whose strange conduct was now beginning to excite the interest of the other passengers.

"Whaddidyuh say-y-y?" demanded the guard.

Benjamin Mehlig stood up.

"I said like hell," replied Benjamin Mehlig. "That's what I said. What do you think of that? Like hell I'll change at 103d Street. I'm going to 157th Street. That's where I'm going."

"Ho!" said the guard. "Not on this train, brother, you ain't."

"Ho!" said Benjamin Mehlig, climbing on a seat. "But I am. On this train. An' don't you call me brother, you—you subway guard."

The train had stopped. It was 103d Street. The passengers gathered around Benjamin Mehlig, who stood on his seat in a corner. Other passengers sensing a murder or a hold-up or some other mildly exciting vicarious adventure, crowded from other cars. People who had left the train got back on. Benjamin Mehlig was now making a speech.

"You're a lot of sheep," said Benjamin Mehlig, the small man. "That's what you are—a lot of sheep. You let a subway guard tell you where to get off the train. You paid your fares, didn't you? You paid to go wherever it is you're going to, didn't you? You're a lot of sheep—all but me. I'm not a sheep. I'm going to stay on this train until it gets to 157th Street. Thank God, I'm not a sheep."

"Yuh look like one," said the guard bitterly.

"I would rather," said Benjamin Mehlig gazing coldly down at the guard—he was still standing on the seat—"look like a sheep than like a subway guard."

Benjamin Mehlig was applauded by the other passengers. The Movement was begun. Other protestants arrived. There were cheers for Benjamin Mehlig, who, standing on his seat, implored every one not to be a sheep.

More guards arrive. The Interborough held a conference. The guard who had originally encountered Benjamin Mehlig's Movement favored an immediate slaughter with as much mayhem as possible thrown in. Calmer counsels prevailed.

"We'll take you people to 110th Street," the spokesman of the guards' conference conceded at last. "You'll have to get off there. This train is going to the car barns."

"No," said Benjamin Mehlig. "Only the sheep will get off at 110th Street. I am not a sheep."

The train moved to 110th Street. Some passengers left. They were going to 110th Street anyway. Benjamin Mehlig remained, remarking at frequent intervals that he was not a sheep.

Another conference and a further compromise. The train would go to 137th Street. Cheers. Mr. Mehlig, the small man, announced that he was prepared to tell the world that he was not a sheep.

At 137th Street every one left the train except Benjamin Mehlig and two others. The faithful disciples of the anti-sheep movement on the subway who stood by the grand old flag were Arthur Weiner, of 134 West 180th Street, and Eleanor Booth Simmons, a writer and suffragist, who was going to Dyckman Street and who also is not a sheep.

The crowd at 137th Street cheered Benjamin Mehlig, Arthur Weiner and Eleanor Booth Simmons. They cheered for themselves. They jeered the guard and the Interborough and the turnstiles and the slot machines. Jeers, cheers; and Benjamin Mehlig, standing on his seat, declining to be a sheep.

"You gotta get out," announced the guards' conference.

"At 157th Street," said Benjamin Mehlig. "Don't kid yourselves that I'm a sheep."

"We'll put you out," said the guards' conference, and the voice of the original guard was heard lifted above all the rest begging to be allowed to get at him.

"You lay a finger on me," said Benjamin Mehlig, "and you'll hear from my lawyers. I got lawyers. Sheep haven't got lawyers, but me, I ain't a sheep."

The train continued. Ten cars. Three passengers, one of them Mr. Mehlig, but none of them sheep.

The train roared through 145th Street and howled into 157th Street. The brakes shrieked. The train, all ten cars of it, came to a stop. The doors were flung open.

Benjamin Mehlig walked out.

"I hope you choke," shouted the guard.

"I am not a sheep," announced Benjamin Mehlig, and went home to supper.

Homo Neanderthalensis
H. L. MENCKEN—*Baltimore Sun*—6/29/1925

Such obscenities as the forthcoming trial of the Tennessee evolutionist, if they serve no other purpose, at least call attention dramatically to the fact that enlightenment, among mankind, is very narrowly dispersed.

It is common to assume that human progress affects everyone—that even the dullest man, in these bright days, knows more than any man of, say, the Eighteenth Century, and is far more civilized. This assumption is quite erroneous. The men of the educated minority, no doubt, know more than their predecessors, and of some of them, perhaps, it may be said that they are more civilized—though I should not like to be put to giving names—but the great masses of men, even in this inspired republic, are precisely where the mob was at the dawn of history. They are ignorant, they are dishonest, they are cowardly, they are ignoble. They know little if anything that is worth knowing, and there is not the slightest sign of a natural desire among them to increase their knowledge.

Such immortal vermin, true enough, get their share of the fruits of human progress, and so they may be said, in a way, to have their part in it. The most ignorant man, when he is ill, may enjoy whatever boons and usufructs modern medicine may offer—that is, provided he is too poor to choose his own doctor. He is free, if he wants to, to take a bath. The literature of the world is at his disposal in public libraries. He may look at works of art. He may hear good music. He has at hand a thousand devices for making life less wearisome and more tolerable: the telephone, railroads, bichloride tablets, newspapers, sewers, correspondence schools, delicatessen. But he had no more to do with bringing these things into the world than the horned cattle in the fields, and he does no more to increase them today than the birds of the air.

On the contrary, he is generally against them, and sometimes with immense violence. Every step in human progress, from the first feeble stirrings in the abyss of time, has been opposed by the great majority of men. Every valuable thing that has been added to the store of man's possessions has been derided by them when it was new, and destroyed by them when they had the power. They have fought every new truth ever heard of, and they have killed every truth-seeker who got into their hands.

The so-called religious organizations which now lead the war against the teaching of evolution are nothing more, at bottom, than conspiracies of the inferior man against his betters. They mirror very accurately his congenital hatred of knowledge, his bitter enmity to the man who knows more than he does, and so gets more out of life. Certainly it cannot have gone unnoticed that their membership is recruited, in the overwhelming main, from the lower orders—that no man of any education or other human dignity belongs to them. What they propose to do, at bottom and in brief, is to make the superior man infamous—by mere abuse if it is sufficient, and if it is not, then by law.

Such organizations, of course, must have leaders; there must be men in them whose ignorance and imbecility are measurably less abject than the ignorance and imbecility of the average. These super-Chandala often attain to a considerable power, especially in democratic states. Their followers trust them and look up to them; sometimes, when the pack is on the loose, it is necessary to conciliate them. But their puissance cannot conceal their incurable inferiority. They belong to the mob as surely as their dupes, and the thing that animates them is precisely the mob's hatred of superiority. Whatever lies above the level of their comprehension is of the devil. A glass of wine delights civilized men; they themselves, drinking it, would get drunk. *Ergo*, wine must be prohibited. The hypothesis of evolution is credited by all men of education; they themselves can't understand it. *Ergo*, its teaching must be put down.

This simple fact explains such phenomena as the Tennessee buffoonery. Nothing else can. We must think of human progress, not as of something going on in the race in general, but as of something going on in a small minority, perpetually beleaguered in a few walled towns. Now and then the horde of barbarians outside breaks through, and we have an armed effort to halt the process. That is, we have a Reformation, a French Revolution, a war for democracy, a Great Awakening. The minority is decimated and driven to cover. But a few survive—and a few are enough to carry on.

The inferior man's reasons for hating knowledge are not hard to discern. He hates it because it is complex—because it puts an unbearable burden upon his meager capacity for taking in ideas. Thus his search is always for short cuts. All superstitions are such short cuts. Their aim is to make the unintelligible simple, and even obvious.

So on what seem to be higher levels. No man who has not had a long and arduous education can understand even the most elementary concepts of modern pathology. But even a hind at the plow can grasp the theory of chiropractic in two lessons. Hence the vast popularity of chiropractic among the submerged— and of osteopathy, Christian Science and other such quackeries with it. They are idiotic, but they are simple—and every man prefers what he can understand to what puzzles and dismays him.

The popularity of Fundamentalism among the inferior orders of men is explicable in exactly the same way. The cosmogonies that educated men toy with are all inordinately complex. To comprehend their veriest outlines requires an immense stock of knowledge, and a habit of thought. It would be as vain to try to teach to peasants or to the city proletariat as it would be to try to teach them to streptococci. But the cosmogony of Genesis is so simple that even a yokel can grasp it. It is set forth in a few phrases. It offers, to an ignorant man, the irresistible reasonableness of the nonsensical. So he accepts it with loud hosannas, and has one more excuse for hating his betters.

Politics and the fine arts repeat the story. The issues that the former throw up are often so complex that, in the present state of human knowledge, they must remain impenetrable, even to the most enlightened men. How much easier to follow a mountebank with a shibboleth—a Coolidge, a Wilson or a Roosevelt! The arts, like the sciences, demand special training, often very difficult. But in jazz there are simple rhythms, comprehensible even to savages.

What all this amounts to is that the human race is divided into two sharply differentiated and mutually antagonistic classes, almost two genera—a small minority that plays with ideas and is capable of taking them in, and a vast majority that finds them painful, and is thus arrayed against them, and against all who have traffic with them. The intellectual heritage of the race belongs to the minority, and to the minority only. The majority has no more to do with it than it has to do with ecclesiastic politics on Mars. In so far as that heritage is apprehended, it is viewed with enmity. But in the main it is not apprehended at all.

That is why Beethoven survives. Of the 110,000,000 so-called human beings who now live in the United States, flogged and crazed by Coolidge, Rotary, the Ku Klux and the newspapers, it is probable that at least 108,000,000 have never heard of him at all. To these immortals, made in God's image, one of the greatest artists the human race has ever produced is not even a name. So far as they are concerned he might as well have died at birth. The gorgeous and incomparable beauties that he created are nothing to them. They get no value out of the fact that he existed. They are completely unaware of what he did in the world, and would not be interested if they were told.

The fact saves good Ludwig's bacon. His music survives because it lies outside the plane of the popular apprehension, like the colors beyond violet or the concept of honor. If it could be brought within range, it would at once arouse hostility. Its complexity would challenge; its lace of moral purpose would affright. Soon there would be a movement to put it down, and Baptist clergymen would range the land denouncing it, and in the end some poor musician, taken in the un-American act of playing it, would be put on trial before a jury of Ku Kluxers, and railroaded to the calaboose.

Lindbergh Lands in Paris

EDWIN L. JAMES—*New York Tribune*—5/21/1927

Lindbergh did it. Twenty minutes after 10 o'clock tonight suddenly and softly there slipped out of the darkness a gray-white airplane as 25,000 pairs of eyes strained toward it. At 10:24 the *Spirit of St. Louis* landed and lines of soldiers, ranks of policemen and stout steel fences went down before a mad rush as irresistible as the tides of ocean.

"Well, I made it," smiled Lindbergh, as the little white monoplane came to a halt in the middle of the field and the first vanguard reached the plane. Lindbergh made a move to jump out. Twenty hands reached for him and lifted him out as if he were a baby. Several thousands in a minute were around the plane. Thousands more broke the barriers of iron rails round the field, cheering wildly.

As he was lifted to the ground Lindbergh was pale and with his hair unkempt, he looked completely worn out. He had strength enough, however, to smile, and waved his hand to the crowd. Soldiers with fixed bayonets were unable to keep back the crowd.

United States Ambassador Herrick was among the first to welcome and congratulate the hero.

A *New York Times* man was one of the first to reach the machine after its graceful descent to the field. Those first to arrive at the plane had a picture that will live in their minds for the rest of their lives. His cap off, his famous locks falling in disarray around his eyes, "Lucky Lindy" sat peering out over the rim of the little cockpit of his machine.

It was high drama. Picture the scene. Almost if not quite 100,000 people were massed on the east side of Le Bourget airfield. Some of them had been there six and seven hours.

Off to the left the giant phare lighthouse of Mount Valarien flashed its guiding light 300 miles into the air. Closer on the left Le Bourget Lighthouse twinkled, and off to the right another giant revolving phare sent its beams high into the heavens.

Big arc lights on all sides with enormous electric glares were flooding the landing field. From time to time rockets rose and burst in varied lights over the field.

Seven thirty, the hour announced for the arrival, had come and gone. Then 8 o'clock came, and no Lindbergh; at 9 o'clock the sun had set but then came reports that Lindbergh had been seen over Cork. Then he had been seen over Valentia in Ireland and then over Plymouth.

Suddenly a message spread like lightning, the aviator had been seen over

Cherbourg. However, remembering the messages telling of Captain Nungesser's flight, the crowd was skeptical.

"One chance in a thousand!" "Oh, he cannot do it without navigating instruments!" "It's a pity, because he was a brave boy." Pessimism had spread over the great throng by 10 o'clock.

The stars came out and a chill wind blew.

Suddenly the field lights flooded their glares onto the landing ground and there came the roar of an airplane's motor. The crowd was still, then began to cheer, but two minutes later the landing glares went dark for the searchlight had identified the plane and it was not Captain Lindbergh's.

Stamping their feet in the cold, the crowd waited patiently. It seemed quite apparent that nearly everyone was willing to wait all night, hoping against hope.

Suddenly—it was 10:16 exactly—another motor roared over the heads of the crowd. In the sky one caught a glimpse of a white-gray plane, and for an instant heard the sound of one. Then it dimmed, and the idea spread that it was yet another disappointment.

Again landing lights glared and almost by the time they had flooded the field the gray-white plane had lighted on the far side nearly half a mile from the crowd. It seemed to stop almost as it hit the ground, so gently did it land.

And then occurred a scene which almost passed description. Two companies of soldiers with fixed bayonets and the Le Bourget field police, reinforced by Paris agents, had held the crowd in good order. But as the lights showed the plane landing, much as if a picture had been thrown on a moving picture screen, there was a mad rush.

The movement of humanity swept over soldiers and by policemen and there was the wild sight of thousands of men and women rushing madly across half a mile of the not too even ground. Soldiers and police tried for one small moment to stem the tide, then they joined it, rushing as madly as anyone else toward the aviator and his plane.

The first people to reach the plane were two workmen of the aviation field and half a dozen Frenchmen.

"Cette fois, ca va!" they cried. (This time, it's done.)

Captain Lindbergh answered:

"Well, I made it."

An instant later he was on the shoulders of half a dozen persons who tried to bear him from the field.

The crowd crushed about the aviator and his progress was halted until a squad of soldiers with fixed bayonets cleared a way for him.

It was two French aviators—Major Pierre Weiss and Sergeant de Troyer— who rescued Captain Lindbergh from the frenzied mob. When it seemed that the excited French men and women would overwhelm the frail figure which was being carried on the shoulders of a half dozen men, the two aviators rushed up with a Renault car and hastily snatching Lindy from the crowd, sped across the field to the commandant's office.

Then followed an almost cruel rush to get near the airman. Women were thrown down and a number trampled badly. The doors of the small building were closed, but the windows were forced by enthusiasts, who were promptly ejected by soldiers.

Spurred on by reports spread in Paris of the approach of the aviator, other thousands began to arrive from the capital. The police estimate that within half an hour after Captain Lindbergh landed there were probably 100,000 storming the little building to get a sight of the idol of the evening.

Suddenly he appeared at a window, waving his helmet. It was then that, amid cheers for him, came five minutes of cheering for Captain Nungesser.

While the gallant aviator was resting in the Aviators' Club part of the crowd turned toward his airplane. It had landed in the pink of condition. Before the police could intervene the spectators turned souvenir mad, had stripped the plane of everything which could be taken off, and some were even cutting pieces of linen from the wings when a squad of soldiers with fixed bayonets quickly surrounded the *Spirit of St. Louis* and guarded it while mechanics wheeled it into a shed, but only after it had been considerably marred.

While the crowd was waiting, Captain Lindbergh was taken away from the field about midnight, to seek a well-earned repose.

The thing that Captain Lindbergh emphasized more than anything else to the American committee which welcomed him and later to newspapermen, was that he felt no special strain.

"I could have gone one-half again as much," he said with conviction.

Ruth for President

WESTBROOK PEGLER—*Chicago Tribune*—10/1/1932

There, in the third ball game of the World Series, at the Cubs' ball yard on the north side yesterday, the people who had the luck to be present saw the supreme performance of the greatest artist the profession of sport has ever produced. Babe Ruth hit two home runs.

Now, Lou Gehrig also hit two home runs, and Jimmy Foxx of the Athletics or any other master mechanic of the business might have hit three or four home runs and you would have gone away with the same impression that a factory tourist receives from an hour of watching a big machine lick labels and stick them on bottles of mouthwash or pop. The machine might awe you, but would you love it?

The people who saw Babe Ruth play that ball game and hit those two home runs against the Cubs came away from the baseball plant with a spiritual memento of the most gorgeous display of humor, athletic art and championship class any performer in any of the games has ever presented.

Bobby Jones? A sportsman, a champion and a gentleman.

Tilden? A splendid player at his game, but over-nice and never intimate with a gallery.

Dempsey? He brought them up screaming madly for or against them, but did he ever make them laugh as he stepped back from some inert hunk with a lacerated face heaving laboriously on the floor?

The Babe is 38 years old, and if you don't know that he is unable to hike as high for fly balls or stoop as nimbly as he used to for rollers coming to him through the grass, that must be just your own fault, because he would not deceive you. As an outfielder he is pretty close to his past tense, which may mean that one more year from now he will be only a pinch-hitter. He has been breaking this news all year to himself and the customers.

Why, when Bill Jurges, the human clay pigeon, hit a short fly to him there in left field and he mauled it about, trying for a shoestring catch, he came up off the turf admitting all as Jurges pulled up at second.

The old Babe stood up, straightened his cap and gesticulated vigorously toward Earl Combs in center. "Hey!" the old Babe waved, "my dogs ain't what they used to be. Don't hit them out to me. Hit to the young guys out there."

The customers behind him in the bleachers were booing him when the ball game began, but they would have voted him president when it was over, and he might not be a half-bad compromise, at that.

Somebody in the crowd tossed out a lemon that hit him in the leg. Now there are sensitive ball players who might have been petulant at that and some stiff-necked ones who could only ignore it, boiling inwardly. But the Babe topped the jest. With graphic gestures, old Mr. Ruth called on them for fair play. If they must hit him with missiles, would they please not hit him on the legs? The legs weren't too good anyway. Would they just as lief hit him on the head? The head was solid and could stand it.

I am telling you that before the ball game began the Babe knew he was going to hit one or more home runs. He had smacked half a dozen balls into the right-field bleachers during his hitting practice and he knew he had the feel of the trick for the day. When his hitting practice was over he waddled over toward the Cubs' dugout, his large abdomen jiggling in spite of his rubber corsets, and yelled at the Cubs sulking down there in the den, "Hey, muggs! You muggs are not going to see the Yankee Stadium any more this year. This World Series is going to be over Sunday afternoon. Four straight."

He turned, rippling with the fun of it and, addressing the Chicago customers behind third base, yelled, "Did you hear what I told them over there? I told them they ain't going back to New York. We lick 'em here, today and tomorrow."

Lou Gehrig was hitting next behind him in practice. Lou's shots were not clearing the infield and he came back from the plate scrutinizing his stick.

"The Babe is on fire," Lou said. "He ought to hit one today. Maybe a couple. I'm not catching them right, but I know what's the trouble. I'm catching them on the end of the club. I ought to catch them about four inches down to make them ride."

The Babe had been humiliating the Cubs publicly throughout the series. They were a lot of Lord Jims to him. They had had a chance to be big fellows when they did the voting on the division of the World Series pool. But for a few dollars' gain they had completely ignored Rogers Hornsby, their manager for most of the year, who is through with baseball now apparently without much to show for his long career, and had held Mark Koenig, their part-time shortstop, to a half share. The Yankees, on the contrary, had been generous, even to ex-Yankees who were traded away months ago, to their deformed bat boy who was run over and hurt by a car early in the season, and to his substitute.

The Cubs may regret their selfishness now that the Yanks by their generosity have made it so conspicuous and the Babe, by his pantomime and repartee, has flung it up to them in public a dozen times in every game. But the Cubs are a Lord Jim ballclub. They had their chance to be big about it. Now, even if they should reapportion their money, it would be too late. The world heard them the first time, through the Babe.

There never was such contempt shown by one antagonist for another as the Babe displayed for the Cubs, and ridicule was his medium.

In the first inning, with Combs and Joe Sewell on base, he sailed his first home run into the bleachers. He hit Charlie Root's earnest pitching with the same easy, playful swing that he had been using against the soft, casual service of a guinea-pig pitcher. The ball would have fallen into the street beyond the bleachers under ordinary conditions, but dropped among the patrons in the temporary seats.

The old Babe came around third base and past the Cubs' dugout yelling comments which were unintelligible to the patrons but plainly discourteous and, pursing his lips, blew them a salute known as the Bronx cheer.

He missed a second home run in the third inning when the ball came down a few feet short of the wire screen, but the masterpiece was only deferred. He hit it in the fifth, a ball that sailed incredibly to the extreme depth of center field and dropped like a perfect mashie shot behind the barrier, long enough to clear it, but with no waste of distance.

Guy Bush, the Cubs' pitcher, was up on the top step of the dugout, jawing back at him as he took his turn at bat this time. Bush pushed back his big ears, funneled his hands to hit mouth, and yelled raspingly at the great man to upset him. The Babe laughed derisively and gestured at him. "Wait, mugg, I'm going to hit one out of the yard." Root threw a strike past him and he held up a finger to Bush, whose ears flapped excitedly as he renewed his insults. Another strike passed him and Bush crawled almost out of the hole to extend his remarks.

The Babe held up two fingers this time. Root wasted two balls and the Babe put up two fingers on his other hand. Then, with a warning gesture of his hand to Bush, he sent him the signal for the customers to see.

"Now," it said, "this is the one. Look!" And that one went riding in the longest home run ever hit in the park.

He licked the Chicago ball club, but he left the people laughing when he said good-bye, and it was a privilege to be present because it is not likely that the scene will ever be repeated in all its elements. Many a hitter may make two home runs, or possibly three in World Series play in years to come, but not the way Babe Ruth made these two. Nor will you ever see an artist call his shot before hitting one of the longest drives ever made on the grounds, in a World Series game, laughing and mocking the enemy with two strikes gone.

The Cinderella Man
DAMON RUNYON—*New York American*—6/14/1935

The fistic fairy tale comes true. James J. Braddock, of New Jersey, "the Cinderella Man" of pugilism, is the new heavyweight champion of the world.

He beats the glamorous Max Baer of California, in a fifteen-round right in the Madison Square Garden Bowl tonight, where no champion has yet successfully defended his title.

UNANIMOUS DECISION
The decision of the referee, Johnny McAvoy, and the judges, Charley Lynch and George Kelly, is unanimous, which is the verdict of practically all the 25,000 spectators, who pay upwards of $200,000 to the see the battle.

It is the greatest pugilistic upset in the modern history of the boxing game.

Brought back from Hasbeenville by the magic wave of the wand of sheer chance, after being such a down-and-outer that he had to go on relief in his home State of New Jersey at $24 per month to provide food for his wife and three children, James J. Braddock at 29 years of age suddenly finds himself occupying the pinnacle of the pugilistic heap, with an utterly new life before him.

Faced 8 to 1 Odds

Coming into the ring on the short end of the unheard-of price of 8 to 1 with even money he does not come out for the tenth round, and with his chances so little regarded that the crowd does not half fill the "graveyard of champions," Braddock fights from the opening bell with the desperation of a man leading a forlorn hope.

He is the slow, patient, plodding type, no longer the puncher he was in his fistic youth, but he is game, and he marches boldly into what the crowd feels is a fistic furnace only to suddenly discover that the fire is all out in the mighty Max Baer.

Old Form is Gone

The latter claims two badly injured hands. He says his fighting tools went back on him early in the battle, and his efforts become so feeble that some of the suspicious souls you always find among the pugilistic following are raising their eyebrows at the finish.

He has absolutely nothing of the form he displayed in his fights against Max Schmeling and Primo Carnera to stave off the already plodding of the man from New Jersey, "the Cinderella Man," who stepped into this picture as a last hope choice of Madison Square Garden to get one final fight out of its contract with Max Baer.

Practically every boxing observer in the country except this writer picked Baer to win by a swift knockout, but we told you that the stage was set for one of the little comedy dramas that fistic fate loves to play against these odds-on choices, that Braddock is an earnest, tough fellow, never knocked out in the ring except what they call "technically," and difficult to knock out.

"Experts" Sit Stunned

The "experts" sit stunned tonight as the battle progresses. They observe Baer's futile efforts and realize that only a miracle can save Baer. The writer thinks Braddock wins a good majority of the rounds with ease. He gets several from the referee because Baer is guilty of backhanding and hitting low, though these blows are unintentional.

Only occasionally is Baer of the magnificent torso, Baer of the many love affairs, and the wisecracks, the comedian tonight as he tries to catch up with the plugging, steady family man from New Jersey, whose aged father sits in the bowl with several other sons, watching the battle. It is a very slow fight at all stages, there is not a knockdown, not a thrill, except in the result, which is bound to thrill anyone who likes to see the unexpected, who likes to see the underdog triumph once in a while.

BUDDY KISSES MAX

As the decision is announced, Braddock stands in the ring swathed in a blue robe. He is surrounded by his wildly excited handlers, a smile curling his bruised lips, and hundreds of his fellow citizens from New Jersey swarm up to the ringside to shake his hand. Baer's brother, the huge Buddy, climbed into the ring and kisses Max, who tries to smile, too, but it is a wry effort. Max realizes from around the tenth round that his title is gone, and he keeps charging and pummeling Braddock around the body with his sore hands but by this time Jim is cool and confident and outboxes Baer. The latter is frequently warned by Johnny McAvoy, the referee, for roughing and other foul tactics.

Max quickly leaves the ring, and the crowd, which is booing and clapping derisively at him through half the fight, gives him a few parting boos.

BAER GETS 42 1/2%

For this fight tonight Baer gets 42 1/2 percent of the receipts against Braddock's 15 percent. Baer has made little money out of the title in the brief year he has held it since he beat Primo Carnera in this very arena.

Braddock has to fairly fight his way through the crowd to get to his dressing room. The crowd is so big he slips away without even taking his usual shower bath.

His victory tonight saves Madison Square Garden's fistic hash to some extent, because Baer was through with the Garden with this fight and Braddock had to sign a contract to give his next fight for the title to the Garden, though he is already under contract to the new Twentieth Century Sporting Club.

When the chance came for Braddock to get the fight with Baer for the title, Mike Jacobs, head of the Twentieth Century, released Jim to the Garden, saying: "I will not stand in the way of a man who has the opportunity of fighting for the championship."

Baer, in his dressing room, says he will never fight again and is going to devote his future to raising white-faced cattle in California, but even while he is saying this, his manager, Ansil Hoffman, is signing with Mike Jacobs to fight the winner of the Joe Louis-Carnera battle in the Fall.

BRADDOCK TO RECOUP

It is doubtful if Braddock will fight again this year, but will devote his time to make a few of the dollars that have been eluding him since he lost his considerable savings in the general crash of '29, had to go back to hard labor and wound up on relief.

A year ago, in this very ring, he stepped in to pick up a small purse that he needed badly by fighting a youngster named Corn Griffin in a preliminary. He was supposed to be a sacrifice to the career of a rising youngster. He was knocked over in the first round, one of the two times Jim has ever been knocked down, and his old-time admirers sighed sadly, recalling his former fistic glory. Braddock got up, made a desperate rally, and flattened Griffin.

FINDS HE'S NOT THROUGH

That decided him that he was not through after all. He fought John Henry Lewis, a Negro from the Pacific Coast, and won a close decision. Then he beat Art Lasky in fifteen rounds. His first act after getting his start was to repay the money he had taken from the relief authorities, so it is said.

The Garden wanted to match Baer with Max Schmeling for the title after Schmeling knocked out Steve Hamas, but Schmeling refused to come here from Germany before September. Meantime, Mike Jacobs had signed up Carnera, the other outstanding contender, and the Garden fell back on Braddock in sheer desperation. It devoted tremendous ballyhoo effort trying to build up the man from New Jersey as a contender, but the pugilistic following eyed the effort with little interest, as the crowd tonight indicates.

AMAZING SPECTACLE

Those who remain away miss nothing, except the amazing spectacle of the transfer of the heavyweight crown from the curly locks of Glamorous Baer to the brown thatched head of Braddock, whose once quite regular features are now somewhat disarranged by his experiences in the ring since he began fighting in 1926, and who has a well-cauliflowered ear.

Braddock, an inarticulate fellow, who does not know how to bluster and play-act like Baer, but whose manager, Joe Gould, is voluble enough for a Huey Long filibuster, has said all along that he thought he would beat Baer, and there is no fear in his heart tonight as he faces the magnificent champion from California, the ex-butcher boy, whose antics have made him one of the most colorful characters the ring has ever known.

BAER GRINS AT BOOS

At the start of the fight, Baer apparently begins half playing with Braddock. Perhaps he has been fooled by the predictions of the experts. The crowd boos him as a showoff, and Baer only grins. For a couple of rounds he keeps up his dilatory tactics, but all the time Braddock is taking the thing seriously and is picking up points by out-boxing Max with a long left and an occasional right-hand chop.

Then, urged by Ancil Hoffman and Dolph Thomas, his handlers, Max starts trying to do a little fighting, only to discover that he cannot reach Braddock with any effectiveness. He claims that it is in the fifth round that his right hand goes. In any event, the fighting gets slower and slower as the rounds pass, and at the finish the experts are agreeing that it is one of the slowest fights in heavyweight history.

THEY WAIT AND WAIT

Perhaps some of them are piqued by their predictions going astray. Baer's admirers keep waiting and waiting for the tiger-like attack that felled the German, Schmeling, and the Italian giant, Carnera, but finally even his best friends can see that Maxie cannot fight tonight, and join the steadily growing Braddock brigade, that starts out with just a few loyal pals from New Jersey. It is an entire army at the close of the battle.

Once Max stops the booing against him by putting on a grotesque and very funny pantomime of a groggy fighter, and raising a big laugh, but when the laugh comes Baer is too far behind to ever catch up, and there is something almost pathetic in his attempt at comedy.

CORNER BEDLAM

Meantime, Braddock's corner, where Joe Gould, his manager, and Whitney Bimstein and Ray Arcel and Doc Robb are clustered behind the ring posts, like a group of frightened men drawn together for mutual protection, is a bedlam as they see Braddock steadily rolling up rounds on the baffled Baer.

They are yelling at McAvoy, the referee, and at Baer, who finally stops fighting, completely exasperated, and stands with his hands down, glaring at the corner, and leaving himself open for a knockout punch from a quicker thinker than Braddock.

Once, in his excitement at what he deems Max's foul treatment of Jim, Joe Gould rushes across the ring, shouting at Baer, but, fortunately, it is between rounds. A second entering a ring during the actual fighting calls for a disqualification of his fighter.

JOHNSTON ELATED

Joe is recalled by the yells of Jimmy Johnston, the Garden boxing director, who is almost beside himself with joy over Braddock's victory, because he hates Max Baer with a deep hatred. Incidentally, Johnston's interest in Braddock's success is heightened by the Garden's contract with the fighter.

At the close of the fight, while the fighters are awaiting the announcement of the decision, the crowd begins filing out, knowing beforehand what the verdict will be, and so ends the fistic fairy tale, as all fairy tales should end, with the poor abused hero finding his pumpkins of failure turned into prancing white steeds of glittering success and his feet incased in the glass slippers of happiness, if you can follow all this twisted metaphor.

Anyway, so ends the strange story of James J. Braddock "the Cinderella Man" of Fistiana.

And you cannot match his story anywhere in the realm of the most fantastic fiction.

Joe Louis Uncovers Dynamite

RICHARD WRIGHT—*New Masses*—10/8/1935

"WUN—TUH—THREE—FOOO—FIIVE—SEEX—SEVEN—EIGHT—NIINE—THUNN!"

Then:

"JOE LOUIS—THE WINNAH!"

On Chicago's South Side five minutes after these words were yelled and Joe Louis' hand was hosted as victor in his four-round go with Max Baer, Negroes poured out of beer taverns, pool rooms, barber shops, rooming houses, and dingy flats and flooded the streets.

"LOUIS! LOUIS! LOUIS!" they yelled and threw their hats away. They snatched newspapers from the stands of astonished Greeks and tore them up, flinging the bits into the air. They wagged their heads. Lawd, they'd never seen or heard the like of it before. They shook the hands of strangers. They clapped one another on the back. It was like a revival. Really, there was a religious feeling in the air. Well, it wasn't exactly a religious feeling, but it was the *thing*, and you could feel it. It was a feeling of unity, of oneness.

Two hours after the fight the area between South Parkway and Prairie Avenue on 47th Street was jammed with no less than twenty-five thousand Negroes, joy-mad and moving so they didn't know where. Clasping hands they formed long writhing snake-lines and wove in and out of traffic. They seeped out of doorways, oozed from alleys, trickled out of tenements, and flowed down the street, a fluid mass of joy. White storekeepers hastily closed their doors against the tidal wave and stood peeping through plate glass with blanched faces.

Something had happened, all right. And it had happened so confoundingly sudden that the whites in the neighborhood were dumb with fear. They felt—you could see it in their faces—that *something* had ripped loose, exploded.

Something which they had long feared and thought was dead. Or if not dead at least so safely buried under the pretense of goodwill that they no longer had need to fear it. Where in the world did it come from? And what was worst of all, how far would it go? Say, what's got into these Negroes?

And the whites and the blacks began to *feel* themselves. The blacks began to remember all the little slights, and discriminations and insults they had suffered; and their hunger too and their misery. And the whites began to search their souls to see if they had been guilty of something, some time, somewhere, against which this wave of feeling was rising.

As the celebration wore on, the younger Negroes began to grow bold. They jumped on the running boards of automobiles going east or west on 47th Street and demanded of the occupants:

"Who yuh fer—Baer or Louis?"

In the stress of the moment it seemed that the answer to the question marked out friend and foe.

A hesitating reply brought waves of scornful laughter. Baer, huh? That was funny. Now, hadn't Joe Louis just whipped Max Baer? Didn't think we had it in us, did you? Thought Joe Louis was scared, didn't you? Scared because Max talked loud and made boasts. We ain't scared either. We'll fight too when the time comes. We'll win, too.

A taxicab driver had his cab wrecked when he tried to put up a show of bravado.

Then they began stopping streetcars. Like a cyclone sweeping through a forest, they went through them, shouting, stamping. Conductors gave up and backed away like children. Everybody had to join this celebration. Some of the people ran out of the cars and stood, pale and trembling, in the crowd. They felt it, too.

In the crush a pocketbook snapped open and money spilled on the street for eager black fingers.

"They stole it from us, anyhow," they said as they picked it up.

When an elderly Negro admonished them, a fist was shaken in his face. Uncle Tom-ing, huh?

"What in hell yuh gotta do wid it?" they wanted to know.

Something had popped loose, all right. And it had come from deep down. Out of the darkness it had leaped from its coil. And nobody could have said just what it was, and nobody wanted to say. Blacks and whites were afraid. But it was a sweet fear, at least for the blacks. It was a mingling of fear and fulfillment. Something dreaded and yet wanted. A something had popped out of a dark hole, something with a hydra-like head, and it was darting forth its tongue.

You stand on the borderline, wondering what's beyond. Then you take one step and you feel a strange, sweet tingling. You take two steps and the feeling becomes keener. You want to feel some more. You break into a run. You know it's dangerous, but you're propelled in spite of yourself.

Four centuries of oppression, of frustrated hopes, of black bitterness, felt even in the bones of the bewildered young, were rising to the surface. Yes, unconsciously they had imputed to the brawny image of Joe Louis all the balked dreams of revenge, all the secretly visualized moments of retaliation. AND HE HAD WON! Good Gawd Almighty! Yes, Jesus, it could be done! Didn't Joe do it? You see, Joe was the consciously-felt symbol. He was the concentrated essence of black triumph over white. And it comes so seldom, so seldom. And what could be sweeter than long nourished hate vicariously gratified? From the symbol of Joe's strength they took strength, and in that moment all fear, all obstacles were wiped out, drowned. They stepped out of the mire of hesitation and irresolution and were free! Invincible! A merciless victor over a fallen foe! Yes, they had felt all that—for a moment. . . .

And then the cops came.

Not the carefully picked white cops who were used to battering the skulls of white workers and intellectuals who came to the South Side to march with the black workers to show their solidarity in the struggle against Mussolini's impending invasion of Ethiopia; oh, no, black cops, but trusted black cops and plenty tough. Cops who knew their business, how to handle delicate situations. They piled out of patrols, swinging clubs.

"Git back! Gawddammit, git back!"

But they were very careful, very careful. They didn't hit anybody. They, too, sensed *something*. And they didn't want to trifle with it. And there's no doubt but that they had been instructed not to. Better go easy here. No telling what might happen. They swung clubs, but pushed the crowd back with their hands.

Finally, the streetcars moved again. The taxis and automobiles could go through. The whites breathed easier. The blood came back to their cheeks.

The Negroes stood on the sidewalks, talking, wondering, looking, breathing hard. They had felt something, and it had been sweet—that feeling. They wanted some more of it, but they were afraid now. The spell was broken.

And about midnight down the street that feeling ebbed, seeping home—flowing back to the beer tavern, the pool room, the café, the barber shop, the dingy flat. Like a sullen river it ran back to its muddy channel, carrying a confused and sentimental memory on its surface, like water-soaked driftwood.

Say, Comrade, here's the wild river that's got to be harnessed and directed. Here's that *something*, that pent-up folk consciousness. Here's a fleeting glimpse of the heart of the Negro, the heart that beats and suffers and hopes—for freedom. Here's that fluid something that's like iron. Here's the real dynamite that Joe Louis uncovered!

London Still Stood This Morning
HELEN KIRKPATRICK—*Chicago Daily News*—9/9/1940

London still stood this morning, which was the greatest surprise to me as I cycled home in the light of early dawn after the most frightening night I have ever spent. But not all of London was still there, and some of the things I saw this morning would scare the wits out of anyone.

When the sirens first shrieked on Saturday, it was evident we were in for something, but dinner proceeded calmly enough. It was when the first screaming bomb started on its downward track that we decided the basement would be healthier.

The whole night was one of moving from the basement to the first floor, with occasional sallies to make sure that no incendiaries had landed on the rooftop.

That was perhaps more frightening than the sound of constant bombs punctuated by guns near and far. For the London air was heavy with the burning smell. The smoke sometimes brought tears to the eyes, and the glow around the horizon certainly looked as though the entire city might be up in flames any minute.

On one occasion I dropped off to sleep on a basement floor and slept probably forty-five minutes, when two screamers sounding as though they had landed right next door brought me, startled, to my feet. A few minutes later a couple of incendiaries arrived just around the comer, but the fire equipment came within seconds.

Most of the time we felt that the entire center of the city had probably been blasted out of existence and we ticked off each hit with "That must be Buckingham Palace—that's Whitehall." It was staggering, to say the least, to cycle for a mile through the heart of London and fail to see even one pane of glass shattered and eventually to find one's own house standing calm and in one piece.

A later tour, however, showed that while none of the bombs hit any objectives we had picked out, they had landed squarely on plenty of places. I walked through areas of rubble and debris in southeastern London this morning that made it seem incredible that anyone could be alive, but they were, and very much so. Fires for the most part were put out or were well under control by early morning.

It was a contrast to find one section of "smart London" that had as bad a dose as the tenement areas. Near one of many of Sir Christopher Wren's masterpieces, houses were gutted structures with windowpanes hanging out, while panes in a church were broken in a million pieces.

It is amazing this morning to see London traffic more like New York theater traffic than the slow dribble it had been during past months, but it is most amazing to see that there is any London to have traffic at all. It is pretty indescribable, too, to find people relatively unshaken after the terrific experience.

Fright becomes so mingled with a deep almost uncontrollable anger that it is hard to know when one stops and the other begins. And on top of it all London is smiling even in the districts where casualties must have been very heavy.

Liberating the City of Light
ERNIE PYLE—Scripps Howard—8/28/1944

PARIS, August 28, 1944—I had thought that for me there could never again be any elation in war. But I had reckoned without the liberation of Paris—I had reckoned without remembering that I might be a part of this richly historic day.

We are in Paris—on the first day—one of the great days of all time. This is being written, as other correspondents are writing their pieces, under an emotional tension, a pent-up semi-delirium.

Our approach to Paris was hectic. We had waited for three days in a nearby town while hourly our reports on what was going on in Paris changed and contradicted themselves. Of a morning it would look as though we were about to break through the German ring around Paris and come to the aid of the brave French Forces of the Interior who were holding parts of the city. By afternoon it would seem the enemy had reinforced until another Stalingrad was developing. We could not bear to think of the destruction of Paris, and yet at times it seemed desperately inevitable.

That was the situation this morning when we left Rambouillet and decided to feel our way timidly toward the very outskirts of Paris. And then, when we were within about eight miles, rumors began to circulate that the French 2nd Armored Division was in the city. We argued for half an hour at a crossroads with a French captain who was holding us up, and finally he freed us and waved us on.

For fifteen minutes we drove through a flat gardenlike country under a magnificent bright sun and amidst greenery, with distant banks of smoke pillaring the horizon ahead and to our left. And then we came gradually into the suburbs, and soon into Paris itself and a pandemonium of surely the greatest mass joy that has ever happened.

* * *

The streets were lined as by Fourth of July parade crowds at home, only this crowd was almost hysterical. The streets of Paris are very wide, and they were packed on each side. The women were all brightly dressed in white or red blouses and colorful peasant skirts, with flowers in their hair and big flashy earrings. Everybody was throwing flowers, and even serpentine.

As our jeep eased through the crowds, thousands of people crowded up, leaving only a narrow corridor, and frantic men, women and children grabbed us and kissed us and shook our hands and beat on our shoulders and slapped our backs and shouted their joy as we passed.

I was in a jeep with Henry Gorrell of the United Press, Capt. Carl Pergler of Washington, D.C., and Corp. Alexander Belon of Amherst, Massachusetts. We all got kissed until we were literally red in the face, and I must say we enjoyed it.

Once when the jeep was simply swamped in human traffic and had to stop, we were swarmed over and hugged and kissed and torn at. Everybody, even beautiful girls, insisted on kissing you on both cheeks. Somehow I got started kissing babies that were held up by their parents, and for a while I looked like a baby-kissing politician going down the street. The fact that I hadn't shaved for days, and was gray-bearded as well as bald-headed, made no difference. Once when we came to a stop, some Frenchman told us there were still snipers shooting, so we put our steel helmets back on.

The people certainly looked well-fed and well-dressed. The streets were lined with green trees and modern buildings. All the stores were closed in holiday. Bicycles were so thick I have an idea there have been plenty of accidents today, with tanks and jeeps overrunning the populace.

We entered Paris via Rue Aristide Briand and Rue d'Orléans. We were slightly apprehensive, but decided it was all right to keep going as long as there were crowds. But finally we were stymied by the people in the streets, and then above the din we heard some not-too-distant explosions—the Germans trying to destroy bridges across the Seine. And then the rattling of machine guns up the street, and that old battlefield whine of high-velocity shells just overhead. Some of us veterans ducked, but the Parisians just laughed and continued to carry on.

There came running over to our jeep a tall, thin, happy woman in a light brown dress, who spoke perfect American.

She was Mrs. Helen Cardon, who lived in Paris for twenty-one years and has not been home to America since 1935. Her husband is an officer in French Army headquarters and home now after two and a half years as a German prisoner. He was with her, in civilian clothes.

Mrs. Cardon has a sister, Mrs. George Swikart, of New York, and I can say here to her relatives in America that she is well and happy. Incidentally, her two children, Edgar and Peter, are the only two American children, she says, who have been in Paris throughout the entire war.

* * *

We entered Paris from due south and the Germans were still battling in the heart of the city along the Seine when we arrived, but they were doomed. There was a full French armored division in the city, plus American troops entering constantly.

The farthest we got in our first hour in Paris was near the Senate building, where some Germans were holed up and firing desperately. So we took a hotel room nearby and decided to write while the others fought. By the time you read this I'm sure Paris will once again be free for Frenchmen, and I'll be out all over town getting my bald head kissed. Of all the days of national joy I've ever witnessed this is the biggest.

The Atomic Bombing of Nagasaki
WILLIAM LAURENCE—*The New York Times*—8/9/1945

We are on our way to bomb the mainland of Japan. Our flying contingent consists of three specially designed B-29 Superforts, and two of these carry no bombs. But our lead plane is on its way with another atomic bomb, the second in three days, concentrating its active substance, and explosive energy equivalent to twenty thousand, and under favorable conditions, forty thousand tons of TNT.

We have several chosen targets. One of these is the great industrial and shipping center of Nagasaki, on the western shore of Kyushu, one of the main islands of the Japanese homeland.

I watched the assembly of this man-made meteor during the past two days and was among the small group of scientists and Army and Navy representatives privileged to be present at the ritual of its loading in the Superfort last night, against a background of threatening black skies torn open at intervals by great lightning flashes.

It is a thing of beauty to behold, this "gadget." In its design went millions of man-hours of what is without a doubt the most concentrated intellectual effort in history. Never before had so much brain power been focused on a single problem.

This atomic bomb is different from the bomb used three days ago with such devastating results on Hiroshima.

I saw the atomic substance before it was placed inside the bomb. By itself it is not at all dangerous to handle. It is only under certain conditions, produced in the bomb assembly, that it can be made to yield up its energy, and even then it gives up only a small fraction of its total contents, a fraction, however, large enough to produce the greatest explosion on earth.

The briefing at midnight revealed the extreme care and the tremendous amount of preparation that had been made to take care of every detail of the mission, in order to make certain that the atomic bomb fully served the purpose for which it was intended. Each target in turn was shown in detailed maps and in aerial photographs. Every detail of the course was rehearsed—navigation, altitude, weather, where to land in emergencies. It came out that the Navy had submarines and rescue craft, known as Dumbos and Superdumbos, stationed at various strategic points in the vicinity of the targets, ready to rescue the fliers in case they were forced to bail out.

The briefing period ended with a moving prayer by the chaplain. We then proceeded to the mess hall for the traditional early-morning breakfast before departure on a bombing mission.

A convoy of trucks took us to the supply building for the special equipment carried on combat missions. This included the Mae West, a parachute, a life boat, an oxygen mask, a flak suit, and a survival vest. We still had a few hours before take-off time but we all went to the flying field and stood around in little groups or sat in jeeps talking rather casually about our mission to the Empire, as the Japanese home islands are known hereabouts.

In command of our mission is Major Charles W. Sweeney, twenty-five, of 124 Hamilton Avenue, North Quincy, Massachusetts. His flagship, carrying the atomic bomb, is named *The Great Artiste*, but the name does not appear on the body of the great silver ship, with its unusually long, four-bladed, orange-tipped propellers. Instead it carried the number 77, and someone remarks that it is "Red" Grange's winning number on the gridiron.

We took off at 3:50 this morning and headed northwest on a straight line for the Empire. The night was cloudy and threatening, with only a few stars here and there breaking through the overcast. The weather report had predicted storms ahead part of the way but clear sailing for the final and climactic stages of our odyssey.

We were about an hour away from our base when the storm broke. Our great ship took some heavy dips through the abysmal darkness around us, but it took these dips much more gracefully than a large commercial airliner, producing a sensation more in the nature of a glide than a "bump," like a great ocean liner riding the waves except that in this case the air waves were much higher and the rhythmic tempo of the glide was much faster.

I noticed a strange eerie light coming through the window high above in the navigator's cabin, and as I peered through the dark all around us I saw a startling phenomenon. The whirling giant propellers had somehow become great luminous disks of blue flame. The same luminous blue flame appeared on the Plexiglas windows in the nose of the ship, and on the tips of the giant wings. It looked as though we were riding the whirlwind through space on a chariot of blue fire.

It was, I surmised, a surcharge of static electricity that had accumulated on the tips of the propellers and on the di-electric material in the plastic windows. One's thoughts dwelt anxiously on the precious cargo in the invisible ship ahead of us. Was there any likelihood of danger that this heavy electric tension in the atmosphere all about us may set it off?

I express my fears to Captain Bock, who seems nonchalant and unperturbed at the controls. He quickly reassures me.

"It is a familiar phenomenon seen often on ships. I have seen it many times on bombing missions. It is known as St. Elmo's Fire."

On we went through the night. We soon rode out the storm and our ship was once again sailing on a smooth course straight ahead, on a direct line to the Empire.

Our altimeter showed that we were traveling through space at a height of seventeen thousand feet. The thermometer registered an outside temperature of thirty-three degrees below zero Centigrade, about thirty below Fahrenheit. Inside our pressurized cabin the temperature was that of a comfortable air-conditioned room and a pressure corresponding to an altitude of eight thousand feet. Captain Bock cautioned me, however, to keep my oxygen mask handy in case of emergency. This, he explained, may mean either something going wrong with the pressure equipment inside the ship or a hole through the cabin by flak.

The first signs of dawn came shortly after five o'clock. Sergeant Curry, of Hoopeston, Illinois, who had been listening steadily on his earphones for radio reports, while maintaining a strict radio silence himself, greeted it by rising to his feet and gazing out the window.

"It's good to see the day," he told me. "I get a feeling of claustrophobia hemmed in in this cabin at night."

He is a typical American youth, looking even younger than his twenty years. It takes no mind reader to read his thoughts.

"It's a long way from Hoopeston, Illinois," I find myself remarking.

"Yep," he replies, as he busies himself decoding a message from outer space.

"Think this atomic bomb will end the war?" he asks hopefully.

"There is a very good chance that this one may do the trick," I assure him, "but if not then the next one or two surely will. Its power is such that no nation can stand up against it very long." This was not my own view. I had heard it expressed all around a few hours earlier, before we took off. To anyone who had seen this man-made fireball in action, as I had less than a month ago in the desert of New Mexico, this view did not sound overoptimistic.

By 5:50 it was really light outside. We had lost our lead ship, but Lieutenant Godfrey, our navigator, informs me that we had arranged for that contingency. We have an assembly point in the sky above the little island of Yakushima, southeast of Kyushu, at 9:10. We are to circle there and wait for the rest of our formation.

Our genial bombardier, Lieutenant Levy, comes over to invite me to take his front-row seat in the transparent nose of the ship and I accept eagerly. From that vantage point in space, seventeen thousand feet above the Pacific, one gets a view of hundreds of miles on all sides, horizontally and vertically. At that height the vast ocean below and the sky above seem to merge into one great sphere.

I was on the inside of that firmament, riding above the giant mountains of white cumulous clouds, letting myself be suspended in infinite space. One hears the whirl of the motors behind one, but soon becomes insignificant against the immensity all around and is before long swallowed by it. There comes a point where space also swallows time and one lives through eternal moments filled with an oppressive loneliness, as though all life had suddenly vanished from the earth and you are the only one left, a lone survivor traveling endlessly through interplanetary space.

My mind soon returns to the mission I am on. Somewhere beyond these vast mountains of white clouds ahead of me there lies Japan, the land of our enemy. In about four hours from now one of its cities, making weapons of war for use against us, will be wiped off the map by the greatest weapon ever made by man: In one tenth of a millionth of a second, a fraction of time immeasurable by any clock, a whirlwind from the skies will pulverize thousands of its buildings and tens of thousands of its inhabitants.

But at this moment no one yet knows which one of the several cities chosen as targets is to be annihilated. The final choice lies with destiny. The winds over Japan will make the decision. If they carry heavy clouds over our primary target, that city will be saved, at least for the time being. None of its inhabitants will ever know that the wind of a benevolent destiny had passed over their heads. But that same wind will doom another city.

Our weather planes ahead of us are on their way to find out where the wind blows. Half an hour before target time we will know what the winds have decided.

Does one feel any pity or compassion for the poor devils about to die? Not when one thinks of Pearl Harbor and of the Death March on Bataan.

Captain Bock informs me that we are about to start our climb to bombing altitude.

He manipulates a few knobs on his control panel to the right of him, and I alternately watch the white clouds and ocean below me and the altimeter on the bombardier's panel. We reached our altitude at nine o'clock. We were then over Japanese waters, close to their mainland. Lieutenant Godfrey motioned to me to look through his radar scope. Before me was the outline of our assembly point. We shall soon meet our lead ship and proceed to the final stage of our journey.

We reached Yakushima at 9:12 and there, about four thousand feet ahead of us, was *The Great Artiste* with its precious load. I saw Lieutenant Godfrey and Sergeant Curry strap on their parachutes and I decided to do likewise.

We started circling. We saw little towns on the coastline, heedless of our presence. We kept on circling, waiting for the third ship in our formation.

It was 9:56 when we began heading for the coastline. Our weather scouts had sent us code messages, deciphered by Sergeant Curry, informing us that both the primary target as well as the secondary were clearly visible.

The winds of destiny seemed to favor certain Japanese cities that must remain nameless. We circled about them again and again and found no opening in the thick umbrella of clouds that covered them. Destiny chose Nagasaki as the ultimate target.

We had been circling for some time when we noticed black puffs of smoke coming through the white clouds directly at us. There were fifteen bursts of flak in rapid succession, all too low. Captain Bock changed his course. There soon followed eight more bursts of flak, right up to our altitude, but by this time we were too far to the left.

We flew southward down the channel and at 11:33 crossed the coastline and headed straight for Nagasaki, about a hundred miles to the west. Here again we circled until we found an opening in the clouds. It was 12:01 and the goal of our mission had arrived.

We heard the prearranged signal on our radio, put on our arc welder's glasses, and watched tensely the maneuverings of the strike ship about half a mile in front of us.

"There she goes!" someone said.

Out of the belly of *The Great Artiste* what looked like a black object came downward.

Captain Bock swung around to get out of range; but even though we were turning away in the opposite direction, and despite the fact that it was broad daylight in our cabin, all of us became aware of a giant flash that broke through the dark barrier of our arc welder's lenses and flooded our cabin with an intense light.

We removed our glasses after the first flash, but the light still lingered on, a bluish-green light that illuminated the entire sky all around. A tremendous blast wave struck our ship and made it tremble from nose to tail. This was followed by four more blasts in rapid succession, each resounding like the boom of cannon fire hitting our plane from all directions.

Observers in the tail of our ship saw a giant ball of fire rise as though from the bowels of the earth, belching forth enormous white smoke rings. Next they saw a giant pillar of purple fire, ten thousand feet high, shooting skyward with enormous speed.

By the time our ship had made another turn in the direction of the atomic explosion the pillar of purple fire had reached the level of our altitude. Only about forty-five seconds had passed. Awestruck, we watched it shoot upward like a meteor coming from the earth instead of from outer space, becoming ever more alive as it climbed skyward through the white clouds. It was no longer smoke, or dust, or even a cloud of fire. It was a living thing, a new species of being, born right before our incredulous eyes.

At one stage of its evolution, covering missions of years in terms of seconds, the entity assumed the form of a giant square totem pole, with its base about three miles long, tapering off to about a mile at the top. Its bottom was brown, its center was amber, its top white. But it was a living totem pole, carved with many grotesque masks grimacing at the earth.

Then, just when it appeared as though the thing has settled down into a state of permanence, there came shooting out of the top a giant mushroom that increased the height of the pillar to a total of forty-five thousand feet. The mushroom top was even more alive than the pillar, seething and boiling in a white fury of creamy foam, sizzling upwards and then descending earthward, a thousand Old Faithful geysers rolled into one.

It kept struggling in an elemental fury, like a creature in the act of breaking the bonds that held it down. In a few seconds it had freed itself from its gigantic stem and floated upward with tremendous speed, its momentum carrying into the stratosphere to a height of about sixty thousand feet.

But no sooner did this happen when another mushroom, smaller in size than the first one, began emerging out of the pillar. It was as though the decapitated monster was growing a new head.

As the first mushroom floated off into the blue it changed its shape into a flowerlike form, its giant petal curving downward, creamy white outside, rose-colored inside. It still retained that shape when we last gazed at it from a distance of about two hundred miles. The boiling pillar of many colors could also be seen at that distance, a giant mountain of jumbled rainbows, in travail. Much living substance had gone into those rainbows. The quivering top of the pillar was protruding a great height through the white clouds, giving the appearance of a monstrous prehistoric creature with a ruff around its neck, a fleecy ruff extending in all directions, as far as the eye could see.

Hope This Is the Last One, Baby
HOMER BIGART—*New York Herald Tribune*—8/16/1945

In a B-29 over Japan, Aug. 15—The radio tells us that the war is over but from where I sit it looks suspiciously like a rumor. A few minutes ago—at 1:32 a.m.—we fire-bombed Kumagaya, a small industrial city behind Tokyo near the northern edge of Kanto Plain. Peace was not official for the Japanese either, for they shot right back at us.

Other fires are raging at Isesaki, another city on the plain, and as we skirt the eastern base of Fujiyama Lieutenant General James Doolittle's B-29s, flying their first mission from the 8th Air Force base on Okinawa, arrive to put the finishing touches on Kumagaya.

I rode in the *City of Saco* (Maine), piloted by First Lieutenant Theodore J. Lamb, twenty-eight, of 103-21 Lefferts Blvd, Richmond Hill, Queens, NY. Like all the rest, Lamb's crew showed the strain of the last five of the uneasy "truces" that left Superforts grounded.

They had thought the war was over. They had passed most of the time around radios, hoping the President would make it official. They did not see that it made much difference whether Emperor Hirohito stayed in power. Had our propaganda not portrayed him as a puppet? Well, then, we could use him just as the warlords had done.

The 314th Bombardment Wing was alerted yesterday morning. At 2:30 p.m., pilots, bombardiers, navigators, radio men, and gunners trooped into the briefing shack to learn that the war was still on. Their target was to be a pathetically small city of little obvious importance, and their commanding officer, Colonel Carl R. Storrie, of Denton, Texas, was at pains to convince them why Kumagaya, with a population of 49,000, had to be burned to the ground.

There were component parts factories of the Nakajima aircraft industry in the town, he said. Moreover, it was an important railway center.

No one wants to die in the closing moments of a war. The wing chaplain, Captain Benjamin Schmidke, of Springfield, Mo., asked the men to pray, and then the group commander jumped into the platform and cried: "This is the last mission. Make it the best we ever ran."

Colonel Storrie was to ride in one of the lead planes, dropping 1,000-pound high explosives in the hope that the defenders of the town would take cover in buildings or underground and then be trapped by a box pattern of fire bombs to be dumped by eighty planes directly behind.

"We've got 'em on the one yard line. Let's push the ball over," the colonel exhorted his men. "This should be the final knockout blow of the war. Put your bombs on the target so that tomorrow the world will have peace."

Even after they were briefed, most of the crewmen hoped and expected that an official armistice would come before the scheduled 5:30 takeoff. They looked at their watches. Two and a half hours to go.

You might expect that the men would be in a sullen, almost mutinous, frame of mind. But morale was surprisingly high.

"Look at the sweat pour off me," cried Major William Marchesi, of 458 Baltic Street, Brooklyn. "I've never sweated out a mission like this one."

A few minutes earlier the Guam radio had interrupted its program with a flash and quoted the Japanese Domei Agency announcement that Emperor Hirohito had accepted the peace terms.

Instantly the whole camp was in an uproar. But then a voice snapped angrily over the squawk box: "What are you trying to do? Smash morale? It's only a rumor."

So the crews drew their equipment—parachutes, Mae West, and flak suits— and got on trucks to go out to the line. We reached the City of Saco at about 4:30 p.m., and there was still nearly an hour to go before our plane, which was to serve as a pathfinder for the raiders, would depart.

We were all very jittery. Radios were blaring in the camp area but they were half a mile from us and all we could catch were the words "Hirohito" and "Truman". For all we knew, the war was over.

Then a headquarters officer came by and told Lieutenant Lamb that the takeoff had been postponed thirty minutes in expectation of some announcement from Washington.

By that time none of us expected to reach Japan, but we knew that unless confirmation came soon the mission would have to take off, and then very likely salvo its bombs and come home when the signal "Utah, Utah, Utah," came through. That was the code agreed upon for calling off operations in the event of an announcement of peace by President Truman.

Lamb's crew began turning the plane's props at 5:45, and we got aboard. "Boy, we're going to kill a lot of fish today," said Sergeant Karl L. Braley, of Saco, Maine. To salvo the bombs at sea is an expensive method of killing fish.

We got San Francisco on the radio. "I hope you boys out there are as happy as we are at this moment," an announcer was saying. "People are yelling and screaming and whistles blowing."

"Yeah," said one of the crewmen disgustedly, "they're screaming and we're flying."

We took off at 6:07.

We saw no white flags when we reached Japanese territory. Back of the cockpit Radioman Staff Sergeant Rosendo D. Del Valle Jr., of El Paso, Texas, strained his ears for the message, "Utah, Utah, Utah." If it came on time, it might save a crew or two, and perhaps thousands of civilians at Kumagaya.

The message never came. Each hour brought us nearer the enemy coast. We caught every news broadcast, listening to hours of intolerable rot in the hope that the announcer would break in with the news that would send us home.

The empire coast was as dark and repellent as ever. Japan was still at war, and not one light showed in the thickly populated Tokyo plain.

Lamb's course was due north to the Kasumiga Lake, then a right angle, turning west for little Kumagaya. It was too late now. There would be bombs on Kumagaya in a few minutes.

Kumagaya is on featureless flats five miles south of the Tone River. It is terribly hard to pick up by radar. There were only two cues to Kumagaya. Directly north of the town was a wide span across the Tone, and a quarter of a mile south of it was a long bridge across the Ara River.

The radar observer, Lieutenant Harold W. Zeisler, of Kankakee, Ill, picked up both bridges in good time and we started the bomb run.

An undercast hit the city almost completely but through occasional rifts I could see a few small fires catching on from the bombs dropped by the two preceding pathfinders.

The Japanese were alert. Searchlights lit the clouds beneath us and two ack-ack guns sent up weak sporadic fire. Thirty miles to the north we saw Japanese searchlights and ack-ack groping for the bombers of another wing attacking Isesaki.

Leaving our target at the mercy of the eighty Superforts following us, we swerved sharply southward along the eastern base of Fujiyamaa [sic.] and reached the sea.

At one point we were within ten miles of Tokyo. The capital was dark.

Every one relaxed. We tried to pick up San Francisco on the radio but couldn't. The gunners took out photos of their wives and girlfriends and said: "Hope this is the last, baby."

This postscript is written at Guam. It was the last raid of the war. We did not know it until we landed at North Field.

A Month After the Atom Bomb: Hiroshima Still Can't Believe It

HOMER BIGART—*New York Herald Tribune*—9/3/1945

HIROSHIMA, JAPAN—We walked today through Hiroshima, where survivors of the first atomic-bomb explosion four weeks ago are still dying at the rate of about one hundred daily from burns and infections which the Japanese doctors seem unable to cure.

The toll from the most terrible weapon ever devised now stands at 53,000 counted dead, 30,000 missing and presumed dead, 13,960 severely wounded and likely to die, and 43,000 wounded. The figures come from Hirokuni Dadai, who, as "chief of thought control" of Hiroshima Prefecture, is supposed to police subversive thinking.

On the morning of Aug. 6 the 340,000 inhabitants of Hiroshima were awakened by the familiar howl of air-raid sirens. The city had never been bombed—it had little industrial importance. The Kure naval base lay only twelve miles to the southeast and American bombers had often gone there to blast the remnants of the imperial navy, or had flown mind-laying or strafing missions over Shimonoseki Strait to the west. Almost daily enemy planes had flown over Hiroshima, but so far the city had been spared.

At 8 a.m. the "all clear" sounded. Crowds emerged from the shallow raid shelters in Military Park and hurried to their jobs in the score of tall, modern, earthquake-proof buildings along the broad Hattchobori, the main business street of the city. Breakfast fires still smoldered in thousands of tiny ovens—presently they were to help to kindle a conflagration.

Very few persons saw the Superfortress when it first appeared more than five miles above the city. Some thought they saw a black object swinging down on a parachute from the plane, but for the most part Hiroshima never knew what hit it.

A Japanese naval officer, Vice-Admiral Masao Kanazawa, at the Kure base said the concussion from the blast twelve miles away was "like the great wind that made the trees sway." His aide, a senior lieutenant who was to accompany us into the city, volunteered that the flash was so bright even in Kure that he was awakened from his sleep. So loud was the explosion that many thought the bomb had landed within Kure.

When Lieutenant Taira Ake, a naval surgeon, reached the city at 2:30 p.m. he found hundreds of wounded still dying unattended in the wrecks and fields of the northern edge of the city. "They didn't look like human beings," he said. "The flesh was burned from their faces and hands, and many were blinded and deaf. . . ."

In the part of the town east of the river the destruction had looked no different from a typical bomb-torn city in Europe. Many buildings were only partly demolished, and the streets were still choked with debris.

But across the river there was only flat, appalling desolation, the starkness accentuated by bare, blackened tree trunks and the occasional shell of a reinforced concrete building.

We drove to Military Park and made a walking tour of the ruins.

By all accounts the bomb seemed to have exploded directly over Military Park. We saw no crater there. Apparently the full force of the explosion was expended laterally.

Aerial photographs had shown no evidence of rubble, leading to the belief that everything in the immediate area of impact had been literally pulverized into dust. But on the ground we saw this was not true. There was rubble everywhere, but much smaller in size than normal.

Approaching the Hattchobori, we passed what had been a block of small shops. We could tell that only because of office safes that lay at regular intervals on sites that retained little else except small bits of iron and tin. Sometimes the safes were blown in.

The steel door of a huge vault in the four-story Geibi Bank was flung open, and the management had installed a temporary padlocked door. All three banking houses—Geibi, Mitsubishi and the Bank of Japan—were conducting business in the sturdy concrete building of the Bank of Japan, which was less damaged than the rest.

We stood uneasily at the corner of the bank building, feeling very much like a youth walking down Main Street in his first long pants. There weren't many people abroad—a thin trickle of shabbily dressed men and women—but all of them stared at us. There was hatred in some glances, but generally more curiosity than hatred. We were representatives of an enemy power that had employed a weapon far more terrible and deadly than poison gas, yet in the four hours we spent in Hiroshima none so much as spat at us, nor threw a stone. . . .

Neither Dadai nor local correspondents who asked for an interview seemed to believe that the atomic bomb would end the war. One of the first questions asked by Japanese newspaper men was: "What effect will the bomb have on future wars?" They also asked whether Hiroshima "would be dangerous for seventy years." We told them we didn't know.

Go for Broke
HODDING CARTER JR.—*Delta Democrat Times*—8/27/1945

Company D of the 168th Regiment which is stationed in Leghorn, Italy, is composed of white troops, some from the East, some from the South, some from the Midwest and West Coast.

Company D made an unusual promise earlier this month. The promise was in the form of a communication to their fellow Americans of the 442nd Infantry Regiment and the 100th Infantry Battalion, whose motto is "Go For Broke," and it was subscribed to unanimously by the men and officers of Company D.

In brief, the communication pledged the help of Company D in convincing "the folks back home that you are fully deserving of all the privileges with which we ourselves are bestowed."

The soldiers with whom that promise was made are Japanese-Americans. In all of the United States Army, no troops have chalked up a better combat record. Their record is so good that these Nisei were selected by General Francis H. Oxx, commander of a military area in which they are stationed, to lead the final victory parade. So they marched, 3,000 strong, at the head of thousands of other Americans, their battle flag with three Presidential unit citationed streamers floating above them, their commander, a Wisconsin white council, leading them.

Some of these Nisei must have been thinking of the soul-shaking days of last October, when they spearheaded the attacks that opened the Vosges Mountain doorway to Strasbourg. Some of them were probably remembering how they, on another bloody day, had snatched the Thirty-Six Division's lost battalion of Texans from encircling Germans. And many of them were bearing scars from those two engagements which had cost the Nisei boys from Hawaii and the West Coast 2,300 casualties.

Perhaps these yellow-skinned Americans, to whose Japanese kinsmen we have administered a terrific and long overdue defeat, were holding their heads a little higher because of the pledge of their white fellow-soldiers and fellow Americans of Company D. Perhaps, when they gazed at their combat flag, the motto "Go For Broke" emblazoned thereon took a different meaning. "Go For Broke" is the Hawaiian-Japanese slang expression for shooting the works in a dice game.

The loyal Nisei have shot the works. From the beginning of the war, they have been on trial, in and out of uniform, in army camps and relocation centers, as combat troops in Europe and as frontline interrogators, propagandists, and combat intelligence personnel in the Pacific where their capture meant prolonged and hideous torture. And even yet they have not satisfied their critics.

It is so easy for a dominant race to explain good or evil, patriotism or treachery, courage or cowardice in terms of skin color. So easy and so tragically wrong. Too many have committed that wrong against the local Nisei, who by the thousands have proved themselves good Americans, even while others of us, by our actions against them, have shown ourselves to be bad Americans. Nor is the end of this misconception in sight. Those Japanese-American soldiers who paraded in Leghorn in commemoration of the defeat of the nation from which their fathers came, will meet other enemies, other obstacles as forbidding as those of war..A lot of people will begin saying, as soon as these boys take off their uniforms, that a "Jap is a Jap," and the Nisei deserve no consideration. A majority won't say or believe this, but an active minority can have its way against an apathetic majority.

It seems to us that the Nisei saying of "Go For Broke" could be adopted by all Americans of good will in the days ahead. We've got to shoot the works in a fight for tolerance. Those boys of Company D point the way. Japan's surrender will be signed aboard the *Missouri* and General McArthur's part will be symbolic "Show Me."

The Rise of the United States
WALTER LIPPMANN—*New York Herald Tribune*—9/11/1945

Thanks to those who gave their lives, and to all who have suffered and toiled, the United States has been delivered from its most dangerous enemies and has been raised to a leading place of power and influence throughout the world. Their achievement is clear and unmistakable amidst all the complications and difficulties of the demobilization and the pacification in the wake of so great a war.

Never before have the young men of any American generation had spread out before them such a prospect of a long peace within which there is so much they can do that is useful and fascinating. There never was a better time than this to be an American and to be young, nor a more interesting one in which to be alive. The time to come is peculiarly their own because they have themselves earned it and done so much to make it possible. They are not merely the heirs of stronger and more resolute forefathers but they are, once again, a generation of explorers, discoverers, and pioneers, who can become the founders of good and enduring things. The opportunity can, of course, be stupidly and lazily missed. But if it is used, as it can be, there is no reason to doubt that this cycle of twentieth-century wars is over, and that Americans have at their disposal all that they need in order to take a foremost part in inaugurating an age that mankind will long remember gratefully.

Great works are not yet for the fainthearted who doubt themselves. Yet only with that humility which opens men's minds to wisdom, can greatness be understood. We have much that we must learn to understand. When a nation rises as suddenly as we have risen in the world, it needs above all to measure its power in the scheme of things. For it is easier to develop great power than it is to know how to use it well. Wisdom always lags behind power, and for the newcomer, which is what we are, the lag is bound to be greater than in an old established state where the exercise of world power is a matter of long experience and settled habit.

Even more than the Soviet Union, which is now resuming its connection with Russia's past, the United States is the newest world power. We have never been a world power before, and we might say that in relation to the world we are just now at the end of our colonial experience and at the beginning of the time when all great affairs are as a matter of course American affairs. For isolationism, as it has persisted in our day, is in essence the view of the colonial who feels that the great affairs of history are not for the likes of him, and that he must live in a world which is ruled mysteriously from afar by others, who are shrewder if less righteous than he is.

An awareness that the great power we now possess is newly acquired is the best antidote we can carry about with us against our moral and political immaturity. There is no more difficult art than to exercise great power well; all the serious military, diplomatic, and economic decisions we have now to take will depend on how correctly we measure our power, how truly we see its possibilities *within* its limitations. That is what Germany and Japan, which also rose suddenly, did not do; those two mighty empires are in ruins because their leaders and their people misjudged their newly acquired power, and so misused it.

Our own position in the world is fully recognized, and our real interests are such that they need never be hidden. But there are many pitfalls for a nation which is not yet accustomed to the exercise of great power. We can be honest with ourselves, then, and recognize that nothing is so tempting as to overestimate one's own influence and to underestimate one's own responsibilities, to be more interested in the rights than in the duties of a powerful state, and like so many of the newly rich and just arrived to be jealously fearful of losing privileges which, in fact, can in the long run be retained only by using them well. Nothing is easier, too, than to dissipate influence by exerting it for trivial or private ends, or to forget that power is not given once and forever but that it has to be replenished continually by the effort which created it in the first place. The wisdom which may make great powers beneficent can be found only with humility, and also the good manners and courtesy of the soul which alone can make great power acceptable to others.

Great as it is, American power is limited. Within its limits, it will be greater or less depending on the ends for which it is used. It is, for example, altogether beyond the limits of any power we possess to dictate to any one of our allies, even the smallest, how it must organize its social and economic order. We can preserve our own order if we improve so that it produces progressively that greater freedom and plenty which we believe it can produce. By providing the results, not by declaiming generalities and making threats, we can offer an example which others may wish to follow if and as they have the means to do so.

In regard to our military power, including the atomic bomb, we must have no illusions whatsoever. It is sufficient, if properly maintained, to make the United States invulnerable to conquest by any other nation. But no military power we can conceivably muster can keep us secure if we dissolve our alliances, if we provoke or permit the other great states to combine against us. Friendly and reliable neighbors on both sides of our ocean frontiers are indispensable to our security and to our peace of mind. It would be as childish as it is churlish to think that because of the atomic bomb, or the prodigious size of our industry, we can now dismiss the friends with whom we fought the good fight side by side.

Nor must we fall into the trap of imagining that the devastating power we brought to bear upon our enemies can be used to enforce our arguments with our allies. Our influence is great, perhaps leading, but it is not commensurate with the alleged fact that we possess a weapon which could, theoretically, kill several hundred thousand people without notice and at one blow. If we are intelligent, we shall never entertain such a monstrous delusion. We could no more use such a weapon in such a way than we could hire thugs to assassinate foreign statesmen with whom we disagree. But if we allow fools among us to brandish the atomic bomb with the idea that it is a political argument, we shall certainly end by convincing the rest of the world that their own safety and dignity compel them to unite against us.

Our power and influence will endure only if we measure them truly and use them for the ends that we have always avowed and can proclaim with pride. We are the latest great power developed by and committed to the tradition of the West. We are among the bearers of this tradition, and we are numbered now among its proudest defenders. That is the polestar by which we must set our course. At the center of that tradition resides the conviction that man's dignity rises from his ability to reason and thus to choose freely the good in preference to evil. We may claim without offense that this inner principle of the Western tradition is not local, tribal, or national, but universal, and in so far as we are its faithful servants, we shall, in learning how to use our power, win the consent of mankind.

Don Larson's Perfect Game
SHIRLEY POVICH—*Washington Post*—10/8/1956

The million-to-one shot came in. Hell froze over. A month of Sundays hit the calendar. Don Larsen today pitched a no-hit, no-run, no-man-reach-first game in a World Series.

On the mound at Yankee Stadium, the same guy who was knocked out in two innings by the Dodgers on Friday, came up today with one for the record books, posting it there in solo grandeur as the only Perfect Game in World Series history.

With it, the Yankee righthander shattered the Dodgers, 2–0, and beat Sal Maglie, while taking 64,519 suspense-limp fans into his act.

First there was mild speculation, then there was hope, then breaths were held in slackened jaws in the late innings as the big mob wondered if the big Yankee righthander could bring off for them the most fabulous of all World Series games.

YANKS GRAB 3-2 SERIES LEAD

He did it, and the Yanks took the Series lead three games to two, to leave the Dodgers as thunderstruck as Larsen himself appeared to be at the finish of his feat.

Larsen whizzed a third strike past pinch-hitter Dale Mitchell in the ninth. That was all. It was over. Automatically, the massive 226-pounder from San Diego started walking from the mound toward the dugout, as pitchers are supposed to do at the finish.

But this time there was a woodenness in his steps and his stride was that of a man in a daze. The spell was broken for Larsen when Yogi Berra stormed on to the infield to embrace him.

It was not Larsen jumping for joy. It was the more demonstrative Berra. His battery-mate leaped full tilt at the big guy. In self-defense, Larsen caught Berra in midair as one would catch a frolicking child, and that's how they made their way toward the Yankee bench, Larsen carrying Berra.

There wasn't a Brooklyn partisan left among the 64,519, it seemed, at the finish. Loyalties to the Dodgers evaporated in sheer enthrallment at the show big Larsen was giving them, for this was a day when the fans could boast that they were there.

So at the finish, Larsen had brought it off, and erected for himself a special throne in baseball's Hall of Fame, with the first Perfect Game pitched in major league baseball since Charlie Robertson of the White Sox against Detroit 34 years ago.

MAGLIE JUST WATCHES

But this was one more special. This one was in a World Series. Three times, pitchers had almost come through with no-hitters, and there were three one hitters in the World Series books, but never a no-man-reach-base classic.

The tragic victim of it all, sitting on the Dodger bench, was sad Sal Maglie, himself a five-hit pitcher today in his bid for a second Series victory over the Yankees. He was out of the game, technically, but he was staying to see it out and it must have been in disbelief that he saw himself beaten by another guy's World Series no-hitter.

Mickey Mantle hit a home run today in the fourth inning and that was all the impetus the Yankees needed, but no game-winning home run ever wound up with such emphatic second-billing as Mantle's this afternoon.

It was an exciting wallop but in the fourth inning only, because after that Larsen was the story today, and the dumbfounded Dodgers could wonder how this same guy who couldn't last out two innings in the second game, could master them so thoroughly today.

He did it with a tremendous assortment of pitches that seemed to have five forward speeds, including a slow one that ought to have been equipped with back-up lights.

Larsen had them in hand all day. He used only 97 pitches, not an abnormally low number because 11 pitches an inning is about normal for a good day's work. But he was the boss from the outset. Only against Pee Wee Reese in the first inning, did he lapse to a three-ball count, and then he struck Reese out. No other Dodger was ever favored with more than two called balls by Umpire Babe Pinelli.

Behind him, his Yankee teammates made three spectacular fielding plays to put Larsen in the Hall of Fame. There was one in the second inning that calls for special description. In the fifth, Mickey Mantle ranged far back into left center to haul in Gil Hodges' long drive with a backhand, shoetop grab that was a beaut. In the eighth, the same Hodges made another bid to break it up, but Third Baseman Andy Carey speared his line drive.

Little did Larsen, the Yankees, the Dodgers or anybody among the 64,519 in the stands suspect that when Jackie Robinson was robbed of a line drive hit in the second inning, the stage was being set for a Perfect Game.

McDougald Saves It

Robinson murdered the ball so hard that Third Baseman Andy Carey barely had time to fling his glove upward in a desperate attempt to get the ball. He could only deflect it. But, luckily, Shortstop Gil McDougald was backing up, and able to grab the ball on one bounce. By a half step, McDougald got Robinson at first base, and Larsen tonight can be grateful that it was not the younger, fleeter Robinson of a few years back but a heavy-legged, 40-year-old Jackie.

As the game wore on, Larsen lost the edge that gave him five strikeouts in the first four innings, and added only two in the last five. He had opened up by slipping called third strikes past both Gilliam and Reese in the first inning.

Came in the sixth, and he got Furillo and Campanella on pops, fanned Maglie, Gilliam, Reese and Snider were easy in the seventh. Robinson tapped out, Hodges lined out and Amoros flied out in the eighth. And now it was the ninth, and the big Scandinavian-American was going for the works with a calm that was exclusive with him.

Furillo gave him a bit of a battle, fouled off four pitches, then flied mildly to Bauer. He got two quick strikes on Campanella, got him on a slow roller to Martin.

Now it was the left-handed Dale Mitchell, pinch-hitting for Maglie.

Ball one came in high. Larsen got a called strike.

On the next pitch, Mitchell swung for strike two.

Then the last pitch of the game: Mitchell started to swing, but didn't go through with it.

But it made no difference because Umpire Pinelli was calling it Strike Number Three, and baseball history was being made.

MAGLIE'S BRILLIANCE FORGOTTEN

Maglie himself was a magnificent figure out there all day, pitching hitless ball and leaving the Yankees a perplexed gang, until suddenly with two out in the fourth, Mickey Mantle, with two strikes called against him, lashed the next pitch on a line into the right field seats to give the Yanks a 1–0 lead.

There was doubt about that Mantle homer because the ball was curving and would it stay fair? It did. In their own half of the inning, the Dodgers had no such luck. Duke Snider's drive into the same seats had curved foul by a few feet. The disgusted Snider eventually took a third strike.

The Dodgers were a luckless gang and Larsen a fortunate fellow in the fifth. Like Mantle, Sandy Amoros lined one into the seats in right, and that one was a near-thing for the Yankees. By what seemed only inches, it curved foul, the umpires ruled.

Going into the sixth, Maglie was pitching a one-hitter . . . Mantle's homer . . . and being out-pitched. The old guy lost some of his stuff in the sixth, though, and the Yankees came up with their other run.

EXTRA RUN UNNECESSARY

Carey led off with a single to center, and Larsen sacrificed him to second on a daring third-strike bunt. Hank Bauer got the run in with a single to left. There might have been a close play at the plate had Amoros come up with the ball cleanly, but he didn't and Carey scored unmolested.

Now there were Yanks still on first and third with only one out, but they could get no more. Hodges made a scintillating pickup of Mantle's smash, stepped on first and threw to home for a double play on Bauer who was trying to score. Bauer was trapped in a run-down and caught despite a low throw by Campanella that caused Robinson to fall into the dirt.

But the Yankees weren't needing any more runs for Larsen today. They didn't even need their second one, because they were getting a pitching job for the books this memorable day in baseball.

Martin Luther King: Where Does He Go from Here?
TED POSTON—*New York Post*—4/14/1957

The buses of Montgomery are no longer segregated. The bombings of Negro churches and homes have, for the moment at least, ceased. And the leader of the historic nonviolent struggle here has received international acclaim as a young man of unusual ability.

But where, at 28, does Martin Luther King Jr. go from here?

The youthful minister pondered the question the other day in his comfortable home here, and his brooding gaze went far beyond the walls of the tastefully furnished living room.

He had returned only the day before from Washington, where he, Roy Wilkins of the NAACP, and A. Philip Randolph, AFL-CIO vice president, had conferred with scores of the most influential Negro leaders in America to plan a May 17 "Pilgrimage of Prayer" to the nation's capital.

His slanted eyes were almost closed as he considered his answers. And then he said:

"Frankly, I don't know."

A pause, and then:

"There's so much remaining to be done here in Montgomery and I feel like I have a responsibility to stay and help get things done. I feel that whatever your job is, you should do it as well as if you thought it was to be your last job. But when you are as young as I am—"

His voice trailed off for the moment. But it was not a new thought for King. Just a year ago, when he had first been firmly catapulted into the headlines, he discussed the problem with Rev. J. Pius Barbour, his friend and mentor at Crozier Theological Seminary.

Barbour teased him about his nationwide publicity, and King said:

"Frankly, I'm worried to death. A man who hits the peak at 27 has a tough job ahead. People will be expecting me to pull rabbits out of the hat for the rest of my life. If I don't or there are no rabbits to be pulled, then they'll say I'm no good."

He reverted to the theme of early success as he discussed his future the other day.

"One of the frustrations of any young man is to approach the heights at such an early age," he said. "The average man reaches this point maybe in his late forties or early fifties.

"But when you reach it so young, your life becomes a kind of decrescendo. You feel yourself fading from the screen at a time you should be starting to work toward your goal.

"And no one knows better than I that no crowds will be waiting outside churches to greet me two years from now when someone invites me to speak."

The question of Martin Luther King's future is not a theoretical one. For he has been receiving offers of jobs and positions across the country.

There has been widespread discussion, for instance, of offering him the presidency of Fisk University in Nashville, to fill the post left vacant by the recent death of Dr. Charles Johnson, one of the country's most responsible Negro spokesmen.

King had heard of the discussion and felt flattered when he was officially "sounded out" on the proposal. But he gave little indication the other day that he might accept such a position.

"I feel a responsibility for continuing my work in the field of civil rights," he said, "and the church offers me more freedom to continue that work.

"When I first entered the ministry, I thought I might like to teach or be an educator like Dr. Benjamin Mays at Morehouse College, who so greatly influenced my life, but I have learned to love the pastorate now and I don't think I would like to leave it.

"I don't think I could have the same kind of freedom I have now if I were a college president. After all, colleges have boards of trustees, and many of the white trustees in the South might feel—and with justification—that my activities might hurt the institution economically."

He paused again and idly fingered the hair of his active little 17-month-old daughter, Yolande Denise ("Yoki"), who had halted her destructive course around the living room to come to rest at his knee. And he rephrased the point.

"I do have a great desire to serve humanity," he said, "but at this particular point, the pulpit gives me an opportunity and a freedom that I wouldn't have in any other sphere of activity."

Although he probably is the only man who hasn't, King said he had not heard of increasing suggestions that he become a national executive of the NAACP and help direct the national fight for civil rights. But he immediately rejected that idea.

"They've got some of the ablest men in the country directing the NAACP right now," he said, "there would be no need of my services there.

"And I feel that it is the duty and responsibility of the clergy to supplement the work of the NAACP. That is why I insisted that every member of my congregation join the local chapter here long before the bus protest began.

"For the NAACP is a vital weapon in our fight for freedom. We must consider our struggle in the courts. Our major victories out there have come through the work of the NAACP.

"One thing the gradualists don't seem to understand is that we are not trying to make people love us when we go to court, we are trying to keep them from killing us.

"At the same time, we must support organizations like the NAACP that are trying to mold public opinion. Legislation changes a man's external relations with other men; education changes them internally."

His own mention of "trying to keep them from killing us" brought King back to the original question of where does he go from here. For he recalled the two attempts to bomb his own home and the danger faced by Yolande and Mrs. Coretta Scott King.

"If ever I get around to thinking about my future," he said, "I must also think of my family. I've got to think of what's best for them also. It is not pleasant to live under the threat of death even if Coretta and I reject such threats personally. But I do have a responsibility to my family, and that must always be a consideration."

The young minister feels deeply about his obligation to Montgomery and is aware of the magnitude of the obstacles still facing Negroes here in their quest for full citizenship. And much of his immediate local activity may be devoted to efforts to establish a bridge of communication between the Negro and white communities here.

"Since *Time* magazine published a cover story on our movement recently," he said, "I think I have observed a lessening of the tensions and feelings against me and the movement itself."

But this means no slackening, of course, of King's Montgomery Improvement Assn.'s efforts to gain full citizenship for all Montgomerians. That was quite evident last Monday night when the still-weekly mass meeting of the former bus boycotters was held in King's Dexter Av. Baptist Church.

Speaker after speaker, King included, stressed the MIA's next local project— the matter of Negro registration and voting. The MIA has long been conducting classes on registration for prospective Negro voters, but now they conduct tests to see how the "students" are progressing.

As Rev. S. S. Seay told the cheering throng Monday night (a throng not as large but as enthusiastic as any which attended the twice-weekly bus boycott meetings for a full year):

"We're going to test you ourselves before you go down there to the board of registrars. And if you pass our test and don't pass theirs, we'll have a good reason to go down there and find out why you don't pass. Knowledge is knowledge and the white folks don't have no corner on it, and we'll find out why you didn't pass just as sure as you are born to die."

Both Seay and the Rev. H. H. Hubbard, another older minister, twitted King that they were making their first appearance in his pulpit since he came to Montgomery in 1954. And both pointed out that Dexter Av. Baptist is an "uppity" Negro church where the shout "Amen" is frowned on.

But James Pierce, the Alabama State College economist and long-time Dexter member, defended his church by saying:

"Dexter Av. may be one of those sophisticated churches, but I'm here to testify that Rev. King has ruined more faces with crying than anybody else I know. Because I almost broke out crying myself yesterday when he preached on his recent trip to the birth of Ghana."

Inferentially, both sides were referring to King's original aversion to the ministry because of his suspicion of the "emotionalism" in religion in Negro churches.

But King no longer fears or rejects that shouting, amen-ing emotionalism. He knows that without it—displayed twice weekly—in different Negro churches here for a full year, the bus boycott movement would never have been a success.

In fact, King's ability to hold all Montgomery's varied Negro factions together for the 12-month struggle was cemented in the near-worship of the elderly, emotional domestics who form the mass backbone of the Montgomery Improvement Assn.

In Martin Luther King Jr., at 28, they see the son they never had or would like to have had. As one lad explained to this writer:

"He makes up to me for all my two boys didn't do. You know, my boys is the biggest whiskey drinkers in Montgomery. But he at least brought them half the way to salvation. During the whole bus protest, they never rode the buses— even if they did save the bus fare to buy more whiskey."

And no one is more aware than King that the die-hards have by no means given up their fight against equal rights for Negroes in Montgomery, even if the arrest of half a dozen suspected arsonists and bombers has outlawed violence momentarily in large sections of the white community.

Just last week, hundreds of Montgomery Negroes received in the mail copies of a four-page tabloid called *The Truth: a Newspaper Devoted to the Rights of All Races*. And it purported to be a Negro newspaper editor by one "Jim White" (as opposed to Jim Crow) with a Post Office Box No. 471 in Wetumpka, Ala.

But even *Time* magazine apparently has been unable to convince the die-hards of the basic intelligence of Negroes in Montgomery. For the badly edited sheet used every nonprofane expression which is repugnant to Negroes while pretending to be a Negro publication.

Practically the whole four pages were devoted to heavy-handed attacks on King. Of his recent trip to Ghana, one story said:

"Members of his congregation have been assessed $25.00 each (they weren't, although some contributed $25.00 for this purpose) to defray his expenses. Some have balked and refused to give anything, others have readily agreed to donate $25.00 to be rid of him for at least a while. There is speculation among many in his congregation that once he is in Africa, a fund will be raised to keep him there."

But the particular gem in *The Truth* was a front-page centered box which was headed: "King Not at Communist Meeting."

The short box story said simply:

"Despite rumors to the contrary, Rev. Martin Luther King was not at the recent meeting of the Communist Party in Chicago. He has been so busy that he cannot attend all meetings."

And this sheet was mailed straight-faced to Negroes exactly 16 months after the first mass meeting at which they voted unanimously to boycott the buses until segregated seating was abolished.

And where does Martin Luther King Jr. go from here?

Nowhere immediately. There's still much to be done in Montgomery.

Jim Brown Beats the Redskins
SHIRLEY POVICH—*Washington Post*—10/31/1960

For 18 minutes the Redskins were enjoying equal rights with the Cleveland Browns yesterday, in the sense that there was no score in the contest. Then it suddenly became unequal in favor of the Browns, who brought along Jim Brown, their rugged colored fullback from Syracuse.

From 25 yards out, Brown was served the ball by Milt Plum on a pitch-out and he integrated the Redskins' goal line with more than deliberate speed, perhaps exceeding the famous Supreme Court decree. Brown fled the 25 yards like a man in an uncommon hurry and the Redskins' goal line, at least, became interracial.

The Redskins were practically ambushed on the play because Brown is Cleveland's man for the inside jobs where the going is heavy and they leave the end running to Bobby Mitchell. Brown swinging around end was a great surprise to the Redskins who now can better understand how Custer felt about it.

The Browns were very sneaky, otherwise. In the second quarter Mitchell swung toward right end with a handoff from Plum but only so far. Then he threw his first pass and it was touchdown, Browns, because Ray Renfro was skulking in the end zone unguarded and caught it. The Cleveland quarterback was Plum full of surprises for the Redskins.

In the beginning, the Redskins themselves were the daring team. On their first play from scrimmage, Ralph Guglielmi passed from his own 15-yard line and made it work to Jim Podoley for seven yards and the crowd of 32,086 was brought up sharply by this tactic. There was a drop in the enthusiasm, though, when two passes later Bobby Franklin of the Browns picked off a pitch aimed at Podoley.

On the fourth down, Cleveland asked Jim Brown to get a touchdown from the six-inch line and at this point the Redskins were wonderful, particularly Don Lawrence and Ralph Fenton. Brown hit the Redskins' line and vice versa. He didn't get the six inches. Lawrence hit him low and Felton hit him high and the Redskins took the ball away from the Browns.

In the first quarter and early in the second, the officials were blowing their whistles against the Browns and coach Paul Brown was furious with them. He started on the field but was whistled off it. Cleveland was twice penalized for clipping with Brown denying his team had transformed Griffith Stadium into a vast clip joint.

Guglielmi pitched the Redskins back to field goal range after the Browns took a 7–0 lead and Bob Khayat booted one from 12 yards out. This was a very mild effort by Khayat who booted a 50-yarder two weeks ago, and on the next kickoff he proved something by kicking 60 yards through the goal posts for a pointless but impressive touchback.

With Coach Mike Nelson's halftime lecture still ringing in their ears, the Redskins came back on the field and were scored on again, almost immediately. The clock showed only a minute and 50 seconds of elapsed time for the third quarter when Gern Nagler was in the end zone with a Plum pass firmly clutched to his bosom. This play covered 53 yards but not the embarrassment of Billy Brewer, the Redskins' pass defense rookie. Guglielmi was getting none of the excellent pass protection of Plum, probably for some reason very fundamental, and in addition he was luckless. A pass he threw at midfield was deflected first by a Redskin then by a Brown before it was snatched by Don Fleming of the Browns. Fleming ran it back 25 yards and Sam Baker improved the Browns' lead to 24–3 by kicking a mere 22-yard field goal.

Plum found Mitchell in motion, and unguarded in the Redskins' secondary a bit later and he reacted splendidly. He passed to Mitchell for a 31-yard gain to the Redskins' three-yard line and on the next play he sent Mitchell around the left end. This was a play well-scouted by the Redskins who know Mitchell's habits. He scored a touchdown.

With their 31–3 lead the Browns were hardly a desperate club in the final quarter but they acted like one and continued to throw passes, even in their own territory, palpably trying to pour it on. They had to punt and served 'em rightly. The Redskins got the ball, and Guglielmi took them to a face-saving touchdown.

Guglielmi threw a pass to Podoley who had the ball wrestled away from him by Ross Fichter of the Browns who promptly fumbled it into the air. Joe Walton grabbed the air-borne fumble for the Redskins and took it to the Browns' seven. Don Bosseler took it over from the one-yard line and the Redskins cut the Browns' lead to 21 points with five minutes left to play.

I Have a Dream
EUGENE PATTERSON—*Atlanta Journal Constitution*—8/30/1963

WASHINGTON—The march was ended. The marble Lincoln brooded over meadows snowy white with litter and placards. In the sudden silence left by 200,000 departed people, the meaning of what had happened here slowly settled into shape. It may have been historic.

It may be that this will be marked down as the date when the Civil Rights movement grew up.

Two upheavals occurred here.

1. Breaking a rising national fever of shrillness and disorder, Negro demonstrators embraced a constructive discipline.

2. Rejecting a further rise of bitterness and anger, Martin Luther King defined a new purpose, expressed in bright hope through love of a country.

What this Negro maturing will mean to a nation that is much in need of both pacification and racial progress will depend on the response of the country, of course. The country saw it happen, and has been handed the challenge.

The reaction of the marching Negro multitude and its leaders was unmistakable. They were proud, awestruck and more than a little bewildered by the implications of the new vein they had struck here. It all seemed slightly accidental.

For the first time the various Negro leaders had concerted their efforts. Those efforts had been getting at ragged cross purposes.

Here, for the first time, the leaders sat down in council. They decided to show the country discipline and order, instead of making a bitter and trouble-fraught march on the Capitol to goad and anger Congress. The crowd obeyed. The council of leaders got together on the march day itself and pressured SNCC's John Lewis to temper a bitter and negative speech he had planned to make. More than preaching, they wanted progress.

But it still would have been just a large turnout of people who came and heard predictable things if Martin Luther King had not gotten carried away to spontaneity by the roars of an electrified crowd. In a few passionate and triumphant moments below the great seated statue of Abraham Lincoln, King swept the marchers to a new vision of the Negro's destiny in America by praising and celebrating America, and lifting their eyes from the "valley of despair" to purple mountain majesties.

"I have a dream," he boomed, again and again, and each dream showed him liberty and pursuit of happiness for all races of Americans soon, from the cliffs of the Rockies to the slopes of the Alleghenies, from Stone Mountain in Georgia to the broad Mississippi. "I have a dream," he roared, weeping, and his dream stretched from sea to shining sea, and all the way from the speaker's stand at the Lincoln Memorial to the far end of a crowd that stretched to the Washington Monument.

The rapt crowd was on its feet, seeing the Negro's dream really wrapped in the red, white and blue, and the answering ovations seemed to seal a very important bond.

King had preached hope, and not despair; faith in the white man, not bitterness; identification with America, not doubt of its capacity for social justice. In this tremendously positive and upbeat moment, he found 200,000 Negro Americans had that dream too, and responded.

How the country will respond is up to its individuals. (On my way home the airliner stewardess said, "I haven't been for this civil rights stuff and I've never liked King. But I watched him on TV, and after it was over I was proud of the Negro and proud of America. I'd thought they were just going to criticize us white people. He made my country seem so beautiful I felt like I wanted to shake his hand.")

I'm the Greatest
RED SMITH—*New York Herald Tribune*—2/26/1964

Cassius Marcellus Clay fought his way out of the horde that swarmed and leaped and shouted in the ring, climbed like a squirrel onto the red velvet ropes and brandished his still-gloved hand aloft.

"Eat your words," he howled to the working press rows. "Eat your words."

Nobody ever had a better right. In a mouth still dry from the excitement of the most astounding upset in many roaring years, the words don't taste good, but they taste better than they read. The words, written here and practically everywhere else until the impossible became unbelievable truth, said Sonny Liston would squash Cassius Clay like a bug when the boy braggart challenged for the heavyweight championship of the world.

The boy braggart is the new champion, and not only because Liston quit in his corner after the sixth round. This incredible kid of twenty-two, only nineteen fights away from the amateurs and altogether untested on boxing's topmost level, was winning going away when Liston gave up with what appeared to be a dislocated shoulder.

He might have been nailed if the bout had continued, but on the evidence of eighteen frenzied minutes, Cassius was entitled to crow, as he did at the top of his voice before Liston retired: "I'm the greatest. I'm gonna upset the world."

"That's right," his camp followers howled. "That's what you're doin."

And he was.

On this score, Clay won four of the six rounds, and in one of the two he lost he was blinded. Apart from the unforeseen ending, that was perhaps the most extraordinary part of the whole evening.

It started between the fourth and fifth rounds. "Floating like a butterfly and stinging like a bee" as he and his stooges had predicted, Cassius had made Liston look like a bull moose plodding through a swamp.

Dancing, running, jabbing, ducking, stopping now and then to pepper the champion's head with potshots in swift combinations, he had won the first, third, and fourth rounds and opened an angry cut under Liston's left eye.

Handlers were swabbing his face in the corner when suddenly he broke into an excited jabber, pushed the sponge away and pawed at his eyes. As the bell rang he sprang up waving a glove aloft as though forgetting that a man can't call a time-out in a prize fight. In the corner, frantic seconds sniffed the sponge suspiciously.

Cassius couldn't fight at all in the fifth, but he could and did show a quality he had never before been asked for. He showed he could take the sternest hooks and heaviest rights Liston could throw—or at least this Liston, whose corner said later that the shoulder had slipped in the first round.

Just pawing feebly at the oncoming champion, Clay rocked under smacking hooks, ducked, rolled, grabbed, and caught one brutal right in the throat. He rode it out, though, and at the end of the round he had ceased to blink.

"You eyes okay, champ," they were screaming from his corner as the round drew to a close. "Everything okay."

He didn't confirm that until after the bell rang for the sixth. Then, getting up from his stool, he looked across the ring, nodded with assurance, and went out to enjoy one of his best rounds, pumping both hands to the head, circling, dancing.

"Get mad, baby," his corner pleaded. "He's retreatin', champ."

It was at the end of this heat that he came back crowing about upsetting the world. Yet he couldn't have known how quickly his words would be confirmed.

Just before the bell for the seventh, Cassius sprang up and waved both hands overhead in a showoff salute to the crowd. He took a step or so forward, as the gong clanged, then leaped high in a war dance of unconfined glee. He had seen what scarcely anybody else in Convention Hall had noticed.

Liston wasn't getting up. Willie Reddish, Sonny's trainer, had his hands spread palms up in a gesture of helplessness. Jack Nilon, the manager, swung his arm in a horizontal sweep, palm down. The fight was over, the championship gone.

Dr. Robert C. Bennett of Detroit, who has treated Liston in the past, hastened into the ring and taped Liston's shoulder. The former champion told him he had felt the shoulder go midway in the first round and the left hand had grown progressively number from then on.

They'll fight again to answer the prodding question of what might have been, and it will be a big one. Although return-bout clauses are frowned upon these days, Bob and Jimmy Nilon, Jack's brothers, have an independent contract with Clay entitling them to name the time, place, and opponent for his first defense.

As Bob Nilon explained this, Clay rode the ropes. "Eat your words," he bawled.

Edward R. Murrow: In Memoriam
JAMES RESTON—*The New York Times*—4/28/1965

Edward R. Murrow lived long enough before he died this week to achieve the two great objectives of a reporter: He endured, survived, and reported the great story of his generation, and in the process he won the respect, admiration, and affection of his profession.

The Second World War produced a great cast of characters, most of whom have been properly celebrated. Roosevelt, Churchill and Stalin are gone. Chiang Kai-shek is now living in the shadow of continental China, which he once commanded, and only de Gaulle of France retains power among that remarkable generation of political leaders formed in the struggle of the two world wars.

The great generals of that time too, like MacArthur and Rommel, have died or, like Eisenhower and Montgomery, have retired; but in addition to these there was in that war a vast company of important but minor characters who played critical roles.

History would have not been the same without them. They were the unknown scientists like Merle Tuve, who invented the proximity fuse and helped win the air war, and Chiefs of Staff like Bedell Smith, and the Foreign Service officers like Chip Bohlen and Peter Loxley of Britain, and on the side, the Boswells of the story, like Ed Murrow of the Columbia Broadcasting System.

It was odd of Ed to die this week at 57—usually his timing was much better. He was born at the right time in North Carolina—therefore he was around to understand the agony of the American South. He went West to the state of Washington as a student and therefore understood the American empire beyond the Rockies; and he came East and stumbled into radio just at the moment when it became the most powerful instrument of communication within and between the continents.

He was part of a remarkable company of reporters from the West: Eric Sevareid, Ed Morgan, Bill Costello, whom Murrow recruited at CBS; Hedley Donovan and Phil Potter, out of Minnesota; Elmer Davis. Ernie Pyle, Tom Stokes, Bill Shirer, Raymond Clapper, Wallace Carroll, Webb Miller, Quentin Reynolds, Wally Deuel, the Mowrers, and many others, including his dearest friend, Raymond Swing, who played such an important part in telling the story of the Old World's agony to America.

But Murrow was the one who was in London at that remarkable period of the Battle of Britain, when all the violence and sensitivities of human life converged, and being both sensitive and courageous himself, he gave the facts and conveyed the feeling and spirit of that time like nobody else.

It is really surprising that he lived to be 57. He was on the rooftops during the bombings of London, and in the bombers over the Ruhr, and on the convoys across the Atlantic from the beginning to the end of the battle. Janet Murrow, his lovely and faithful wife, and Casey, his son, never really knew where he was most of the time, but somehow he survived.

In the process, he became a symbol to his colleagues and a prominent public figure in his country, where there was something else about him that increased his influence. He had style. He was handsome. He dressed with that calculated conservative casualness that marked John Kennedy. He was not a distinguished writer, but he talked in symbols and he did so with a voice of doom.

It is no wonder that the British, who know something about the glory and tragedy of life, knighted him when they knew he was dying of cancer at the end. Their main hope in the darkest days of the German bombardment of London was that the New World would somehow understand and come to the rescue of the Old, and if anybody made the New World understand, it was Murrow.

He hated the commercial rat race of the television networks, and fought their emphasis on what he regarded as the frivolities rather than the great issues of life, and talked constantly of escaping back into the small college atmosphere from which he came. He never made it, and probably wouldn't have liked it if he had.

Those who knew him best admired him most. He was a reporter of the old school and a performer of the new. In radio and television, there is no written permanent record. Only the memory of the listener remains. And the memory of Ed Murrow will remain for a long time among people who remember the terrible and wonderful days of the Battle of Britain.

Boys Will Be Heroes
WILLIAM F. BUCKLEY—Universal Press Syndicate—8/24/1965

The best explanation I ever heard for man's compulsive race to get to the moon was offered by a shrewd and attractive lady, wife of a law school don at the University of Indiana. "Don't you understand?" she asked, after the company had worn each other down with elaborate scientific explanations. They wheeled toward her. "Boys will be boys."

The rhetoric, of course, can be escalated without difficulty, making the statement read: "Men will be men." That takes the hint of mischief out of it all, but it is much better with the mischief left in. Because there is a bit of mischief in adventure, and men who go off grandiloquently to meet their destiny often feel a trace of the excitement a boy feels when he goes out for the first time on an overnight hike. There is, of course, no fun at all in the pursuit of adventure if, as so often is the case, you die en route. No fun at all, when you feel fear, and loneliness and helplessness. It is man's capacity to expose himself to the certainty that he will be lonely and afraid that makes possible great adventures of the human spirit.

And it takes a boyish zest for adventure for staid and middle-aged men to engage in such a dazzling adventure as Robert Manry's aboard *Tinkerbelle*, the 13½-foot converted dinghy in which he crossed the Atlantic Ocean, covering in eighty days 3,200 miles. The chances of surviving such a voyage were less than the chance our astronauts will survive their orbits around the planet, covering, in one-tenth the time, a distance 1,000 times as long.

The astronauts are to prove to us that heavenly rendezvous are possible between assorted flying objects and that man's body can endure eight days of weightlessness and immobility. Mr. Manry proved that a few planks of wood, none of them more than 13½ feet long, and strips of cloth, made by a single carpenter of moderate skill, can, using only nature's power, transport a man across the most treacherous ocean in the world.

One feels nothing but admiration for the astronauts. Theirs is, above all, a mission to press their fragile bodies against the unknown and in an experiment so mechanized that they are left with little to do except to obey the signals they hear. It must put a special tax on the spirit to be left with so little latitude. Mr. Manry, by contrast, had great latitude. He could point the nose of his boat in any direction he chose, except in the direction the wind was coming from, and he could leave both sails up, or take down one of them, or take down both of them, or trim one or both, or drag his sea anchor. An almost infinite number of possibilities. And if he made a serious mistake, he would drown. And he might have drowned anyway, because a truly determined sea will not respect the right of so frail a challenger to claim safe passage across the haunted area.

Mr. Manry, who is almost fifty and makes his living as a copyreader in Cleveland, knew enough of the literature of the sea to know that for every sailor the sea is the enemy, that it must be treated as the enemy, and that the enemy is formidable enough to have wrecked whole navies in her time. And the astronauts know that nothing in the world is more mysterious than science, that the most fastidious preparations, projections and calculations are sometimes confounded by utterly inexplicable scientific backtalk or because someone didn't turn the screwdriver hard enough.

Even so, boys will be boys, and some boys have the makings of heroes: Astronaut Gordon Cooper has reported that "once, in the middle of the night, at an altitude of over 150 miles, over the middle of the Indian Ocean," he prayed. Mr. Manry may have had room in his cluttered dinghy for the thirty-third Psalm: By the word of the Lord, the heavens were established, and all the power of them by the spirit of His mouth.

Gathering together the waters of the sea, as in a vessel, laying up the depths in storehouses.

You're Joe Namath
JIMMY CANNON—*New York Post*—11/15/1968

You're Joe Namath who has it all. The garish pad in airline-hostess country on the East Side of New York is for laughs. Modeling mink coats turns a dollar. So does shaving off the Fu Manchu mustache on television for a razor company.

Horseplaying is for kicks. The wow-wee chicks are terrific. The mod rags are sharp. The sideburns testify you're with it. The piece of the chain of short-order restaurants is solid. But you picked up another big prize this week. You own the respect of your own kind.

The people who count measure you as the most valuable player in the American Football League. The coaches and football reporters in separate elections bestowed greatness on you. The players on the Jets decided you did more than anyone on the team this year. There isn't any doubt. You belong with Bart Starr and Johnny Unitas.

The other teams caught 28 of your passes last year. They intercepted 17 this season, 10 of them in two games with Buffalo and Denver. Now you throw the ball away when your receivers are surrounded. You don't pitch it when the other people might catch it.

That's why the bookmakers have made the Jets favorites over Oakland for the championship of the American League this Sunday. You're the difference. It is as great a tribute to you as all the trophies and accolades.

You claim the Jets' improved defense was the reason for changing your style. Once you felt you couldn't afford to waste a pass. Now you can take your time. You say you ground the ball because you know the defensive unit will get it back for you.

This is your best year as a quarterback but you have thrown fewer passes for fewer touchdowns and fewer yards than in 1967. The Jets also scored two more touchdowns by rushing than they did by passing. You are gambling less. You shoot for sure things.

Some Jets resented your friendship with Sonny Werblin, who ran the club before he sold his stock. They figured you were pampered. They placed you sixth last year when it came time to honor the most valuable player on the team. Obviously, they felt they were wrong because you were their choice as offensive captain when the season started.

You had rough years. The line would break in front of you and the other team would drown you in their rush. You had your cheekbone fractured by Oakland. Kansas City's strong men, such as Buck Buchanan, used Sherman Plunkett as a bowling ball and would throw him at you. This year Sam Walton has been installed in his place. Until the last couple of games he has been steady and unmovable. But Dave Herman may be switched into his position this Sunday.

There were reports of friction between you and Weeb Ewbank who coaches the team. But since Werblin departed, the relationship appears to have improved. It isn't one of affection. But you seem to realize that Ewbank is an intelligent and often imaginative coach. He brought Unitas into professional football at Baltimore when he also won two championships. He has always praised you as a spectacular quarterback.

You have the style of a great athlete. It is beyond ability. It is what Babe Ruth had and Jack Dempsey still holds on to, although most of the people who want his autograph weren't born when he was fighting. It was the way Ray Robinson dances up a flight of ring stairs. It is Willie Mays doing the basket catch. It is Wilt Chamberlain sitting in his car behind his chauffeur. It is Bill Russell in his swirling cape. It is what a man is, and the joy of life.

It is what splits Bo Belinsky out from Denny McLain. They both force the ball reporters to write about them. But McLain won 31 games, and no one is exciting in the minors where Belinsky went because he couldn't win. Some do it like Jimmy Brown with a haughty silence. You tell your side of it with fierce candor. The truth is a rare commodity in your game.

The buffs at Shea Stadium have been cruel. There was an afternoon when one of them flung a container of hot coffee in your face. They swore at you when you had difficult days. You talked back to them in interviews. You never asked for chivalry. You agreed with them that you had incompetent Sundays. But you reprimanded them for their viciousness. All that's gone. You are the most popular athlete in New York.

You are paid to suffer. Your legs are slashed by pain. The needle deadens it temporarily. The fluid has to be drained out of your knees after most games. You don't showboat about it. But the stories keep describing you as a good-time swinger moving around in the go-go joints. This happens. But you are a football player. You are a man of cold Sunday afternoons. You do your work in the daytime. The night doesn't intrude.

The season started right for you. In the first game there was six minutes to go against Kansas City and it was third down and 11 yards to go with the ball on your own 5-yard line. The Jets led by one point. You held the ball for six minutes, and killed the clock. This is what being a quarterback is all about. The club responds to you. You dominate it. You're Joe Namath who has it all.

Moon Launching Brings Mood of Reflection
LACEY FOSBURGH—*The New York Times*—7/17/1969

At 9:32 a.m. Eastern daylight time yesterday, when exhaust and flames filled the air at Cape Kennedy and the rocket carrying three men to the moon was lifted off the ground, dawn was just reaching the western shores of the United States.

As new light moved along the California beaches and touched the hills, people rose and switched on their television sets. In open-air markets in San Francisco, others already at work by 6:32 a.m. stood in silence amid the flounder and mackerel or asters and roses and listened: "Five, four, three . . ."

Far away in the flat lowlands south of San Diego, Albert J. Gilman, assistant chief of the patrol that polices the border between California and Mexico at Tijuana, sat alone at a television set in his darkened living room.

"I just couldn't believe I was actually watching history in the making," he said, "but I was there. I was part of it. I saw it happen."

Several miles away drivers waiting to go through customs listened to the countdown on their car radios. Others crossing the border on foot stopped at dilapidated gasoline stations along the highway to share the moment with strangers.

"It's so thrilling, maybe the engine will explode," cried an elderly woman with blue hair as she twirled the dice in her hand. The blackjack and roulette tables in the 24-hour casino at Caesars Palace in Las Vegas were empty at 6:32 as the hundreds of gamblers and tourists picked up their cards and stood spellbound in front of six television sets.

At 7:32 a.m. in northern Wyoming, a heavy white fog was lifting at the Valley Ranch in the small hamlet of Valley Cowhands in the barn and wranglers herding horses in the hills, with no radios or TV sets, interrupted their work to honor the take-off.

"WE FEEL SO CLOSE"

"We feel so close to the moon shot out here, because we're so close to the stars and the sky," said Dr. Oakleigh Thorn, the owner of the ranch.

"Last night," he went on, "we sat out under the trees like we do most every summer night and looked at the moon. We talked about how extraordinary it is that now man is going to that white, white place which has always seemed so untouchable and remote.

"I think we all felt it was strange," he continued, "to be sitting here where our lives are so close to nature and to know that man has been so able to extend himself that he can reach the moon."

"Four, three, two . . ."

At 7:32 about 50 cadets hovered around one television set in a small lounge at the Air Force Academy in Colorado Springs. Normal 7:30 classes had been postponed to allow cadets to watch the launching.

WANTS TO GO TO MARS

"Everybody held his breath," said Angus J. MacDonald, a 20-year-old senior who hopes to be an astronaut. "We couldn't believe it was actually going to happen. Then, as the spaceship lifted off the ground, we began to cheer and clap and yell and scream. I guess you could say it was like our team winning a football game."

"I stood there watching that ship and listening to the words. 'Five, four, three . . .' and all I could think about was myself and Mars. I want to be the one to go there. I got to be."

At 8:32 in Biloxi, Miss., Michael Haver, a 22-year-old University of Mississippi Law School student, had been waiting in his living room overlooking the languid waters of the Gulf of Mexico for two hours.

"Four, three, two . . ."

"It means different things to different people," he said. "It makes me think about the adventurous nature man has. What is it that makes him always want to see more, do more?"

In the Biloxi harbor, where large fishing boats jostle each other even at that late hour, the fishermen paused on the wharf to hear the final countdown. They stood on the oil-streaked docks holding transistors. Even in the shrimp and oyster canneries nearby, the sounds of the blast-off mingled with the sounds of the machinery.

In Tennessee, tobacco farmers picking small pink flowers from the tobacco plant and dropping them on the dusty soil shared the big moment with the world because someone had a transistor.

"Four, three, two, one."

"It's the birth, the beginning of a new age," said a young teacher in Washington, D.C., who asked not to be named. "The astronauts didn't just go to the moon. All our minds went to the moon and intellectually man's horizons have jumped leaps and bounds beyond the historical situation they've always been confined to."

Jackie's Debut
MIKE ROYKO—*Chicago Sun-Times*—10/25/1972

[Mike Royko wrote this reminiscence on the day of Jackie Robinson's death.]

All that Saturday, the wise men of the neighborhood, who sat in chairs on the sidewalk outside the tavern, had talked about what it would do to baseball.

I hung around and listened because baseball was about the most important thing in the world, and if anything was going to ruin it, I was worried.

Most of the things they said, I didn't understand, although it all sounded terrible. But could one man bring such ruin?

They said he could and would. And the next day he was going to be in Wrigley Field for the first time, on the same diamond as Hack, Nicholson, Cavarretta, Schmitz, Pafko, and all my other idols.

I had to see Jackie Robinson, the man who was going to somehow wreck everything. So the next day, another kid and I started walking to the ballpark early.

We always walked to save the streetcar fare. It was five or six miles, but I felt about baseball the way Abe Lincoln felt about education.

Usually we could get there just at noon, find a seat in the grandstand, and watch some batting practice. But not that Sunday, May 18, 1947.

By noon, Wrigley Field was almost filled. The crowd outside spilled off the sidewalk and into the streets. Scalpers were asking top dollar for box seats and getting it.

I had never seen anything like it. Not just the size, although it was a new record, more than 47,000. But this was twenty-five years ago, and in 1947 few blacks were seen in the Loop, much less up in the white North Side at a Cubs game.

That day, they came by the thousands, pouring off the northbound Ls and out of their cars.

They didn't wear baseball-game clothes. They had on church clothes and funeral clothes—suits, white shirts, ties, gleaming shoes, and straw hats. I've never seen so many straw hats.

As big as it was, the crowd was orderly. Almost unnaturally so. People didn't jostle each other.

The whites tried to look as if nothing unusual was happening, while the blacks tried to look casual and dignified. So everybody looked slightly ill at ease.

For most, it was probably the first time they had been that close to each other in such great numbers.

We managed to get in, scramble up onto the ramp, and find a place to stand behind the last row of grandstand seats. Then they shut the gates. No place remained to stand.

Robinson came up in the first inning. I remember the sound. It wasn't the shrill, teenage cry you now hear, or an excited gut roar. They applauded, long, rolling applause. A tall, middle-aged black man stood next to me, a smile of almost painful joy on his face, beating his palms together so hard they must have hurt.

When Robinson stepped into the batter's box, it was as if someone had flicked a switch. The place went silent.

He swung at the first pitch and they erupted as if he had knocked it over the wall. But it was only a high foul that dropped into the box seats. I remember thinking it was strange that a foul could make that many people happy. When he struck out, the low moan was genuine.

I've forgotten most of the details of the game, other than that the Dodgers won and Robinson didn't get a hit or do anything special, although he was cheered on every swing and every routine play.

Just before the Cub reached first, he swerved to his left. And as he got to the bag, he seemed to slam his foot down hard at Robinson's foot.

It was obvious to everyone that he was trying to run into him or spike him. Robinson took the throw and got clear at the last instant.

I was shocked. That Cub, a hometown boy, was my biggest hero. It was not only an unheroic stunt but it seemed a rude thing to do in front of people who would cheer for a foul ball. I didn't understand why he had done it. It wasn't at all big league.

I didn't know that while the white fans were relatively polite, the Cubs and most other teams kept up a steady stream of racial abuse from the dugout. I thought that all they did down there was talk about how good Wheaties are.

Late in the game, Robinson was up again, and he hit another foul ball. This time it came into the stands low and fast, in our direction. Somebody in the seats grabbed for it, but it caromed off his hand and kept coming. There was a flurry of arms as the ball kept bouncing, and suddenly it was between me and my pal. We both grabbed. I had a baseball.

The two of us stood there examining it and chortling. A genuine major-league baseball that had actually been gripped and thrown by a Cub pitcher, hit by a Dodger batter. What a possession.

Then I heard the voice say: "Would you consider selling that?"

It was the black man who had applauded so fiercely.

I mumbled something. I didn't want to sell it.

"I'll give you ten dollars for it," he said.

Ten dollars. I couldn't believe it. I didn't know what ten dollars could buy because I'd never had that much money. But I knew that a lot of men in the neighborhood considered sixty dollars a week to be good pay.

I handed it to him, and he paid me with ten $1 bills.

When I left the ball park, with that much money in my pocket, I was sure that Jackie Robinson wasn't bad for the game.

Since then, I've regretted a few times that I didn't keep the ball. Or that I hadn't given it to him free. I didn't know, then, how hard he probably had to work for that ten dollars.

But Tuesday I was glad I had sold it to him. And if that man is still around, and has that baseball, I'm sure he thinks it was worth every cent.

Super Hero
WELLS TWOMBLY—*San Francisco Examiner*—1/2/1973

In nature, there are certain movements so swift and so graceful that no mortal can adequately describe what has taken place. In the upper branches of a fir tree, a squirrel goes bounding from level to level, his eyes focused on the horizon, his heart pounding gently with the vibrations of the earth itself. Beyond a copse of birches, a doe stirs. Somewhere inside her she knows that a hunter is waiting, hip-deep in the snow. Swiftly, she turns and goes leaping through the drifts.

No man living is skillful enough to describe exactly how Roberto Clemente moved through the meadows of our land for 18 summers. His was a special style and grace. It was a smooth motion, fluid and compact. Most of the people who bought tickets to watch him play right field for the Pittsburgh Pirates never seemed to appreciate what he could do. They accepted it. But they never appreciated it. Pay $3.50 and see Roberto do the impossible. He was brilliant, to use a phrase that doesn't really do justice to his memory.

No athlete of Clemente's quality has been taken for granted quite so shamelessly. The customers applauded him like human beings who had seen too much television. Magic was dead. The super-sensational was too ordinary. Perfection was their birthright. They paid their money and they sat there as baseballs went sailing off toward a glove that never made a mistake. It was far too easy, far too sweet. Roberto just couldn't make the game of baseball look hard enough.

Hit the ball to right at Pittsburgh and forget it. Try to run to second on that slim figure in the outfield and you could count on the ball being there ahead of you. It was so lovely, so automatic that God Himself must have designed the play. Offensively, Clemente was one of the best of his generation. He rated right there with Mickey Mantle, Stan Musial, Willie Mays, Henry Aaron, etc. He was a walking immortal. He ran. He threw. He hit.

Trouble was that Roberto Clemente could never communicate with his true self. It was his opinion that newspapermen had a stringent pecking order. They regarded baseball players in the following way: On top were the American whites, followed rapidly by the American blacks. Next were the Latin whites. Way down at the bottom were the Latin blacks. They were nobody's children.

"I feel that I would be considered to be a much better athlete if I were not a Latin black," he told a newspaperman one sorrowful evening in Pittsburgh two years ago when the Pirates were winning the World Series.

"I play as good as anybody. Maybe I play as good as anybody who plays the game. But I am not loved. I don't need to be loved. I just wish that it would happen. There are many people like me who would like that to happen. I wish it for them. Do you know what I mean?"

Trouble was that few people truly understood what he was talking about. Even his colleagues on the Pittsburgh Pirates admitted that they weren't sure how to take him. They didn't know if he was a self-serving egotist or a humanitarian who honestly loved his neighbors. Always Roberto Clemente seemed to be tiptoeing along a chalk line.

"This was the most decent man I've ever known," said pitcher Steve Blass. "And nobody ever seemed to understand him. Maybe there was a language barrier, I don't know. He was absolutely selfless. He'd talk about his physical problems and writers would make jokes. What he was trying to say was that Latins and blacks play hurt just like everybody else. They didn't get that. They said he was a hypochondriac."

When the Pirates got into the World Series, Clemente got a dozen hits. He was splendid beyond belief. After each game he would talk seriously to writers. Certainly he wanted credit for himself. Why? Not for personal glory, but because he wanted a forum for his beliefs. He had this wild notion about a sports city in his native Puerto Rico where indigent children could live. They could grow to manhood with the high ideals of competitive athletes to guide them. Their whole lives would be changed by the opportunity to play games, to get a decent meal, to wear clean clothes.

"This is my dream," he said. "I do not know exactly what this sports city will be like, but it will be beautiful. It will be open to everybody. No matter what they are. After I open the first one in Puerto Rico I will open others. I will do this thing because that is what God meant me to do. Baseball is just something that will give me a chance to do this."

And Roberto Clemente believed he had this mission to perform for mankind. When the Governor of Puerto Rico asked him to head the island's relief fund for the Managua earthquake victims, he threw himself into the project with a passion.

Here was one of the finest baseball players who ever lived and he went from door to door in the richer sections of San Juan, asking for donations. He raised $150,000 in cash and thousands extra in material goods. Roberto filled up the Santurce ball park with clothing and food. Clemente said he would personally take them to Nicaragua. He meant it.

The time came to transport those items. The airplane rose slowly from the runway, headed out to sea, made a desperate turn, and fell into the water. Thus died a humanitarian. Thus died a real man. Thus died a very fine baseball player. Not necessarily in that order.

A Salute to Gilliam
JIM MURRAY—*Los Angeles Times*—10/13/1978

I guess my favorite all-time athlete—certainly, ballplayer—was Jim Gilliam.

This is not a post-mortem. I have said it to interviewers, broadcast and print, over the years. I said it while Jim was alive. I lumped him with Ben Hogan. He liked that. He also deserved that.

The reason was simple: I admire most the athletes who didn't wake up one morning with their skill and didn't have to do a damn thing about it to excel. As Jerry Barber, the golfer, said one day to a pupil on the driving range, "Look,

Sam Snead rolled out of bed one day with his swing. You and I have to work at it."

Jimmy had to work at it. God didn't give him much of a head start. There were plenty of guys in the neighborhood who could run faster, hit harder, jump higher and dress better. God gave Jim Gilliam qualities that didn't show in a track meet. Patience. Determination. Discipline. Guts. Jim Gilliam was the kind of guy you'd want to get stuck in a submarine with.

Don't misunderstand me. Jim Gilliam wasn't a mediocre ballplayer. He was very, very good. Better than almost every big league infielder in the game in the '30s and early '40s.

But you see, God not only didn't give Jim Gilliam Honus Wagner's arm, Babe Ruth's swing or Ty Cobb's eye. He didn't even give him the same color skin. Jimmy was bucking into a pat hand right from the start. And he played his cards that way.

The Baltimore Elite (pronounced "Ee-light") Giants were disappointed in him. Not flashy enough. He didn't have any gaudy routines, any hot-dog bat flips or home run struts. Jimmy played it straight. Jimmy wanted to be a ballplayer, not an end man.

They said his arm was too weak for third base. So he shifted to second. They said he was sucker for a curveball right-handed. So he made himself a switch hitter. They wanted his cap to fly off, his feet to shuffle or his teeth to show. Jimmy told them if they wanted a tap dancer, try Hollywood. As for him, he intended to become a big leaguer.

He became one. One of the best. A joy to watch. As dependable as tomorrow, as quiet as a forest. He outwaited the flashy guys with the buck-and-wing acts and, when they couldn't solve the curveball often enough to go into their act, Jimmy stepped in. The big leagues isn't a floor show and Jimmy was a big leaguer.

He lived in New York but you never found him in any clubs called "Paradise" or "The Kitty Club." That wasn't Jimmy's style. Between games he studies hitting. At the foot of Jackie Robinson.

Much was made of the fact that Jimmy wasn't bitter. Jim Gilliam didn't think he had anything to be bitter about. The Reverend Jesse Jackson hit it right on the nose at the eulogy when he said: "Jim Gilliam gave much to his world but he didn't expect much in return."

A point has been missed about Jim Gilliam, though. A lot of people think he was short-changed in not being named a manager by now. But it didn't bother Jimmy that much. I know. Because he told me. You say, What else would he tell you? But that's not the way it was with Jim Gilliam. He never bothered to lie. About anything. You got nine innings of truth from him, too. And Jim Gilliam was happy in what he did. The old Dodger pitcher, Joe Black, confided ruefully at the funeral about the time he tried to get Jim Gilliam to join him at the Greyhound Bus Company. Recalls Joe: "Jim said to me, 'Joe, you know how far I went in school. No way I could get up in front of all those people and tell them what to do. I'm not qualified.'"

Jim Gilliam was not going to be any man's token. He was going to stay where he was needed—in a baseball uniform. One of Jimmy's favorite sayings was "Never play the other man's game." Jimmy moved within his limitations. He never underestimated anybody. Or overestimated them, for that matter. Jimmy read the pitch.

He took pitches so that Maury Wills could set base-stealing records. Not for Maury, for the Dodgers. He stepped aside as each succeeding "phee-nom" would come along to take his job. One of the first times I ever sat with Jimmy was in a coffee shop back in 1961 as we discussed some now-forgotten young hopeful who was supposed to take over his position. The road to Spokane was clogged with rookies Jimmy sent back to the minors. He never rejoiced in it. He hoped they would come through. They didn't.

He played seven positions on the ballclub and, as Casey Stengel once said, "each one better than the last."

The author, Roger Kahn, a few years ago, wrote a melancholy tome titled *The Boys of Summer*. It was about the 1953 Dodgers, a star-crossed club, the first desegregated team in baseball history, bedeviled by undeserved misfortune. Death and personal tragedy dogged the lives of the individuals—Gil Hodges, Jackie Robinson, Billy Cox, Carl Erskine. Jim Gilliam is the latest. Dead at 49, he makes it seem a ship's company pursued by ill fate.

This is probably the first World Series ever played with a tenth man in one lineup. The Dodgers take the field with a "19" etched in black sewed on their uniform sleeves. It is not a reminder to win. It is a reminder to play well, to play fair and do your best at all times. The number "19" has always stood for that on the Dodgers. The number "19" has stood for a man who was my friend, your friend, baseball's friend, humanity's friend—an American, a major leaguer, a class act all the way.

Two thousand people don't show up for a league president. But Jim Gilliam was more representative of baseball than any league president. Gilliam was as true baseball as "Take Me out to the Ball Game." He thought he was lucky to be a Dodger. I thought it was the other way round. And, as he reaches home plate sooner than almost everybody else as usual, I am sure Gil Hodges, Jackie Robinson and the rest of the Boys of Summer will be crowded around there waiting for him with arms outstretched as Junior comes in, standing up as usual.

It Could Happen Only in Hollywood
JIM MURRAY—*Los Angeles Times*—10/16/1988

Well, you can believe that if you want to.

As for me, I know a Warner Bros. movie when I see one. I've been around this town long enough to spot a hokey movie script.

I mean, this is *Rambo IV*, right? That was Sylvester Stallone that came out of the dugout in the ninth inning of Game 1 of the 1988 World Series. That wasn't a real player?

Believe this one and you'll think *Superman* is a documentary.

The country is never going to buy it. This is the thing Hollywood does best. But it never happens in real life. In real life, the hero pops up in this situation. In an Italian movie, he dies. He doesn't hit a last-minute home run with 2 outs and 2 strikes and the best relief pitcher in baseball throwing. This is John Wayne saving the fort stuff. Errol Flynn taking the Burma Road.

A guy who can hardly walk hits a ball where he doesn't have to. A few minutes before, he's sitting in a tub of ice like a broken-down racehorse.

Kirk Gibson is the biggest bargain since Alaska. He should be on crutches—or at least a cane. He wasn't even introduced to the World Series crowd in the pregame ceremonies. He wasn't even in the dugout till the game got dramatic. Some people were surprised he was in uniform. Some were surprised he was upright.

The odds against his hitting a home run in this situation were about the odds of winning a lottery. The manager was just milking the situation, trying to keep the crowd from walking out early. No one seriously expected a guy with two unhinged knees to get a hit, never mind *the* hit.

Here was the situation: The Oakland Athletics, who are less a team than a packet of mastodons, baseball's answer to a massed artillery attack, had the game all but won, ahead by 1 with 2 out, 1 on.

Somehow, a quartet of Dodger pitchers had held this mass of muscle to 4 measly runs. The Dodgers had somehow pasted together 3. They got 2 of them when Mickey (Himself) Hatcher who may be himself a figment of the sound stages, hit his second home run of the year.

Oakland got back 4 when Jose Canseco hit his 46th homer of the year.

So, the score was 4–3, favor of Oakland. Two were out, the crowds were streaming out, the traffic jam was starting, when pinch-hitter Mike Davis drew a walk.

Out of the dugout came Our Hero. Tom Mix, Frank Merriwell, the Gipper never had a better part.

The wonder was, they didn't have to carry him up there. There should have been a star in the East or lightning playing around his forehead the way this postseason has been going for Kirk Gibson. He had posted the most devastating .154 average in the history of playoffs (his slugging average is .800) this fall. Every hit he gets wins a game. Three out of three of them have been home runs.

A World Series crowd doesn't know much about baseball. But a Hollywood crowd knows all about happy endings. They know an MGM finish when they scent one, too. They began to holler and scream.

You wanted to say, "OK, nice touch," to the manager, Tommy Lasorda, but you wanted to tell the crowd, "Grow up! This isn't Disneyland."

On the mound, Oakland pitcher Dennis Eckersley didn't believe in fairy tales or Horatio Alger Jr. dime novel plots, either. Nor did Oakland Manager Tony La Russa.

If they did, they would have walked Kirk Gibson. Even when the count went to 3 and 2, they were putting their money on logic, reason, percentages.

Hah!

Eckersley threw a here-hit-this! pitch.

If you saw *Sands of Iwo Jima*, *Rio Hondo* or even *Singing in the Rain*, you know what happened. When last seen the ball was headed to the moon.

Fadeout. Up the music. Roll the credits. The guys in the white hats win again. The big bad rustlers from Oakland, the hit men, the seat-breakers, had to stand there helplessly while the good guys won again.

It had everything but a schoolmarm and a dog. Or Gibson riding slowly off into the sunset.

You knew it would happen. A movie is 9 reels of disaster and calamity befalling the star. But the last act finds him getting fanned into consciousness by his horse and led by Rin Tin Tin to where the outlaw has his fiancee and he rescues her in the nick of time, the ninth inning, so to speak. It's the way we do things here in Hollywood. You have to figure that's what happened. Somewhere out there, the screenwriter in the sky brought in this ending where the hero takes a called Strike 3 while everybody cries. Or he pops up to the pitcher. But somewhere out there, C.B. or L.B. takes a disgusted look and says, "You call this a picture! What's this dreck! Take it back and write me something for Doug Fairbanks and Mary Pickford, something that'll sell in Dubuque. When I want a 3-handkerchief picture I'll remake *Camille*."

Well, look at it this way: You got a better explanation for what happened at Dodger Stadium Saturday night? You believe it, do you?!

Nah!!

His Dreams Belong to the Next Generation
DIANE GRIEGO ERWIN—*Orange County Register*—5/25/1989

His brow furrowed and the crow's-feet deepened as he struggled to understand. There was little doubt. He was confused.

The busy information clerk at the Department of Motor Vehicles in Santa Ana didn't notice.

"You need to go over there," she said, pointing across the room to the sea of people waiting. "I already told you."

It was 11 a.m. Her patience was shot for the morning.

The man pulled at the waistband of his beige work pants and scratched his sun-aged face. He stared at her, stalling for time as he tried to understand, but afraid to say he didn't.

He left, returned. The next clerk didn't speak Spanish either.

"Why can't they learn English?" she grumbled to me, the next in line.

"He probably won't," I said. "But maybe his kids will."

I had to say it. My father had been one of those kids. The ones who learn English although their parents speak Spanish at home. Schools back then didn't offer special programs; some people have told me that nuns rapped their knuckles with a ruler if they spoke Spanish—even on the playground. They learned English quickly and well that way.

But the information clerks didn't know all this, so they couldn't understand the man with the sun-aged face like I did.

I watched as he leaned against a wall where about 15 men waited. Many wore work pants and that same face, deeply lined from too much sun and too many worries.

I asked Luis Manuel Delgado why he waited.

"The lady who speaks Spanish has gone to lunch," he said.

There was no irritation in his voice, no anger at the time wasted. It was simply a fact.

I pointed out that the clerks hadn't treated him very nicely. Didn't that anger him? I wondered.

"I should know how to speak English," he said with a quiet simplicity. "This is the United States."

Delgado, 46, said he works long hours and doesn't leave in time to attend adult English classes.

He came to the United States in 1973 because two brothers and three uncles had migrated here and found better lives than the ones they left in Mexico.

Delgado worked as a bricklayer and saved enough money so his wife and two children could join him after 2½ years. An uncle paid for the other two children to come.

A lifetime renter and a nobody by social standards, Delgado has big dreams for his children. He hopes they are respected by their peers and become property owners. In his old age, maybe he will live comfortably in a house owned by one of his children.

Meanwhile, he works hard and long to educate his kids. They are his future. "I am here for my children," he said proudly.

I was right about Luis Manuel Delgado.

"My kids are very good," he said. "They get good marks in school. They speak English. No accent. One wants to be a doctor.

"When they first came here I told them to study English and learn it well. Don't let them treat you like a donkey like they treat your papa."

I asked him if it didn't hurt, being treated *como un burro*, like he said.

"No, I am not a donkey and my children know it. They know I do all this for them. They are proud of me. Nothing anyone else says or does can make me sad when they have pride in me.

"And they will never be donkeys."

He nodded toward the stressed-out information clerks busily shuffling papers behind the government-issued desk. "And they won't work here," he said. "This is donkey work."

From Selma to Berlin
DOROTHY GILLIAM—*Washington Post*—11/13/1989

Long before the Berlin Wall finally crumbled Thursday, we watched in amazement as East Germans peacefully marched, defied the state police and sang "We Shall Overcome."

In recent weeks in South Africa, as the protest ban that had muzzled but failed to stop black protesters was lifted, blacks who once were slammed into jail cells for singing the black nationalist anthem walked down the street singing freedom songs. Their favorite hymn, sung while white police officers looked at them passively, was "We Shall Overcome."

In Lusaka, Zambia, they sang it. In Southeast Washington earlier this year, Barbara Bush joined a group of District schoolchildren in singing it. And in a Frederick, Md., protest against the Ku Klux Klan, "We Shall Overcome" was the anthem of choice.

It's axiomatic that this song associated with the 1960s civil rights movement has become an international anthem and has inspired freedom struggles around the world.

But the singing and swaying are only part of the story.

The types of resistance taught by Mahatma Gandhi and the Rev. Martin Luther King Jr. have been shown to have an international appeal. As the waves of freedom today wash over people around the world, these men and their followers have been the heroic models.

Although the Tiananmen Square revolt was brutally halted, some Chinese students were clearly using the Gandhian and King methods of nonviolent protest, unity of purpose and a turning away from terrorism.

In Hungary, Poland, East Germany, even the Soviet Union itself, people have marched peacefully in protest against an old order.

Something universal is blowing in the wind as we are seeing a crumbling of the communist systems under a thirst for freedom.

That the catalyst was in part the American civil rights movement is a fact to be lauded. It is ironic that those who were called communists during the U.S. struggle against segregation should hear their song sung as the communist system is being dismantled.

The U.S. civil rights movement was arguably American television's biggest domestic story. Part of the reason the world was able to observe this evolution was increased travel and the advent of world media during the past quarter century.

Even Mikhail Gorbachev is an heir of the tradition. Because of the people who have been motivated by the principles lived and taught by Gandhi and King, Gorbachev has been forced to acquiesce in the drive for individual freedom now being seen throughout Eastern Europe. Indeed, the international outcome of the civil rights movement may be a fire that has never been put out.

Gorbachev is a realist, but there is little reason to believe that he would have encouraged diversity without the groundswell of freedom demands coming from Eastern Europe. The speed with which these events have taken place belies the many years of quiet struggle that have gone into the earthshaking events of recent days.

This period may become known as one when tradition was set aside and new things were being looked for, when people were willing to demand and accept change in ways not before seen in this century.

When the history of the era is written, it must be recorded that a brown man from India and a black man from Georgia were the leaders for change that shook the world, and that their methods inspired millions in their struggles for freedom.

Conviction of Their Courage
MARY MCGRORY—*Washington Post*—6/28/1990

In the last seven months, three ex-convicts have paraded through Congress to give the members a lesson in leadership. They presented no formulas, no answers. They provoked huzzahs and uncomfortable questions in our officials: "How much am I willing to sacrifice?" and "Is it worth it?"

What Lech Walesa, Vaclav Havel and Nelson Mandela have in common, beyond conscience and conviction, is time spent in jail. That and the fact that they were caught up in causes larger than themselves.

"They are willing to die for what they believe," mused Sen. David L. Boren (D-Okla.), a supercautious conservative and unlikely Mandela fan. "We're not willing to risk one bad poll."

Walesa and Havel spent shorter terms, but the circumstances were comparable. Walesa could have stopped organizing Solidarity. He chose not to. Havel, a playwright, could have gone along with the commissars in Czechoslovakia—and a majority of his countrymen—on human rights. He didn't.

And Mandela, because he held the anti-apartheid cause more dear than personal freedom, stayed in prison for twenty-seven years, coming out, finally, on his own terms. He is, with his straight back and his straight talk, something of a miracle, and an argument for long incarceration. His incandescent quality was such that he got standing ovations all over. Even people who deplored his taste in allies, his anachronistic bent towards violence, were impressed.

All three forswore that most crippling of emotions, self-pity. None of them, in madly acclaimed join session speeches, mentioned their suffering. A Democrat who voted against the flag-burning amendment or a Republican who swallowed George Bush's taxes, carries on more. Mayor Marion Barry, on trial for drug possession and perjury, sees himself as a martyr.

But members of his entourage who had talked with Mandela's fellow prisoners say that he lived a structured, highly disciplined life, totally engaged as a college president and political organizer. A fitness fanatic, he got up at 3:00 A.M. to do calisthenics in his cell; relaying messages through the people who brought the food, he presided over unending seminars for fellow ANC inmates; drew up a curriculum for those, like so many blacks, deprived of education, and organized each cellblock under an ANC captain.

It isn't appearance that determines esteem. To be sure, Mandela, scion of a royal family, walks like a king, but Walesa is stocky and Havel is slight. Moral stature comes in all sizes.

Friends of the South American government have tried to rally the right to indignation over Mandela's singular preference in allies. "Yasser Arafat, Colonel Gadhafi, Fidel Castro, support our struggle to the hilt," he forthrightly replied.

"I wish he hadn't said that," says Boren, "but I can understand it—you never turn your back on the people who were for you when nobody else was."

Boren, an ardent defender of the CIA, the agency said to have fingered Mandela for the South African police, made a trip to South Africa in 1989 and is the first to say he hasn't been the same since.

It is one thing to see red-necked southern sheriffs in their inefficient way practicing discrimination, but in South Africa it is efficient and official. Meeting Albertina Sisulu [wife of then-jailed ANC leader Walter Sisulu] was "the single most radicalizing experience of my life."

Boren went to New York to greet Mandela and was struck by his "inner peace—so rare in our system, especially in politics."

Is oratory the key? Probably not. Walesa, who came last November, had the House chamber rocking with enthusiasm for a real, live profile in courage, addressed the assemblage in a man-to-man manner, saying bluntly that Poland appreciated kind words but really needed money. Havel treated them to a literary masterpiece, an exquisite exposition of moral responsibility and Europe's determination to be a civilizing force again.

Mandela's luminous face set off a storm; the place was packed with people just palpitating to applaud. His accented English was somewhat hard to follow, and his speech was more conventional than, say, his beguiling rebuke to President Bush on the subject of ANC armed struggle the day before.

He spoke of the Constitution. It's what we have that our imported heroes don't. We have a peerless system of government that forbids the kind of oppression that they suffered. It may be why we don't really need heroes.

When Jordan Cried Behind Closed Doors
BOB GREENE—*Chicago Tribune*—5/15/1991

"I went to my room and I closed the door and I cried," Michael Jordan said. "For a while I couldn't stop. Even though there was no one else home at the time, I kept the door shut. It was important to me that no one hear me or see me."

Now the National Basketball Association playoffs are entering their most exciting and dramatic phase. Jordan's likeness and electronic image are everywhere; sometimes it seems he is as much logo as he is human.

In a sense, Jordan owns the world. To me, though, perhaps the most remarkable part of the Jordan story is the fact that, as a sophomore in high school, he was cut from his school's basketball team. I kept wondering about how it affected him at the time it happened. Back then, he didn't know that someday he was going to be Michael Jordan. Back then, he wanted to play with the others, and was told that he wasn't good enough.

One evening, as we sat and talked in the hours before a Bulls game, he spoke about it. I wasn't surprised that Jordan remembered every detail. How could he not? Back then he had no idea what was going to happen to him in the years ahead.

"For about two weeks, every boy who had tried out for the basketball team knew what day the cut list was going to go up," Jordan said. "We knew that it was going to be posted in the gym. In the morning.

"So that morning we all went in there, and the list was up. I had a friend, and we went in to look at the list together.

"We stood there and looked for our names. If your name was on the list, you were still on the team. If your name wasn't on the list, you were cut. His name was on the list. He made it. Mine wasn't on the list."

As we talked, other members of the Bulls walked past—Scottie Pippen, Horace Grant, John Paxson, Bill Cartwright. Jordan's voice was soft, and he nodded hello to each of them and continued with his memories.

"I looked and looked for my name," he said. "It was almost as if I thought that if I didn't stop looking, it would be there."

Was the list in descending order of talent? Were the best players at the top of the list, with the marginal players at the bottom?

"No," Jordan said, as if envisioning the list anew. "It was alphabetical. I looked at the H's, and the I's, and the J's, and the K's, and I wasn't there, and I went back up and started over again. But I wasn't there. I went through the day numb. I sat through my classes. I had to wait until after school to go home. That's when I hurried to my house and I closed the door of my room and I cried so hard. It was all I wanted—to play on that team.

"My mother was at work, so I waited until she got home, and then I told her. She knew before I said anything that something was wrong, and I told her that I had been cut from the team. When you tell your mom something like that the tears start again, and the two of you have an aftercry together."

At the end of that basketball season, Jordan said, he asked the coach if he could ride the bus with the team to the district tournament. Just to watch the other boys play.

"The coach told me no," Jordan said. "But I asked again, and he said I could come. But when we got to the tournament gym, he said he didn't know if I could go in. He told me that the only way I could go in was to carry the players' uniforms.

"So that's what I did. I walked into the building carrying the uniforms for the players who had made the team. What made me feel the worst about that was that my parents had come to watch the tournament, and when they saw me walking in carrying the uniforms, they thought I was being given a chance to play.

"That's what hurt me. They thought I was being given a chance. But I was just carrying the clothes for the others."

He is the best basketball player in the world; he is very likely the best basketball player who ever lived. If you ever wondered why he continues to work so hard, the answer may lie in this story. It is doubtful that any other professional athlete was ever cut from a high school team. The men who make it to the pros have always been the best on every playground, the best in every class, the best in every school.

"It's OK, though," Jordan said. "It's probably good that it happened."

Good?

"I think so," he said. It was almost time for him to go upstairs onto the Stadium floor and hear the amazing, shuddering roar that comes from the crowd every time they catch sight of him.

"It was good because it made me know what disappointment felt like," he said. "And I knew that I didn't want to have that feeling ever again."

Amid the Graves, Gratitude Lives On
MIKE BARNICLE—*Boston Globe*—6/7/1994

ST. JAMES, FRANCE—On a stunning, cloudless afternoon, when the green grass of the low, rolling hills flowed like a brilliant emerald wave in the soft breeze, a long ribbon of schoolchildren marched in procession to honor 4,410 American boys buried beneath 28 acres of French soil liberated with their blood 50 summers ago.

More than 4,000 boys and girls had been summoned from this agricultural region 12 miles from the Normandy coast and they all walked in silence, each carrying a white cardboard box containing a single white dove.

It was well before the pageantry involving world politicians began yesterday at places named Pointe du Hoc and Omaha Beach, and there were no famous people present to give speeches. Instead, farmers and office workers, housewives and schoolteachers, young French families and frail grandparents came by foot and by car from miles around to pray, stand or simply stare at the graves of so many assembled strangers whom they never knew, never met but never forgot.

In the blue sky above the startling cemetery, a lone French paratrooper dressed in the uniform of the 82nd Airborne drifted lazily down to the sacred ground below. As he landed, a little girl took his hand and led him toward the chapel at the edge of all the marble headstones where the two of them joined the major of St. James, several local dignitaries and a few members of the French and American military as they saluted history's fallen legions.

A band played the national anthems of both countries. Then the children, one by one, stood alongside all the stone monuments and placed a lovely, lonesome daisy on top of every grave. All was quiet as the children opened the boxes and momentarily held the doves in innocent hands before releasing them in unison, the white birds soaring off in squadron toward England and ports all these brave dead boys sailed from at the start of their last summer, 1944, from Massachusetts. And their names represent a unique cultural tapestry. In death they blend together, all of them beyond prejudice, envy or the resentments that often weigh us down today. A few of them were: Douglas Perry, Robert Cahill, Ralph Parenteau, Robert Lamb, Vartan Panagian, James Huard, Alfred Cloutier, Herman Lindsey Jr., William LeClair, Clifford Oliver Jr., Walter Potter, Carl Savlone, James Starr, Joseph Tuohey, William Walsh, Edgar Whittaker, Daniel Esposito, Lucien La Croix, George Nawn, Thomas Duffy, Stephen Jakstis, Frank Mello, Bronis Lipskis, Michael Halprin, Nathan Gurwitz, Edward Drakopolos, William Breed, Neil Manning, Francis X. Kelly and Earnest W. Prussman from West Newton who, on Sept. 8, 1944, won the Medal of Honor when he destroyed two German machine gun bunkers before being killed by enemy gunfire.

You wonder now, all these years later, what the dead might have done: Who among them would have been doctors saving lives, teachers strengthening young minds, laborers building roads and cities, homes and highways, farmers growing crops, salesmen, police, firefighters. You wonder about the children some of them left and the families they were denied. You wonder about the parents of the 20 sets of brothers buried here, side by side, and how anyone could ever handle such great eternal grief.

These are the heroes who all died young. They missed sunsets and baptisms. They went without 50 World Series and 50 New Year's Eves. They never stood at the door, anxiously waiting for a daughter's first date to arrive or witnessed their kids' junior proms and college graduations. They never saw men landing on the moon or a fax machine. They were not allowed to walk on a beach with the girls they loved or hold the hands of grandchildren who would have asked about their great crusade.

In our increasingly selfish country where everything and nearly everyone is part of some special interest, where defining any enemy or current threat to live or moral values is as difficult as peering through the murky fog that envelopes this French coast, it is stunning to realize that these 4,410 and millions of others sailed to certain danger with no thought of conquest or profit. They came because they were asked and because they were needed.

And today the French here do their best to remember. The local people, far from the glamour of Paris, live in an area of centuries-old villages where nearly everyone still depends on the land. These citizens are the French equivalent of our Midwesterners, open, honest and grateful for what they have been given.

For the past few weekends, they have come in droves to the American cemetery. While D-Day has become a television spectacle in the United States, these simple folks who manage to get by without 100 cable channels, CNN, MTV, microwaves and ATM machines on every block recall their history and those who helped them. Unlike so many of us at home, geography never insulated them from sacrifice.

Now, as the sun began to set, the people began to leave the cemetery in groups of twos and threes, quietly, with respect, the way you would leave a church or temple after prayer. And as they headed toward their cars and homes and their rural lives, the only sounds in the gathering dusk were the bark of a single dog, the crowing of a rooster somewhere in the distance and the rustle of the wind that provides these boys eternal companionship.

Hero Builds a Life After Pal's Death

MIKE MCALARY—*New York Daily News*—11/14/1994

We met over blood. The youngest member of his Brooklyn gang, Jose Luis Lebron, age 14, had just missed his first meeting with the Killer Blunt Squad. Someone had called the kid in dead.

Lebron was nicknamed Race because he could outrun capture. He robbed somebody in Bushwick Park of $10 at gunpoint and then sprinted away. A cop caught up to Race, who had just handed off the gun. The cop ordered Race to freeze.

The kid went to his pocket. Maybe he was trying to get rid of the money. The cop misread his panic and fired. Race could not outrun a bullet. He fell dead right there. It was front page news on Feb 1, 1990: POLICE KILL B'KLYN TEEN.

His blood ran down the sidewalk, over the curb and into the gutter. In the morning, a kid named Lofty spray-painted his epitaph at the bloody spot in a quick, crude hand:

A friend is one who comes in when the whole world has gone out. Lefty. KB-Squad.

We stood there for a moment, sizing each other up. It is an old dance between reporter and subject, the crime scene waltz. Lefty was wearing jeans and gang colors. It was his gang. I was wearing the uniform of my place, too—a suit. Finally, Lefty talked.

The gang leader and another kid, Fur, were smoking, swearing hard and spitting, which is how young men handle war. Mostly they talk about smoking weed. The gang was even named after weed.

After a while, the blood and the murders run together. Murder is too ordinary to have meaning any more. I moved on to the next atrocity, the next corner. The death of Race, and the name Lefty were quickly forgotten.

And then, nearly five years later, in the middle of an election turned to anger over killing and revenge, a letter arrived. It was mailed Oct. 17 from an Army base in Germany by Herminlo Vargas, 26, an American soldier. Years ago, Vargas was Lefty from the KBSquad. The former gang leader is now a specialist assigned to the 127th Adjutant General Company.

"While it may surprise you to know that I have kept an article of yours written for the Daily News *for almost five years, the article has had a profound meaning to me and has served me as an inspiration in turning my life around. . . .*

"As a powerful gang leader, I recruited Race into our posse, KBSquad, at the age of 13, the age when most boys in Bushwick are vulnerable. On the 30th of January, 1990, he skipped his first posse meeting at Bushwick Park. On this day he had a date with death, but how were we to presume it?

"The next morning in complete disarray, I walked back to the same street corner with a can of spray paint . . . Mr. McAlary, it was at that point we met.

"I remember all of this as if it happened yesterday, but I have been away since then serving my country, my city, and my people. Doing all the right things and sacrificing all of the good things in the process. I left everything I knew and everything I loved behind when I left Bushwick in April 1990 to join the Army. . . .

"Growing up in Brooklyn gave me that tough mentality, after all war is war. I wanted to redeem myself, earn society's respect, and most importantly I was determined not to let Jose Lebron's death be in vain.

"Today I am a proud recipient of three Army achievement awards, one Good Conduct Medal, one national defense medal, the Army's physical fitness patch and soldier of the year for the U.S. European Command in Germany—the greatest honor for any soldier.

"My turnaround has allowed me to live longer, form a family, travel the world and come in touch with different walks of life. I've earned social status, respect and admiration from those who know me best. I now see life as I do, as a result of Race's death and your article."

There are more words, all of them breathing. The success is soaring, wonderful and rare. Last week, I called the hero in Germany. We talked about the old days and some of the old violence.

"All of the guys from the gang are dead or in jail," he said.

And then he remembered the first time he saw a man shot. The gang was robbing a guy we knew from the neighborhood at the Jefferson St. subway station. I was told, if the guy resists, we shoot him. We shot him in the kneecaps and legs.

"I put my hands over my eyes," Lefty recalled. "Later, I started to hold my own gun."

The letter from the one-time Brooklyn gang leader turned American soldier makes my depression go away. In the midst of all this divisive talk, you need some one to stand and cheer. I am humbled by his talent. Sure, as a columnist you can get people indicted and even free the wrongly accused. That is what you do. But from now on, I know, at least once, I wrote a story that mattered.

All She Has, $150,000, Is Going to a University
RICK BRAGG—*The New York Times*—8/13/1995

HATTIESBURG, MISS.—Oseola McCarty spent a lifetime making other people look nice. Day after day, for most of her 87 years, she took in bundles of dirty clothes and made them clean and neat for parties she never attended, weddings to which she was never invited, graduations she never saw.

She had quit school in the sixth grade to go to work, never married, never had children and never learned to drive because there was never any place in particular she wanted to go. All she ever had was the work, which she saw as a blessing. Too many other black people in rural Mississippi did not have even that.

She spent almost nothing, living in her old family home, cutting the toes out of shoes if they did not fit right and binding her ragged Bible with Scotch tape to keep Corinthians from falling out. Over the decades, her pay—mostly dollar bills and change—grew to more than $150,000.

"More than I could ever use," Miss McCarty said the other day without a trace of self-pity. So she is giving her money away, to finance scholarships for black students at the University of Southern Mississippi here in her hometown, where tuition is $2,400 a year.

"I wanted to share my wealth with the children," said Miss McCarty, whose only real regret is that she never went back to school. "I never minded work, but I was always so busy, busy. Maybe I can make it so the children don't have to work like I did."

People in Hattiesburg call her donation the Gift. She made it, in part, in anticipation of her death.

As she sat in her warm, dark living room, she talked of that death matter-of-factly, the same way she talked about the possibility of an afternoon thundershower. To her, the Gift was a preparation, like closing the bedroom windows to keep the rain from blowing in on the bedspread.

"I know it won't be too many years before I pass on," she said, "and I just figured the money would do them a lot more good than it would me."

Her donation has piqued interest around the nation. In a few short days, Oseola McCarty, the washerwoman, has risen from obscurity to a notice she does not understand. She sits in her little frame house, just blocks from the university, and patiently greets the reporters, business leaders and others who line up outside her door.

"I live where I want to live, and I live the way I want to live," she said. "I couldn't drive a car if I had one. I'm too old to go to college. So I planned to do this. I planned it myself."

It has been only three decades since the university integrated. "My race used to not get to go to that college," she said. "But now they can."

When asked why she had picked this university instead of a predominantly black institution, she said, "Because it's here; it's close."

While Miss McCarty does not want a building named for her or a statue in her honor, she would like one thing in return: to attend the graduation of a student who made it through college because of her gift. "I'd like to see it," she said.

Business leaders in Hattiesburg, 110 miles northeast of New Orleans, plan to match her $150,000, said Bill Pace, the executive director of the University of Southern Mississippi Foundation, which administers donations to the school.

"I've been in the business 24 years now, in private fund-raising," Mr. Pace said. "And this is the first time I've experienced anything like this from an individual who simply was not affluent, did not have the resources and yet gave substantially. In fact, she gave almost everything she has.

"No one approached her from the university; she approached us. She's seen the poverty, the young people who have struggled, who need an education. She is the most unselfish individual I have ever met."

Although some details are still being worked out, the $300,000—Miss McCarty's money and the matching sum—will finance scholarships into the indefinite future. The only stipulation is that the beneficiaries be black and live in southern Mississippi.

The college has already awarded a $1,000 scholarship in Miss McCarty's name to an 18-year-old honors student from Hattiesburg, Stephanie Bullock.

Miss Bullock's grandmother, Ledrester Hayes, sat in Miss McCarty's tiny living room the other day and thanked her. Later, when Miss McCarty left the room, Mrs. Hayes shook her head in wonder.

"I thought she would be some little old rich lady with a fine car and a fine house and clothes," she said. "I was a seamstress myself, worked two jobs. I know what it's like to work like she did, and she gave it away."

The Oseola McCarty Scholarship Fund bears the name of a woman who bought her first air-conditioner just three years ago and even now turns it on only when company comes. Miss McCarty also does not mind that her tiny black-and-white television set gets only one channel, because she never watches anyway. She complains that her electricity bill is too high and says she never subscribed to a newspaper because it cost too much.

The pace of Miss McCarty's walks about the neighborhood is slowed now, and she misses more Sundays than she would like at Friendship Baptist Church. Arthritis has left her hands stiff and numb. For the first time in almost 80 years, her independence is threatened.

"Since I was a child, I've been working," washing the clothes of doctors, lawyers, teachers, police officers, she said. "But I can't do it no more. I can't work like I used to."

She is 5 feet tall and would weigh 100 pounds with rocks in her pockets. Her voice is so soft that it disappears in the squeak of the screen door and the hum of the air-conditioner.

She comes from a wide place in the road called Shubuta, Miss., a farming town outside Meridian, not far from the Alabama line. She quit school, she said, when the grandmother who reared her became ill and needed care.

"I would have gone back," she said, "but the people in my class had done gone on, and I was too big. I wanted to be with my class." So she worked, and almost every dollar went into the bank. In time, all her immediate family died. "And I didn't have nobody," she said. "But I stayed busy."

She took a short vacation once, as a young woman, to Niagara Falls. The roar of the water scared her. "Seemed like the world was coming to an end," she said.

She stayed home, mostly, after that. She has lived alone since 1967.

Earlier this year her banker asked what she wanted done with her money when she passed on. She told him that she wanted to give it to the university, now rather than later; she set aside just enough to live on.

She says she does not want to depend on anyone after all these years, but she may have little choice. She has been informally adopted by the first young person whose life was changed by her gift.

As a young woman, Stephanie Bullock's mother wanted to go to the University of Southern Mississippi. But that was during the height of the integration battles, and if she had tried her father might have lost his job with the city.

It looked as if Stephanie's own dream of going to the university would also be snuffed out, for lack of money. Although she was president of her senior class in high school and had grades that were among the best there, she fell just short of getting an academic scholarship. Miss Bullock said her family earned too much money to qualify for most Federal grants but not enough to send her to the university.

Then, last week, she learned that the university was giving her $1,000, in Miss McCarty's name. "It was a total miracle," she said, "and an honor."

She visited Miss McCarty to thank her personally and told her that she planned to "adopt" her. Now she visits regularly, offering to drive Miss McCarty around and filling a space in the tiny woman's home that has been empty for decades.

She feels a little pressure, she concedes, not to fail the woman who helped her. "I was thinking how amazing it was that she made all that money doing laundry," said Miss Bullock, who plans to major in business.

She counts on Miss McCarty's being there four years from now, when she graduates.

My Favorite Teacher
THOMAS L. FRIEDMAN—*The New York Times*—1/9/2001

Last Sunday's *New York Times Magazine* published its annual review of people who died last year who left a particular mark on the world. I am sure all readers have their own such list. I certainly do. Indeed, someone who made the most important difference in my life died last year—my high school journalism teacher, Hattie M. Steinberg.

I grew up in a small suburb of Minneapolis, and Hattie was the legendary journalism teacher at St. Louis Park High School, Room 313. I took her Intro to Journalism course in 10th grade, back in 1969, and have never needed, or taken, another course in journalism since. She was that good.

Hattie was a woman who believed that the secret for success in life was getting the fundamentals right. And boy, she pounded the fundamentals of journalism into her students—not simply how to write a lead or accurately transcribe a quote, but, more important, how to comport yourself in a professional way and to always do quality work.

To this day, when I forget to wear a tie on assignment, I think of Hattie scolding me. I once interviewed an ad exec for our high school paper who used a four-letter word. We debated whether to run it. Hattie ruled yes. That ad man almost lost his job when it appeared. She wanted to teach us about consequences.

Hattie was the toughest teacher I ever had. After you took her journalism course in 10th grade, you tried out for the paper, *The Echo*, which she supervised. Competition was fierce. In 11th grade, I didn't quite come up to her writing standards, so she made me business manager, selling ads to the local pizza parlors. That year, though, she let me write one story. It was about an Israeli general who had been a hero in the Six-Day War, who was giving a lecture at the University of Minnesota. I covered his lecture and interviewed him briefly. His name was Ariel Sharon. First story I ever got published."

Those of us on the paper, and the yearbook that she also supervised, lived in Hattie's classroom. We hung out there before and after school. Now, you have to understand, Hattie was a single woman, nearing 60 at the time, and this was the 1960's. She was the polar opposite of "cool," but we hung around her classroom like it was a malt shop and she was Wolfman Jack. None of us could have articulated it then, but it was because we enjoyed being harangued by her, disciplined by her and taught by her. She was a woman of clarity in an age of uncertainty.

We remained friends for 30 years, and she followed, bragged about and critiqued every twist in my career. After she died, her friends sent me a pile of my stories that she had saved over the years. Indeed, her students were her family—only closer. Judy Harrington, one of Hattie's former students, remarked about other friends who were on Hattie's newspapers and yearbooks: "We all graduated 41 years ago; and yet nearly each day in our lives something comes up—some mental image, some admonition that makes us think of Hattie."

Judy also told the story of one of Hattie's last birthday parties, when one man said he had to leave early to take his daughter somewhere. "Sit down," said Hattie. "You're not leaving yet. She can just be a little late."

That was my teacher! I sit up straight just thinkin' about her.

Among the fundamentals Hattie introduced me to was *The New York Times*. Every morning it was delivered to Room 313. I had never seen it before then. Real journalists, she taught us, start their day by reading *The Times* and columnists like Anthony Lewis and James Reston.

I have been thinking about Hattie a lot this year, not just because she died on July 31, but because the lessons she imparted seem so relevant now. We've just gone through this huge dot-com-Internet-globalization bubble—during which a lot of smart people got carried away and forgot the fundamentals of how you build a profitable company, a lasting portfolio, a nation state or a thriving student. It turns out that the real secret of success in the information age is what it always was: fundamentals—reading, writing and arithmetic, church, synagogue and mosque, the rule of law and good governance.

The Internet can make you smarter, but it can't make you smart. It can extend your reach, but it will never tell you what to say at a P.T.A. meeting. These fundamentals cannot be downloaded. You can only upload them, the old-fashioned way, one by one, in places like Room 313 at St. Louis Park High. I only regret that I didn't write this column when the woman who taught me all that was still alive.

Fighting for Life, 50 Floors Up
Jim Dwyer—*The New York Times*—10/9/2001

Now memories orbit around small things. None of the other window washers liked his old green bucket, but Jan Demczur, who worked inside 1 World Trade Center, found its rectangular mouth perfect for dipping and wetting his squeegee in one motion. So on the morning of the 11th, as he waited at the 44th-floor Sky Lobby to connect with elevators for higher floors, bucket and squeegee dangled from the end of his arm.

The time was 8:47 a.m. With five other men—Shivam Iyer, John Paczkowski, George Phoenix, Colin Richardson and another man whose identity could not be learned—Mr. Demczur (pronounced DEM-sir) boarded Car 69-A, an express elevator that stopped on floors 67 through 74.

The car rose, but before it reached its first landing, "We felt a muted thud," Mr. Iyer said. "The building shook. The elevator swung from side to side, like a pendulum."

Then it plunged. In the car, someone punched an emergency stop button. At that moment—8:48 a.m.—1 World Trade Center had entered the final 100 minutes of its existence. No one knew the clock was running, least of all the men trapped inside Car 69-A; they were as cut off 500 feet in the sky as if they had been trapped 500 feet underwater.

They did not know their lives would depend on a simple tool.

After 10 minutes, a live voice delivered a blunt message over the intercom. There had been an explosion. Then the intercom went silent. Smoke seeped into the elevator cabin. One man cursed skyscrapers. Mr. Phoenix, the tallest, a Port Authority engineer, poked for a ceiling hatch. Others pried apart the car doors, propping them open with the long wooden handle of Mr. Demczur's squeegee.

There was no exit.

They faced a wall, stenciled with the number "50." That particular elevator bank did not serve the 50th floor, so there was no need for an opening. To escape, they would have to make one themselves.

Mr. Demczur felt the wall. Sheetrock. Having worked in construction in his early days as a Polish immigrant, he knew that it could be cut with a sharp knife. No one had a knife.

From his bucket, Mr. Demczur drew his squeegee. He slid its metal edge against the wall, back and forth, over and over. He was spelled by the other men. Against the smoke, they breathed through handkerchiefs dampened in a container of milk Mr. Phoenix had just bought.

Sheetrock comes in panels about one inch thick, Mr. Demczur recalled. They cut an inch, then two inches. Mr. Demczur's hand ached. As he carved into the third panel, his hand shook, he fumbled the squeegee and it dropped down the shaft.

He had one tool left: a short metal squeegee handle. They carried on, with fists, feet and handle, cutting an irregular rectangle about 12 by 18 inches. Finally, they hit a layer of white tiles. A bathroom. They broke the tiles.

One by one, the men squirmed through the opening, headfirst, sideways, popping onto the floor near a sink. Mr. Demczur turned back. "I said, 'Pass my bucket out,'" he recalled.

By then, about 9:30, the 50th floor was already deserted, except for firefighters, astonished to see the six men emerge. "I think it was Engine Company 5," Mr. Iyer said. "They hustled us to the staircase."

On the excruciating single-file descent through the smoke, someone teased Mr. Demczur about bringing his bucket. "The company might not order me another one," he replied. At the 15th floor, Mr. Iyer said: "We heard a thunderous, metallic roar. I thought our lives had surely ended then." The south tower was collapsing. It was 9:59. Mr. Demczur dropped his bucket. The firefighters shouted to hurry.

At 23 minutes past 10, they burst onto the street, ran for phones, sipped oxygen and, five minutes later, fled as the north tower collapsed. Their escape had taken 95 of the 100 minutes. "It took up to one and a half minutes to clear each floor, longer at the lower levels," said Mr. Iyer, an engineer with the Port Authority. "If the elevator had stopped at the 60th floor, instead of the 50th, we would have been five minutes too late.

"And that man with the squeegee. He was like our guardian angel."

Since that day, Mr. Demczur has stayed home with his wife and children. He has pieced together the faces of the missing with the men and women he knew in the stations of his old life: the security guard at the Japanese bank on the 93rd floor, who used to let him in at 6:30; the people at Carr Futures on 92; the head of the Port Authority. Their faces keep him awake at night, he says.

His hands, the one that held the squeegee and the other that carried the bucket, shake with absence.

Welcome Back, Duke
PEGGY NOONAN—*Wall Street Journal*—10/12/2001

A few weeks ago I wrote a column called "God Is Back," about how, within a day of the events of September 11, my city was awash in religious imagery—prayer cards, statues of saints. It all culminated, in a way, in the discovery of the steel-girder cross that emerged last week from the wreckage—unbent, unbroken, unmelted, perfectly proportioned and duly blessed by a Catholic friar on the request of the rescue workers, who seemed to see meaning in the cross's existence. So do I.

My son, a teenager, finds this hilarious, as does one of my best friends. They have teased me, to my delight, but I have told them, "Boys, this whole story is about good and evil, about the clash of good and evil." If you are of a certain cast of mind, it is of course meaningful that the face of the Evil One seemed to emerge with a roar from the furnace that was Tower One. You have seen the Associated Press photo, and the photos that followed: the evil face roared out of the building with an ugly howl—and then in a snap of the fingers it lost form and force and disappeared. If you are of a certain cast of mind it is of course meaningful that the cross, which to those of its faith is imperishable, did not disappear. It was not crushed by the millions of tons of concrete that crashed down upon it, did not melt in the furnace. It rose from the rubble, still there, intact.

For the ignorant, the superstitious and me (and maybe you), the face of the Evil One was revealed, and died; for the ignorant, the superstitious and me (and maybe you), the cross survived. This is how God speaks to us. He is saying, "I am." He is saying, "I am here." He is saying, "And the force of all the evil of all the world will not bury me."

I believe this quite literally. But then I am experiencing September 11 not as a political event but as a spiritual event.

And, of course, a cultural one, which gets me to my topic.

It is not only that God is back, but that men are back. A certain style of manliness is once again being honored and celebrated in our country since September 11. You might say it suddenly emerged from the rubble of the past quarter century, and emerged when a certain kind of man came forth to get our great country out of the fix it was in.

I am speaking of masculine men, men who push things and pull things and haul things and build things, men who charge up the stairs in a hundred pounds of gear and tell everyone else where to go to be safe. Men who are welders, who do construction, men who are cops and firemen. They are all of them, one way or another, the men who put the fire out, the men who are digging the rubble out, and the men who will build whatever takes its place.

And their style is back in style. We are experiencing a new respect for their old-fashioned masculinity, a new respect for physical courage, for strength and for the willingness to use both for the good of others.

You didn't have to be a fireman to be one of the manly men of Sept. 11. Those businessmen on flight 93, which was supposed to hit Washington, the businessmen who didn't live by their hands or their backs but who found out what was happening to their country, said goodbye to the people they loved, snapped the cell phone shut and said, "Let's roll." Those were tough men, the ones who forced that plane down in Pennsylvania. They were tough, brave guys.

Let me tell you when I first realized what I'm saying. On Friday, September 14, I went with friends down to the staging area on the West Side Highway where all the trucks filled with guys coming off a 12-hour shift at ground zero would pass by. They were tough, rough men, the grunts of the city—construction workers and electrical workers and cops and emergency medical worker and firemen.

I joined a group that was just standing there as the truck convoys went by. And all we did was cheer. We all wanted to do some kind of volunteer work but there was nothing left to do, so we stood and cheered those who were doing. The trucks would go by and we'd cheer and wave and shout "God bless you!" and "We love you!" We waved flags and signs, clapped and threw kisses, and we meant it: *We loved these men.* And as the workers would go by—they would wave to us from their trucks and buses, and smile and nod—I realized that a lot of them were men who hadn't been applauded since the day they danced to their song with their bride at the wedding.

And suddenly I looked around me at all of us who were cheering. And saw who we were. Investment bankers! Orthodontists! Magazine editors! In my group, a lawyer, a columnist and a writer. We had been the kings and queens of the city, respected professionals in a city that respects its professional class. And this night we were nobody. We were so useless, all we could do was applaud the somebodies, the workers who, unlike us, had not been applauded much in their lives.

And now they were saving our city.

I turned to my friend and said, "I have seen the grunts of New York become kings and queens of the City." I was so moved and, oddly I guess, grateful. Because they'd always been the people who ran the place, who kept it going, they'd just never been given their due. But now—"And the last shall be first"—we were making up for it.

It may seem that I am really talking about class—the professional classes have a new appreciation for the working class men of Lodi, N.J., or Astoria, Queens. But what I'm attempting to talk about is actual manliness, which often seems tied up with class issues, as they say, but isn't always by any means the same thing.

Here's what I'm trying to say: Once about 10 years ago there was a story—you might have read it in your local tabloid, or a supermarket tabloid like the *National Enquirer*—about an American man and woman who were on their honeymoon in Australia or New Zealand. They were swimming in the ocean, the water chest-high. From nowhere came a shark. The shark went straight for the woman, opened its jaws. Do you know what the man did? He punched the shark in the head. He punched it and punched it again. He did not do brilliant commentary on the shark, he did not share his sensitive feelings about the shark, he did not make wry observations about the shark, he punched the shark in the head. So the shark let go of his wife and went straight for him. And it killed him. The wife survived to tell the story of what her husband had done. He had tried to deck the shark. I told my friends: That's what a wonderful man is, a man who will try to deck the shark.

I don't know what the guy did for a living, but he had a very old-fashioned sense of what it is to be a man, and I think that sense is coming back into style because of who saved us on September 11, and that is very good for our country.

Why? Well, manliness wins wars. Strength and guts plus brains and spirit wins wars. But also, you know what follows manliness? The gentleman. The return of manliness will bring a return of gentlemanliness, for a simple reason: masculine men are almost by definition gentlemen. Example: If you're a woman and you go to a faculty meeting at an Ivy League University you'll have to fight with a male intellectual for a chair, but I assure you that if you go to a Knights of Columbus Hall, the men inside (cops, firemen, insurance agents) will rise to offer you a seat. Because they are manly men, and gentlemen.

It is hard to be a man. I am certain of it; to be a man in this world is not easy. I know you are thinking, *But it's not easy to be a woman*, and you are so right. But women get to complain and make others feel bad about their plight. Men have to suck it up. Good men suck it up and remain good-natured, constructive and helpful; less-good men become the kind of men who are spoofed on "The Man Show"—babe-watching, dope-smoking nihilists. (Nihilism is not manly, it is the last refuge of sissies.)

I should discuss how manliness and its brother, gentlemanliness, went out of style. I know, because I was there. In fact, I may have done it. I remember exactly when: It was in the mid-'70s, and I was in my midtwenties, and a big, nice, middle-aged man got up from his seat to help me haul a big piece of luggage into the overhead luggage space on a plane. I was a feminist, and knew our rules and rants. "I can do it myself," I snapped.

It was important that he know women are strong. It was even more important, it turns out, that I know I was a jackass, but I didn't. I embarrassed a nice man who was attempting to help a lady. I wasn't lady enough to let him. I bet he never offered to help a lady again. I bet he became an intellectual, or a writer, and not a good man like a fireman or a businessman who says, "Let's roll."

But perhaps it wasn't just me. I was there in America, as a child, when John Wayne was a hero, and a symbol of American manliness. He was strong, and silent. And I was there in America when they killed John Wayne by a thousand cuts. A lot of people killed him—not only feminists but peaceniks, leftists, intellectuals, others. You could even say it was Woody Allen who did it, through laughter and an endearing admission of his own nervousness and fear. He made nervousness and fearfulness the admired style. He made not being able to deck the shark, but doing the funniest commentary on not decking the shark, seem... cool.

But when we killed John Wayne, you know who we were left with. We were left with John Wayne's friendly-antagonist sidekick in the old John Ford movies, Barry Fitzgerald. The small, nervous, gossiping neighborhood commentator Barry Fitzgerald, who wanted to talk about everything and do nothing.

This was not progress. It was not improvement.

I missed John Wayne.

But now I think . . . he's back. I think he returned on September 11. I think he ran up the stairs, threw the kid over his back like a sack of potatoes, came back down and shoveled rubble. I think he's in Afghanistan now, saying, with his slow swagger and simmering silence, "Yer in a whole lotta trouble now, Osama-boy."

I think he's back in style. And none too soon.

Welcome back, Duke.

And once again: Thank you, men of September 11.

Pope John Paul II: Bigger Than the Nobel
DAVID BROOKS—*The New York Times*—10/11/2003

I can't imagine he cares, but Pope John Paul II, who has had a more profound influence on more people than any other living human being, is never going to win the Nobel Peace Prize.

For years, prize watchers have felt that the Norwegian committee would have no choice but to give him the award, even if he does have unfashionable views on abortion. And this, oddsmakers predicted, was his year. His health is fragile, and his fervent opposition to the war in Iraq would have pleased the impeccably liberal committee.

But I like to think the members of the committee understood the central truth, that they could not give the prize to John Paul. He is too big and complex for their award. The project he is engaged in—still engaged in—defies their categories.

Instructed by faith, trained by the hard history of Central Europe, the young Karol Wojtyla came to believe that "the evil of our times consists in the first place in a kind of degradation, indeed in a pulverization, of the fundamental uniqueness in each person." The Nazis tried to reduce individuals to their racial makeup, the Marxists to their class status.

John Paul II dedicated his life to the defense of the whole and the indivisible dignity of each person. At the core of each individual, he believes, is the moral need to seek truth.

The "fundamental error of socialism," he writes, "is anthropological." It tries to pare down human beings into something narrower and more degraded than they really are. It tries to crush, among other things, their search for God.

So when John Paul II went to Poland and Cuba early in his papacy, he told the crowds, "You are not who they say you are." The result was a cultural revolution. One young Polish student, quoted in George Weigel's biography, *Witness to Hope*, heard the teaching and realized, "Now what I wanted to do was to live without being a liar."

The pope has tried to defend the dignity of personhood in all spheres, and this has meant that he does not conform to ordinary political categories.

While respecting private property, he has been suspicious of the utilitarian calculus of capitalism, and embraced welfare state policies that put him far to the left.

Defending the dignity of life from the moment of conception to the moment of death, he has fought abortion, euthanasia and the scientific refashioning of human nature, putting himself on the side of conservatives.

His main achievement has been to remind us—Catholics and even us non-Catholics—that you can't pare people down. We do this all the time without realizing it. When we write for newspapers, or talk in public, we generally speak as if democracy and freedom are ends in themselves. We give our heroes prizes for curing diseases and clearing land mines.

Those things, grand as they are, are insufficient, the pope is always insisting. Democracy is just a system. Freedom is just an opportunity to do good or bad. The essence of life is not long life, but true life.

The pope is always taking us out of our secular comfort zone and dragging us toward ultimate issues. You can't talk about politics, economics, science, philosophy or war, he argues, while conveniently averting your eyes from God and ultimate truth.

In its statement lauding this year's winner, Shirin Ebadi, the Norwegian Nobel Committee celebrates her commitment to dialogue and democracy. But where the authors of that statement stop thinking is where the pope picks up.

Dialogues toward what truth? Democracy for what? He understands we will never persuade a radical Islamist to give up his absolute grip on what he sees as God's truth if all we are offering is a tepid dialogue on the need to get along. We need to show him truth with tolerance. This is the challenge of the increasingly religious 21st century, and the pope, a philosopher more than an activist, is far out ahead.

Shirin Ebadi is obviously a courageous person, doing vitally important work. Nothing takes away from her heroism. But when history looks back on our era, Pope John Paul II will be recognized as the giant of the age, as the one individual who did the most to place democracy and freedom at the service of the highest human goals.

A Gambler Sees Beyond the Jackpot
DAN BARRY—*The New York Times*—5/6/2006

Victor Ramdin considered the cards dealt to him.

Around him stood hundreds of people watching this hand of the Foxwoods Poker Classic. Across from him sat a Yale student so gifted he could teach a doctoral program in Texas Hold 'Em. And now, in his hands, promising everything and nothing, the jack of spades and the ace of fast-beating hearts.

Mr. Ramdin, 38, whose pleasant smile masks a killer's instinct, considered the odds, among them: the chances that as a hard-working Guyanese immigrant from the Bronx, he would take up poker and within three years be vying for a $1.3 million jackpot in a casino in eastern Connecticut. Ten to one? Million to one?

The Yale man, Alex Jacob, signaled all in, which meant that he was dedicating all his chips to this hand of Texas Hold 'Em. Mr. Ramdin called, which meant that they would dispense with bluffing and expose their cards.

Mr. Jacob revealed the king of diamonds and the jack of clubs. Mr. Ramdin showed his ace and his jack.

The dealer placed three cards—community cards, to be used by both players—face up on the table: the three of spades, the queen of hearts, and the seven of hearts. Nothing favoring either player, really. Two more cards to go before a winner could be determined.

Seventeen years ago, Mr. Ramdin entered this country illegally and worked, and worked. He became a guard at the city morgue, but was so spooked that he quit after his first day, never to return for his check. Then he got a job packing and delivering fish all day, after which, he recalled, he would board the subway "and nobody would stick around."

He managed his mother's grocery store in the Bronx. He saved up and started a 99-cent store. He helped family members with other businesses, and started investing in real estate. Along the way he got his green card, and became an American citizen.

He began to play poker with friends. It appealed to his compulsive nature, which was already manifesting itself in the way he drank, shot pool, played darts. Most of all, he liked how success equaled cash.

Poker became everything. He entered qualifying rounds for tournaments to try to win, of course, but also to learn from veteran players. He made mental notes of what card combinations they favored, of when they called and when they bluffed. He learned to detect the "tell" of other players—the scratch of the nose, the dart of the eyes—that betrayed their feelings about the cards in their hands.

The dealer presented the next card, the eight of spades. Mr. Ramdin's ace gave him the best hand. The only way he could lose was if the seventh and last card—"the river," they call it—was a king that would give Mr. Jacob a winning pair.

Earlier in the week, while he was checking into the casino's hotel, Mr. Ramdin overheard a distraught woman telling the clerk that her bus had left without her and that she needed a room. But the clerk told her the hotel was booked solid.

Seeing no other play, Mr. Ramdin arranged to have the woman stay in the room reserved for him, while he doubled up with a poker-playing friend. The next day, at a point in the tournament when he was down to $3,000, the grateful woman appeared as if from a dream. I'm praying for you, she told him. You will win.

He took heart in her words; he had plans for some of the winnings.

Finally, the river. The dealer turned over the last card of the last hand in the four-day tournament: the jack of hearts—not a king!—which meant that Victor Ramdin, Guyanese immigrant from the Bronx, held the winning hand of a pair of jacks with an ace kicker. With the flick of one card, he was $1.3 million richer.

"I jumped straight over the table," he recalled.

But the story does not end with Mr. Ramdin on that table four weeks ago in Connecticut. In addition to being a poker player, in addition to owning a 99-cent store, he is a philanthropist, having worked closely with Guyana Watch, a nonprofit organization that tries to meet the medical needs of poor children in Guyana.

After winning the Foxwoods tournament, he put to work that estimable mind of his, the one forever whirring with calculations. He determined that with $200,000 of his prize money, he could pay for heart surgery for 10 children from his native country.

With one call, 10 new hands were dealt. All hearts.

Post-Cancer Life: Precious, Priceless
REGINA BRETT—*Cleveland Plain Dealer*—2/18/2007

The commercial nearly knocked me off the couch.

There he was, the world's most famous cancer survivor, taunting the disease that could have killed him.

Or was he thanking it?

I couldn't tell.

Lance Armstrong stared into the camera and said, "Remember me, cancer? You made me who I am today."

Armstrong got cancer in 1996. He won his first Tour de France in 1999, then won six more.

But thank cancer? Could I?

Cancer and I met nine years ago Monday. I woke from a surgical biopsy on Feb. 19, 1998, to a new life. Everything before that fell on the other side of the timeline of life. B.C. Before Cancer.

Nine years have passed.

Nine precious years.

The first year was a blur. By the time you recover from surgery, it's time for four rounds of chemo. By the time your hair is starting to grow back, it's time for six weeks of radiation.

By the time you get your energy back, you're into year two.

That's when it hit me. Damn, I had cancer.

A new life unfolded as the fuzz of chemo brain cleared.

Before cancer, I acted out of guilt and fear. I had to finish every book, movie, argument.

Now? Life is too short.

Before cancer, I worried about gray hair, wrinkles and gravity. Now? I get to grow old.

Before cancer, I held grudges, replayed bad home movies, poked old wounds.

Now? Nothing is more important than faith, family and finding joy in this day. In my wallet, I carry a picture of me bald to remind me that every day above ground is a good day.

Before cancer, I could go days without looking at the stars. Weeks without calling my best friends. Months without talking to my sisters and brothers.

Cancer made me tougher.

Sinus infection? Flu? Pulled muscle? Easy breezy Japanesy. Pain? So what. Fear? Who cares.

Cancer made me bolder.

I speak up more and care less about what people think.

When it came to friends, cancer separated the weak from the strong. Some didn't make the cut.

Cancer didn't make my husband love me more. He couldn't love me more. But cancer made me better at receiving his love.

I've grown fond of the color pink. Grown closer to all my nieces and nephews.

I got to see my stepsons graduate and chase their dreams.

I got to see my daughter marry a wonderful man and pursue a career with the National Cancer Institute. Within two minutes of meeting people, she urges them to quit smoking, go for a mammogram and get a colonoscopy.

My battle with cancer took her to the front lines. She stayed there to fight for others.

"Your cancer made me who I am," she told me last week. "It shaped my whole career, my passion for what I do. It gave me my script."

She reminded me why it's important to talk about surviving. It's an obligation we 10 million cancer survivors in America share.

Are we cured? In remission? Who knows? We all got the wake-up call, and we aren't going back to sleep.

Am I cured? Nine years says yes, but I look at it this way: I got a daily reprieve—and I'm not wasting a minute of it.

Remember me, cancer?

Didn't think so.

I've changed too much.

The Last Lecture
Jeffrey Zaslow—*Wall Street Journal*—9/20/2007

Randy Pausch, a Carnegie Mellon University computer-science professor, was about to give a lecture Tuesday afternoon, but before he said a word, he received a standing ovation from 400 students and colleagues.

He motioned to them to sit down. "Make me earn it," he said.

They had come to see him give what was billed as his "last lecture." This is a common title for talks on college campuses today. Schools such as Stanford and the University of Alabama have mounted "Last Lecture Series," in which top professors are asked to think deeply about what matters to them and to give hypothetical final talks. For the audience, the question to be mulled is this: What wisdom would we impart to the world if we knew it was our last chance?

It can be an intriguing hour, watching healthy professors consider their demise and ruminate over subjects dear to them. At the University of Northern Iowa, instructor Penny O'Connor recently titled her lecture "Get Over Yourself." At Cornell, Ellis Hanson, who teaches a course titled "Desire," spoke about sex and technology.

At Carnegie Mellon, however, Dr. Pausch's speech was more than just an academic exercise. The 46-year-old father of three has pancreatic cancer and expects to live for just a few months. His lecture, using images on a giant screen, turned out to be a rollicking and riveting journey through the lessons of his life.

He began by showing his CT scans, revealing 10 tumors on his liver. But after that, he talked about living. If anyone expected him to be morose, he said, "I'm sorry to disappoint you." He then dropped to the floor and did one-handed pushups.

Clicking through photos of himself as a boy, he talked about his childhood dreams: to win giant stuffed animals at carnivals, to walk in zero gravity, to design Disney rides, to write a World Book entry. By adulthood, he had achieved each goal. As proof, he had students carry out all the huge stuffed animals he'd won in his life, which he gave to audience members. After all, he doesn't need them anymore.

He paid tribute to his techie background. "I've experienced a deathbed conversion," he said, smiling. "I just bought a Macintosh." Flashing his rejection letters on the screen, he talked about setbacks in his career, repeating: "Brick walls are there for a reason. They let us prove how badly we want things." He encouraged us to be patient with others. "Wait long enough, and people will surprise and impress you." After showing photos of his childhood bedroom, decorated with mathematical notations he'd drawn on the walls, he said: "If your kids want to paint their bedrooms, as a favor to me, let 'em do it."

While displaying photos of his bosses and students over the years, he said that helping others fulfill their dreams is even more fun than achieving your own. He talked of requiring his students to create videogames without sex and violence. "You'd be surprised how many 19-year-old boys run out of ideas when you take those possibilities away," he said, but they all rose to the challenge.

He also saluted his parents, who let him make his childhood bedroom his domain, even if his wall etchings hurt the home's resale value. He knew his mom was proud of him when he got his Ph.D., he said, despite how she'd introduce him: "This is my son. He's a doctor, but not the kind who helps people."

He then spoke about his legacy. Considered one of the nation's foremost teachers of video-game and virtual-reality technology, he helped develop "Alice," a Carnegie Mellon software project that allows people to easily create 3-D animations. It had one million downloads in the past year, and usage is expected to soar.

"Like Moses, I get to see the Promised Land, but I don't get to step foot in it," Dr. Pausch said. "That's OK. I will live on in Alice."

Many people have given last speeches without realizing it. The day before he was killed, Martin Luther King Jr. spoke prophetically: "Like anybody, I would like to live a long life. Longevity has its place." He talked of how he had seen the Promised Land, even though "I may not get there with you."

Dr. Pausch's lecture, in the same way, became a call to his colleagues and students to go on without him and do great things. But he was also addressing those closer to his heart.

Near the end of his talk, he had a cake brought out for his wife, whose birthday was the day before. As she cried and they embraced on stage, the audience sang "Happy Birthday," many wiping away their own tears.

Dr. Pausch's speech was taped so his children, ages 5, 2 and 1, can watch it when they're older. His last words in his last lecture were simple: "This was for my kids." Then those of us in the audience rose for one last standing ovation.

Being Albee
MICHAEL RIEDEL—*New York Post*—3/12/2008

Edward Albee is 80 today.

And he's going to work.

The celebrated playwright is directing revivals of his early one-acts *The American Dream* and *The Sandbox*, opening March 25 at the Cherry Lane Theatre.

After that, he goes into rehearsals for *Occupant*, about his late friend sculptor Louise Nevelson. It stars Mercedes Ruehl and opens in June at the Signature Theatre.

Then it's on to the Broadway transfer of his new play *Me, Myself and I*, about identical twins, that opened to raves last month at Princeton's McCarter Theatre.

And just as soon as his schedule allows, he's returning to one of his favorite places on Earth—Easter Island—to spend three weeks writing a play set there called *Silence*.

"I've been to some impressive places," Albee says. "Egypt was impressive. So was the Yucatan and my first glacier. But Easter Island, out in the Pacific, a thousand miles away from anything—wow! The silence is amazing."

In the twilight of his life, Albee isn't coasting on his Pulitzers (three), his Tonys (two) or even his proclamation from the mayor designating today Edward Albee Day in New York City.

The proclamation sits on the kitchen floor, propped against the wall, in the spacious Harrison Street loft he bought 35 years ago for $40,000 and shares with his kitten, Abby, who darts merrily about his vast collection of African art.

The Tonys and the Pulitzers aren't on view. Nor are any posters from his 31 plays, among them *Who's Afraid of Virginia Woolf? A Delicate Balance, Tiny Alice* and *Seascape*.

"When I was young, I was always embarrassed to go into theater people's apartments and see all their posters on the walls," he says. "I decided that, if I ever got a poster or an award, I would never put it up.

"Well, maybe I'll put up *The Man Who Had Three Arms*," he adds, referring to his most notorious Broadway flop, which resulted in a 15-year banishment of sorts from the commercial New York theater. He returned, triumphantly, in 1994 with the Pulitzer Prize–winning *Three Tall Women*.

"I've always thought I write fairly decent plays, even the ones the critics don't like," Albee says. "I would never let a play open that I didn't think was OK. I have a fairly good sense of my talent. Anybody in the American theater has got to be that way. Look what they [the critics] did to Tennessee Williams. They killed Bill Inge."

(Inge has made a posthumous comeback with the hit revival of *Come Back, Little Sheba* at the Manhattan Theater Club.)

"Actually, it was psychiatry that killed Bill Inge," Albee continues. "He was an alcoholic and a closeted gay guy who wrote good plays. Then he went to a psychiatrist and never wrote another good play. Back in those days, psychiatrists tried to 'adjust' you to society."

Albee, who usually has a store of witty, if enigmatic, responses to reporters' questions, is surprisingly candid these days.

He misses his lover of 35 years, artist Jonathan Thomas, who died in 2005 after a long battle with cancer.

"I learned something important about dying, about a slow death, as

Jonathan's was," Albee says. "What I learned was: Never forget who's dying. It's not about you. It's always about them.

"And I learned something about grief: It never ends. It's like a third arm."

Albee's made a few stabs at dating since Jonathan's death. But the one relationship he's had recently ended.

"He was 50 years younger than I am, which has its problems," Albee says, dryly. "And he was a writer. It didn't work. I don't think I'll have another relationship. And that's OK. Besides, I can't offer a person more than 10 years.

"Am I lonely? Probably. Yes. I want Jonathan back."

As for his own death, Albee says: "Well, I'm not looking forward to it. Woody Allen has all the best lines about dying, to which I can only add that it's a terrible waste of time.

"I have some plays to finish. Maybe I'll be allowed to go after that. Maybe if I stop writing a play, I'll die."

Nobody's Perfect, but They Were Good
PEGGY NOONAN—*Wall Street Journal*—6/4/2010

We needed some happy news this week, and I think we got it. But first, a journey back in time.

It was Monday, July 4, 1983, a painfully hot day, 94 degrees when the game began. We were at Yankee Stadium, and the Yanks were playing their ancestral foes, the Boston Red Sox. More than 40,000 people filled the stands. My friend George and I had seats in the upper decks, where people were waving programs against the heat, eating hot dogs, drinking beer and—oh, innocent days— smoking. In fact it was the smoking that made me realize something was going on.

The Yankees' pitcher, Dave Righetti, who'd bounced from the majors to the minors and back again, was having a good game, striking out seven of the first nine hitters. The Yanks were scoring; the Red Sox were doing nothing. Suddenly, around the sixth or seventh inning, I realized the boisterous crowd had turned quieter. George was chain-smoking with a look of fierce intensity. "What's happening?" I asked him. "Don't say it," he replied. "If you say it, you jinx it." He said some other things, talking in a kind of code, and I realized: This may be a no-hitter. We may be witnessing history.

Now I'm watching not only the game but everyone around me. Fathers are with their kids, and you can tell they're starting to think: "I have given my son a great gift today." Just down from us was an old man, 75 or so, tall, slim and white-haired. I never saw him say a word to anyone, and throughout the game there was an empty seat beside him. I thought: He's got a wife in the hospital and she told him to take the afternoon off; he'd bought the tickets before she got sick, and he's here by himself. He was so distracted and lonely-looking but inning by inning the game started to capture him, and the last few innings he couldn't sit down.

Everyone else in New York was at the beach for the three-day weekend, but around us were regular people, working people who didn't have enough to be at the Jersey Shore or out on the island, but who had enough for a baseball game. Also there were die-hard fans holding their game cards. Meaning everyone who was there deserved to be there, everyone who got the gift deserved it. It was one of those moments where life is just.

Twenty-five years later, on July 3, 2008, Anthony McCarron of New York's *Daily News* wrote of the final moments of the game. Righetti is facing the final batter, Wade Boggs, and is worried he'll tap the ball toward first and beat him to the bag. At the plate, Boggs is thinking, "If I get a hit here, with two out in the ninth inning, and break this thing up, I'm probably not getting out of here alive." As Mr. McCarron wrote, Righetti "snapped off a crisp slider, Boggs struck out swinging," and Righetti flung his arms out in joy.

The crowd exploded, they wouldn't stop jumping and cheering, and later they filled the bars around the stadium. It was raucous, joyful. Everyone acted as if they were related, because it is a beautiful thing when you witness history together. It's unifying.

Only later would it be noted that it wasn't only Independence Day, and a home game, and the Red Sox, it was the anniversary of Lou Gehrig's 1939 farewell speech. So it was fitting everyone left feeling like the luckiest man on the face of the earth.

I bet you know where I'm going.

It was Wednesday night of this week, and it was a heartbreaker, and you have seen the videotape. Comerica Park in Detroit, the Tigers vs. the Cleveland Indians, and on the mound is Tigers pitcher Armando Galarraga, 28. In his brief Major League career, he has not pitched a complete game, never mind a perfect one but here he is. He's retired 26 straight batters. It's two outs in the ninth with just one to go, one out between him and history. Indians shortstop Jason Donald is at the plate. Donald hits a grounder between first and second. Miguel Cabrera, the Tigers first baseman, fields it as Galarraga sprints to first. The pitcher takes the throw from Cabrera and steps on the base. Donald crosses it just a step later. Galarraga gets this look of joy. And the umpire blows it. He calls Donald safe. Everyone is shocked.

It's everything that follows that blunder that makes the story great.

When Galarraga hears the call, he looks puzzled, surprised. But he's composed and calm, and he smiles, as if accepting fate. Others run to the ump and begin to yell, but Galarraga just walks back to the mound to finish the job. Which he does, grounding out the next batter. The game is over.

The umpire, Jim Joyce, 54, left the field and watches the videotape. He saw that he'd made a mistake and took immediate responsibility. He went straight to the clubhouse where he personally apologized to Galarraga. Then he told the press, "I just cost the kid a perfect game." He said, "I thought [Donald] beat the throw. I was convinced he beat the throw until I saw the replay. It was the biggest call of my career."

Galarraga told reporters he felt worse for Joyce than he felt for himself. At first, reacting to the game in the clubhouse, he'd criticized Joyce. But after Joyce apologized, Galarraga said, "You don't see an umpire after the game come out and say, 'Hey, let me tell you I'm sorry.'" He said, "He felt really bad." He noted Joyce had come straight over as soon as he knew he'd made the wrong call.

What was sweet and surprising was that all the principals in the story comported themselves as fully formed adults, with patience, grace and dignity. And in doing so, Galarraga and Joyce showed kids How to Do It.

A lot of adults don't teach kids this now, because the adults themselves don't know how to do it. There's a mentoring gap, an instruction gap in our country. We don't put forward a template because we don't know the template. So everyone imitates TV, where victors dance in the end zone, where winners shoot their arms in the air and distort their face and yell "Whoooaahhh," and where victims of an injustice scream, cry, say bitter things, and beat the ground with their fists. Everyone has come to believe this is authentic. It is authentically babyish. Everyone thinks it's honest. It's honestly undignified, self-indulgent, weak and embarrassing.

Galarraga and Joyce couldn't have known it when they went to work Wednesday, but they were going to show children in an unforgettable way that a victim of injustice can react with compassion, and a person who makes a mistake can admit and declare it. Joyce especially was a relief, not spinning or digging in his heels. I wish he hadn't sworn. Nobody's perfect.

Thursday afternoon the Tigers met the Indians again in Comerica Park. Armando Galarraga got a standing ovation. In a small masterpiece of public relations, Detroit's own General Motors gave him a brand new red Corvette. Galarraga brought out the lineup card and gave it to the umpire—Jim Joyce, who had been offered the day off but chose to work.

Fans came with signs that said, "It was perfect."

It was.

ABOUT THE COLUMNISTS

MITCH ALBOM (1958–)—Mitch Albom is a columnist, author, radio host, television commentator, screenwriter, playwright, musician, and philanthropist. He splits his twice-weekly column for the *Detroit Free Press* between sports and civic issues. His books include the best-selling *Tuesdays with Morrie*. Albom has been named best sports columnist thirteen times and best feature writer seven times by the Associated Press. His advice to fellow newspaper journalists confronting competition with Cable TV, the Internet, and talk radio: "We have to arrest the readers' attention. . . . When we do what we do best, which is stylize, write, detail, flow, extrapolate, then we win, because they can never do that."

STEWART ALSOP (1914–1974)—The influential brothers Stewart and Joseph Alsop started the syndicated column Matter of Fact in 1945. Anticommunist abroad and anti-anti-Communist at home, they help define the contours of cold war–era policy, coining terms such as "Hawks" and "Doves." A play about Joseph Alsop, *The Columnist*, debuted on Broadway in 2012, with John Lithgow portraying Joseph and Boyd Gaines playing Stewart. "As columnists," they wrote, "we always regard ourselves as reporters. We tried . . . never to print a column lacking at least one previously unpublished and significant item of factual information." Stewart finished his career writing a column for *Newsweek*.

PAUL AVERY (1934–2000)—Portrayed by Robert Downey Jr. in the movie *Zodiac*, Paul Avery was the San Francisco reporter and columnist who achieved national renown for his involvement in the Zodiac Killer case as well as the Patti Hearst kidnapping trial. A legendary local character with a pronounced fondness for smoking and drinking, he was directly threatened by the Zodiac Killer in one of the letters he sent Avery. Colleagues at the *Chronicle* responded by wearing buttons reading "I am not Paul Avery."

MIKE BARNICLE (1943–)—Barnicle is to Boston what Royko was to Chicago and Breslin is to New York—an authentic voice who comes to symbolize a great city. Almost a generation younger than Breslin & Co., Barnicle's column with the *Boston Globe* ran from 1973 to 1998. He has subsequently written for the *Daily News* and the *Boston Herald*, logging an estimated four thousand columns in the process. He is also a frequent guest on MSNBC's *Morning Joe* as well as a featured interview in Ken Burns's *Baseball: the 10th Inning* documentary.

DAN BARRY (1958–)—Born and raised in Queens, New York, Dan Barry won a Pulitzer for investigative reporting at the *Providence Journal-Bulletin* before returning home to *The New York Times*, where he ran the paper's City Hall and Police bureaus. He currently writes the paper's This Land column, which explores lesser-known corners of America.

DAVE BARRY (1947–)—The Pulitzer Prize–winning humorist for the *Miami Herald* proved so popular that he gave up his column in 2005 to concentrate on writing profitable books and spending time with his family. He has said that he worked seven days a week making his column sound like he "dashed it off while carpet-chewing drunk." Barry won the Pulitzer Prize in 1988. Barry has defined a sense of humor as "a measurement of the extent to which we realize that we are trapped in a world almost totally devoid of reason. Laughter is how we express the anxiety we feel at this knowledge."

MEYER BERGER (1898–1959)—Meyer Berger started *The New York Times'* long-running About New York column in 1939. A master of local color and street-level storytelling, Berger won the Pulitzer Prize in 1950 for his feature detailing a murder spree in Camden perpetrated by a war vet named Howard Unruh. Berger gave the prize money to Unruh's mother. Some of his best work was posthumously anthologized in *Meyer Berger's New York*.

HOMER BIGART (1907–1991)—A two-time Pulitzer Prize winner, Homer Bigart was among the most honored and respected journalists of his time. Beginning at the *New York Herald Tribune* in 1929, he was a shy and private man with a pronounced stutter and a healthy instinct to doubt the "official version" of events. He found fame as a war correspondent in three successive American conflicts, and won praise from *Newsweek* as "the best war correspondent of an embattled generation" as well as "the hardest kind of worker and the fairest kind of competitor."

WINIFRED BLACK (1863–1936)—Daughter of the Civil War general Benjamin Sweet, Winifred Sweet Black Bonfils was raised in Wisconsin and became an early star of the Hearst papers, based in the *San Francisco Examiner*. She was the first reporter on the scene after the hurricane that destroyed Galveston. "I'm proud of being, in a very humble way, a member of the good old newspaper gang," she once wrote. "The kindest-hearted, quickest-witted, clearest-eyed, most courageous assemblage of people I have ever had the honor and the good fortune to know."

NELLIE BLY (1864–1922)—Perhaps the most celebrated investigative journalist of her time, Nellie Bly circumnavigated the globe in seventy-two days, besting the fictional record established by the Jules Verne novel, *Around the World in Eighty Days*. Born Elizabeth Jane Cochran in Pennsylvania, she began her newspaper career writing for the *Pittsburgh Dispatch*, joining Joseph Pulitzer's *New York World* in 1887. Her first celebrated story involved getting herself institutionalized for insanity at New York's notorious Blackwell's Island to expose the abuses of female inmates, an exposé published as "10 Days in a Madhouse." She married a multimillionaire industrialist forty years her senior in 1895 and retired from reporting, eventually running his business and applying for several patents. After facing bankruptcy because of embezzlement, she covered the outbreak of World War I from the front lines. Bly's exploits have been the subject of a Broadway play and a made-for-TV movie.

RICK BRAGG (1959–)—Rick Bragg, born in Alabama, grew up in the tiny town of Possum Trot before embarking on a career at *The New York Times* that included stints in Haiti and covering major stories like the terrorist bombing of the Oklahoma City federal building. He was suspended for two weeks in 2005 for putting his byline on a story largely written and researched by an assistant. He has won dozens of journalism prizes, including the 1996 Pulitzer for feature writing, and has authored five books.

JIMMY BRESLIN (1930–)—The archetypal New York newspaper columnist, he is regarded by his contemporaries as one of the all-time greats. The Queens native inspired a generation of writers with his front-page columns and recurring characters. Breslin's best work found uncommon angles to breaking news—interviewing the attending emergency room surgeon after JFK's assassination or the cop who piled John Lennon's dying body into the back of his patrol car. Breslin grew to embody many stereotypes—the hard-drinking, chain-smoking newsman, brilliant but bullshit intolerant, rumpled but hyperliterate and able to write on deadline like an unsentimental angel. Says Breslin: "Rage is the only quality which has kept me, or anybody I have ever studied, writing columns for newspapers."

REGINA BRETT (1956–)—A *Cleveland Plain Dealer* columnist, Brett's candid account of overcoming a breast cancer diagnosis in 1998 made her column an inspiration to readers. Initially, her columns ran in the *Akron Beacon Journal*, where she won a National Headliner Award. Brett has written over two thousand columns in her career and hosts a radio show. Her column 45 Life Lessons went viral online and is often misattributed to a ninety-year-old woman. She was a Pulitzer Prize Finalist for Commentary in 2008 and 2009. Her first book, *God Never Blinks: 50 Lessons for Life's Little Detours*, was published in April 2010.

NOAH BROOKS (1830–1903)—A journalist, editor, and author who chronicled the rise of the Republican Party and the Lincoln administration firsthand, Noah Brooks was born in Maine and died in California. His 258 Civil War–era dispatches for the *Sacramento Daily Union* were collected in the 1998 book *Lincoln Observed*.

HEYWOOD BROUN (1888–1939)—Perhaps the preeminent liberal columnist of his day, Broun was a Harvard dropout and the founding president of the American Newspaper Guild. His talents allowed him to tackle subjects ranging from art to sports to war to politics—and he was an outspoken advocate of the idea that journalism could help solve society's ills. During the Great Depression, he used his column as an occasional employment agency, helping to find work for roughly one thousand individuals. In 1930, he ran for Congress unsuccessfully as a Socialist. An easygoing man of appetites, he was a member of the storied Algonquin Round Table and a friend of the Marx Brothers. He wrote more than a dozen books and was a frequent voice on the radio. Broun died suddenly a week after his fifty-first birthday. More than three thousand mourners crowded St. Patrick's Cathedral.

Art Buchwald (1925–2007)—A syndicated satirist for more than fifty years, Art Buchwald published more than thirty books and won the Pulitzer Prize for Commentary in 1982. The son of Austrian-Hungarian immigrants, Buchwald ran away from home to join the Marines during World War II. After attending the University of Southern California on the GI Bill, Buchwald decamped for France, where he began writing a humor column. In 1962, he transferred his column to the United States under the title Capitol Punishment. His writing riffed off newspaper headlines, extending narratives to absurd extremes and adding new characters—for example, God speaking to Richard Nixon as Watergate unfolds. When once asked why he chose to write humor, Buchwald replied, "Getting even. I am constantly trying to avenge hurts from the past." After his death in 2007, a video obituary was posted online, beginning with the columnist beaming into the camera, saying: "Hi. I'm Art Buchwald, and I just died."

William F. Buckley Jr. (1925–2008)—Godfather of the modern conservative movement, Buckley was a prolific author, bon vivant, ideological entrepreneur, television host, onetime mayoral candidate, and founder of the *National Review*. Through his United Press Syndicate column, Buckley wrote three pieces a week that reached 350 papers. His vivid personality disarmed (some) critics while galvanizing a movement; his intellectual achievement was to reshape the landscape of American political debate without sacrificing the breadth of his interests or enthusiasms. "If there is a common thread in Buckley's writings," George Will wrote in the preface of the posthumous column anthology *Athwart History*, "it is the compatibility of seriousness, even occasional indignation, with an unfailing sense of merriment about the pleasures of intellectual combat."

Jimmy Cannon (1909–1973)—Greenwich Village–born Jimmy Cannon gained his fame writing sports columns for New York dailies and for a time was the highest-paid sportswriter in the nation, making $1,000 a week. His range and access was aided by friendships with the hard-drinking rich and famous, including Frank Sinatra and Ernest Hemingway. Fellow New York columnist Pete Hamill paid Cannon tribute by writing: "It was Cannon who made me want to be a newspaper man. He wrote a sports column, but it was always more than that. In some ways the hero of the column was its style, an undisciplined personal mixture of New York street talk, soaring elegance, Hemingway and Algren, deep Celtic feeling, city loneliness, prohibition violence, and a personal belief in honor."

Hodding Carter Jr. (1907–1972)—The editor of the *Greenville Delta Democrat Times*, Carter was a leading progressive voice of the New South during the end of segregation. Raised in a prominent anti–Huey Long Louisiana family, Carter continued the tradition of bucking against the powers of the South. He won the Pulitzer Prize in 1946 for a group of editorials such as "Go for Broke," which defended the rights of Japanese-American soldiers returning home from serving in the European war. A close friend and political ally of Robert F. Kennedy, Carter was with him the day before he died and punched a fellow passenger on a flight who gloated at the news of RFK's assassination.

IRVIN S. COBB (1876–1944)—Paducah, Kentucky's most famous native son spent most of his adult life in New York City among the most celebrated newspapermen, humorists, and short-story writers of his time, writing some sixty books and three hundred stories. He got his first big break with an eyewitness account of the assassination of Kentucky governor William Goebel and soon joined the *New York World* as a reporter and columnist. His coverage of the murder of famed architect Stanford White and the subsequent first "trial of the century" set the standard of the age. Upon his death, instructions for his funeral were subsequently found in a desk drawer, sealing his renown as a beloved and iconoclastic raconteur. It read in part: "Above all I want no long faces and no show of grief at the burying ground. . . . In deference to the faith of our dear mother who was through her lifetime a loyal though never bigoted communicant of that congregation, perhaps the current pastor of the First Presbyterian Church would consent to read the Twenty-third Psalm, which was her favorite passage in the Scriptures and is mine since it contains no charnel words, no morbid mouthings about corruption and decay and, being mercifully without creed or dogma, carries no threat of eternal hell-fire for those parties we do not like, no direct promise of a heaven which, if one may judge by the people who are surest of going there, must be a powerfully dull place, populated to a considerable and uncomfortable degree by prigs, time-servers and unpleasantly aggressive individuals. Hell may have a worse climate but undoubtedly the company is sprightlier."

JOSEPH COOKMAN (1899–1944)—Born in England and raised in New York, Joseph Cookman was one of the founders of the Newspaper Guild and one of the most celebrated newspapermen of his time. He served in World War I and turned down a career as a steel salesman to pursue journalism in New York City. While investigating the expansion of gangster Dutch Schultz's gambling empire, Cookman was severely beaten in an unsuccessful attempt to get him to back off the story. He founded the Newspaper Guild in 1933 with Heywood Broun and other contemporaries. He died of tuberculosis.

RICHARD BEN CRAMER (1950–)—Perhaps best known for his nonfiction epics *What It Takes* and *Joe DiMaggio: A Hero's Life*, Cramer is also a Pulitzer Prize–winning international reporter, writing dispatches from the Middle East and Europe for the *Philadelphia Inquirer* and the *Baltimore Sun*. His magazine work, especially *Esquire* profiles of the Boston Red Sox's Ted Williams and Baltimore mayor William Donald Schaefer are also considered modern classics of magazine writing. An extended interview with the reclusive Cramer is featured in 2005's *The New New Journalism*. He lives in Maryland.

MICHAEL DALY (1951–)—Daly was the first American born in his family. He attended sixteen grammar schools in six years. He is a graduate of Yale University. He was a longtime columnist with the *New York Daily News* and was a finalist for the Pulitzer Prize in 2001 for his columns on 9/11. He is a recipient of the Francis Medal, bestowed by the Holy Name Province of the Order of Friars Minor. He has also written for *New York Magazine*, *The Atlantic Monthly*, *Rolling Stone*, and the *Village Voice*. He is the author of a novel, *Under Ground*, and of a biography, *The Book of Mychal*. He lives in Brooklyn with his wife and two daughters.

RICHARD HARDING DAVIS (1864–1916)—The pioneering war correspondent and columnist helped create the image of the swashbuckling international reporter, writing of bullets that sound like "humming-birds on a warm summer's day." He first made his name covering the devastation of the Johnstown Flood and then focused his attention overseas, often becoming a part of the action he chronicled. Davis participated in his friend Teddy Roosevelt's charge up San Juan Hill in the Spanish-American War, being named an honorary Rough Rider in its aftermath. Davis helped establish Roosevelt's fame and had become a celebrity in his own right. He authored many thinly veiled fictional accounts of his adventures, including *Captain Macklin* and *Real Soldiers of Fortune*. He died suddenly at his home in Mount Kisco, New York, shortly before his fifty-second birthday.

LINDSAY DENISON (1873–1934)—A year after graduating in Yale's class of 1895, Lindsay Denison became a reporter at the *New York Sun*, where he drew the job of following Theodore Roosevelt's campaign for governor, and followed him across the country in 1900, as TR campaigned for vice president. Years later, as a forty-three-year-old writer with the *New York Evening World*, Denison—determined to be in Europe for the fast-approaching war—volunteered for the army and managed, despite his age and gray hair, to get stationed in France during World War I before returning home to the *Evening World*.

BRADY DENNIS (1977–)—A national economics reporter for the *Washington Post*, this North Carolina native first achieved prominence for a series of eight stories published in the *St. Petersburg Times'* occasional series 300 Words, for which he won the 2006 Ernie Pyle Award for human interest writing. He worked as Bob Woodward's research assistant on *The War Within: A Secret White House History, 2006–2008*. He was a finalist for the 2009 Pulitzer Prize.

PETE DEXTER (1943–)—A National Book Award–winning novelist for *Paris Trout* in 1988, Pete Dexter first made his name as a columnist for the *Philadelphia Daily News* and the *Sacramento Bee* in the 1970s and '80s. His wry, self-effacing style fronted a razor-sharp mind that enjoyed confrontation. His reported columns show remarkable range—alternately compassionate, cold-eyed, and funny. The best of his newspaper work was collected in the highly recommended 2007 book *Paper Trails*.

MAUREEN DOWD (1952–)—The Pulitzer Prize–winning *New York Times* columnist is known for her jaunty, personality-driven political columns. A native of Washington D.C., she began work at the *Washington Star* and became the White House correspondent for the *Times* during the first Bush administration. She was given a column upon the retirement of Anna Quindlen and won the Pulitzer Prize in 1999 and the Damon Runyon Award in 2000.

JIM DWYER (1957–)—Jim Dwyer is a native New Yorker whose early work included a three-year stint as a columnist writing about the city's subway system. He wrote and reported for *Newsday* and the *New York Daily News* (winning Pulitzers at both), joining *The New York Times*, where he is currently a Metro columnist. Dwyer's books include *102 Minutes*, an account of the destruction of the World Trade Center in the terrorist attack of September 11, 2001.

FREDERICK B. EDWARDS (1887–1959)—A local reporter and columnist for the *New York Herald Tribune*.

NORA EPHRON (1941–2012)—Nora Ephron joined with friends in publishing a fake newspaper during a 1963 strike by the International Typographical Union that shut down four New York City newspapers, including the *New York Post*. Ephron's parodies of *Post* columnists caught the eye of then publisher Dorothy Schiff, who offered Ephron a job at the paper. She piled up accolades as a columnist, essayist, and, later, screenwriter of Hollywood blockbusters including *When Harry Met Sally*, *Sleepless in Seattle*, and the director of *You've Got Mail*. Her death in 2012 was met with an outpouring of grief, appreciation and tributes

DIANE GRIEGO ERWIN (1959–)—Diane Griego Erwin got hooked on journalism as an undergraduate at Chico State University in California, after which she ended up at the *Denver Post*, where in her first year on the job—at age twenty-five—she was part of a team that won the 1985 Pulitzer Prize for Public Service. A few years later, at twenty-nine, she became the first female columnist at the *Orange County Register*, and in 1994 she joined the *Sacramento Bee* as a star columnist. Erwin resigned in disgrace after it was found that she fabricated more than forty individuals in columns for the *Sacramento Bee*. "Journalism is like quicksand," she once said. "Put your foot in it, and good luck getting out."

JOHN FETTERMAN (1920–1975)—A lifelong Kentuckian and two-time Pulitzer Prize winner for the Louisville Courier Journal, Fetterman was lauded for his story, "PFC Gibson Comes Home" and a series on strip mining. He was the author of *Stinking Creek*. He daughter Mindy Fetterman became a reporter, columnist and editor in her own right.

LACEY FOSBURGH (1942–1993)—A writer of fact and fiction, Lacey Fosburgh was a leading reporter of the baby boom generation and one of the few journalists to ever interview the reclusive author of *Catcher in the Rye*, J. D. Salinger. She was married to the ex-husband of folk singer Joan Baez, David Harris, and had a daughter named Sophie. A New York City native, Fosburgh was educated at the Brearly School and Sarah Lawrence College. She was a staff reporter for *The New York Times* from 1968 through 1973. Her books include *Closing Time: The True Story of the "Goodbar" Murder*, *Old Money*, and *India Gate*. She died of breast cancer at the age of fifty.

GENE FOWLER (1890–1960)—A legendary newspaperman, screenwriter, novelist, and biographer, Fowler was perhaps most famous among his contemporaries for "ribald escapades that matched anything he wrote." Fowler himself admitted that he was "too proud to pretend chastity when there was no chastity in his soul." Born in Colorado, Eugene Fowler worked as a taxidermist and telegraph clerk before working at a printer's office and then the *Denver Post*. His fellow Coloradan, Damon Runyon, recruited him to join William Randolph Hearst's *New York American*. He covered crime, sports, and local politics, with a hard-boiled style like this: "She laid her wanton red head on her lover's breast, then plugged him through the heart." He later wrote a biography of his friend and drinking partner John Barrymore, *Good Night, Sweet Prince*, and later became the subject of a biography, *The Life and Legend of Gene Fowler* by H. Allen Smith. "Set things down fairly and honestly and without pulling punches," Fowler advised. "Put in the faults, the eccentricities, and those things which some unthinking persons blush to recall, but which are the very essence of true biography."

THOMAS L. FRIEDMAN (1953–)—A Minnesota native turned prophet of globalization and three-time Pulitzer Prize winner, Tom Friedman's *New York Times* column is read around the world. Becoming Beirut Bureau Chief six weeks before the Israeli invasion of Lebanon in 1982, Friedman's frontline reporting gave him enduring insights into the Middle East conflicts, bringing his first Pulitzer and forming the basis of his award-winning book *From Beirut to Jerusalem*, ultimately translated into twenty-five languages. He then served as the *Times'* Chief Diplomatic Correspondent during the end the cold war and revived the paper's Foreign Affairs column in 1995. Friedman's other best-selling books include *The Lexus and the Olive Tree* and *The World Is Flat*.

DOROTHY GILLIAM (1936–)—The first African-American reporter hired by the *Washington Post*, Dorothy Gilliam began writing her column in 1979. Born in Memphis, Tennessee, educated at the Columbia Journalism School, and married to the abstract artist Sam Gilliam, Dorothy served as the president of the National Association of Black Journalists in the mid-1990s. She was the author of the 1976 biography *Paul Robeson, All-American*. She was awarded the Washington Press Club's Lifetime Achievement Award in 2010.

HARRY GOLDEN (1902–1981)—Founder, editor, publisher, and writer of the *Carolina Israelite*, Harry Golden was born in the Ukraine and raised on New York's Lower East Side. After losing his job in the stock-market crash of 1929 and serving three years for mail fraud in a federal penitentiary, Golden moved to Charlotte, North Carolina. His irregularly published newspaper combined humor, Jewish folklore, and contemporary politics, including Golden's support for civil rights in the still segregated South, the subject of his most famous column, "The Vertical Negro Plan." His collection *Only in America* became a national bestseller as Golden's unabashed patriotism and humorous approach to social criticism made him a beloved figure in his lifetime. The *New York Post* proclaimed: "His is the voice of sanity amid the braying of jackals. He combines the cool lucidity of a Montaigne with the gusto of a pushcart peddler."

ELLEN GOODMAN (1941–)—Perhaps the first feminist of the baby boom generation with a nationally syndicated column, Ellen Goodman won the Pulitzer Prize for Commentary in 1980, at the ripe age of thirty-nine. A graduate of Radcliffe College, she first worked for *Newsweek* as a researcher and then began a column at the *Detroit Free Press*, soon moving back to Boston to begin her legendary column for the *Boston Globe*. Blending humor with self-referential reflections on the different stages of life facing the baby boomers, Goodman authored many best-selling books before retiring in 2010.

BOB GREENE (1947–)—Robert Bernard "Bob" Greene was a twenty-four-year veteran of the *Chicago Tribune*, where he won numerous awards for his columns before resigning in 2002. Greene's friendship with basketball great Michael Jordan provided material for many columns as well as one or two of his many books. He resigned from the *Chicago Tribune* and currently writes a weekly column for CNN.com.

CLYDE HABERMAN (1945–)—A metro columnist and foreign correspondent for *The New York Times*, Clyde Haberman writes columns that captured the strange rhythms of civic life. A 1966 graduate of City College, he joined the military during the Vietnam War. He worked the City Hall desk before serving as Tokyo bureau chief and being stationed in Rome and Jerusalem. Upon returning to the United States, he wrote the NYC column for sixteen years before beginning a four-day-a-week online column called "The Day." Haberman's post-9/11 column, "60s Lessons on How Not to Wave the Flag," is taught in journalism schools. He is the father of political journalist Maggie Haberman.

PETE HAMILL (1935–)—Pete Hamill began delivering newspapers in Brooklyn and became one of the most respected journalists of his generation. He started as a columnist for the *New York Post* in 1965 and ultimately went on to serve as editor of that newspaper as well as its rival, the *Daily News*. He has written a celebrated memoir, *A Drinking Life*, numerous New York City–based novels (*Snow in August, Forever*), and two anthologies of his journalism, *Irrational Ravings* (1971) and *Piecework* (1996). He even won a Grammy for writing the liner notes to Bob Dylan's classic *Blood on the Tracks*. Hamill is the recipient of numerous awards, including the Ernie Pyle Lifetime Achievement Award from the National Society of Newspaper Columnists and the A. J. Liebling Lifetime Achievement Award from the Boxing Writers of America.

BEN HECHT (1894–1964)—The *Chicago Daily News* columnist became a pioneering Hollywood screenwriter, using his journalist experience to cowrite *The Front Page* and other award-winning films. The son of Russian-Jewish immigrants, Hecht served as a war correspondent in Berlin from 1918 to 1919. Upon returning to the *Daily News*, Hecht proposed a column, to be called One Thousand and One Afternoons, composing a short-story each day, rooted in reportage. His real-world experience made him attractive to Hollywood, where he stayed for the remainder of his life, writing or assisting with the scripts of *Gone with the Wind* (uncredited), *Gunga Din*, *His Girl Friday*, and *Wuthering Heights*. He wrote and directed the film *Angels over Broadway* and was active in Zionist causes that aided the creation of the state of Israel.

RICH HEILAND (1946–)—Rich Heiland was a reporter, columnist, editor, and publisher at a number of newspapers during the 1970s and '80s. He was honored with a Pulitzer Prize in 1975 as part of the team that covered the tornadoes in Xenia, Ohio. In 1985 he won the National Newspaper Association's award for best serious columnist for a paper with circulation under fifteen thousand.

ERNEST HEMINGWAY (1899–1961)—The archetypal American novelist began as a newspaper reporter for the *Kansas City Star* and the *Toronto Star*, filing dispatches from Chicago, Paris, Barcelona, and cities in Germany. Much of Hemingway's journalism is captured in the anthology *By-Line: Ernest Hemingway*. In later years, with his reputation established, Hemingway occasionally filed features and columns from war zones for *The New York Times*. He credited the *Kansas City Star*'s style guide for providing the foundation of his writing: "Use short sentences. Use short first paragraphs. Use vigorous English. Be positive, not negative."

DANIEL HENNINGER (1946–)—The deputy editor of the *Wall Street Journal* editorial board, Henninger writes the weekly Wonderland column. He shared the *Wall Street Journal*'s Pulitzer Prize award for coverage of the terrorist attacks of September 11 and was a Pulitzer finalist for editorial writing in 1987 and 1996. He has won numerous journalistic awards.

CARL HIAASEN (1953–)—A columnist, novelist, and humorist, Carl Hiaasen captures the absurdity of his native Florida's excesses. A *Miami Herald* columnist since 1985, Hiaasen is among the most versatile contemporary columnists, touching on politics, corruption, crime, corporate greed, and environmental devastation. Two collections of his columns have been published to date: *Kick Ass* and *Paradise Screwed*. On the job of writing a column, Hiaasen believes: "You just cover a lot of territory and you do it aggressively and you do it fairly and you don't play favorites and you don't take any prisoners. It's the old school of slash-and-burn metropolitan column writing. You just kick ass. That's what you do. And that's what they pay you to do."

LORENA A. HICKOK (1893–1968)—Lorena Hickok is perhaps best known today, if at all, as the intimate friend of Eleanor Roosevelt. But Hickok was a pioneering female journalist who proved an ability to compete on daily deadline. She rose from local Midwest papers to covering the 1932 Roosevelt campaign for the Associated Press. She resigned that position in 1933, citing an inability to be objective about the Roosevelts. She was subsequently hired by the Federal Emergency Relief Administration and toured the country filing reports on the program's impact on people. Suffering from diabetes, she moved into the White House during FDR's third term. She wrote several books, including several biographies for children, and coauthored a book with Eleanor Roosevelt called *Ladies of Courage*.

MARGUERITE HIGGINS (1920–1966)—The first woman to win the Pulitzer Prize for war correspondence was born in Hong Kong and grew up in Oakland, California. She worked for the *New York Herald Tribune* for more than twenty years, working as a war correspondent from 1944 until the end of the war, including her harrowing account of the liberation of Dachau. She was appointed Berlin bureau chief in 1947 and Tokyo bureau chief in 1950. She won her Pulitzer in 1951 for frontline coverage of the Korean War including a celebrated account of the invasion of Inchon. She began writing a three-times weekly column for *Newsday* in 1963, syndicated in ninety newspapers. She died of a tropical disease covering the Vietnam War. Her papers are archived at Syracuse University.

MOLLY IVINS (1944–2007)— A Texas humorist and fighting liberal, Molly Ivins always gave her readers a good time. A columnist for the *Dallas Times Herald*, the *Fort Worth Star-Telegram*, and Creators' Syndicate, Ivins pulled no punches, as when she remarked that Pat Buchanan's "Culture War" speech at the 1992 Republican convention "probably sounded better in the original German." But she could also express powerful, understated sentiment, as with her classic column A Short Story about the Vietnam War Memorial. In books such as *Molly Ivins Can't Say That, Can She?* she expressed her love of her Lone Star State even as she mocked its excesses, saying, "God gave me Texas politics to write about. How can I not be funny?" This defiant left-libertarian died of breast cancer while still in her prime, but she left a rollicking legacy. "So keep fightin' for freedom and justice, beloveds, but don't you forget to have fun doin' it," she once advised. "Lord, let your laughter ring forth. Be outrageous, ridicule the fraidy-cats, rejoice in all the oddities that freedom can produce. And when you get through kickin' ass and celebratin' the sheer joy of a good fight, be sure to tell those who come after how much fun it was."

EDWIN L. JAMES (1890–1951)—James became a newspaper legend as managing editor of the *New York Times* from 1932 to 1951. He earned his stripes as a young man when the paper sent him abroad after just three years on the job, to serve as chief army reporter during World War I. No less a competitor than Damon Runyon called him "probably one of the greatest correspondents on the American front." As the paper's Paris bureau chief in the 1920s, James was the confidant of the word's leading diplomats and generals, turning up in Brussels, Prague, London, Washington, or any other place from which he could tell, in his words, "the daily story of the progress of mankind."

MICHAEL KELLY (1957–2003)—Armed with piercing insight and perfect pitch, Michael Kelly was one of the best political and culture writers of his generation. A frequent contributor to the pages of the *Washington Post*, Kelly was the editor of *The New Republic* and *The Atlantic Monthly*. He was the author of *Martyr's Day* and the posthumous collection *Things Worth Fighting For*. He died covering the 2003 invasion of Iraq. Even a quick survey of his writing will instill an appreciation of his rare talent. As Robert Vare wrote, "Mike's voice was a musical instrument that he played in many different keys."

MURRAY KEMPTON (1917–1997)—He began as a copyboy for H. L. Mencken and became a newspaper legend in his own right. Four days a week for almost forty years, Murray Kempton graced New York City newspaper pages, first at the *New York Post* and then finishing his career at *Newsday*. He was known for a courtly personal style, riding a bicycle around New York in a three-piece suit, listening to Bach on headphones. His writing could be wise, kind, and incisive. It was collected in *America Comes of Middle Age* and *Rebellions, Perversities, and Main Events*. As David Remnick wrote in 1994: "Murray Kempton is the greatest of all living newspapermen and his beat stretches from the Vatican to the social clubs of the Mob. He is a moralist who does not preach: an artist who reports."

COLBERT KING (1939–)—Colbert King took his time getting into journalism, spending decades as a banker and as a government official holding posts in the departments of State and Treasury, including a stint as U.S. executive director of the World Bank. Along the way, the Washington, D.C., native spent a stint helping to draft legislation giving D.C. limited home rule. He joined the *Washington Post* editorial board in 1990 and began writing a weekly column that won the 2003 Pulitzer Prize for Commentary.

HELEN KIRKPATRICK (1909–1997)—One of the best-known frontline journalists of the Second World War, Helen Kirkpatrick moved to Europe after her graduation from Smith College. She worked for various newspapers and started her own publication in London, the *Whitehall News*, which Winston Churchill subscribed to due to its editorial policy of opposing dictatorships. She warned that the Munich Pact could incite war rather than stop it. When the London Blitz occurred, Kirkpatrick was working for the *Chicago Daily News*. During the liberation of France, she rode into Paris on a tank. She also scaled Hitler's Bavarian bunker the Eagle's Nest, and stole a frying pan to cook field rations. She covered the Nuremberg trials and returned to the United States in the 1950s, where she married a trustee of her alma mater and lived a subsequent comfortable life of civic engagement in California.

NICHOLAS D. KRISTOF (1960-) The two-time Pulitzer-prize winning *New York Times* columnist's official bio states that he "has lived on four continents, reported on six, and traveled to more than 140 countries, plus all 50 states, every Chinese province and every main Japanese island. He's also one of the very few Americans to be at least a two-time visitor to every member of the Axis of Evil." In 1990, he and his wife Sheryl WuDunn won a Pulitzer Prize for reporting on the Tiananmen Square massacre. Together, they are the authors of three books, including *Half the Sky: From Oppression to Opportunity for Women Worldwide*. In 2006, Kristof won the Pulitzer Prize for commentary, earning accolades "for his graphic, deeply reported columns that, at personal risk, focused attention on genocide in Darfur and that gave voice to the voiceless in other parts of the world." Kristof was the subject of a 2009 documentary, "Reporter," and established himself as an early adaptor of digital journalism, becoming the first *Times* columnist to blog and use Twitter. "I'm not surprised to see him emerge as the moral conscience of our generation of journalists," said his one-time college classmate Jeffrey Toobin. "I am surprised to see him as the Indiana Jones of our generation of journalists."

JACK LAIT (1883–1954)—Editor of the *New York Daily Mirror*, Jack Lait was a journalistic renaissance man who worked as a reporter, columnist, cartoonist, and author. His column All in the Family ran for two decades and his cartoon *Gus and Gussie* was available between 1925 and 1930. Lait was perhaps best known for his series of best-selling Confidential books—*Washington Confidential, Chicago Confidential*, and *New York Confidential*—the latter of which became a 1955 film and short-lived television series.

WILLIAM L. LAURENCE (1888–1977)—Born in Lithuania and educated at Harvard, William Laurence was the premier science journalist of his time. He served in the Army Signal Corps during World War I and earned a law degree before becoming a newspaperman. Working for the *New York Times*, Laurence was granted unprecedented access to the tests of the atomic bomb and its detonation over Nagasaki, a journey that is reprinted in this book. He chronicled the atomic age, aided by a well-placed source, Dr. Robert J. Oppenheimer. He retired to Majorca in the late 1960s and died there.

WALTER LIPPMANN (1889–1974)—Perhaps the premiere pundit at the heart of the American Century, Walter Lippmann wrote a column that ran from 1931 to 1971. He was a counselor to presidents whose work was carefully read by all who worked in the corridors of power. As a student at Harvard, he studied under George Santayana and William James and served as an assistant to Lincoln Steffens. He later helped draft Woodrow Wilson's Fourteen Points and served on the staff of General Pershing in Army Intelligence. He was an editor at *The New Republic* and the *New York World* before starting his syndicated column Today and Tomorrow. He wrote over forty books, including the 1922 classic (and controversial) *Public Opinion*. "We have missed the meaning of history, then, if today we are 'Jeffersonians' opposed to 'Hamiltonians' or vice versa," Lippmann wrote in a 1943 column titled The Living Past. "To be partisan today as between Jefferson and Hamilton is like arguing whether men or women are more necessary to the procreation of the race."

JACK LONDON (1876–1916)—Novelist, short-story writer, and journalist, Jack London inspired generations of American authors in the twentieth century. A California native and dedicated Bohemian, he challenged the conventions of his day. Among his best-known works are *Call of the Wild, The Sea Wolf*, and *To Build a Fire*. "Don't loaf and invite inspiration," he advised. "Light out after it with a club, and if you don't get it you will nonetheless get something that looks remarkably like it."

STEVE LOPEZ (1953–)—An award-winning columnist at the *Los Angeles Times* and *Philadelphia Inquirer*, Steve Lopez is the son of Spanish and Italian immigrants. His work has been anthologized in *Land of Giants* and he has written three novels to date. His series of columns about his friendship with the homeless and schizophrenic bassist Nathaniel Anthony Ayers inspired *The Soloist*, a 2009 film starring Robert Downey Jr. and Jamie Foxx. "I've always tried to keep readers wondering what might be next, whether it's a postcard from a corner of a forgotten neighborhood, someone's struggle against the system, or a good chop to the teeth of a public official," Lopez says. "I used to listen to Thelonious Monk when I wrote, just to remind myself there's no point in doing it if you can't find a way to write like no one else and make a story your own."

MIKE MCALARY (1957–1998)—Lauded for his "bulletproof swagger and unyielding reporting," Mike McAlary died at age forty-one, months after he was awarded the Pulitzer Prize for Commentary in honor of his columns on the abuse of Abner Louima at the hands of New York City police officers. Two plays have been written about McAlary since his untimely death from colon cancer, Dan Klores's *The Wood* and Nora Ephron's *Lucky Guy*.

MARY MCGRORY (1918–2004)—The Boston native worked her way up from being a secretary at the *Boston Herald Traveler* to becoming one of the most influential and admired Washington columnists of her era. From the army-McCarthy hearings to the Kennedy administration to Watergate, McGrory's presence was a Washington staple and her column captured the tone of the times. She worked for the *Washington Star* until it folded and then moved to the *Washington Post*, writing her column until shortly before her death. She won the Pulitzer Prize in 1975 for her columns on Watergate.

HERBERT L. MATTHEWS (1900–1977)—A bookish man who became a celebrated war correspondent, after graduating Columbia University Herbert Matthews joined *The New York Times*. In 1931, he went overseas to the Paris bureau, covering the Italian invasion of Ethiopia and, most famously, the Spanish Civil War. He lived in Madrid and became known for his detailed dispatches as well as his Republican sympathies. Along with Ernest Hemingway and Martha Gellhorn, he became one of the best-known chroniclers of that war, warning the world about the rise of fascism. In World War II, he was briefly jailed by the Italians and narrowly survived a Nazi shell that killed three colleagues. He subsequently joined *The New York Times* editorial board. His career ended on a controversial note, when he was duped by Fidel Castro into reporting that Cuban revolutionary forces did not have communist sympathies.

H. L. MENCKEN (1880–1956)—The "Sage of Baltimore" is among the most revered American columnists: a transcendent skeptic, an equal opportunity offender. Writing for the *Baltimore Sun* and cofounding *The American Mercury*, Henry Louis Mencken courted controversy as a critic and satirist. He was particularly impatient with the ignorance that paraded as populism and the politicians who catered to it. His coverage of the Scopes Monkey trial brought him national renown, and he was the thinly veiled inspiration for the character E. K. Hornbeck played by Gene Kelly in the film *Inherit the Wind*. He wrote over forty books, many of which are still in print. "A newspaper reporter, in those remote days," he wrote in his memoir *Newspaper Days*, "had a grand and gaudy time of it, with no call to envy any man."

H. P. MOORE (1884–1965)—Working more than a half-century in the newspaper business, H.P. Moore never exceeded the success of his first big scoop. Working as a nineteen-year-old freelance reporter in Norfolk, he had travelled to Kitty Hawk with a friend and seen the Wright Brothers preparing for their historic flight. He asked to be told when and if they achieved their goal and some twenty minutes after the first flight occurred he received a telegram and began piecing together the story for publication. He was first but the story contained numerous inaccuracies. Nonetheless, Moore would recount the big scoop amid some controversy for the rest of his career.

JIM MURRAY (1919–1998)—The longtime *Los Angeles Times* sports columnist was so beloved that Ronald Reagan showed up at a tribute dinner to offer ten minutes of unscripted remarks. A 1990 winner of the Pulitzer Prize for Commentary, Murray filed his last column on the day he died. Looking back gratefully at a life in sportswriting, he said, "Somebody had to sit on the curb and watch the parade go by."

JACK NEWFIELD (1938–2004)—This modern muckraker wrote for the *Village Voice* for twenty-four years before bringing his column to *New York Daily News*, the *New York Post*, and the *New York Sun*. He was the author of ten books, received the George Polk Award for Investigative Journalism in 1980, and won an Emmy for his documentary on Don King in 1991. A friend and confidant of Bobby Kennedy and Muhammad Ali, he was unafraid of taking on the rich, powerful, and corrupt. When eccentric millionaire Abe Hirschfeld bought the *New York Post* in 1993, Newfield's column about his new boss asked "Who Is This Nut?" "I do have an underlying set of principles," Newfield wrote when he was ill with cancer. "Tell the truth no matter what. . . . Also, I tend to defend underdogs and the powerless. I often find the official version of events is not the true story. I have never wanted to be a stenographer for those in power."

PEGGY NOONAN (1950–)—The *Wall Street Journal* columnist began her career as a writer and producer for CBS News. She was a special assistant and speechwriter for President Ronald Reagan. Her memoir of his administration, *What I Saw at the Revolution*, has become a classic. Noonan's eight books to date include a biography of Ronald Reagan, *When Character Was King*; a biography of Pope John Paul II, *John Paul the Great*; and *Patriotic Grace: What It Is and Why We Need It Now*.

FRANK WARD O'MALLEY (1875–1932)—A legendary reporter for the *New York Sun*, Frank Ward O'Malley was regarded as the best of his age, admired by his colleagues and readers. His range extended from humor to straight reporting and he was known to find inspiration in the saloons and steakhouses of Manhattan. His celebrated sob story of 1907, recounting the senseless murder of a policeman, was written after O'Malley got the story from the officer's mother. According to newspaper lore, a Westchester commuter was so taken by the story that he stood up to read it to his fellow train-riders and was again moved to tears. O'Malley is credited with the quotation, "Life is just one damned thing after another."

FRANK DEL OLMO (1948–2004)—Frank del Olmo started as an intern at the *Los Angeles Times* and stayed for nearly thirty-four years, taking turns as a staff writer, editorial writer, and assistant to the editor of the *Times*—the latter position making him the first Latino added to the paper's masthead. Along the way, del Olmo scored a Pulitzer Prize for Public Service in 1984 and wrote columns about southern California's Latino community. He died of a heart attack in his office at the *Times* in 2004—and right up to that final day provided a clear, powerful voice in the City of Angels.

KATHLEEN PARKER (1952–)—A voice of sanity from South Carolina, Kathleen Parker captures the common sense of Main Street America in her columns to the Washington Post. Witty, sly, and self-effacing, Parker's center-right sensibility keeps her political opponents from successfully stereotyping her. She won the H. L. Mencken Award for commentary in 1993 writing for the *Orlando Sentinel*, and the Pulitzer Prize in 2010.

EUGENE PATTERSON (1923–)—The Georgia-born editor of the *Atlanta Constitution* in the turbulent 1960s also published a column seven days a week. During World War II, he served as a tank platoon leader in General Patton's Third Army. After his time in Atlanta, Patterson served as Managing Editor of the *Washington Post* and the *St. Petersburg Times* as well as head of the Poynter Institute. A collection of his work —*The Changing South of Gene Patterson: Journalism and Civil Rights, 1960–1968*— was published in 2002. "I was regarded as a Southern turncoat by many of my critics," Patterson said. "But I didn't think I was. I thought I was leading us in the direction the South had to go, which was toward justice."

WESTBROOK PEGLER (1894–1969)—One of the most talented and widely read columnists of his time, Pegler had fighting spirit that shone through in prose of uncommon wit and clarity. In his prime, he was an equal opportunity offender, criticizing Democrats and Republicans as well as Communists and Fascists with equal enthusiasm. Targets of his attacks were said to have been "Peglerized." In 1938, *Time* magazine wrote, "Pegler's place as the great dissenter for the common man is unchallenged." In 1941, Pegler became the first columnist to win a Pulitzer Prize for Reporting, uncovering criminal racketeering in labor unions. Pegler lost a libel suit in 1954 and was fired by the Hearst syndicate in 1962. He once commented to his friend Murray Kempton that his increasing unhinged-ness did not start with his hatred of Eleanor Roosevelt: "It began when I quit sports and went cosmic. It finished when I began writing on Monday to be printed on Friday." As alcoholism consumed him, he moved further and further to the right, ending his distinguished career writing for a journal published by the John Birch Society. The subject of at least two biographies, Pegler's work was also anthologized in should-be classics like *T'ain't Right* and *The Dissenting Opinions of Mr. Westbrook Pegler.*

TED POSTON (1906–1974)—By the time the *New York Post* hired Ted Poston in 1945, he had made a national name for himself as a columnist for the black-owned *Pittsburgh Courier* and city editor of the Harlem-based *Amsterdam News.* During World War II he served in the War Information Office and was part of President Franklin Delano Roosevelt's "black cabinet," an informal collection of men who advised FDR about African-American life and issues. Returning to journalism after the war, he covered the early years of the civil rights movement, winning a Polk Award for National Reporting in 1949.

SHIRLEY POVICH (1905–1998)—For over seventy-five years, Shirley Povich wrote for the *Washington Post*—as enduring a relationship as American journalism is ever likely to see. He became the nation's youngest sports columnist at age twenty and continued his column for the next seventy-one years, ceasing only for military service during World War II. His ledes are the stuff of legend—for example, here is Povich after witnessing Don Larson's perfect game in the 1956 World Series. "The million-to-one shot came in. Hell froze over. A month of Sundays hit the calendar. Don Larsen today pitched a no-hit, no-run, no-man-reaches-first game in a World Series." He and his wife, Ethyl, were the parents of television journalist Maury Povich and two other children, David and Lynn. Many of his best columns were collected in his acclaimed memoir *All Those Mornings . . . at The Post.*

ERNIE PYLE (1900–1945)—The GI journalist and the patron saint of war correspondents, Ernie Pyle penned the syndicated Scripps Howard column that brought the facts and feel of the Second World War to the home front. He lived on the front lines with the troops—"the God-Damned Infantry," as he christened them. His columns had the informal style of a letter back home, but they did not shy away from the cold facts. His column The Death of Captain Waskow is among the best writing to come out of the war. Previously, Pyle studied at Indiana University and worked as the nation's first aviation columnist before buying a home in Albuquerque. He wrote a column encouraging Congress to pay active-duty soldiers an additional $10 a month as "combat pay," leading to the passage of the proposal, known as the Ernie Pyle Bill. On April 18, 1945, Pyle was killed by Japanese machine-gun fire on the island of Ie Shima, off the coast of Okinawa. His last words to a soldier standing next to him were, "Are you all right?" Soldiers erected a gravesite monument that read, "At this spot the 77th Infantry Division lost a buddy, Ernie Pyle." His wartime journalism was collected in four books: *Ernie Pyle in England, Here Is Your War, Brave Men,* and *Last Chapter.*

JAMES RESTON (1909–1995)—The Scottish-born Reston twice won the Pulitzer Prize for his work at *The New York Times* and received the Presidential Medal of Freedom.

He served as a longtime columnist as well as executive editor of the *Times*. He was sometimes accused of being too close to those in power, but he was also included in President Richard Nixon's enemies list. In his "retirement," Reston bought and ran the weekly *Vineyard Gazette*. He wrote several books, including a collection of columns called *Sketches in the Sand* and a memoir, *Deadline*. "[Reston] felt that journalism and government were integral parts of the fabric of the country," wrote Reston's biographer John F. Stacks in 2002's *Scotty*, "working in different ways toward the same goal: helping the country deal with threats to its health and survival from abroad and at home."

GRANTLAND RICE (1880–1954)—He was known as "the Dean of American sportswriters" and helped the American sports column evolve, adopting a literary style and becoming a star in his own right. The Tennessee native's syndicated column, The Sportlight, shone on the athletic heroes of his day—Babe Ruth, Jack Dempsey, Seabiscuit, and, especially, the Notre Dame backfield he christened "The Four Horsemen." At the end of his career, Rice estimated that he'd written an average of three thousand words a day and traveled fifteen thousand miles a year in pursuit of good stories. He was the play-by-play announcer of the 1922 World Series, the first broadcast in its entirety. He also wrote verse, at least one line of which lodged itself in the American consciousness: "When the One Great Scorer comes to mark against your name / He writes—not that you won or lost—but how you played the game."

MICHAEL RIEDEL (1969–)—Mark Riedel has covered Broadway since the early 1990s, primarily for the *New York Post*. A native of Geneseo, New York, he is the cohost of *Theater Talk* on PBS and CUNY-TV. He graduated from Columbia University with a BA in history.

WILL ROGERS (1879–1935)—This cowboy philosopher, humorist, and movie star was among the most beloved celebrities of his day. His column, Will Rogers Says, was syndicated by *The New York Times*. Will was beloved for his "cool mind and warm heart," offering wisdom that harkened back to his Oklahoma roots. Among his enduring aphorisms: "I never met a man I didn't like" and "everybody is ignorant, only on different subjects." An early aviation enthusiast (often typing his columns out en route), Rogers was killed in an Alaskan crash with aviator Wiley Post. He was mourned in cities and small towns from the East Coast to the West.

ANDY ROONEY (1919–2011)—Best-known as the cantankerous essayist on CBS's *60 Minutes*, Andy Rooney was also a lifelong reporter and newspaper columnist. He covered the Second World War from the front lines, alongside Ernie Pyle and Walter Cronkite. He authored a number of best-selling books and column collections, writing three columns a week for Tribune Media Services and appearing on television until retiring a month before he died.

A. M. ROSENTHAL (1922–2006)—Abraham Michael Rosenthal spent a storied and sometimes stormy career at *The New York Times* in various positions, winning the

Pulitzer Prize in 1960 for his stories from behind the Iron Curtain. After graduating from City College, he worked primarily as a foreign correspondent during the 1940s and 1950s. Rosenthal served as managing editor of *The New York Times* from 1969 to 1977 and afterward as executive editor. He coined what became known as the "Rosenthal Rule": "I don't care if my reporters are fucking elephants, as long as they aren't covering the circus." His nationally syndicated column On My Mind began in 1986. He was awarded the Presidential Medal of Freedom in 2002.

MIKE ROYKO (1932–1997)—For more than forty years, Mike Royko was the voice of Chicago. He grew up over his family's tavern and began writing a five-day-a-week column in 1956, switching newspapers three times but never leaving the Windy City. He challenged City Hall and celebrated the little guy, especially those who gathered at his favorite watering hole, the Billy Goat Tavern. Syndicated in over six hundred papers, Royko created characters to tell his stories, including Slats Grobnik, and was the first to call California's Jerry Brown "Governor Moonbeam." Jimmy Breslin called him "the best journalist of his time" and Royko won the Pulitzer Prize for Commentary in 1972. Royko's only book was an unflattering look at Chicago's longtime mayor Richard Daley, titled *Boss*, but columns were collected in two posthumous anthologies. Royko's memorial service was held on a sunny day in Wrigley Field.

VERMONT ROYSTER (1914–1996)—A North Carolina native, the northeasterly-named Vermont Connecticut Royster won his first Pulitzer in 1951, for editorial writing. He later became editor of the *Wall Street Journal* and began a weekly column after his retirement in 1971. An early champion of the rise of Ronald Reagan, he was also a frequent commentator on television, notably on CBS's *Spectrum* program. He was awarded the Presidential Medal of Freedom by Ronald Reagan in 1986. The citation read: "His common sense exploded the pretensions of 'expert opinion,' and his compelling eloquence warned of the evils of society loosed from its moorings in faith. The voice of the American people can be heard in his prose— honest, open, proud, and free."

DAMON RUNYON (1884–1946)—Best known today as the author of *Guys and Dolls*, this chronicler of Broadway's characters was born in Pueblo, Colorado, in the waning days of the Wild West. He established his column at the *New York American*, establishing himself as one of the most versatile and distinctive columnists in U.S. history, developing a dialogue style known to devotees as "Runyonese." Runyon covered crime, politics, war, humor, and sports with equal mastery. On one notable adventure, he rode into Mexico with General Pershing on the hunt for Pancho Villa. His short stories were developed into nearly a dozen feature films and more than fifty radio plays, making Runyon one of the wealthiest writers of the time. Runyon was an inveterate gambler and night owl who nonetheless gave up drinking at age thirty in exchange for the hand of the first of his two wives. After his death due to cancer, courtesy of a heavy smoking habit, his ashes were scattered over Manhattan and a still enduring cancer research fund was established in his name.

RUBEN SALAZAR (1928–1970—A pioneering Mexican-American journalist and columnist for the *Los Angeles Times*, Rueben Salazar was mistakenly killed by a LAPD Sheriff's deputy during a march against the Vietnam War. Born in Cuidad Juarez, Mexico, Salazar moved to Texas, served in the U.S. Army and began work as a reporter at the El Paso Times. He joined the *Los Angeles Times* in 1959, becoming one of the first Latino journalists to cover the Hispanic community for a mainstream American newspaper. He covered the Vietnam War and served as news director for KMEX. He was killed when a tear gas canister was fired indiscriminately into the Silver Dollar Café, where Salazar was resting during protests that turned violent. The canister struck him in the head, killing him instantly. Salazar was posthumously awarded the Robert F. Kennedy Journalism Award and became one of five journalists of the 20th Century honored with a U.S. Stamp.

GEORGE S. SCHUYLER (1895–1977)—Schuyler began professional life as a columnist and editor of the socialist *Messenger* newspaper and a business manager of the NAACP before dropping Left-leaning philosophy for his true calling as a conservative satirist, most of it spent as a columnist for the black-owned *Pittsburgh Courier*. His wicked pen drew the admiration of H. L. Mencken, who published Schuyler frequently in *The American Mercury* and once said of Schuyler: "I am more and more convinced that he is the most competent editorial writer now in practice in this great free republic." As he migrated rightward, Schuyler stirred outrage with a blistering 1964 attack on Martin Luther King for receiving the Nobel Prize that appeared in the *Manchester Union Leader*—and rendered Schuyler an outcast, reduced to writing occasional essays for the John Birch Society.

JOHN L. SMITH (1960–)—The chronicler of Casino-land, Smith has written four columns a week for the *Las Vegas Review-Journal* since 1988. His character studies involve "aging boxers, two-bit mobsters, bookmakers, loan sharks and waitresses at Denny's—preferably a combination of two or more." He has written a dozen books to date, including an anthology of his columns titled *On the Boulevard*.

MERRIMAN SMITH (1913–1970)—"The 20th Century's finest performance by one reporter on a breaking news story," was how Merriman Smith's account of the JFK assassination was described in the pages of the *American Journalism Review* almost a half-century later. Smith was a lifelong newspaper man and UPI's White House correspondent from 1941 through the 1960s. He cover the death of FDR and the end of World War Two—but it was his coverage of November 22, 1961 that earned him the Pulitzer Prize. He was awarded the Medal of Freedom by President Lyndon Johnson. Smith wrestled with alcoholism for much of his life and suffered the death of a son in Vietnam. He died by suicide in 1970 and is buried in Arlington Cemetery.

RED SMITH (1905–1982)—Walter "Red" Smith's 1976 Pulitzer Prize for Commentary cited "the erudition, the literary quality, the vitality and freshness of viewpoint" he brought to the most widely syndicated sports column of his time. Writing about sports for five decades and covering forty-five World Series, Smith didn't become a columnist until age forty and reached *The New York Times* at age sixty-five. But his excellence was appreciated by readers and competitors alike, especially given his five-day-a-week output. His *New York Times* colleague Dave Anderson paid tribute to Smith the day after his death, writing: "Red Smith was, quite simply, the best sportswriter. Put the emphasis on 'writer.' Of those who have written sports for a living, no one else ever had the command of the language, the turn of the phrase, the subtlety of the skewer as he did."

JOHN STEINBECK (1902–1968)—The Nobel-prize-winning author of *The Grapes of Wrath*, *East of Eden* and *Travels with Charley*, found much of his literary inspiration by working as a journalist. Born in Salinas, California, on the Monterey Peninsula, Steinbeck attended Stanford University but left before graduation to pursue a writing career. His first book was *Cup of Gold*, but he did not find widespread critical of commercial success until *Tortilla Flat*, published in 1935. His coverage of the Dust Bowl migrant community for the *San Francisco Examiner* informed the *Grapes of Wrath* and was named one of the 100 greatest works of journalism of the 20th Century by NYU. Toward the end of his life, Steinbeck lived in Sag Harbor, New York. The National Steinbeck Center, in Salinas, is the only U.S. museum dedicated to a single writer.

BRET STEPHENS (1973–)—The foreign affairs columnist of the *Wall Street Journal* and deputy editorial page editor also served as the editor of the *Jerusalem Post* from 2002 to 2004, the youngest person to hold that position. Raised in Mexico City by American parents, Stephens is a graduate of Middlesex School, the University of Chicago, and the London School of Economics.

DOROTHY THOMPSON (1893–1961)—Sometimes called "The First Lady of American Journalism," Dorothy Thompson was the most influential female columnist of the 1930s and '40s. A pioneer in her field, she was the Berlin bureau chief for the *New York Post* in the late 1920s and became an early and outspoken opponent of the Nazis' rise. She was the first foreign journalist to be expelled from Germany, in 1934. Her syndicated column On the Record began in 1936, and she simultaneously served as an NBC radio correspondent, reaching 8 million readers and 5 million listeners. When Hitler invaded Poland in 1939, she spoke on the radio for fifteen consecutive nights denouncing the action and the world war, which she had warned was coming. Married for a time to the novelist Sinclair Lewis, Thompson was a charismatic and colorful figure who had affairs with both men and women. Among her aphorisms: "Only when we are no longer afraid do we begin to live."

WELLS TWOMBLY (1935–1977)—Named one of the six best sportswriters in the nation by *Esquire* magazine in 1974, Wells Twombly wrote inventive columns that graced the *San Francisco Examiner* six days a week until his untimely death at age forty-one. His work was anthologized in *Best Sports Stories* for sixteen of the twenty years of his professional career. "There Was Only One Casey" was included in the anthology *The Best American Sports Writing of the Century*. "I try to be as literate as I can be. Anybody who writes down to a reader in this age of higher education is living in the past," Twombly once commented. "I don't want anybody skimming through anything I write. I've been battling the Who-What-Where-Why-When and KISS (Keep it Simple Stupid) crowd ever since I started. Lord, we're in a war with television. I try to recreate scenes for readers, take them places where even the damned camera can't go."

HENRY G. WALES (1888–?)—One of the few war correspondents to cover both the first and second world wars with equally celebrated dispatches, Wales was injured in the line of duty. His scoops included the death of Mata Hari, the 1919 peace negotiations and the landing of Charles Lindbergh in Paris, where he was the first reporter to greet the aviator.

MAURINE DALLAS WATKINS (1896–1969)—As a young journalist for the *Chicago Tribune*, Maurine Watkins found material to support a lifetime of theater and screenwriting. Her coverage of two jazz age murderesses, Beulah Annan and Velma Kelly, became Roxie Hart and Velma Kelly in a play Watkins originally wrote at Yale Drama School. It first became a film in 1942 and then was adapted into the musical *Chicago* by Bob Fosse after Watkins's death. She wrote numerous screenplays during her lifetime, including *Libeled Lady* and *Professional Sweetheart*. In later years, she lived in seclusion, her face disfigured by cancer, finding solace as a born-again Christian. She donated her multimillion-dollar estate to the endowed chairs in classical Greek and Latin at a number of universities. The film version of the musical *Chicago* won best picture in 2002.

TOM WICKER (1926–2011)—A native of Hamlet, North Carolina, he rose to national prominence on November 22, 1963, when he was covering President Kennedy's trip to Dallas and dictated the front-page story of the assassination over the phone. Nine months later he became Washington bureau chief of the *Times*. In 1966, he started a column for the paper, which he continued until 1991. Wicker was the author of 10 books, including *On Press* and *A Time to Die* about the Attica prison riots.

GEORGE WILL (1941–)—This conservative columnist and author is one of the most widely syndicated writers today. The son of an Illinois philosophy professor and a long-suffering Chicago Cubs fan, Will has been an eloquent, steady, and civil source of intellectual consistency for the conservative movement since the 1970s. Among Will's aphorisms: "The four most important words in politics are: up to a point."

HARVEY T. WOODRUFF (1876–1937)—The sports editor of the *Chicago Tribune*, who penned the popular In the Wake of the News column for a time, Woodruff was one of the premier chroniclers of the Black Sox scandal of the thrown 1919 World Series.

RICHARD WRIGHT (1908–1960)—The acclaimed author of *Native Son* and *Black Boy*, Wright grew up in Mississippi and moved to Chicago as a young man to become a writer. There he joined a John Reed Club and then the Communist Party. He wrote for the party paper *New Masses* and became the Harlem editor of *The Daily Worker*. His memoirs and novels soon brought him success and widespread acclaim as well as a Guggenheim Fellowship. He moved to Paris after the Second World War and befriended Camus and Sartre. He died there in 1960.

DICK YOUNG (1917–1987)—An iconic and abrasive sportswriter, Young wrote for the *New York Daily News* for more than forty years. He was elected to the Baseball Hall of Fame writer's wing in 1978. After his death, *The New York Times* described his style: "With all the subtlety of a knee in the groin, Dick Young made people gasp. . . . He could be vicious, ignorant, trivial and callous, but for many years he was the epitome of the brash, unyielding yet sentimental Damon Runyon sportswriter."

JEFFREY ZASLOW (1958–2012)—As a twenty-nine-year-old writer, Zaslow won a contest to select a successor to fill the advice column slot at the *Chicago Sun-Times* that was long held by the legendary Ann Landers. He was twice named best columnist by the National Society of Newspaper Columnists for his work at the *Wall Street Journal*, and authored a string of best-selling nonfiction books. One of them, *The Last Lecture*, based on the column included in this volume, has sold more than 5 million copies. Zaslow died in a car accident in January 2012. He was widely mourned.

ACKNOWLEDGMENTS

We would like to thank our agent, Ed Victor, and our publisher, Peter Mayer at the Overlook Press as well as the whole Overlook team, especially our editor Dan Crissman and publicist Jack Lamplough.

As with the first volume of *Deadline Artists*, the columns in this book were selected with the help of many individuals and organizations, including Roy Peter Clark of the Poynter Institute, Rick Mastroianni of the Newseum, The National Society of Newspaper Columnists, Steve Shepard of the CUNY Journalism School, William Grueskin of Columbia School of Journalism, Mike Barnicle, Jimmy Breslin, Pete Hamill, Eugene Patterson, Ben Pollock and John L. Smith. Chloe Bakalar and Stephanie Lowe provided valuable help in researching and transcribing the columns in this volume. Reynolds Avlon worked as our photo editor and helped with photo research as did Amy Pereira. Special thanks to everyone who emailed in their suggestions through our website, DeadlineArtists.com.

Among the many books we surveyed were *The Column* by Hallam Walker Davis (1926); *The Columnists: A Surgical Survey* by Charles Fisher (1944); *A Treasury of Great Reporting* by Louis L. Snyder & Richard B. Morris (1949); *A Treasury of American Political Humor* by Leonard C. Lewin; *Pundits, Poets and Wits* by Karl E. Meyer (1990); *The American Newspaper Column* by Sam G. Riley (1998); *Biographical Dictionary of American Newspaper Columnists* by Sam G. Riley; *Crusaders, Scoundrels, Journalists: The Newseum's Most Intriguing Newspeople*, edited by Eric Newton (1999).

A special thanks to our friend and one-time colleague, Jack Newfield, who was an inspiration and a sounding board as this project was first conceived.

We'd like to thank our co-workers at the *Daily Beast*, *Newsweek*, CNN, *The Daily*, the *New York Post*, and NY1, And of course, our families and friends.

John: I want to thank my bride Margaret for her love and support—she is beautiful and bright in every way. My parents can never be thanked enough for their lifetime of encouragement—and my brother Reynolds, cousin Alex, aunts, uncles, godparents and especially my grandmother Toula Carvelas Phillips, for giving me the blessing of an amazing family. Thanks to Tina Brown, Harry Evans, Kathy O'Hearn, Mark Allen, Harry Siegel, Damon Linker, Andrew Kirk and everyone at NewsBeast. At CNN, I want to especially thank Bart Feder, Ken Jautz, Mark Whitaker, Amy Entelis, Wil Surratt, Erin Burnett, Susie Xu, Mark Preston, Sam Feist, Michelle Jaconi, Janelle Rodriguez, Lucy Spiegel, Rich Galant—and everyone on the OutFront team. To all my friends—and you know who you are—thank you, always.

Jesse: I would like to thank all of my colleagues at *The Daily* for teaching me what journalism in the digital age can be. I would like to thank Rupert Murdoch, Col Allan, and all of my colleagues at the *New York Post*, the *Daily Telegraph*, and *The Sun* for teaching me what journalism should be. To my family—John, Judy, Jack, Hilary, Kate and Francois—thank you for making me who I am, and always supporting me. To my bride, Rebecca . . . well, I would need another book to say it all. You are my soul.

Errol: I would like to thank my parents, Ed and Tomi Louis, my wife, Juanita Scarlett, and our son, Noah, for their love and support. I also thank my inspired and dependable sisters—Pamela Louis, Lisa Burton and Ellen Louis—and my dear brother, Edward. I do not have space here to name all the members of the very large Scarlett, Hawkins, Maloney and Louis clans, but this book is dedicated to all of them, and to Eric Daniels, Fred Moten, Alan Jackson, Mark Winston Griffith, Stefano Harney and the Revs. Taharka Robinson and Karim Camara. I am also grateful to my work family at NY1 News, one of the finest newsrooms in America.